Accounting Policies and Procedures Manual

Update Service

BECOME A SUBSCRIBER!
Did you purchase this product from a bookstore?

If you did, it's important for you to become a subscriber. John Wiley & Sons, Inc. may publish, on a periodic basis, supplements and new editions to reflect the latest changes in the subject matter that you ***need to know*** in order to stay competitive in this ever-changing industry. By contacting the Wiley office nearest you, you'll receive any current update at no additional charge. In addition, you'll receive future updates and revised or related volumes on a 30-day examination review.

If you purchased this product directly from John Wiley & Sons, Inc., we have already recorded your subscription for this update service.

To become a subscriber, please call **1-800-225-5945** or send your name, company name (if applicable), address, and the title of the product to:

mailing address: **Supplement Department**
                                     John Wiley & Sons, Inc.
                                     One Wiley Drive
                                     Somerset, NJ 08875

e-mail: **subscriber@wiley.com**
fax: **1-732-302-2300**
online: **www.wiley.com**

For customers outside the United States, please contact the Wiley office nearest you:

Professional & Reference Division	John Wiley & Sons, Ltd.
John Wiley & Sons Canada, Ltd.	Baffins Lane
22 Worcester Road	Chichester
Rexdale, Ontario M9W 1L1	West Sussex, PO19 1UD
CANADA	ENGLAND
(416) 675-3580	Phone: (44) 1243 779777
Phone: 1-800-567-4797	Fax: (44) 1243 770638
Fax: 1-800-565-6802	cs-books@wiley.com.uk
canada@jwiley.com	
Jacaranda Wiley Ltd.	John Wiley & Sons (SEA) Pte. Ltd.
PRT Division	37 Jalan Pemimpin
P.O. Box 174	Block B # 05-04
North Ryde, NSW 2113	Union Industrial Building
AUSTRALIA	SINGAPORE 2057
Phone: (02) 805-1100	Phone: (65) 258-1157
Fax: (02) 805-1597	Fax: (65) 463-4604
headoffice@jacwiley.com.au	enquiry@wiley.com.sg

Accounting Policies and Procedures Manual

Fifth Edition

A Blueprint for Running an Effective and Efficient Department

Steven M. Bragg

BICENTENNIAL
1807
WILEY
2007
BICENTENNIAL

John Wiley & Sons, Inc.

Note: The previous edition of this is titled *Design and Maintenance of Accounting Manuals: A Blueprint for Running an Effective and Efficient Department, Fourth Edition*

Library of Congress Cataloging-in-Publication Data

Bragg, Steven M.
    Accounting policies and procedures manual : a blueprint for
running an effective and efficient department / Steven M. Bragg. – 5th ed.
        p. cm.
    Rev. ed. of: Design and maintenance of accounting manuals /
Steven M. Bragg, Harry L. Brown. 4th ed. c2003.
    Includes index.
    ISBN 978-0-470-14662-0 (cloth/website)
1. Accounting–Handbooks, manuals, etc. – Authorship. I.
Bragg. Steven M. Design and maintenance of accounting manuals.
II. Title.
    HF5636.B8315 2007
    808.066657–dc22
    2007025170

Printed in the United States of America

10 9 8 7 6 5 4 3 2 1

In memory of Wheaton, who always wanted to
write an accounting book and sail around the world
(not necessarily in that order).

Contents

Preface

Lack of adequate documentation is one of the largest pitfalls facing any accounting system. One of four excuses is usually given: (1) nobody reads it, (2) the hands-on approach in which each person teaches another is a better method, (3) written policies and procedures are too confining, and (4) nobody has the time to write documentation. In a constantly changing accounting world, none of these excuses can stand very long.

If an accounting staff and company executives are to be fully informed, this flood of material must be read and, when necessary, related to the accounting operations at your company. The dissemination of information on this scale cannot be handled orally or with periodic meetings and brief memos to the staff involved. Thus, there is a need for clear, consistent documentation to describe the accounting system being used, the principles involved, the policies that management wishes enforced, and the procedures describing what is to be done and how it is to be performed on a daily basis.

This book covers the development, implementation, and maintenance of 13 different accounting manuals. Two of these are mandatory: the *general accounting manual* that describes account coding schemes and how to code accounting transactions, and *the policy/procedure statement* system that provides full information to anyone needing to know a company's accounting policies and the procedures to maintain them.

The other 11 manuals are optional, but as you read about them you will find that they supplement and complement the primary accounting documentation; they are the lubricant of the accounting system, and as such are useful for increasing the efficiency of operations. If none of the following manuals are developed, certain portions of each will appear in the basic manuals but in less depth. They are as follows:

1. *Corporate policies manual*. Contains nearly 250 policies used to govern all functional areas of the accounting department.
2. *Purchasing card manual*. Describes all policies and procedures needed to operate an effective purchasing card program.
3. *Accounting controls manual*. Contains nearly 400 controls that can be used to ensure that accounting transactions are completed with a minimal number of exceptions, and that the probability of fraud is reduced.
4. *Period-end manual*. Describes the actions, reports, and schedules to be completed in sufficient detail to assure that the period-end closing is accurate, consistent, usable, and timely.
5. *Budgeting manual*. Describes the specific steps to be followed to create the annual budget, as well as task responsibilities by position.
6. *Property accounting manual*. Shows the forms that should be filled in and stored in order to maintain a proper database of all corporate fixed assets, describing when items were purchased or constructed, where they are located, and how they were disposed of.

7. **Forms manual**. Describes every form in detail—its use, limitations, and how to complete it.

8. **Document management manual**. Describes how to index, store, and dispose of information related to the accounting function.

9. **User manual**. Provides information to non-accountant employees who are involved in initiating or adding to an accounting document. This manual provides a list of employees by function, a condensed chart of accounts, and instructions for completing specific forms that are later used by the accounting department, such as the employee expense report.

10. **Information technology manual**. A condensation of portions of the technical computer processing instructions that accountants must handle, which can extend to basic operating procedures for the information technology staff.

11. **Human resources manual**. Contains a list of all policies related to human resources activities, as well as specific procedures required to perform operations within the human resources department.

This book gives the reader a wide variety of real-life examples for constructing all of the manuals just noted, as well as pertinent advice on how to write clearly, construct easy-to-use manuals, and issue both paper-based and electronic manuals. It should be the one-stop solution for anyone constructing accounting manuals.

September 2007
Centennial, Colorado

Acknowledgments

My background in procedures development stems entirely from a number of years in the consulting division of Ernst & Young, which employed many of the finest writers in the United States, including Janice "Red Pen" Roehl. Jan, you emptied a few red pens correcting my habits, and I appreciate the help.

About the Author

Steven Bragg, CPA, CMA, CIA, CPIM, has been the chief financial officer or controller of four companies, as well as a consulting manager at Ernst & Young and auditor at Deloitte & Touche. He received a Master's degree in Finance from Bentley College, an MBA from Babson College, and a Bachelor's degree in Economics from the University of Maine. He has been the two-time president of the Colorado Mountain Club, and is an avid alpine skier, mountain biker, and certified master diver. Mr. Bragg resides in Centennial, Colorado. He has written the following books through John Wiley & Sons:

Accounting and Finance for Your Small Business

Accounting Best Practices

Accounting Control Best Practices

Accounting Reference Desktop

Billing and Collections Best Practices

Business Ratios and Formulas

Controller's Guide to Costing

Controller's Guide to Planning and Controlling Operations

Controller's Guide: Roles and Responsibilities for the New Controller

Controllership

Cost Accounting

Design and Maintenance of Accounting Manuals

Essentials of Payroll

Fast Close

Financial Analysis

GAAP Guide

GAAP Policies and Procedures Manual

Inventory Accounting

Inventory Best Practices

Just-in-Time Accounting

Management Accounting Best Practices

Managing Explosive Corporate Growth

Outsourcing

Payroll Accounting

Payroll Best Practices

Revenue Recognition

Sales and Operations for Your Small Business

The Controller's Function

The New CFO Financial Leadership Manual

The Ultimate Accountants' Reference

Throughput Accounting

Also:

Advanced Accounting Systems (Institute of Internal Auditors)

Run the Rockies (CMC Press)

Free Online Resources by Steve Bragg

Steve issues a free accounting best practices newsletter and an accounting best practices podcast. You can sign up for both at www.stevebragg.com, or access the podcast through iTunes.

About the Web Site

As a purchaser of this book, *Accounting Policies and Procedures Manual: A Blueprint for Running an Effective and Efficient Department, 5th Edition,* you have access to the supporting Web site:

www.wiley.com/go/manual

The Web site contains files for the manuals that appear in this book (see Contents) as well as two additional manuals: Informational Technological Manual and Human Resources Manual. This material is provided in Word format in order for you to modify.

The password to enter this site is: accounting

Accounting Policies and Procedures Manual

Chapter 1

ACCOUNTING MANUALS

1.1 INTRODUCTION

Ask a dozen accountants to name the major method of communicating in their accounting operations and they will probably describe the accounting manual. However, you will get 12 answers about what the manual is, varying from a simple listing of account names and numbers to an academic treatise of the philosophy and practice of accounting as used in that particular environment.

In its simplest form, the accounting manual documents the meaning of sets of descriptive numbers used in an organized manner to record, summarize, and report information. It may contain descriptions of one or more of the systems and procedures that explain the basic accounting structure of the enterprise.

However, the manual can be much more than numbers and definitions. It may contain organization charts to show responsibility and lines of authority, policy, formulas, clerical procedures, special industry terminology, data processing rules and procedures, forms descriptions and uses, and so on. It is the general map through which one can learn to travel through a company's operations.

Every business enterprise has an accounting system, from the self-employed person operating a small business out of his or her home to charitable, not-for-profit organizations, educational institutions, governmental agencies, industrial and service companies, and so on. The system may be completely undocumented, possibly just a checkbook and a list of receipts, or it may be an elaborate, difficult-to-maintain, small library of books and manuals used by large national and international companies.

An accounting manual has three basic purposes: to answer questions, to instruct accounting personnel, and to provide consistent reporting of business transactions. As a printed document, it must be useful and, more importantly, *used*. Therefore, it should be *formal*—not in the sense of being rigid and unyielding, but in the sense of being complete and consistent.

It should be available to all who need it or think they need it. Certainly, the accounting staff needs the manual. Also, line supervisors, managers, and others who submit accounting data should have the manual available to them.

It should always be *current,* a condition requiring a method of publishing changes, additions, and deletions very quickly (see the discussion of electronic methods of distribution in Chapter 4). Finally, the manual should be *easy to use* as a tool to answer questions of consistency, accuracy, and clarity of presentation.

A word of warning: Unless the contents of a manual are to be used exclusively by accountants in the accounting operation, the accountants must turn *their* terminology into *our* terminology—that is, terminology that can be understood by non-accountant users of the manual. Avoid accounting jargon at all times.

For reference purposes, *accounting manual,* as used in this book, includes all the modules described in this chapter. The reader has the choice of developing selected modules and combining them into one accounting manual or maintaining each one as a separate manual. The modules are:

- General accounting manual
- Corporate policies manual
- Accounting procedures
- Purchasing card manual
- Accounting controls manual
- Year-end manual
- Budgeting manual
- Property accounting manual
- Forms manual
- Document management manual
- User manual
- Information technology manual
- Human resources manual

Each of these modules is briefly described in the following sections, and more fully described in the indicated chapters.

1.2 GENERAL ACCOUNTING MANUAL

The general accounting manual includes a general description of the overall accounting system, the chart of accounts, account descriptions, activities calendars for the accounting staffing, accounting policies, and descriptions of the key process cycles. Parts of the general accounting manual are usually included in the user manual to provide account coding information to other departments, such as purchasing and receiving, so that they can code transaction documents or otherwise provide accounting information. The general accounting manual is covered in Chapter 2.

The chart of accounts is the basic underlying account code structure that is used to record information in the general ledger. To create the chart, one prepares a list of every account number and name, which should include every asset, liability, ownership, income, and expense item. Then a one or two sentence definition is written for each line item in the chart of accounts. The list of definitions developed here will be the primary reference of permitted actions—and, more importantly, those that are not permitted—in each account being used. If divisions or departments are included in the corporate structure, then the account code structure can be stretched into a longer format to accommodate codes that can be traced to specific operating entities within the organization.

Job descriptions are extremely useful for determining which employee positions are responsible for which tasks, as well as to form a basis for periodic job reviews. These descriptions are most easily compiled by interviewing the staff members to see what they already do; on an ongoing basis, the descriptions can be adjusted to shift work among personnel to achieve increased levels of efficiency.

An activities calendar should be constructed not only for the entire department but also for each person within it. An activity calendar should itemize exactly which tasks should be completed on each day of the month. It forms the basis for task assignments within the accounting department, and is an excellent visual tool for managing the department's function. The calendar will be in a constant state of flux, as work tasks are constantly shifted among different staff members or moved to different time slots to create a balanced work flow for the department as a whole.

A more complete manual would contain a section on accounting principles and general procedures. For example, the company might indicate that it follows a published industry account numbering and format procedure, or that it operates in accordance with control guidelines laid down by the American Institute of Certified Public Accountants (AICPA).

Finally, the manual may contain flowcharts of the principal process cycles used by the company (such as the purchasing and order fulfillment cycles) as well as related procedures. The documentation of these key underlying activities gives the reader a broad conceptual overview of how the key accounting activities work, and how documents flow from function to function in order to complete tasks.

1.3 CORPORATE POLICIES MANUAL

Corporate policies are needed to set up boundaries within which transactions are to be accepted, and for how those transactions are to be processed. Policies are necessary components of a comprehensive system of controls and form an integral part of a company's risk management system. Chapter 5 contains nearly 250 policies for many transactional areas, including cash, hedges, barter transactions, inventory valuation, intangible assets, research and development costs, investments, debt extinguishment, warrants, lease terminations, dividends, options, and foreign currency translations. Though not all of these policies will be needed by any one company, a selection of the policies could form the foundation of a company's corporate policies manual.

1.4 ACCOUNTING PROCEDURES

The accounting procedures used must be clearly stated in a consistent format. To aid in the construction of such a manual, Chapter 3 itemizes a number of key writing, style, and mechanics guidelines. It also describes how to create an understandable flowchart that can accompany a procedure, including the most common direction of flow and types of graphics to use. The chapter also notes how to calculate and interpret read-ability statistics for a procedure. In addition to these general guidelines, the chapter describes how to lay out a simple procedure format and accompanying header, which are used in all subsequent chapters whenever example procedures are shown. Next, we cover the key work steps needed to construct a procedures manual, itemizing the process flow required to ensure that the information contained within a procedure is accurate. Finally, there is an itemization of suggested procedures that can be used. This list is by no means complete, because accounting systems will vary widely by industry, and even between companies within the same industry; nonetheless, it provides a core set of procedures that can be expanded upon to create a complete set of company-specific procedures.

With the basic procedure construction information in hand, one can then proceed to the creation of actual accounting procedures. Chapter 6 assists in this process by presenting a long list of actual procedures. They are summarized into the following categories for easy reference:

- Acquisitions
- Billing
- Budgeting
- Credit
- Financial statement preparation
- Fixed asset transactions
- Funds management
- Internal auditing
- Payroll
- Purchasing

The majority of the procedures were taken from the procedures manuals of several real companies that use different software packages and operate in different industries. Consequently, some of the most detailed information listed in the procedures will only be applicable to very specific situations, and must be modified to meet the reader's needs. Other procedures, such as those applying to acquisitions and budgeting, are more broad-based and can be applied to one's existing systems with comparatively little modification.

1.5 PURCHASING CARD MANUAL

A purchasing card program is an integral part of the purchasing program of many companies, since it usually results in a substantial reduction in the cost of acquiring goods and services. However, most such programs are informal, and can lead to purchasing abuses or excessive expenditures. The purchasing card manual shown in Chapter 7 itemizes how to set up a purchasing card program, as well as what forms are to be used to ensure that purchases are made in the appropriate amounts by authorized purchasers and that all purchases have been assigned to the correct cost centers.

1.6 ACCOUNTING CONTROLS MANUAL

In the era of the Sarbanes-Oxley Act, where adequate control systems are mandatory for publicly held companies, an accounting controls manual is not only a good idea, but should also be a cornerstone of a risk management program. Chapter 8 contains a list of nearly 400 controls that can be assembled into a controls manual, which in turn should be integrated into individual accounting procedures. It is advantageous to separately itemize controls in an accounting controls manual, since a risk manager or auditor can more easily peruse the document to ascertain the types of controls being used.

1.7 YEAR-END MANUAL

The year-end manual is probably better described as a year-end assignments list. It defines all of the tasks that must be accomplished at the end of a company's fiscal year to close the books and prepare the required accounting statements, schedules, and narrative for the annual report.

Once prepared, the year-end manual is updated annually for any changes in the fiscal year-end closing procedures. Such changes come about by a change in management, a change in auditors, or an expansion or contraction of year-end procedures caused by a change in accounting systems. The revised year-end manual is usually issued one or two months before the fiscal year-end to every employee assigned to complete one or more closing tasks. The manual is sometimes assembled in cooperation with the outside auditors, and working papers or schedules required by them are included as tasks. The year-end and period-end manuals are discussed in Chapter 9, which covers specific closing activities, the soft close, and closing procedures that are tailored to specific accounting positions.

1.8 BUDGETING MANUAL

Most organizations of any size spend a considerable amount of time creating budgets for at least the upcoming year, and perhaps for multiple years. If so, they have found that this is a complex and highly iterative process that impacts virtually every part of a company. In Chapter 10, we present the system of interlocking budgets and describe how they are structured so that one can see how information is first assembled for the sales budget. This information then cascades down into a series of "cost of goods sold" budgets that determine targeted inventory levels, purchasing volumes, production targets, and requirements for facilities as well as direct labor. After these steps are completed, budgets for supporting functions—such as general, administrative, and marketing—are added to the set of budgeting documents. The chapter contains a complete example of these interlocking budgets, as well as a discussion of flex budgeting, under which the supporting budgets all automatically change if revenue levels vary from the initial budgeted level. There is also coverage of the budgeting process and how budgets can be used as an integral part of corporate control systems.

1.9 PROPERTY ACCOUNTING MANUAL

The typical organization only tracks its fixed assets through some bare-bones entries in a depreciation calculation that itemizes the general type of asset, when it was purchased, what it cost, and the amount of its monthly depreciation. However, there are many other details that should be tracked, such as the presence of warranties that can be used in the event of a product failure, the location of each asset, and contact information about suppliers. A truly comprehensive set of information about each fixed asset is recorded in the property accounting manual, which is described in Chapter 11.

The chapter describes how to accumulate costs for projects that are being developed in-house with a project cost report. It also describes how to collect and organize information about land projects, which require the accumulation of special information such as legal descriptions, zoning classifications, and assessed value. There are additional discussions and different forms to cover land improvement projects, building projects, and the purchase of factory equipment, office equipment, vehicles, leasehold improvements, and leases. The chapter concludes with a complete example of a property accounting manual, showing the indexing, procedures, cost sheets, and instructions for the completion of each form.

1.10 FORMS MANUAL

Forms are the vehicles that carry information and approvals throughout the accounting map. They record the authorization and the purpose of a transaction and what actions are accomplished, such as buying, selling, making, biding, moving, adding, deleting, changing, and so forth. Forms are the foundation of computerized data processing activities. Developing and maintaining a forms manual need not be difficult or burdensome.

Chapter 12 provides a form survey worksheet to identify needed forms, presents a number of basic rules for creating forms, and then shows how to create form descriptions and compile them into a formal forms manual.

1.11 DOCUMENT MANAGEMENT MANUAL

Accounting departments are exceptionally good at creating paperwork, but typically experience considerable difficulty in indexing, storing, and disposing of it once it has been created. The document management manual shown in Chapter 13 contains policies and procedures that show how to handle these functions. The result should be a more organized accounting department where needed paperwork is readily available, less-necessary items are filed away, and there is a regimented system for disposing of outdated documents.

1.12 USER MANUAL

The user manual is most useful in companies where non-accountants initiate or prepare original accounting forms or documents that provide accounting information to the general accounting operation. Examples of such transactions are the hiring or termination of an employee or the submission of an expense report for reimbursement. Other examples of user manual procedures are petty cash reports, receiving reports, shipping documents, branch sales and activity, requests for special supplier payments such as subscriptions, dues, contractual services performed locally, and so on.

This manual can be general in nature or may contain specific abstracts from the general manual, forms manual, and policy/procedure statements. Usually it contains abstracts from other manuals, so it can be easy to prepare. It is designed for mass distribution to departments or individuals who use or prepare accounting documents, initiate account transaction coding, have some knowledge of the accounting process, or receive summary accounting reports. It can also be used as a training tool for non-accounting supervisors, secretaries, and others who are involved in adding or checking data on accounting input documents.

Instructions for creating a user manual, as well as a complete example of such a manual, are shown in Chapter 14.

1.13 INFORMATION TECHNOLOGY MANUAL

This manual has limited distribution, principally to the accounting and information technology staff members who are responsible for submitting forms and data to computer operations for data entry, processing, storage, and retrieval of the data for accounting use, as well as those responsible for ongoing computer system maintenance and development. This manual is unique in that it contains both forms descriptions and procedures. It may also contain details of file record contents and codes used, descriptions of output reports, and the data and calculations used to report each item on an output information report. The information technology manual is addressed in Chapter 15.

Chapter 15 provides a comprehensive set of policies related to systems development, which are:

- Project charter standards

- Work plan standards

- Project team roles and responsibilities

- Risk management standards

- Project status reporting standards

- Issue management standards

- Project completion debriefing standards

The policies can be easily adapted to one's needs with minimal modification. The chapter also contains a series of procedures covering a variety of tasks in the areas of computer system maintenance, the setup of new employees with computers, and the primary tasks involved in the development of new computer systems.

In addition to the fundamental components of the information technology manual, the chapter also covers the use of system survey reports to conduct an inventory of computer systems, as well as a computer reports questionnaire to see if long-standing reports can be reduced or eliminated from use. The chapter also covers the key elements of documentation for database tables and output reports. It finishes with a discussion of the key elements that should be included in a disaster recovery manual, which may be a separate manual or contained within the main information technology manual.

1.14   HUMAN RESOURCES MANUAL

As was the case for the information technology function, the human resources function is frequently under the supervision of the controller of chief financial officer, especially in smaller firms. Consequently, Chapter 16 is included so that one can see a comprehensive list of 28 human resources policies and 11 procedures that can be used to process the variety of transactions related to the payment of employees. Examples of policies included in the chapter are termination, grievance, sexual harassment, and jury duty. The employee pay procedures include the processing of changes to employee pay, cafeteria plan deductions, garnishments, and terminations.

1.15   ISO 9000 QUALITY STANDARDS

With the growth of international trade, particularly in raw materials and parts, customers are demanding assurances that distant suppliers are producing quality products. In an effort to provide that assurance, the International Standards Organization (ISO) issued the ISO 9000 quality standards. Acquiring certification is a lengthy process, but has proven to be necessary for those companies wishing to operate on a global basis.

During the ISO certification process, companies have learned the risk of having poor documentation and documentation practices. Many have therefore had to make significant changes in documentation to achieve certification.

ISO 9000 highlights the importance of comprehensive and well-written manuals for the production of quality products. The same is true for accounting. The quality of the output of the accounting system also depends on sound documentation practices. Accountants and particularly auditors have taken a leadership role here. The AICPA has issued the *Statement of Auditing Standard 55*. The *Consideration of Internal Structure in the Financial Statement Audit and Internal Control—Integrated Framework* is published by the Committee of Sponsoring Organizations (COSO) of the Treadway Commission. Both acknowledge the importance of documentation in the internal control structure.

There are several ISO standards. ISO 9000-1, *Quality Management and Quality Assurance Standards—Guidelines for Selection and Use* provides an overview of ISO 9000. ISO standards 9001, 9002, and 9003 provide quality assurance standards for manufacturers as well as service organizations.

All ISO 9000 standards require quality system documentation. ISO 9000 Quality System Standard 4.2.2, "Quality System Documentation," states that "all the quality system elements, requirements, and provisions should be clearly documented in a systematic and orderly manner." This very general statement was given more detail in ISO 9004 Standard 17.2, "Quality Documentation," which stated the following:

> The system should require that sufficient documentation be available to follow the achievement of the required product quality and the effective operation of the quality management system. Appropriate sub-contractor documentation should be included. All documentation should be legible, dated (including revision dates), clean, readily identifiable and maintained in an orderly manner. Data may be hard copy or stored in a computer.
>
> In addition the quality management system should provide a method for removing and/or disposing of documentation used in the manufacture of products when that documentation has become out of date. The following are examples of types of documents requiring control: drawings; specifications; blueprints; inspection instructions; test procedures; work instructions; operation sheets; quality manual; operational procedures; quality assurance procedures.

The standard explains that the quality manual can be one document supported by several tiers of other documents, each becoming progressively more detailed. For example, there may be an overall system manual and one or more specific procedural manuals. Together, these documents define the complete quality system. This standard is expounded upon in a handbook published by the ISO, *Documentation and Information,* and ISO 10013, *Guidelines for Developing Quality Manuals.*

The ISO 9004-2, "Guidelines for Services," describes the standard documentation system. Standard 5.4.3.1 states that the appropriate quality system documentation includes:

> (a) Quality manual: This should provide a description of the quality system as a permanent reference. It should contain the quality policy; the quality objectives; the structure of the organization, including responsibilities; a description of the quality system, including all elements and provisions that form part of it; the quality practices of the organization; the structure and distribution of the quality system documentation . . .

This standard is followed by Standard 5.4.3.2, "Documentation Control." This standard requires that documentation be legible, dated, clear, and readily identifiable, and that it carry authorization status. Methods should be established to control the issuance, distribution, and revision of documents. The methods should ensure that documents are "approved by authorized personnel; released and made available in the areas where information is needed; understood and acceptable to users; reviewed for necessary revision; removed when obsolete."

The ISO standards cited here require firms to maintain a "quality manual." Companies are not required to maintain an accounting manual, but we certainly recommend that every firm have one. Also, a firm's auditors expect an accounting manual, because adequate documentation is described by Statement of Auditing Standard (SAS) 55 as one of the primary control procedures and thus is an integral part of the control structure.

Again, the ISO standards suggest that the quality manual be one document, supported by several tiers of other documents, each becoming progressively more detailed. The ISO gives the example of an overall system manual and one or more specific procedural manuals, which together define the complete quality system. This book describes a system in which a company's accounting manual is composed of multiple modules that include the general accounting manual, accounting procedures, year-end or period-end manual, budgeting manual, property accounting manual, forms manual, user manual, information technology manual, and human resources manual. This is just one possible design, but is quite similar to that recommended by the ISO for the quality manual.

ISO 9000 requires that the quality manual contain the quality policy as well as the quality objectives. Most accounting manuals explain a firm's accounting policies, but many accounting manuals fail to provide a statement of the objectives of the accounting system. This would be a positive addition to the manual. Such a provision might include a mission statement for the accounting department, a vision statement, and some specific strategies that the department has adopted to reach the vision.

This section illustrated that ISO 9000 standards call for the documentation of quality systems, which includes a quality manual. With this knowledge in hand, accountants can offer their expertise in documentation to their firm's quality control function. Accountants in firms that are undergoing ISO 9000 certification can also learn from the quality control function, as recommendations for changes in the quality documentation may have an impact on company-wide procedures, especially in purchasing. For further information on ISO 9000 and the ISO in general, see the ISO site on the World Wide Web at www.iso.ch.

1.16 IN THE BEGINNING

To begin improving the current accounting system documentation, one should determine the strengths and weaknesses of the current documentation. To do this, questionnaires should be sent to the controller, the professional accountants on the staff, the clerical personnel in accounting, and the managers of departments related to accounting but not part of the accounting department. These departments generally are purchasing, shipping, receiving, finance, and human resources, as well as any other department that furnishes information to accounting.

Exhibit 1.1 is a questionnaire for determining the current status and use of an accounting manual. One form should be used for each separate manual. Enter the general name of the manual, the date that the form must be returned to the person designated to summarize the data, and the department or name of that person (who may also be a consultant). The employee receiving the questionnaire completes the form as follows:

- If the designated manual is not used at all by the recipient, it should be left blank and returned. If used, the frequency of use should be checked.

- A section should address some of the common problems with documentation. These questions are answered "yes" or "no," along with an example to illustrate any "no" answers.

- The recipients answer each use with "yes" or "no" and enter a final overall rating of the manual being surveyed.

```
MANUAL: General Accounting Manual

Name of Reviewer _____ Title _____ Dept._____

  I. __ Check here if your position does not require use of this accounting
        manual. Then stop your work on this questionnaire and return it to the
        address below.

        How often does your position require you to use this accounting manual?
        Check the appropriate frequency.
        _____ Daily
        _____ Several times per week
        _____ One or two times per week
        _____ Several times per month
        _____ One or two times per month
        _____ Several times per year
        _____ One or two times per year

 II.    For this manual, did you find any of the following? Give a specific example
        of any item marked "No" on the other side of this form.

        1. Manual was not readily available.          _____ Yes      _____ No
        2. Information needed was missing.             _____ Yes      _____ No
        3. Information was not clearly written.        _____ Yes      _____ No
        4. Contained terms and jargon I did not know.  _____ Yes      _____ No
        5. Information was difficult to locate.        _____ Yes      _____ No
        6. Information was not current.                _____ Yes      _____ No
        7. Other problems                              _____ Yes      _____ No

III.    Rate how useful the manual is for each of its uses. (Use a 10-point scale,
        where a 1 is not at all useful and a 10 is tremendously useful.)

        Use                                                          Rating
        a. Training new personnel                                    _____
        b. Ensuring uniformity and consistency of reports            _____
        c. Evaluating controls                                       _____
        d. Communicating new policies, procedures, and information   _____
        e. Overall rating                                            _____
        f. Other uses (please list):                                 _____


                            (date)            Controller's Office
Return completed form by _____ to _____
```

Exhibit 1.1 Current Accounting Documentation Questionnaire

1.   Manual _____   Person Responsible _____

     Brief description of the contents of the manual:

2.   What is the distribution of the manual (who has manuals)?

3.   Describe the format of the manual. Are manuals distributed in printed form or
     part of an electronic document system? If they are distributed on electronic
     media, describe the system used.

4.   If the manual is updated, how often? How is the update accomplished?

5.   Are there other sources of documentation of the accounting function/system
     besides the manual described above?

6.   Is there anything in this documentation that you feel is a major weakness? If
     yes, describe.

7.   SUMMARY OF QUESTIONNAIRES: How was the accounting documentation rated on a
     10-point scale, where 1 is not at all useful and 10 is tremendously useful?
     _____ Controller.
     _____ Average of all accounting professional staff.
     _____ Average of managers of departments related to accounting.
     _____ Average of all accounting department clerical staff.

8.   Does it appear that there is a need for more documentation? Explain.

Exhibit 1.2   Summary of Current Accounting Documentation

Exhibit 1.2 is the Summary of Current Accounting Documentation, which is compiled by the person designated to do so. This person should be knowledgeable about the current documentation and may be the principal writer. The reviewer completes this form as follows:

- Enter the formal name of the manual, the person responsible for maintaining its contents and distribution lists, and a brief description of the manual being surveyed.

- Enter the normal distribution of the manual in general terms, such as accounting personnel or designated departments.

- Describe the general format of the manual, such as numbered sections, indexing, and general layout. Also describe how the manual is available via electronic media or some other method.

- Describe how the manual is updated. Is it edited and changed periodically, such as each year, or are only new items distributed as needed?

- Describe any other possible sources of documentation, such as file folders of examples of transactions or forms, or textbooks.

- Describe anything the reviewer thinks may be a major weakness. (The principal weaknesses are listed in the questionnaire.)

- Summarize individual questionnaires for the groups shown. There should be some weighting of each user group. Also, the yes-no answers to question two of the individual questionnaires should be summarized to determine whether there are definite patterns of weakness.

- Enter an opinion about whether improved documentation is needed, with explanations of what principal weaknesses were discovered.

Once the survey is completed and discussed with appropriate personnel such as the chief financial officer, controller, and treasurer, the task to develop new documentation can begin.

1.17 PROCEDURES TO WRITE AND CHANGE PROCEDURES

Though many people want to sit down at a computer and immediately start writing procedures, this usually leads to a set of documents with poor formatting and inconsistent writing. When such documents are issued, readers find them difficult to read, so many ignore them, thereby voiding the purpose of the procedures.

A better way to approach procedure writing is to first create procedures that describe not only how to create a new procedure, but also how to update an existing one. These two tasks are documented in the sample procedures shown in Exhibits 1.3 and 1.4.

Policy/Procedure Statement	Retrieval No.:	PROC-01
Brasto Publishing	Page:	1 of 1
	Issue Date:	10/28/0X
Subject: How to Write a Procedure	Supersedes:	N/A

1.   PURPOSE AND SCOPE
This procedure is used by any employees who require some assistance in
determining the methodology for creating a new procedure.

2.   RESPONSIBILITIES
WRITER   **Staff Writer**

3.   PROCEDURES
3.1   WRITER   **Access Procedure Template**
Go to the Word subdirectory and access the template file for a procedure. Fill in the blanks
on the form and give it to the controller to be entered into the corporate procedures database.
The blanks on the form include the following areas:
1. *Purpose and Scope*. List the reason for the procedure and specify who is expected to use it.
2. *Definitions*. Describe any words used in the procedure that readers may not be familiar with.
3. *Responsibilities*. List the employee positions that are responsible for completing
various steps in the procedure.
4. *Procedures*. List all the steps in the procedure. The level of detail should be sufficient
for a user to complete the described steps without having to ask for additional assistance.
5. *References*. Note any related procedures or documents that the user should refer
to that will help in understanding this procedure.
6. *Records*. Note where the documents (if any) resulting from this procedure are to be stored,
as well as where documents needed for it are located.
7. *Governing Policies*. List the policies that set boundaries for activities described
in this procedure.

3.2   WRITER   **Review Document**
Issue the preliminary procedure document back to all employees who are involved with
the activities described within it, and ask them to review its content. Be sure to specify a due date.

3.3   WRITER   **Enter Adjustment**s
Once the revised procedure document is returned, enter all adjustments into the database, print
the final version, and release it to all personnel who are listed on the approved distribution list.
Put a hard copy of the new procedure in the master procedures manual.

Exhibit 1.3   How to Write a Procedure Statement

Policy/Procedure Statement	Retrieval No.:	PROC-02
Brasto Publishing	Page:	1 of 1
	Issue Date:	10/28/0X
	Supersedes:	N/A
Subject: How to Change an Existing Procedure		

1. **PURPOSE AND SCOPE**

   This procedure is used to facilitate an orderly change in an existing procedure.

2. **RESPONSIBILITIES**

   USER   **Procedure User**

   WRITER   **Staff Writer**

3. **PROCEDURES**

   3.1   USER   **Copy the Procedure**

   Fill out the procedure change notice and make any changes to the procedure. Alternatively, obtain a hard copy of the existing procedure and mark any changes directly onto it in red ink.

   3.2   USER   **Turn in the Request Form**

   Turn in the request form to the procedure writer. Keep a copy for your records in case the original is mislaid.

   3.3   WRITER   **Input Data Changes**

   Enter the requested changes to the procedure. Give the rough draft to the user who requested the change and ask that it be proofed for errors. When the procedure is returned, make any additional changes and print out the final version.

   3.4   WRITER   **Distribute the Procedure**

   Release the procedure to all employees who are on the distribution list for this procedure. File a copy of the revised procedure in the master procedures manual.

Exhibit 1.4   How to Change an Existing Procedure Statement

Chapter 2

GENERAL ACCOUNTING MANUAL

2.1 INTRODUCTION

The general accounting manual is intended for the use of the accounting staff, both at the headquarters location and at any outlying locations that may have somewhat less broad-based accounting functionality. It may also be requested by internal and external auditors, who use it as input to their decisions to test the level of control on various types of company transactions. In rare cases, it may also be used as evidence in legal disputes, such as when a company must prove its level of controls if accused under the Foreign Corrupt Practices Act.

The manual is most efficiently produced if it is printed in a single standard format, rather than being subdivided for people or locations having limited accounting responsibilities. However, in situations where the number of documented transactions is excessively large, it may make sense to separate the documents into orderly groupings for specific recipients so that a limited number of standard manuals can be issued, rather than a complete set.

There are a variety of documents that may be included in the general accounting manual. The decision to include or exclude a document should, to some degree, be based on the number of times that documents are needed. For example, if an assistant controller is constantly being pestered with questions about what account codes to use for various transactions, then it makes sense to include a set of standard journal entries in the manual. However, if information is constantly being revised, then it should be distributed separately, rather than being contained within the manual. For example, a company phone list should be updated separately, as employee departures and new hires will call for ongoing updates. Another reason for including information in the manual is that it is part of a new employee's training. For example, a transaction that describes the basic entry of accounts payable invoices into the computer system is useful to a new hire, even though this may become second nature within a week and will never be used again. This type of document needs to be included simply as a reference for those employees whose skill levels are still ramping up.

The contents of the general accounting manual usually include the chart of accounts, because this is a useful reference tool for making general ledger entries. It should also include accounting term definitions; these may be standard terms found in any accounting text, but should also include terms noted in a company's accounting software package so that new users of the system will understand the meaning of particular data entry fields. The manual should also include job descriptions for all accounting positions so that each person knows his or her responsibilities. There should also be an activities calendar for each position, which is an extremely useful way to keep the accounting staff informed of their duties on particular days of the month. Another useful addition is a complete set of corporate policies that apply to the accounting department. This information is usually supplemented by an overview of all key process cycles and their supporting procedures, which typically form the bulk of the manual. These documents give users crucial information about what transactions are allowed, how they fit into the greater scheme of linked procedures throughout the company, and how each procedure must be completed. The following sections describe the contents of each section of the general accounting manual.

2.2 CHART OF ACCOUNTS[1]

This section covers the types of account numbering formats that can be used to construct a chart of accounts, and also lists sample charts of accounts that use each of the formats. All of the charts of accounts shown follow the same general sequence of account coding, which itemizes the accounts in the balance sheet first, and the income statement second. That sequence is as follows:

- Current assets
- Fixed assets
- Other assets
- Current liabilities
- Long-term liabilities
- Equity accounts
- Revenue
- Cost of goods sold
- Selling, general, and administrative expenses
- Income taxes
- Extraordinary items

---

[1] Much of this section is from *Ultimate Accounts' Reference*, Steven Bragg, copyright ©2006 John Wiley & Sons. This material is used by permission of John Wiley & Sons, Inc.

(a)   Three-Digit Account Code Structure

A three-digit account code structure allows one to create a numerical sequence of accounts that contains up to 1,000 potential accounts. It is useful for small businesses that have no predefined departments or divisions that must be broken out separately. A sample chart of accounts using this format is shown below:

Account Number	Description
010	Cash
020	Petty cash
030	Accounts receivable
040	Reserve for bad debts
050	Marketable securities
060	Raw materials inventory
070	Work-in-process inventory
080	Finished goods inventory
090	Reserve for obsolete inventory
100	Fixed assets—Computer equipment
110	Fixed assets—Computer software
120	Fixed assets—Furniture and fixtures
130	Fixed assets—Leasehold improvements
140	Fixed assets—Machinery
150	Accumulated depreciation—Computer equipment
160	Accumulated depreciation—Computer software
170	Accumulated depreciation—Furniture and fixtures
180	Accumulated depreciation—Leasehold improvements
190	Accumulated depreciation—Machinery
200	Other assets
300	Accounts payable
310	Accrued payroll liability
320	Accrued vacation liability
330	Accrued expenses liability—Other
340	Unremitted sales taxes
350	Unremitted pension payments
360	Short-term notes payable
370	Other short-term liabilities
400	Long-term notes payable
500	Capital stock
510	Retained earnings
600	Revenue
700	Cost of goods sold—Materials
710	Cost of goods sold—Direct labor
720	Cost of goods sold—Manufacturing supplies
730	Cost of goods sold—Applied overhead
800	Bank charges
805	Benefits
810	Depreciation
815	Insurance
825	Office supplies
830	Salaries and wages
835	Telephones
840	Training

Account Number	Description
845	Travel and entertainment
850	Utilities
855	Other expenses
860	Interest expense
900	Extraordinary items

Notice how each clearly definable block of accounts begins with a different set of account numbers. For example, current liabilities begin with "300," revenues begin with "600," and cost of goods sold items begin with "700." This not only makes it easier to navigate through the chart of accounts, but is also mandated by many computerized accounting software packages.

(b) Five-Digit Account Code Structure

A five-digit account code structure is designed for those organizations with clearly defined departments, each of which is tracked with a separate income statement. This format uses the same account codes for the balance sheet accounts that we just saw for three-digit account codes, but replicates at least the operating expenses for each department (and sometimes for the revenue accounts, too). An example of this format is as follows, using the engineering and sales departments to illustrate the duplication of accounts:

Account Number	Department	Description
00-010	xxx	Cash
00-020	xxx	Petty cash
00-030	xxx	Accounts receivable
00-040	xxx	Reserve for bad debts
00-050	xxx	Marketable securities
00-060	xxx	Raw materials inventory
00-070	xxx	Work-in-process inventory
00-080	xxx	Finished goods inventory
00-090	xxx	Reserve for obsolete inventory
00-100	xxx	Fixed assets—Computer equipment
00-110	xxx	Fixed assets—Computer software
00-120	xxx	Fixed assets—Furniture and fixtures
00-130	xxx	Fixed assets—Leasehold improvements
00-140	xxx	Fixed assets—Machinery
00-150	xxx	Accumulated depreciation—Computer equipment
00-160	xxx	Accumulated depreciation—Computer software
00-170	xxx	Accumulated depreciation—Furniture and fixtures
00-180	xxx	Accumulated depreciation—Leasehold improvements
00-190	xxx	Accumulated depreciation—Machinery
00-200	xxx	Other assets
00-300	xxx	Accounts payable
00-310	xxx	Accrued payroll liability
00-320	xxx	Accrued vacation liability
00-330	xxx	Accrued expenses liability—Other
00-340	xxx	Unremitted sales taxes

00-350	xxx	Unremitted pension payments
00-360	xxx	Short-term notes payable
00-370	xxx	Other short term liabilities
00-400	xxx	Long-term notes payable
00-500	xxx	Capital stock
00-510	xxx	Retained earnings
00-600	xxx	Revenue
00-700	xxx	Cost of goods sold—Materials
00-710	xxx	Cost of goods sold—Direct labor
00-720	xxx	Cost of goods sold—Manufacturing supplies
00-730	xxx	Cost of goods sold—Applied overhead
10-800	Engineering	Bank charges
10-805	Engineering	Benefits
10-810	Engineering	Depreciation
10-815	Engineering	Insurance
10-825	Engineering	Office supplies
10-830	Engineering	Salaries and wages
10-835	Engineering	Telephones
10-840	Engineering	Training
10-845	Engineering	Travel and entertainment
10-850	Engineering	Utilities
10-855	Engineering	Other expenses
10-860	Engineering	Interest expense
20-800	Sales	Bank charges
20-805	Sales	Benefits
20-810	Sales	Depreciation
20-815	Sales	Insurance
20-825	Sales	Office supplies
20-830	Sales	Salaries and wages
20-835	Sales	Telephones
20-840	Sales	Training
20-845	Sales	Travel and entertainment
20-850	Sales	Utilities
20-855	Sales	Other expenses
20-860	Sales	Interest expense
00-900	xxx	Extraordinary items

In this example, all expense accounts are replicated for every department. This does not mean, however, that all accounts must be *used* for every department. For example, it is most unlikely that bank charges will be ascribed to either the engineering or sales departments. Accordingly, those accounts that are not to be used can be rendered inactive in the accounting system so that they never appear in the general ledger.

(c)   Seven-Digit Account Code Structure

A seven-digit account code structure is used by those companies that not only have multiple departments, but also multiple divisions or locations, for each of which the management team wants to record separate accounting information. This requires the same coding structure used for the five-digit system, except that two digits are placed in front of the code to signify a different company division. These new digits also apply to balance sheet accounts, because most organizations will want to track assets and liabilities by division. The following chart of accounts, which identifies accounts for divisions in Atlanta and Seattle, continues to use the engineering and sales departments as an example of how the seven-digit account code structure is compiled.

Account No.	Division	Department	Description
10-00-010	Atlanta	xxx	Cash
10-00-020	Atlanta	xxx	Petty cash
10-00-030	Atlanta	xxx	Accounts receivable
10-00-040	Atlanta	xxx	Reserve for bad debts
10-00-050	Atlanta	xxx	Marketable securities
10-00-060	Atlanta	xxx	Raw materials inventory
10-00-070	Atlanta	xxx	Work-in-process inventory
10-00-080	Atlanta	xxx	Finished goods inventory
10-00-090	Atlanta	xxx	Reserve for obsolete inventory
10-00-100	Atlanta	xxx	Fixed assets—Computer equipment
10-00-110	Atlanta	xxx	Fixed assets—Computer software
10-00-120	Atlanta	xxx	Fixed assets—Furniture and fixtures
10-00-130	Atlanta	xxx	Fixed assets—Leasehold improvements
10-00-140	Atlanta	xxx	Fixed assets—Machinery
10-00-150	Atlanta	xxx	Accumulated depreciation—Computer equipment
10-00-160	Atlanta	xxx	Accumulated depreciation—Computer software
10-00-170	Atlanta	xxx	Accumulated depreciation— Furniture and fixtures
10-00-180	Atlanta	xxx	Accumulated depreciation—Leasehold improvements
10-00-190	Atlanta	xxx	Accumulated depreciation—Machinery
10-00-200	Atlanta	xxx	Other assets
10-00-300	Atlanta	xxx	Accounts payable
10-00-310	Atlanta	xxx	Accrued payroll liability
10-00-320	Atlanta	xxx	Accrued vacation liability
10-00-330	Atlanta	xxx	Accrued expenses liability—Other
10-00-340	Atlanta	xxx	Unremitted sales taxes
10-00-350	Atlanta	xxx	Unremitted pension payments
10-00-360	Atlanta	xxx	Short term notes payable
10-00-370	Atlanta	xxx	Other short-term liabilities
10-00-400	Atlanta	xxx	Long-term notes payable
10-00-500	Atlanta	xxx	Capital stock
10-00-510	Atlanta	xxx	Retained earnings
10-00-600	Atlanta	xxx	Revenue
10-00-700	Atlanta	xxx	Cost of goods sold—Materials
10-00-710	Atlanta	xxx	Cost of goods sold—Direct labor
10-00-720	Atlanta	xxx	Cost of goods sold—Manufacturing supplies
10-00-730	Atlanta	xxx	Cost of goods sold—Applied overhead
10-10-800	Atlanta	Engineering	Bank charges
10-10-805	Atlanta	Engineering	Benefits
10-10-810	Atlanta	Engineering	Depreciation
10-10-815	Atlanta	Engineering	Insurance
10-10-825	Atlanta	Engineering	Office supplies
10-10-830	Atlanta	Engineering	Salaries and wages
10-10-835	Atlanta	Engineering	Telephones
10-10-840	Atlanta	Engineering	Training
10-10-845	Atlanta	Engineering	Travel and entertainment
10-10-850	Atlanta	Engineering	Utilities

10-10-855	Atlanta	Engineering	Other expenses
10-10-860	Atlanta	Engineering	Interest expense
10-20-800	Atlanta	Sales	Bank charges
10-20-805	Atlanta	Sales	Benefits
10-20-810	Atlanta	Sales	Depreciation
10-20-815	Atlanta	Sales	Insurance
10-20-825	Atlanta	Sales	Office supplies
10-20-830	Atlanta	Sales	Salaries and wages
10-20-835	Atlanta	Sales	Telephones
10-20-840	Atlanta	Sales	Training
10-20-845	Atlanta	Sales	Travel and entertainment
10-20-850	Atlanta	Sales	Utilities
10-20-855	Atlanta	Sales	Other expenses
10-20-860	Atlanta	Sales	Interest expense
10-00-900	Atlanta	xxx	Extraordinary items
20-00-010	Seattle	xxx	Cash
20-00-020	Seattle	xxx	Petty cash
20-00-030	Seattle	xxx	Accounts receivable
20-00-040	Seattle	xxx	Reserve for bad debts
20-00-050	Seattle	xxx	Marketable securities
20-00-060	Seattle	xxx	Raw materials inventory
20-00-070	Seattle	xxx	Work-in-process inventory
20-00-080	Seattle	xxx	Finished goods inventory
20-00-090	Seattle	xxx	Reserve for obsolete inventory
20-00-100	Seattle	xxx	Fixed assets—Computer equipment
20-00-110	Seattle	xxx	Fixed assets—Computer software
20-00-120	Seattle	xxx	Fixed assets—Furniture and fixtures
20-00-130	Seattle	xxx	Fixed assets—Leasehold improvements
20-00-140	Seattle	xxx	Fixed assets—Machinery
20-00-150	Seattle	xxx	Accumulated depreciation—Computer equipment
20-00-160	Seattle	xxx	Accumulated depreciation—Computer software
20-00-170	Seattle	xxx	Accumulated depreciation—Furniture and fixtures
20-00-180	Seattle	xxx	Accumulated depreciation—Leasehold improvements
20-00-190	Seattle	xxx	Accumulated depreciation—Machinery
20-00-200	Seattle	xxx	Other assets
20-00-300	Seattle	xxx	Accounts payable
20-00-310	Seattle	xxx	Accrued payroll liability
20-00-320	Seattle	xxx	Accrued vacation liability
20-00-330	Seattle	xxx	Accrued expenses liability—Other
20-00-340	Seattle	xxx	Unremitted sales taxes
20-00-350	Seattle	xxx	Unremitted pension payments
20-00-360	Seattle	xxx	Short-term notes payable
20-00-370	Seattle	xxx	Other short-term liabilities
20-00-400	Seattle	xxx	Long-term notes payable
20-00-500	Seattle	xxx	Capital stock
20-00-510	Seattle	xxx	Retained earnings
20-00-600	Seattle	xxx	Revenue
20-00-700	Seattle	xxx	Cost of goods sold—Materials
20-00-710	Seattle	xxx	Cost of goods sold—Direct labor
20-00-720	Seattle	xxx	Cost of goods sold—Manufacturing supplies
20-00-730	Seattle	xxx	Cost of goods sold—Applied overhead
20-10-800	Seattle	Engineering	Engineering—Bank charges
20-10-805	Seattle	Engineering	Engineering—Benefits
20-10-810	Seattle	Engineering	Engineering—Depreciation

Account No.	Division	Department	Description
20-10-815	Seattle	Engineering	Engineering—Insurance
20-10-825	Seattle	Engineering	Engineering—Office supplies
20-10-830	Seattle	Engineering	Engineering—Salaries and wages
20-10-835	Seattle	Engineering	Engineering—Telephones
20-10-840	Seattle	Engineering	Engineering—Training
20-10-845	Seattle	Engineering	Engineering—Travel and entertainment
20-10-850	Seattle	Engineering	Engineering—Utilities
20-10-855	Seattle	Engineering	Engineering—Other expenses
20-10-860	Seattle	Engineering	Engineering—Interest expense
20-20-800	Seattle	Sales	Sales—Bank charges
20-20-805	Seattle	Sales	Sales—Benefits
20-20-810	Seattle	Sales	Sales—Depreciation
20-20-815	Seattle	Sales	Sales—Insurance
20-20-825	Seattle	Sales	Sales—Office supplies
20-20-830	Seattle	Sales	Sales—Salaries and wages
20-20-835	Seattle	Sales	Sales—Telephones
20-20-840	Seattle	Sales	Sales—Training
20-20-845	Seattle	Sales	Sales—Travel and entertainment
20-20-850	Seattle	Sales	Sales—Utilities
20-20-855	Seattle	Sales	Sales—Other expenses
20-20-860	Seattle	Sales	Sales—Interest expense
20-00-900	Seattle	xxx	Extraordinary items

Any of the preceding account codes will be eventually used in a journal entry, for which a standard form should be used such as the one shown in Exhibit 2.1. The form requires both an approval signature and description of the entry, thereby ensuring adequate documentation and evidence that the entry is necessary. There is also space at the bottom of the entry for references to additional exchange rate information, in case foreign exchange is involved.

2.3 ACCOUNTING TERM DEFINITIONS

Though it is not necessary to include an entire dictionary of accounting terms in the general accounting manual, it is useful to include those that are commonly used within the company's transactions, as well as those that appear in its accounting software. Of particular importance are those terms that are unique to the industry within which the company operates. For example, the oil and gas, software, and movie industries have special terminology that cannot be learned through regular accounting classes.

Definitions should be concise and meaningful. One or two sentences of definition are usually sufficient. Because the definitions are references sources, they should be developed for quick and easy look-up. For example, the definition for "fixed asset" may be listed under "A," using the header "Asset, fixed." If a user goes to the "F" section of the definitions, there should be a referral statement, such as "Fixed asset, *see* Asset, fixed. This standard indexing method should make it as easy as possible to find a specific definition. An example of a series of accounting term definitions is as follows:[2]

---

[2]Definitions are from *Cost Accounting: A Comprehensive Guide*, Steven Bragg copyright ©2001 John Wiley & Sons. This material is used by permission of John Wiley & Sons, Inc.

Journal Entry Form

Date: _____   Approval: _____

Account No.	Account Name	Debit	Credit
_____	_____	_____	_____
_____	_____	_____	_____
_____	_____	_____	_____
_____	_____	_____	_____
_____	_____	_____	_____
_____	_____	_____	_____

Reason for journal entry: _____
_____
_____

Exchange rate used: _____
Exchange rate source document: _____
Date of source document: _____

Exhibit 2.1   Journal Entry Form

Backflushing. A method for recognizing incurred costs from the production process that records transactions at the point when production is completed, rather than when materials are released from the warehouse area.

Batch cost. A cost that is incurred when a group of products or services are produced, and which cannot be identified to specific products or services within each group.

Benchmarking. The process of comparing a company's processes and outputs to those of other organizations to determine the "best of class," which a company can then emulate internally to improve its profitability, efficiency, or competitive position.

Bill of materials. A listing of the quantities of all parts and subassemblies that comprise a product. It frequently includes additional information, such as the standard scrap rate to be expected when using each component. It is of great value for a number of applications, such as backflushing and product costing.

Book inventory. The amount of money invested in inventory, as per a company's accounting records. It is comprised of the beginning inventory balance, plus the cost of any receipts, less the cost of sold or scrapped inventory. It may be significantly different from the actual on-hand inventory, if the two are not periodically reconciled.

Book value. An asset's original cost, less any depreciation that has been subsequently incurred.

By-product, *see* Joint production.

A different approach to the inclusion of accounting term definitions in the manual is to define every account listed in the chart of accounts. By doing so, any accounting personnel who are responsible for entering transactions into either the general ledger or its supporting journals will have a better idea of which accounts should be used. This can save a great deal of time later on, when incorrectly applied transactions must be researched and corrected. The following sample definitions are used for the three-digit sample chart of accounts that was described earlier in this chapter.

Account Number	Name	Definition
010	Cash	Money deposited at the bank. If there are restrictions on deposited cash, then it is accounted for as a long-term asset.
020	Petty cash	Money retained in the petty cash box.
030	Accounts receivable	Money due from customers for services received or products shipped, but not yet received. If there are amounts due from officers or employees, these moneys are listed under "other accounts receivable."
040	Reserve for bad debts	A reserve fund that is held as a contingency against the nonpayment of outstanding accounts receivable. This account should always have a credit balance.
050	Marketable securities	Cash that is invested in easily traded equity or debt securities. The cost of acquiring these securities is included in the account.
060	Raw materials inventory	The amount of materials kept on hand for eventual inclusion in finished goods. All freight costs associated with the acquisition of raw materials are included in this account.
070	Work-in-process inventory	The cost of partially completed units of production. Costs stored in this account include raw materials, and any raw materials or overhead used to date.
080	Finished goods inventory	The cost of completed products that have not yet been shipped to customers. Costs stored in this account include all raw materials, direct labor, and overhead used during the production process.
090	Reserve for obsolete inventory	A reserve fund that is held as a contingency against the eventual write-off of any types of inventory that no longer have a resale value.
100	Fixed assets— Computer equipment	Purchased computer equipment exceeding the corporate capitalization limit that has an expected life of greater than one year.
110	Fixed assets— Computer software	Purchased computer software exceeding the corporate capitalization limit that has an expected life of greater than one year.
120	Fixed assets— Furniture and fixtures	Purchased furniture exceeding the corporate capitalization limit that has an expected life of greater than one year.

130	Fixed assets—Leasehold improvements	Improvements made by the company to its leased properties, exceeding the corporate capitalization limit, that has an expected life of greater than one year.
140	Fixed assets—Machinery	Purchased production equipment exceeding the corporate capitalization limit that has an expected life of greater than one year.
150	Accumulated depreciation—Computer equipment	The total of all depreciation charged against the computer equipment fixed asset account, net of disposed assets. This account has a credit balance.
160	Accumulated depreciation—Computer software	The total of all depreciation charged against the computer software fixed asset account, net of disposed assets. This account has a credit balance.
170	Accumulated depreciation—Furniture and fixtures	The total of all depreciation charged against the furniture and fixtures fixed asset account, net of disposed assets. This account has a credit balance.
180	Accumulated depreciation—Leasehold improvements	The total of all depreciation charged against the leasehold improvement fixed asset account, net of disposed assets. This account has a credit balance.
190	Accumulated depreciation—Machinery	The total of all depreciation charged against the machinery fixed asset account, net of disposed assets. This account has a credit balance.
200	Other assets	An account in which minor asset items are stored that do not fit into any other asset account categories.
300	Accounts payable	Both billed and accrued commitments to pay suppliers for services rendered or products shipped to the company.
310	Accrued payroll liability	An obligation to pay wages to employees, but which has not yet been paid.
320	Accrued vacation liability	An obligation to pay for earned vacation time to employees, but which has not yet been paid.
330	Accrued expenses liability—Other	An account in which minor accrued expenses are stored, or those accrued expenses are stored, that do not occur on a recurring basis.
340	Unremitted sales taxes	Sales taxes to government entities that are a company obligation to make as a result of selling products or services into the geographic areas governed by those entities, but which have not yet been made.
350	Unremitted pension payments	Pensions payments that are an obligation of the company to make into the employee pension fund, but which have not yet been made.
360	Short-term notes payable	Debt obligations that are due for payment in less than one year.
370	Other short-term liabilities	An account in which minor liability items are stored that do not fit into any other liability account categories.
400	Long-term notes payable	Debt obligations that are due for payment in more than one year.
500	Capital stock	The amount of funds received from investors in exchange for the issuance of common or preferred stock.
510	Retained earnings	Total corporate earnings since the creation of the company, less dividends and any prior period adjustments.
600	Revenue	The sale of products or services, or receipts from investments, such as interest, royalties, or dividends.

Account Number	Name	Definition
700	Cost of goods sold—Materials	The direct cost of materials associated with the sale of a tangible product. This includes all materials listed on a product's bill of materials, plus all scrap incurred during production, less the resale value of any by-products.
710	Cost of goods sold—Direct labor	The labor expense required to produce a product or service, which is limited to assembly labor.
720	Cost of goods sold—Manufacturing supplies	The cost of supplies consumed when a product is manufactured. This includes all incidental machinery maintenance supplies and packaging materials.
730	Cost of goods sold—Applied overhead	The cost of manufacturing, excluding materials, direct labor, and supplies. Includes depreciation on manufacturing equipment and facilities, as well as factory administration, indirect labor, maintenance, production employees' benefits, quality control and inspection, production facility rent, repair expenses, rework labor, and spoilage.
800	Bank charges	The expense associated with credit card fees, bank service charges, and the cost of printing checks.
805	Benefits	The expense associated with medical insurance, dental insurance, long-term and short-term disability insurance, and health club reimbursement fees. All employee payroll deductions to co-pay benefits should be credited against this account.
810	Depreciation	The expense associated with the periodic reduction of the value of fixed assets, in accordance with a standard value-reduction methodology.
815	Insurance	The expense associated with key-man life insurance, business insurance, and workers' compensation insurance.
825	Office supplies	The expense associated with miscellaneous tangible office purchases, such as paper products, printer cartridges, and diskettes.
830	Salaries and wages	The expense associated with employee pay, which includes salaries, wages, severance payments, signing bonuses, and accrued wages.
835	Telephones	The expense associated with "800" phone service, incoming phone lines, and cell phones. The cost of phone equipment is charged either to office supplies or to fixed assets, depending upon the dollar-value purchased.
840	Training	The expense associated with outsourced training suppliers, tests, and purchased training materials. It does not include travel costs associated with employee travel to training classes, nor the salary cost of inhouse training personnel.
845	Travel and entertainment	The expense associated with the travel of either employees or reimbursed contractors. Includes air fare, lodging, parking, and meals.
850	Utilities	The expense associated with water, heat, waste removal, and electricity fees charged by utilities.
855	Other expenses	Includes all incidental expenses under $500 that do not readily fall into any other category. Consult with the assistant controller before making entries into this account.

| 860 | Interest expense | The expense associated with the interest cost of revolving debt, interest on late payments to suppliers, and outstanding company bonds. Also includes accrued interest on unpaid interest expenses. |
| 900 | Extraordinary items | Any expense that is both unusual and infrequent, such as a gain on a troubled debt restructuring or the loss of foreign assets due to governmental expropriation. No entries to this account are allowed without the controller's approval. |

Other definitions for accounts that are commonly used by the accounting staff include:

Travel and Subsistence

- *Meals and lodging.* Includes meals and lodging costs (hotel, motel, etc.) in accordance with company policy for reimbursement. Per diem allowances for meals and lodging are included here.

- *Travel in private vehicle.* Includes travel in employee-owned vehicles at the currently approved mileage reimbursement rate.

- *Travel in rented vehicle.* Includes daily car rental fees from outside providers.

- *Travel in public carrier.* Includes air, bus, and train travel.

- *Travel in motor pool vehicles.* Includes charges for the use of company-owned vehicles at the approved rates. Costs of air travel for the company-owned air plane are included here.

- *Other travel costs.* Includes such incidental expenses as tips, telephone calls, taxis, tolls, and parking while on a company-authorized trip. Tips on meals are included in meal costs.

- *Conference and registration fees.* Includes registration fees for seminars, work shops, conferences, and similar meetings. Tuition for schools and workshops is included here. If meals and lodging fees included in registration fees cannot be separated, then they are included here.

Communications

- *Postage.* Includes postage charges for mailing, as well as service and rental fees for postage machines, and periodic service fees charged by online postage providers.

- *Express postage.* Includes all freight costs for express delivery services, including pickup fees.

- *Cell phones.* Includes the basic monthly fees, as well as roaming charges, for all issued cell phones.

- *Telephone local service.* Includes the basic monthly charges for all phones.

- *Telephone long distance.* Includes the charges for all long distance services, including the WATS line, line rentals, and telegraph charges.

- *Telephone installation and maintenance.* Includes all charges for the installation of phones and subsequent maintenance of the phone system.

Marketing

- *Advertising*. Includes the cost of classified advertising for employee hiring, as well as required advertising for published purchasing bids.

- *Publicity and public information*. Includes the cost of radio, television, and live shows promoting the company, as well as related layout and copy costs.

Rents

- *Rental of buildings and floor space*. Includes payments to others for buildings, rooms for events, and floor space in buildings for special events. Rental of housing facilities and meeting rooms is included here.

- *Rental of computer equipment*. Includes the rental or lease cost of computer software and equipment, such as payments on operating leases.

- *Other rentals*. Includes any rental that cannot be recorded in other rental accounts.

Repairs and Maintenance

- *Repairs, streets and parking*. Includes repairs and other maintenance on roads, streets, drives, and parking lots.

- *Repairs, building and grounds*. Includes wages and material costs of repairing, cleaning, and maintaining buildings and grounds. Outside contractor costs for this purpose are recorded here.

- *Repairs, office equipment*. Includes the costs of repairing and maintaining office equipment such as furniture, copiers, and facsimile machines. It does not include maintenance on the phone system.

- *Maintenance contracts, equipment*. Includes the annual contract costs for maintenance contracts on office equipment.

- *Repairing and servicing other equipment*. Includes the costs of repairing and servicing machinery, engineering equipment, laboratory equipment, shop equipment, and other equipment not classified in the preceding repair accounts.

Fees, Professional

- *Engineering fees*. Includes out-of-pocket fees for professional engineering services.

- *Auditing fees*. Includes the costs of auditing fees to outside independent auditors. Other incidental costs of the audit, such as supplies, telephone, postage and printing charges related to the audit, are included here.

- *Medical fees*. Includes direct payments to others for medical services, including preemployment physicals and lab tests.

- *Legal fees*. Includes all fees paid to attorneys, appraisers, notaries, and witnesses, in addition to court costs and legal document recording fees.

- *Laboratory and testing fees.* Includes outside laboratory fees and fees paid to outside agencies for testing services other than medical services.

- *Consultant expense reimbursements.* Includes travel costs paid to consultants and other nonemployees.

Other Contractual Services

- *Insurance and fidelity bonds.* Includes the cost of all casualty and liability insurance and fidelity bond coverages.

- *Dues.* Includes approved dues for company memberships in professional organizations.

- *Subscriptions.* Includes the cost of subscriptions to newspapers, magazines, and periodicals.

- *Computer software acquisitions.* Includes the initial cost of acquiring operating or systems software packages. Included is the purchase price, related freight, and software manuals.

- *Computer software maintenance.* Includes the annual maintenance fees to maintain purchased software systems.

Maintenance Supplies

- *Land improvement supplies.* Includes asphalt, cement, joint fillers, curbing, and so forth used in repairing or replacing roads, sidewalks, and parking lots on company property.

- *Building construction supplies.* Includes lumber, caulking, steel, fabricated metal parts, flooring, ceiling tiles, plaster, lime, and other materials used in repairing or renovating buildings.

- *Paints and preservatives.* Includes interior and exterior paints, wood preservatives, and road striping materials used for remodeling or maintenance.

- *Hardware, plumbing, and electrical supplies.* Includes all hardware, plumbing parts and accessories, and electrical wire or parts, including lights used in maintaining or renovating buildings.

- *Custodial supplies and cleaning agents.* Includes all custodial supplies of an expendable nature, such as cloths, brooms, cleaning compounds, mops, or pails.

Office Supplies

- *Printing, binding, and padding.* Includes the cost of printing, binding, and padding paid to outside contractors.

- *Duplication and reproduction.* Includes the paper, toner, and other supplies used in the company copy machines.

- *Office supplies.* Includes all office supplies and materials, such as pens, paper, pencils, staples, paper clips, and so forth.

Equipment Supplies

- *Fuels.* Includes vehicle fuels (gasoline, diesel fuel, propane) purchased for motor pool vehicles or airplanes.

- *Lubricating oils and greases.* Includes lubricating oils and greases used for all vehicles and machinery.

- *Tires and tubes.* Includes the purchase of tires and tubes for all vehicles in the company motor pool.

- *Repair and replacement parts.* Includes the purchase of vehicle and machinery repair and replacement parts and supplies.

- *Shop supplies.* Includes the cost of shop supplies, such as shop rags, windshield cleaner, glues and cements, brushes, degreasers, solvents, and so forth, used in equipment repair and maintenance operations.

- *Small tools.* Includes small tools used in manufacturing operations that are below the corporate capitalization limit.

2.4 JOB DESCRIPTIONS

A key management task is determining who is responsible for each task. Otherwise there is no way to control the flow of activities or know who should be contacted about fixing problems. The typical departmental structure typically includes one or more assistant controllers reporting to the controller, each of whom is responsible for a selected set of functional areas, such as accounts payable and accounts receivable, or cost accounting and the general ledger. Below these personnel are a number of accountants and clerks. Within these reporting relationships, it is necessary to define the exact job description of each position, which should be included in the general accounting manual. The format used for each job description should identify a position by title, rather than by the name of the person currently holding the job, so that the manual does not have to be changed every time a person switches positions. Here are examples of job descriptions that should be included:

Controller[3]

Reports to: Chief Financial Officer

Responsibilities	Timing
Accounting	
Assist in the annual audit as required	Annual
Develop accounting policies and procedures	Ongoing
Ensure that accounts payable are paid on time	Daily
Ensure that accounts receivable are collected promptly	Daily
Ensure that all economical payable discounts are taken	Daily
Ensure that billings are issued promptly	Daily
Ensure that job costs are calculated	Ongoing
Ensure that bank reconciliations are completed	Monthly
Issue financial statements	Monthly

[3] Source: *Controllership: The Work of the Managerial Accountant*, 7th Edition, Janice Roehl-Anderson and Steven Bragg, copyright ©2004 John Wiley & Sons. This material is used by permission of John Wiley & Sons, Inc.

Maintain an orderly accounting filing system	Ongoing
Maintain the chart of accounts	Ongoing
Manage outsourced functions	Ongoing
Manage the accounting staff	Ongoing
Manage the budgeting process	Annual
Prepare the annual budget	Annual
Process payroll in a timely manner	Bi-weekly
Provide financial analyses as needed	Ongoing
Review systems for control weaknesses	Ongoing

Finance

Arrange for banking services	Ongoing
Arrange for debt financing	Ongoing
Conduct public offerings	As needed
Invest excess cash	Daily
Invest pension funds	Monthly
Issue credit to customers	As needed
Maintain insurance coverage	Annual
Maintain lender relations	Ongoing
Manage the finance staff	Daily
Monitor cash balances	Daily

Assistant Controller, Transactions

Reports to: Controller

Responsibilities	Timing
Manage the accounts payable process	Ongoing
Manage the accounts receivable process	Ongoing
Manage the payroll process	Ongoing
Use best practices to increase transactional efficiency	Ongoing
Take all viable supplier discounts	Weekly
Ensure that payments are authorized and accompanying deliveries are received prior to payment	Daily
Issue invoices to customers in a timely manner	Daily
Obtain payment from customers in a timely manner	Daily
Create an efficient time keeping system	Ongoing
Issue payments to employees in a timely manner	Bi-weekly
Make payroll tax payments in a timely manner	Monthly

Assistant Controller, Financial Reporting

Reports to: Controller

Responsibilities	Timing
Create financial statements	Monthly
Create footnotes to financial statements	Monthly
Create SEC reports	Quarterly
Monitor changes in generally accepted accounting principles	Ongoing
Present financial results to the management team	Monthly
Create systems for efficient reporting process	Ongoing
Create the annual budget	Annual
Create internal management reports	Ongoing

Assistant Controller, Cost and Tax Accounting

Reports to: Controller

Responsibilities	Timing
Manage the cost and taxation staff	Ongoing
Devise tax strategies	Ongoing
Create tax data collection systems	As needed
Complete required tax forms in a timely manner	As needed
Update the company sales tax database as tax rates change	As needed
Negotiate with tax authorities over tax payment issues	As needed
Review adequacy of costing systems	Quarterly
Report on costing variances	Monthly
Report on overhead allocation variances	Monthly
Report on margins and break-even points	Monthly
Report on capital budgeting requests	Ongoing
Assist in development of the budget	Annual
Analyze new product margins	Ongoing

Accounts Payable Clerk

Reports to: Assistant Controller, Transactions

Responsibilities	Timing
Match supplier invoices to purchase orders and receiving documents	Daily
Take all viable supplier discounts	Daily
Obtain approvals for supplier invoices	Daily
Pay supplier invoices when due	Weekly
Research supplier requests for payment	As needed

Billings Clerk

Reports to: Assistant Controller, Transactions

Responsibilities	Timing
Issue invoices to customers	Daily
Contact customers about overdue invoices	Daily
Issue monthly customer statements	Monthly
Resolve billing discrepancies with customers	As needed
Process cash receipts	Daily
Recommend bad debt write-offs	As needed

Payroll Clerk

Reports to: Assistant Controller, Transactions

Responsibilities	Timing
Collect time cards from employees	Weekly
Obtain supervisory approval of time card discrepancies	Weekly
Obtain overtime approvals	Weekly
Process garnishment requests	As needed
Process employee advances and paybacks	As needed
Print and issue paychecks	Bi-weekly
Issue direct deposit tapes to the bank	Bi-weekly
Deposit payroll taxes	Monthly

General Ledger Accountant

Reports to: Assistant Controller, Financial Reporting

Responsibilities	Timing
Create a system of recurring journal entries	Annual
Calculate and enter all adjusting journal entries	Monthly
Provide detailed analysis of accounts to auditors	Annual
Create financial statements	Monthly
Assist in writing footnotes to financial statements	Monthly
Assist in completing SEC reports	Quarterly

Financial Analyst

Reports to: Assistant Controller, Financial Reporting

Responsibilities	Timing
Provide analysis of investment vehicles	Ongoing
Review financing options	Ongoing
Review capital expenditure proposals	Ongoing
Review acquisition candidates	Ongoing
Provide ratio analysis of company results	Monthly

Tax Accountant

Reports to: Assistant Controller, Cost and Tax Accounting

Responsibilities	Timing
Devise tax strategies for management approval	Ongoing
Create tax data collection systems	As needed
Complete required tax forms in a timely manner	As needed
Update the company sales tax database as tax rates change	As needed
Manage audits by taxation authorities	As needed
Negotiate with tax authorities over tax payment issues	As needed

Cost Accountant[4]

Reports to: Assistant Controller, Cost and Tax Accounting

Responsibilities	Timing
System Tasks	
Review adequacy of activity-based costing system	Quarterly
Review adequacy of data collection systems	Quarterly
Review system costs and benefits	Quarterly
Audit costing systems	Monthly
Analysis and Reporting Tasks	
Report on product target costing variances	Monthly
Report on activity-based costing overhead allocations	Monthly
Report on break-even points by product and division	Monthly
Report on margins by product and division	Monthly
Report on periodic variance analyses	Monthly
Report on special topics as assigned	Ongoing
Report on capital budgeting requests	Ongoing
Assist in development of the budget	Annual
Pricing Tasks	
Work with marketing staff to update product pricing	Ongoing

Bookkeeper

Reports to: Company Owner

Responsibilities	Timing
Calculate attendance bonus	Bi-weekly
Close software modules following the monthly close	Monthly
Compile 401 (k) census information	Annual
Complete bank reconciliation	Monthly
Conduct job costing	Ongoing
Create financial statements	Monthly
Cut manual checks and enter them into the computer	Ongoing
Enter accounts payable into compute and cut checks	Weekly
Enter time cards and pay rate changes into computer	Weekly
Issue 401 (k) payments to mutual fund	Monthly
Issue paychecks	Bi-weekly
Match accounts payable documents	Daily
Post accounts receivable payments	Daily
Process employee expenses	Ongoing
Reconcile petty cash	Monthly
Store backup information on fixed assets	Ongoing
Track warranty expense detail	Ongoing

Note that the last job description presented, the bookkeeper, was independent of the hierarchical structure assumed for all of the preceding positions. Rather than reporting to someone else in the accounting or finance department, this person usually reports directly to the business owner, because a bookkeeper is usually only used in very small businesses which only need one or two accounting positions.

---

[4]Source: *Cost Accounting: A Comprehensive Guide*, Steven Bragg, copyright ©2001 John Wiley & Sons. This material is used by permission of John Wiley & Sons, Inc.

2.5 ACTIVITIES CALENDAR

The general accounting manual can also include a set of activities calendars. This is a listing of what special events occur on certain days of the year, such as tax report submissions or investor letters. It is extremely useful as a memory jogger so that the accounting staff does not forget to complete certain nonrepetitive key activities. There is usually a summary-level activities calendar for the entire year; dates from this calendar are then transferred to a monthly calendar that is more detailed in nature, and which contains events that tend to be more repetitive within the month. These calendars may be split up by job position so that each person in the department has an uncluttered view of his or her responsibilities over the course of the year. Examples of annual and monthly activities calendars are shown in Exhibits 2.2 and 2.3

2.6 ACCOUNTING POLICIES

A policy can be described as an anticipated or required course of action that is used to guide both present and future decisions. In short, it is a goal. The general outlines of many procedures will be guided by one or more corporate policies. Given the large number of procedures used in the accounting area, one would expect to see a reasonably large list of policies.

A complete set of accounting policies can be listed in the general accounting manual, or individual policies can be placed in the procedures manual near the procedures most

January	**February**	**March**	**April**
1st Commissions	1st Commissions	1st Commissions	1st Commissions
5th CO Sales Tax License	28th Trademark Review	15th 401(k) Enrollment	15th GSA Sales Report
10th 1099 Forms			20th NV Sales Tax
15th NM Sales Tax Report			29th Investor Letter
15th GSA Sales Report			
20th NV Sales Tax			
29th Investor Letter			
May	**June**	**July**	**August**
1st Commissions	1st Commissions	1st Commissions	1st Commissions
31st Trademark Review	15th 401(k) Enrollment	15th NM Sales Tax Report	10th VETS-100 Report
		15th GSA Sales Report	31st Trademark Review
		20th NV Sales Tax	
		29th Investor Letter	
September	**October**	**November**	**December**
1st Commissions	1st Commissions	1st Commissions	1st Commissions
15th 401(k) Enrollment	15th GSA Sales Report	30th Budget	15th 401(k) Enrollment
	20th NV Sales Tax	30th Trademark Review	23rd Add incremental life insurance to paychecks in last payroll
	29th Investor Letter		27th Update Annual Pay Report
			30th Issue W-9 Mailing

Exhibit 2.2 Annual Activities Calendar

Sunday	Monday	Tuesday	Wednesday	Thursday	Friday	Saturday
					1 Weekly Invoice Review **Pay Rent** Commission Calculation	**2**
3	**4** Overtime Report Remaining Billable Hours Production Hours Not Billed Report Open Jobs Report	**5** Review Job Costing **Colorado Sales Tax Verify Deductions**	**6** **Verify Life Insurance Verify Medical Enrolls Verify Deductions**	**7** Department Meeting Flash Report Sales Report	**8** Weekly Invoice Review **Payroll Processing**	**9**
10	**11** Overtime Report Remaining Billable Hours Production Hours Not Billed Report Open Jobs Report	**12** Review Job Costing	**13** Issue Vacation Notices	**14** Department Meeting Flash Report Sales Report	**15** Weekly Invoice Review Hand Out Paychecks Cash Forecast	**16**
17	**18** Overtime Report Remaining Billable Hours Production Hours Not Billed Report Open Jobs Report	**19** Review Job Costing	**20**	**21** Department Meeting Flash Report Sales Report	**22** Weekly Invoice Review **Payroll Processing Manager's Off-Site**	**23**
24	**25** Overtime Report Remaining Billable Hours Production Hours Not Billed Report Open Jobs Report	**26** Review Job Costing **Investor Letter**	**27**	**28** Hand Out Paychecks **Cash Forecast Payroll Summary** Sales Report Flash Report Trademark Review		

Exhibit 2.3 Monthly Activities Calendar

closely related to each policy. The author's preference is to keep the policy list in the general accounting manual for easy access by readers, rather than spreading it out over many pages.

The following list represents a general overview of the types of policies that should be contained within the general accounting manual:

Accounts Payable[5]

- Any supplier invoice within 5% of the price indicated on the buyer's purchase order requires no additional authorization to pay.

Document Archival

- Use the following format to determine when to dispose of old records:

Type of Record	Retention
Accounts payable ledgers/schedules	7 years
Advertisement for a job opening	1 year
Capital stock records	Permanent
Checks (canceled)	7 years
Deeds, mortgages, bills of sale	Permanent
Earnings per week	3 years
Financial statements	Permanent
General ledgers (year-end)	Permanent
Hiring records	1 year from date record made or personnel action taken, whichever is later
Insurance/pension/retirement plans	1 year after termination
Invoices to customers	7 years
Minute books, including bylaws and charter	Permanent
Payroll records—Employment data	3 years from termination
Physical/medical examinations	Duration of employment, plus 30 years
Property records	Permanent
Sales and purchase records	3 years
Stock and bond certificates (canceled)	7 years
Subsidiary ledgers	7 years
Tax returns	Permanent
Time cards	3 years

Fixed Assets

- The minimum dollar amount above which expenses are capitalized is $2,000.

- Any member of the management committee can approve an expenditure for amounts of $5,000 or less if the item was already listed in the annual budget.

- Any capital expenditure exceeding $5,000 requires the approval of the president, plus all expenditures not already listed in the annual budget, regardless of the amount.

- Every production machine shall be assigned a salvage value of 25% of the purchase price.

Investments

- Retirement funds shall not be invested in the company's securities, or those of its subsidiaries or affiliates.

---

[5] Source: *Accounting Best Practices*, 2nd Edition, Steven Bragg, copyright ©2001 John Wiley & Sons. This material is used by permission of John Wiley & Sons, Inc.

- No more than 10% of invested funds should be invested in any one security.

- No more than 15% of invested funds shall be invested in any one industry.

- The return on investment target for invested funds is to match the Standard & Poor's 500 Index.

- Investments must be made in marketable securities.

- Investment activity is prohibited in the areas of short sales, puts, calls, straddles, hedges, or margin purchases.

Logistics

- Any items arriving at the receiving dock without a purchase order number will be rejected.

Risk Management[6]

- The company will obtain insurance only from companies with an A.M. Best rating of at least B++.

- All self-insurance plans will be covered by an umbrella policy that covers all losses exceeding $50,000.

- No insurance may be obtained from captive insurance companies.

- The company must always have current insurance for the following categories, and in the stated amounts:

    - Director's and officer's insurance, $5 million.

    - Commercial property insurance, matching the replacement value of all structures and inventory.

    - Business interruption insurance, sufficient for four months of operations.

Travel and Entertainment

- All reimbursements require a receipt.

- Employees must show all receipts for travel advances within one week of travel, or the advance will be considered a salary advance.

- Only coach air fares will be reimbursed.

- There is no movie reimbursement.

- There is no reimbursement for commuting miles.

- There is no reimbursement for lunch mileage.

---

[6]The risk management policies are from *Controllership: The Work of the Managerial Accountant*, 7th Edition, Janice Roehl-Anderson and Steven Bragg, copyright ©2004 John Wiley & Sons. This material is used by permission of John Wiley & Sons, Inc.

2.7 PROCESS CYCLE DESCRIPTIONS

The accounting manual typically contains a great many procedures, but does not enumerate how they are linked together to form complete process cycles. A process cycle is the complete set of transactions associated with an activity. Showing a user how a specific procedure is incorporated into a process cycle makes it much easier to understand why the procedure is needed. It is also useful for both external and internal auditors, who can see what controls have been incorporated into specific procedures, and how these controls are linked into the process cycles. Consequently, a summary-level overview of all major process cycles is an extremely useful component of the accounting manual.

An example of a process cycle is the purchasing cycle. This begins with the ordering of goods by the purchasing department, continues with the receipt of those goods by the warehouse staff, and ends with payment for them by the accounts payable staff. Examples of other major process cycles are the billing cycle and order fulfillment cycle. There are also many lesser cycles that have a less pervasive influence throughout a company, such as cycles for quality, maintenance, and contracts.

A key aspect of nearly all process cycles is that the activities associated with them cross over multiple departmental boundaries. Whenever this happens, there is a potential loss of data that can affect the completion of the transactions. To continue with the purchasing cycle example, the purchase order generated by the purchasing department may never arrive at the receiving dock, resulting in the erroneous rejection of materials. Similarly, the received goods may never be entered in the inventory database, resulting in their sitting in a corner unused. Further, the receiving documentation may never be sent to the accounting department, resulting in the nonpayment of supplier billings. Thus, possible failures in the overall process cycles can occur as information moves between departments.

The best way to avoid these problems is for the controller to take over the review of process cycles by regularly examining the points in the cycles where errors are likely to occur. Though this function falls outside the boundaries of most individual departments, the controller is the person most frequently called upon to take on this task, given the accounting department's familiarity with systems in general and transactions in particular.

This section describes a number of procedures that are commonly used to spot problems in the transfer of information between departments for major process cycles. They are:

- Compare billings to the shipping log.
- Review rush freight.
- Review suppliers with no activity.
- Delete old purchase orders.
- Review suppliers with early payment discounts.
- Review blanket purchase orders.
- Review customers with no activity.
- Review old open orders.
- Review pricing errors.
- Review small orders.

Policy/Procedure Statement	Procedure No.:	701
Brasto Publishing	Page:	1 of 1
	Issue Date:	10/28/0X
	Revision Date:	None
Subject: Monthly Journal Entry Review		

COMPARE BILLINGS TO THE SHIPPING LOG

1. PURPOSE AND SCOPE

This procedure is used by the accounts receivable clerk to verify that shipments are matched by the same number of invoices to customers so that no billings are missing or duplicated.

2. RESPONSIBILITIES

ACC RECV   **Accounts Receivable Clerk**

3. PROCEDURES

3.1   ACC RECV   **Obtain the Shipping Log**

Go to the warehouse and make a copy of the shipping log for the previous week. Alternatively (if available), access this information online through the receiving system and print out the shipping log.

3.2   ACC RECV   **Verify Information**

Match the shipments listed on the shipping log to invoices issued during the same period. Note all exceptions in the shipping log for missing billings. Also, note on invoices any incorrect quantities that were billed, as well as "leftover" invoices for which there is no shipping record.

3.3   ACC RECV   **Bill for Missing Invoices**

Using the list of shipments for which there are no corresponding invoices, go to the shipping department and obtain bills of lading for the unbilled shipments. If these are not available, determine which freight carrier shipped the items and obtain shipping traces on them. Then create invoices, mail a copy to the customer, and attach the proof of delivery to the company's copy of the invoice. File the company's copy in the accounting files.

3.4   ACC RECV   **Issue Credits for Duplicate Invoices**

Using the list of invoices for which no corresponding shipment is recorded in the shipping log, go back to the company's copy of these invoices and see if there is any bill of lading or other proof of delivery attached to the invoice. If not, call the shipping department to verify that no such documentation exists there. If not, issue a credit to eliminate these invoices.

3.5   ACC RECV   **Adjust Incorrect Invoices**

Using the list of invoices for which the quantity of product billed is different from the quantity shipped, go back to the company's copy of the invoice and check the attached bill of lading to determine the actual quantity shipped. If the quantity is different, verify this with the shipping department, and then either issue a credit (if the quantity billed was too high) or an additional invoice (if the quantity billed was too low).

Policy/Procedure Statement	Procedure No.:	702
Brasto Publishing	Page:	1 of 1
	Issue Date:	10/28/0X
	Revision Date:	None
Subject: **Monthly Journal Entry Review**		

REVIEW RUSH FREIGHT

1.   PURPOSE AND SCOPE

This procedure is used by the financial analyst to determine the amount and type of any rush freight services used by a company to either receive or send materials.

2.   RESPONSIBILITIES

ANALYST   **Financial Analyst**

3.   PROCEDURES

3.1   ANALYST   **Access the Freight Account**

Go to the freight account in the computer for each department. If the total amount for the month is less than $100, ignore the account. Otherwise, write down the total department freight and go to the next step.

3.2   ANALYST   **Access Detail Freight Amounts**

Go to the accounting software and call up the detail for each freight expenditure. This information should include the date of expenditure, the name of the authorizing person, and the name of the freight carrier.

3.3   ANALYST   **Summarize Freight Information**

Enter this detailed freight information into the FREIGHT.XLS spreadsheet. List all the freight for each department and summarize the dollar amounts. The totals in this spreadsheet should match the freight expense totals for each department, as noted in the general ledger. List all rush freight charges in bold font; these charges are noted in the underlying expense detail as being either from a rush freight company, or designated as rush freight by a standard freight company.

3.4   ANALYST   **Distribute Freight Information**

Distribute the freight report to each department manager, as well as the controller and chief operating officer.

3.5   ANALYST   **Track Freight Expenses on a Graph**

Enter the total freight cost by department on a graph, showing the expense for the last 12 months for each department. The intention in using this chart is to show managers any improvement (or lack thereof) in their management of this expense. Distribute the graph to all department managers, the controller, and the chief operating officer.

Policy/Procedure Statement	Procedure No.:	703
	Page:	1 of 1
	Issue Date:	10/28/0X
Brasto Publishing	Revision Date:	None
Subject: Monthly Journal Entry Review		

REVIEW SUPPLIERS WITH NO ACTIVITY

1. **PURPOSE AND SCOPE**

   This procedure is used by the financial analyst to determine which suppliers are no longer used by the company. The logistics manager uses the resulting list to determine which suppliers can be removed from the company database.

2. **RESPONSIBILITIES**

   ANALYST   **Financial Analyst**

3. **PROCEDURES**

   3.1   ANALYST   **Extract Supplier Usage Information**

   Go to the accounting software and run an extract file that shows all suppliers currently in the database, as well as the last dates on which the company purchased supplies from them. This is the SUPPLIER extract, which dumps into an Excel file of the same name.

   3.2   ANALYST   **Summarize Supplier Usage Information**

   Enter the Excel program and access the SUPPLIER spreadsheet. Sort the records based on the last date on which purchases were made from a supplier. Delete all suppliers from the spreadsheet for whom there are purchase dates within the last two years. Print the remaining list of suppliers on the spreadsheet. This list constitutes those suppliers with whom the company is no longer doing business.

   3.3   ANALYST   **Issue Supplier Report**

   Give the supplier spreadsheet report to the purchasing manager, with a request to mark those suppliers who can be deleted from the list, and to return it to the financial analyst.

   3.4   ANALYST   **Delete Suppliers from Database**

   Upon receipt of the approved list, go into the Suppliers screen in the accounting software. Call up each supplier record that was marked on the supplier report, and delete each of those suppliers. File the report in the "Deleted Suppliers" folder, which is located in the front of the accounts payable records.

Policy/Procedure Statement	Procedure No.:	704
	Page:	1 of 1
Brasto Publishing	Issue Date:	10/28/0X
	Revision Date:	None
Subject: **Monthly Journal Entry Review**		

DELETE OLD PURCHASE ORDERS

1. PURPOSE AND SCOPE

This procedure is used by the financial analyst to determine which purchase orders are still open, but are not going to be filled. The logistics manager uses this information to close down old purchase orders.

2. RESPONSIBILITIES

ANALYST   **Financial Analyst**

3. PROCEDURES

3.1 ANALYST   **Extract Open Purchase Order Information**

Go to the accounting software and generate an extract of all open purchase orders in the database. This information dumps into an Excel spreadsheet called PURCHORD and contains each purchase order number, supplier name, date on which it was created, and a flag to indicate if it is a blanket purchase order.

3.2 ANALYST   **Summarize Purchase Order Information**

Enter the Excel program and access the PURCHORD spreadsheet. Sort the records based on the date of each purchase order. Delete from the spreadsheet all purchase orders for which the creation date is within the last six months. Also delete all purchase orders for which there is a blanket purchase order flag (as these may be open and valid for more than a year). Print the remaining list of purchase orders on the spreadsheet, which should thus include all old orders that may be subject to deletion.

3.3 ANALYST   **Issue Open Purchase Order Report**

Forward the open purchase order spreadsheet to the purchasing manager, with a request to mark all purchase orders on the list that should be closed and then to return the list to the financial analyst.

3.4 ANALYST   **Delete Open Purchase Orders**

Upon receipt of the approved list, go into the PURCHASE ORDER screen in the accounting software. Call up each purchase order record that was marked on the report and delete each one. File the report in the "Deleted Purchase Orders" folder, which is located in the front of the accounts payable records.

Policy/Procedure Statement	Procedure No.:	705
	Page:	1 of 1
Brasto Publishing	Issue Date:	10/28/0X
	Revision Date:	None
Subject: Monthly Journal Entry Review		

REVIEW SUPPLIERS WITH EARLY PAYMENT DISCOUNTS

1. PURPOSE AND SCOPE

This procedure is used by the financial analyst to determine how many suppliers currently allow early payment discounts by the company. The logistics manager uses this information to ask suppliers for new or larger discounts.

2. RESPONSIBILITIES

ANALYST   **Financial Analyst**

3. PROCEDURES

3.1   ANALYST   **Extract Discount Information**

Go to the accounting software and select the "Suppliers Extract" option. Select for all suppliers, and extract to an Excel file format.

3.2   ANALYST   **Sort the Discount Information**

Sort the Excel file on the discount field so that the largest discounts are at the top and the smallest at the bottom.

3.3   ANALYST   **Issue the Discounts Report**

Print out the report and issue it to the purchasing manager with a standard request to attempt to obtain discounts from more suppliers, as well as to increase the discount amounts from suppliers that already grant them.

3.4   ANALYST   **Update Discounts Information**

If any changes to discounts are submitted by the purchasing manager, go to the SUPPLIER MASTER screen in the accounting software and update the discount field with the new information for those suppliers needing changes.

3.5   ANALYST   **Record Discounts Statistics**

Go to the Process_Stats Excel file and enter the total number of supplier discounts for the month into the statistics page.

Policy/Procedure Statement	Procedure No.:	706
	Page:	1 of 1
Brasto Publishing	Issue Date:	10/28/0X
	Revision Date:	None
Subject: Monthly Journal Entry Review		

REVIEW BLANKET PURCHASE ORDERS

1.   PURPOSE AND SCOPE

This procedure is used by the financial analyst to determine how many blanket purchase orders are currently open, and with how many suppliers these are used. The resulting information is used by the logistics manager to increase the number of blanket purchase orders.

2.   RESPONSIBILITIES

ANALYST   **Financial Analyst**

3.   PROCEDURES

3.1   ANALYST   **Extract Blanket Purchase Order Information**

Go to the accounting software and select the "Blanket Purchase Orders Extract" option. Select for all purchase orders, and extract to an Excel file format.

3.2   ANALYST   **Sort the Blanket Purchase Order Information**

Access Excel and call up the extract of blanket purchase order information. Format the spreadsheet based on a copy of the last blanket purchase order report that was issued in the previous month. Print the report.

3.3   ANALYST   **Issue the Blanket Purchase Order Report**

Issue the blanket purchase order report to the purchasing manager with a request to add more blanket purchase orders than are currently recorded. The purchasing manager can enter any new blanket purchase orders directly; there is no need for the financial analyst to do so.

3.4   ANALYST   **Record Blanket Purchase Order Information**

Go to the Process_Stats Excel file and enter the total number of blanket purchase orders for the month into the statistics page.

Policy/Procedure Statement	Procedure No.:	707
	Page:	1 of 1
Brasto Publishing	Issue Date:	10/28/0X
	Revision Date:	None
Subject: Monthly Journal Entry Review		

REVIEW CUSTOMERS WITH NO ACTIVITY

1. PURPOSE AND SCOPE

This procedure is used by the financial analyst to determine which customers have not placed orders with the company. The sales manager uses this information to determine which customers can be removed from the customer database.

2. RESPONSIBILITIES

ANALYST   **Financial Analyst**

3. PROCEDURES

3.1 ANALYST   **Extract Customer Information**

Go to the accounting software and select the "Customers Extract" option. Select for all customers, and extract to an Excel file format.

3.2 ANALYST   **Determine Inactive Customers**

Access Excel and call up the EXTRACT spreadsheet. Sort the report based on activity dates so that the oldest dates are at the top of the report. Review the fields in the report that list the last dates on which the company shipped anything to a customer or received payment from one. If the most recent date in either column is less than two years ago, delete the record. This will leave a list of customers with whom the company has had no business in at least two years.

3.3 ANALYST   **Report on Inactive Customers**

Print the spreadsheet and issue it to the sales manager with a request to mark those customers who should be deleted from the accounting database.

3.4 ANALYST   **Delete Inactive Customers**

Once the report is received back from the sales manager, go to the CUSTOMER MASTER screen in the accounting database and delete those customers who have been so marked by the sales manager in the report.

3.5 ANALYST   **Record Customer Statistics**

Go to the Process_Stats Excel file and enter the total number of inactive customers for the month into the statistics page.

Policy/Procedure Statement	Procedure No.:	708
	Page:	1 of 1
Brasto Publishing	Issue Date:	10/28/0X
	Revision Date:	None
Subject: Monthly Journal Entry Review		

REVIEW OLD OPEN ORDERS

1.   PURPOSE AND SCOPE

This procedure is used by the financial analyst to locate those customer orders that are still open but no longer need to be filled, so that they can be closed down.

2.   RESPONSIBILITIES

ANALYST   **Financial Analyst**

3. PROCEDURES

3.1   ANALYST   **Extract Open Orders Information**

Go to the accounting software and select the "Open Orders Extract" option. Select for all open orders, and extract to an Excel file format.

3.2   ANALYST   **Locate Old Open Orders**

Go to Excel and open the EXTRACT file. Sort it for orders that have been open for at least one month, and delete all but these records.

3.3   ANALYST   **Report on Old Open Orders**

Add headings to the report, as well as a column for the names of the customer service staff who are responsible for each customer. Print the report and issue it to them, with a note to either close the orders or shift their due dates forward into a future time period.

3.4   ANALYST   **Close Old Open Orders**

If the customer service staff cannot do so, assist them in closing the orders or shifting their due dates through the ORDER ENTRY screen in the accounting software.

3.5   ANALYST   **Record Open Order Statistics**

Go to the Process_Stats Excel file and enter the total number of old open orders for the month into the statistics page.

Policy/Procedure Statement	Procedure No.:	709
	Page:	1 of 1
	Issue Date:	10/28/0X
Brasto Publishing	Revision Date:	None
Subject: Monthly Journal Entry Review		

REVIEW PRICING ERRORS

1. **PURPOSE AND SCOPE**

   This procedure is used by the financial analyst to determine the number of credits issued to customers that are based on pricing problems, and the nature of the pricing errors.

2. **RESPONSIBILITIES**

   ANALYST   **Financial Analyst**

3. **PROCEDURES**

3.1   ANALYST   **Review Existing Credits**

Go to the accounting software and select the "Invoices Extract" option. Select for all invoices in the previous month, and extract to an Excel file format.

3.2   ANALYST   **Extract Pricing Error Information**

Sort the Excel file for invoices with credit balances and delete all other invoices from the file. Then search the description field for each remaining credit for wording regarding a pricing error. Retain these records and delete all others. Print the spreadsheet.

3.3   ANALYST   **Create Pricing Error Report**

Go to the Price_Error Excel spreadsheet and clear out the information in it from the previous month, except for headings and totals. Then enter the new credit information from the extract spreadsheet you just printed. This information includes the credit number, credit amount, customer name, correct price, actual price charged, the differences between the two, the quantity of product to which the incorrect pricing applies, the grand total pricing error, and the initials of the customer service person who made the entry. When finished, print the Price_Error report.

3.4   ANALYST   **Distribute Report**

Distribute the report to the sales manager, controller, president, and chief operating officer.

3.5   ANALYST   **Record Pricing Error Statistics**

Go to the process_Stats Excel file and enter the total number of pricing errors for the month into the statistics page.

Policy/Procedure Statement	Procedure No.:	710
	Page:	1 of 1
	Issue Date:	10/28/0X
Brasto Publishing	Revision Date.	None
Subject: Monthly Journal Entry Review		

REVIEW SMALL ORDERS

1.   PURPOSE AND SCOPE

The procedure is used by the financial analyst to determine which customers habitually place small orders. This information is useful in determining pricing changes for customers, or whether some customers should be dropped.

2.   RESPONSIBILITIES

ANALYST   **Financial Analyst**

3.   PROCEDURES

3.1   ANALYST   **Extract Invoice Information**

Go to the accounting software and select the "Orders Extract" option. Select for all orders in the previous month, and extract to an Excel file format.

3.2   ANALYST   **Select Small Order Information**

Go to Excel and open the ORDERS EXTRACT file. Sort on the order dollar amount, and delete all records except those that are equal to or less than $500.

3.3   ANALYST   **Create Report**

Sort the Excel file again by customer name so that the number of small orders for each customer can be easily determined. Then print the report. Go to the Small_Order Excel file, which lists the grand total of small orders by customer for the last year in a grid format, and enter the data from the first spreadsheet into this format. Print the report.

3.4   ANALYST   **Issue The Report**

Issue the report to the sales manager, controller, president, and chief operating officer.

3.5   ANALYST   **Update Small Order Statistics**

Go to the Process_Stats Excel file and enter the total number of small orders for the month into the statistics page.

2.8 ACCOUNTING PROCEDURES

It is extremely important to create an environment within the accounting department that results in the consistent processing of all accounting transactions so that resulting financial statements are comparable for all time periods and across all corporate divisions. Another result is error-free transactions that require little ongoing review or correction by the senior accounting staff, which results in a more efficient department. Further, both internal and external auditors will test the accuracy of these transactions from time to time, and will gain a high degree of confidence in the accuracy of company-reported transactions if they are consistently completed. In addition, consistent transaction usage results in better conformance with generally accepted accounting principles (GAAP), so a company will not require restatement of certain transactions for GAAP conformance purposes. For all of these reasons, it is critical to use a standard set of accounting procedures for all regular accounting transactions.

A complete set of accounting procedures may be included within the general accounting manual. However, if the business entity is a large one, there may be so many procedures that they are subdivided by job position or process cycle, and distributed separately.

In the next chapter, we will review the various types of procedures and how they are formatted, as well as examine a checklist of suggested procedures and a number of related examples.

Chapter 3

PROCEDURE STATEMENTS

3.1 INTRODUCTION

A procedure is a standard method for accomplishing a task, usually composed of a series of steps that are followed in a definite, regular order. A typical procedure identifies the purpose for completing it, as well as what job position is responsible for each task within it and how each task is to be completed.

A procedures manual usually only contains the most commonly used procedures, because the inclusion of every possible procedure would require a great deal of time and effort. The reason for this long delay is that, in addition to initiating, checking, approving, distributing, calculating, balancing, and other accounting activities, there are also many forms that each person completes on a regular basis, which may require input from multiple departments. Documenting all of this is a considerable task. Consequently, it is not uncommon to target for documentation only a few of the most important procedures for inclusion in the initial procedures manual, and then add more procedures to subsequent releases of the manual if there is a cost-effective reason for doing so.

In this chapter, we will review the format of a procedure, as well as the writing style and writing mechanics used to create its content. The chapter also covers the basic work steps needed to create a procedure, and a detailed list of possible procedures that may be worthy of inclusion in a procedures manual.

3.2 WRITING STYLE

Clarity and readability are much more important than style, perfect grammar, and a large vocabulary. One should ensure that readers can easily understand the contents

Standard Outline	Roman Numeral Outline	Arabic Numeral Outline
I.	I.	1.
A.	II.	10.
1.	IV.	50.
2.	V.	75.
a.	VI.	100.
b.	VII.	125.
B.	VIII.	150.
II.	XI.	175.

Exhibit 3.1   Different Types of Outline Formats

of a procedure. To this end, consistent use of outlining and active verbs, and avoiding distracting grammar errors, will ensure overall readability.

A typical procedure is composed of a number of logical steps. If these steps are presented in a paragraph format, the reader can become confused about which steps to complete next. To avoid this problem, one should split the text into an outline format, which lets the reader easily move through the various processing steps of a procedure. Exhibit 3.1 shows three outline formats.

The standard outline format is the most flexible approach when there are many sublayers of activities within a procedure. For example, a major processing step for the accounts payable function is "Create Checks," which could be listed as Roman numeral "I." Within the check creation step may be several additional substeps, such as document matching, obtaining final approvals, and printing checks. There may be additional steps within these substeps. The resulting outline is:

I. Create checks.

   A. Match supporting documents.

      1. Obtain receiving documents.

      2. Obtain purchase orders.

      3. Obtain supplier invoices.

      4. Compare all documents and note variances.

         a. Contact supplier over quantity variances.

         b. Contact purchasing over pricing variances.

   B. Obtain final approvals.

      1. Obtain department manager approval if <$10,000.

      2. Obtain president approval if <$100,000.

      3. Obtain board approval if $100,000+.

   C. Print checks.

An outline format makes it much easier to follow a long or complex procedure. If the procedure is shorter or has minimal complexity, then either the Roman numeral or Arabic numeral outlines listed in Exhibit 3.1 can be used. In all cases, one should line up the periods vertically within the outline, so that the text forms a pleasing straight vertical line down the left side of each text block.

No matter what type of outline is used, there must always be at least two of each type of character. For example, there cannot be I without a following II, an A without a following B, or a 1 without a following 2. If outline step "I. Create checks" was followed by "A. Match supporting documents," there must also be a step B. Otherwise, step A would be renamed "II. Match supporting documents."

Outlining is the written version of a flowchart. The mechanics of flowcharting are covered later in section 3.4.

Misspelling is much less of a problem with the advent of automated spell checkers. For example, Microsoft Word can be set to automatically check spellings as soon as they are typed. To set up this function, go to the Tools command in the Word menu, and select the Options command. This will bring up a tiled set of command boxes. Select the Spelling & Grammar box. Select the "Check Spelling as You Type" box, and click OK. Word will then put a wavy red line underneath any word for which there appears to be an incorrect spelling. One can then position the cursor over the word and press the right mouse button, which will bring up a range of alternate spellings from which a selection can be made.

One should use active verbs whenever possible to forcibly push the reader through the narrative of the procedure. The best way to illustrate the problem is with the following examples:

Inactive Version	Active Version
The reader is advised to regularly review documents for mistakes.	Review documents for mistakes.
The receiving log is compared by the accounts payable clerk to the on-hand inventory at month-end.	Verify that all receipts are present in the inventory.

By shifting the verb to the beginning of the sentence, one can create much more active and vibrant sentences. Accountants commonly use these active verbs:

Accrue	Cancel	Correct	Extend
Accumulate	Charge	Credit	File
Approve	Check	Decide	Issue
Authorize	Compare	Enter	Locate
Obtain	Reconcile	Review	Total
Prepare	Record	Run	Verify
Receive	Request	Send	Write off

A few common grammar rules also must be mentioned here. Microsoft Word can conduct a grammar check during the writing task, so one does not have to have a grammar and style book on hand at all times. To activate the grammar checker in Word, go to the Tools command in the Word menu, and select the Options command. This will bring up a tiled set of command boxes. Select the Spelling & Grammar box. Select the "Check grammar as you type" box, and click OK. Word will then put a wavy line underneath any sentence or portion of a sentence for which there appears to be incorrect grammar. One can then position the cursor over the indicated area and press the right mouse button to determine the type of problem. To avoid total reliance on the grammar checker, one should remember the following rules:

- *Abbreviations.* Spell out the abbreviations *lb., oz., ft.,* and *in.* as pound, ounce, foot or feet, and inches. However, some common abbreviations are permitted when used with numbers, such as 50 mph or 1800 rpm.

- *Almost, only, nearly.* Place these modifiers immediately before the words they modify. For example, change "this system nearly costs $10,000" to "this system costs nearly $10,000."

- *Ampersand.* Only use the ampersand (&) in organization names that have this abbreviation in their official titles.

- *Apostrophe.* To form a possessive, place the apostrophe before the final "s" for a singular noun; place it after the final "s" to make a plural noun possessive. Do not use it in numeric dates (such as 1990s), but use it when numerals are omitted from dates ('90s). Omit the apostrophe when an acronym is plural (VCRs).

- *Exclamation point.* When it doubt, leave it out. When using it, you are essentially shouting at the reader.

- *Of.* Avoid using "of" after the words *all, outside, inside,* and so on. Thus, *all of the books* can be reduced to *all the books.*

- *Quotation marks.* Always place quotation marks outside an ending comma, period, exclamation point, or question mark.

- *There is, there are.* Omit these stock phrases if they begin a sentence. Thus, *There is a problem with this journal entry* becomes *This journal entry has a problem.*

Accounting procedures are full of numbers. One should be aware of the rules for including numbers in sentences, and follow them consistently:

- Do not begin a sentence with a number. For example, state "17 facilities follow this procedure" as "Seventeen facilities follow this procedure."

- Spell out numbers one through nine, and use numerals for anything larger. For example, "Eight vice presidents follow the 23 procedures in this manual." Follow this rule until you reach 1 million, and then describe the zeros in a number with words—for example, $32 million.

- Precede decimals of less than one with a zero, such as 0.7%.

A key issue when writing a procedure is one's ability to keep the resulting document as easy to read as possible. Clarity of writing can be quantified to some extent by using the readability scoring system in Microsoft Word. This scoring system itemizes the number of words per sentence, as well as the number of characters per word, to derive a readability index called the Flesch Reading Ease measure. A score of 100 indicates an

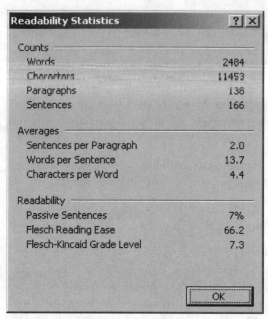

Exhibit 3.2   Readability Statistics Results for a Word Document

extremely easy-to-read document; measurements closer to zero indicate increasing levels of reading difficulty. A score of 60 to 70 is considered acceptable for most documents. This measurement can also be converted into the Flesch-Kincaid Grade Score, which converts the Flesch Reading Ease measure into the comparable grade school level of education required to read the document. For example, a score of 7 indicates that someone with a seventh grade education can read the procedure.

To compile the readability information in a Word document, go to the Tools command in the menu bar, access the Options command, and select the Spelling & Grammar option. Then check the Show Readability Statistics box and click on the OK button to close the command box. Run the spell checker for the document; when the spell check is complete, a readability statistics box will appear. An example of this box is shown in Exhibit 3.2.

A reasonable target is a Flesch-Kincaid Grade Level score of no higher than 12, preferably closer to 8. If the score is too high, consider splitting long sentences into smaller ones; a paragraph containing just one sentence may indicate a sentence-length problem. Also, consider replacing any words exceeding two syllables with shorter synonyms. These steps can greatly increase a procedure's clarity.

3.3   WRITING MECHANICS

The mechanics of writing include the paper, type style, hardware, method of reproduction, use of logos, numbering schemes, indexes, and headlining related to the completion of a procedure. These guidelines provide some rules for each of these items.

- *Color.* Use colors to denote different accounting purposes. Avoid a lack of contrast between colors, such as using blue ink on blue, brown on brown, or black on dark gray.

- *Distribution.* Note the job title or department to which the procedure is to be distributed. This will assist in distributing the procedure.

- *Issue date.* List the actual date on which the procedure was released. This tells a reader if the date on the procedure that he or she is reading matches the date of the most recent release.

- *Logos.* Include the company logo on all forms and procedures as often as possible. The logo tends to make the reader accept the material as *our* procedure, and lends an official status to the document.

- *Margins.* Use a one-inch margin on both sides of any page, as well as at the bottom. If the top margin contains a logo or other information, then use a top margin of a half inch; otherwise, use a one-inch margin at the top of the page.

- *Page numbering.* Number all pages in the form "Page 1 of 2" so that readers can see how many pages are supposed to be included in a procedure, and can thereby see if any are missing.

- *Paper.* Do not use paper that is so flimsy that text on the back side can be seen through it. To avoid this problem, consider using at least 24-pound bond paper. Most photocopy paper is adequate for one-sided printing.

- *Retrieval numbers.* Assign a permanent retrieval number to a document when it is first created, which (as the name implies) can be used to retrieve it from storage. This number also can be used as the identifying file name where the document is stored in the computer system. If not many documents are expected to be included in the procedures manual, then the retrieval number can be as short as three digits, and might be divided in the following manner to leave room for the documents of all departments:

Number Range	Department to Which Numbers Are Assigned
000–099	Accounting
100–199	Purchasing
200–299	Human Resources
300–399	Treasurer
400–499	Sales
500–599	Engineering
600–699	Production/Materials Handling
700–799	Advertising/Public Relations
800–999	Reserved for future use

This scheme breaks down in larger organizations, where there may be many departments and a multitude of forms and procedures. In these cases, it is better to identify the department with a two-digit number, followed by a hyphen, followed by a three- or four-digit number that identifies the document. For example, here are the number ranges that could be used within the accounting department, with the department being assigned an overall code of 10:

Number Range	Functions to Which Numbers Are Assigned
10–000 thru 099	Accounting—Controller
10–100 thru 199	Accounting—Accounts Payable
10–200 thru 299	Accounting—Accounts Receivable
10–300 thru 399	Accounting—Budget
10–400 thru 499	Accounting—Cost Accounting
10–500 thru 599	Accounting—Payroll
10–600 thru 699	Accounting—Purchasing

- *Supersedes.* If a new procedure supersedes a previous one, note the retrieval number of the procedure being eliminated so that the recipient can purge it from the existing procedures manual.

- *Type size.* Use the standard Times New Roman font. Avoid using cursives that imitate handwriting, fancy Old English type, square-faced type, or all-capital type, because they are difficult to read.

3.4 FLOWCHARTING FOR A PROCEDURES MANUAL

(a) Introduction

Flowcharts are a valuable addition to any manual that describes the flow of steps in a process. In the following sections, we review when flowcharts should (and should not) be added to a manual, as well as their basic components and proper layout. A series of examples cover the more basic process flows for the major accounting transactions.

(b) When to Use Flowcharts

Flowcharts should only be used in a minority of situations where the subject matter is so complex that a lengthy written document may not convey the key information to a user without a number of repetitions. This situation most commonly arises when there are many decision points in a process, where a person can move down a number of alternative paths within a procedure. An example of a multidecision process is shown in Exhibit 3.3, where an employee must make several decisions to determine the correct outcome to a credit analysis situation.

By converting this example into the flowchart format shown in Exhibit 3.4, we can greatly simplify the decision-making process for the user of the procedure. However, this conversion can result in the loss of some detailed information that was included in the written procedure, as there is not sufficient room in the flowchart. In this instance, the underlined wording in Exhibit 3.3 relates to a method of reducing the amount of credit granted, which cannot fit into the existing flowchart format. To avoid this problem, the original written procedure can be simplified to avoid these "text overhang" problems; the size and complexity of the flowchart can be expanded to include all possible text; or a reference notation can be added to the flowchart that will send the reader back to the written version of the procedure for additional information.

Besides bringing clarity to complex procedures, the flowchart is also very useful for constructing a written procedure. By plotting the steps in a flowchart format while

```
Credit Approval Procedure:

  Upon receipt of a request for credit, follow these se-
  quential steps:

    1.  Is the credit request for less than $500? If so,
        grant the request at once.

    2.  If not, then go to the Dun & Bradstreet database
        and print out a Business Information Report on
        the prospective customer.

    3.  Is the average amount of payment days listed on
        the Business Information Report less than 40?
        If so, grant a credit level equal to the median
        amount listed on the report, reduced by the im-
        pact of the top 10 percent of credit levels shown
        on the report.

    4.  Is the average amount of payment days between 39
        and 50? If so, reduce the credit level calculated
        in the last step by five percent for every pay-
        ment day in excess of 40 days.

    5.  Is the average amount of payment days on the
        report 50 or higher? If so, reject the credit
        request.
```

Exhibit 3.3   Decision Points in a Procedure

producing the written procedure, one can more easily identify decision points and ensure that all possible variations have been accounted for. Thus, the flowchart introduces more rigor into procedure writing. When it is not intended for later inclusion in the accounting manual, a flowchart may be discarded after the written procedure has been completed.

The flowchart is of particular use for training new employees. An instructor can use it as a teaching tool to walk users through a procedure. The same reasoning applies if the workforce's primary language is not the same as the one in which a procedure has been written, or if the level of employee education is relatively low, because a flowchart is much easier to understand than a written procedure.

A flowchart can also be used as a disposable check-off sheet. For example, an extremely complex procedure can be made much easier for the person performing it if that person checks off each item on the flowchart as he or she progresses through the various procedural steps. This usage can become a formal one, where the user signs off on the flowchart when a procedure is completed to provide proof of completion.

There are also situations in which flowcharts are not worth the effort to construct. One such case is when the underlying procedure is so simple, or so well written, that few readers would refer to the flowchart for additional clarification. Another situation is when there are so many changes to the underlying procedure over time that there is some risk that the details in the accompanying flowchart will not be appropriately revised, resulting

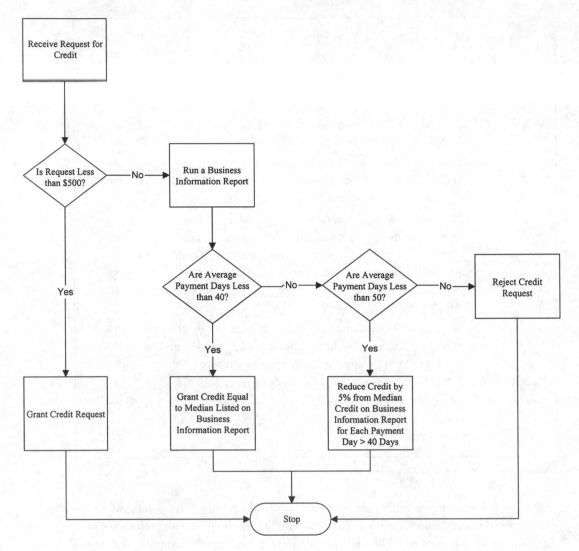

Exhibit 3.4 Decision Points in a Flowchart

in conflicting instructions between the two documents. A final issue is that an excessive amount of flowcharting will result in a considerable increase in the size of an accounting manual; if there is an objective to create a leaner manual, then an editor may view a large number of flowcharts as being excessive duplication of existing written procedures and throw them out.

Despite these few problems, the selective use of flowcharts can greatly increase the user's level of comprehension of more complex procedures, and they remain highly recommended for that purpose.

(c) Flowcharting Symbols

Many symbols can be used to create a flowchart. However, one must focus on user comprehension—will they know what all of the symbols mean? Probably not—their training may not include flowchart symbols. Accordingly, only a few symbols should

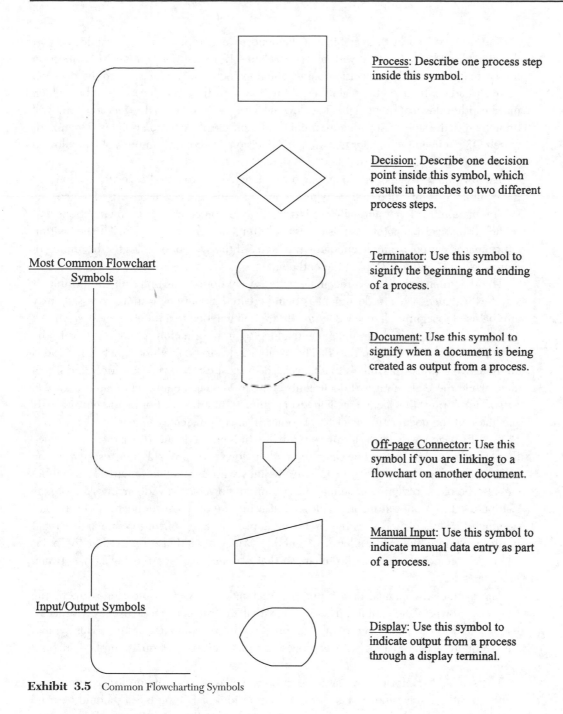

Exhibit 3.5 Common Flowcharting Symbols

be used to describe the majority of flowchart activities. The key items are noted in Exhibit 3.5.

By far the most common flowchart symbol is the rectangle, which signifies a process step. If something can be described with a verb, then it is probably a process step. For example, "compare receiving log to supplier invoices" and "issue financial report to investors" are both valid process descriptions that might be found within a process symbol.

The next symbol in the exhibit is a diamond, which represents a decision point. A decision should be answered with a "yes" or "no." If a statement ends with a question mark, then it is probably a decision point. The flowline for a "yes" answer to the decision point should continue on the main flow of the flowchart from the decision symbol, which may be either down or to the right. The flowline for a "no" answer to the decision point will branch off to the side for separate treatment. An example of a decision point is "Document match OK?" Given the smaller text area in a decision symbol, the amount of text allowed is quite small, so brevity is crucial.

The terminator symbol is a long, narrow rectangle with rounded corners (as shown in the exhibit). It is intended to show where a process ends, but can also be used to show its beginning point. It is not normally used to signify end points for all the side junctions that branch from decision points, as this tends to clutter a flowchart too much. The text within a terminator symbol is simple enough—use "start" if the symbol signifies the beginning of a process, and "end" or "stop" at the end point.

The document symbol is a rectangle with a wavy bottom, as noted in the exhibit. It signifies instances when a document is being created as output from a process. It may also be used to signify when key documents are being added to a process, such as when a document is being taken out of a file and added to an information packet (such as in the accounts payable matching process). This symbol tends to be used too much, which adds an excessive number of symbols to a flowchart. In most cases, it is best to only add it to a chart when there are multipart documents being used, and the flowchart can clarify who gets which copy of the document. The text entered within this symbol should only identify the name of the document, such as "Customer Invoice (pink copy)."

The off-page connector is a square symbol with a pointed end. It is a cross-reference that signifies a shift in the flowchart to another flowchart, probably because either the existing flowchart is too large, or it logically links with another flowchart. This symbol can also be used to signify incoming linkages into a flowchart; a wide arrow symbol may also be used to represent incoming flows, but using the off-page connector in both roles eliminates a symbol, and so is the preferred approach. Each off-page connector should be uniquely identified with a letter or number, which should also be used at the point where it connects to another flowchart so that a reader can see the linkages between flowcharts.

The symbol for manual data input is a rectangle whose top line slopes up to the right (as shown in the exhibit). This signifies that the previous step (usually a process) has resulted in the manual entry of data, probably into a computer system. This symbol can frequently be replaced with a process symbol because action is implied in both cases.

The symbol for information that appears on a display is a two-dimensional representation of a cathode-ray tube, and is shown at the bottom of Exhibit 3.5. It should be used only in cases in which the process flow must describe the dissemination of information to the user from a computer terminal.

Of the symbols described here, by far the most common ones used are the process, decision, terminator, and off-page connector. The document symbol will appear from time to time, but the input/output symbols for manual input and data display are falling into disuse. The general rule when using any of these symbols is to keep the number of different types to an absolute minimum so that readers can spend their time interpreting the process flow that they represent, rather than guessing at what they are.

(d) Flow of the Flowchart

Having gone over the types of symbols to include in a flowchart, the next step is to understand the general layout and flow of the flowchart.

The general flow of information should be either from top to bottom or from left to right. A flowchart ideally should be attached to a set of documents that are printed in portrait mode, so the flowchart should also be in portrait mode; this means that the greatest amount of space on the page is from top to bottom, which makes this the most common direction of flow. Whenever a flowchart contains a decision point, there will be a second flow that juts out from one side of the decision symbol. These contingent flows can be charted to either side of the main flow, depending on space considerations; common practice tends to shift them to the right side of the flowchart (if constructing a top-down flowchart) or on the bottom (if constructing a left-to-right flowchart).

When using a decision symbol, the "yes" answer that flows out of the symbol should generally follow the main flow of the process, while "no" answers are shunted off into contingencies on either side of the main process flow. This type of standardization allows a user to follow the diagram more easily if he or she becomes accustomed to always having positive results associated with the main process flow—if there were to be a mix of "yes" and "no" answers in the main flow, then it would take much longer to comprehend the information contained within a flowchart. However, if this convention is used, then it must be followed 100% of the time, for a reader who is accustomed to it may easily pass over a decision point with a different process flow, which may result in an incorrect transaction.

A final point is to only address actions and decisions within a flowchart. By reducing or eliminating the presence of symbols related to inputs, outputs, obvious decisions, or process steps with no discernible activity, a greatly streamlined product that is clear and easily understandable will result. The only case in which this rule can be ignored is when multipart forms are used, as the flowchart format can be very useful for noting which form copies go to which users. To illustrate the points made in this section, Exhibit 3.6 shows a flowchart that follows no rules, and Exhibit 3.7 shows a much cleaner version that contains approximately the same information as Exhibit 3.6, but with standard formatting rules.

Exhibit 3.6 contains a number of excess symbols and improper formatting. For example, there are no fewer than three processes to schedule and hold a meeting—these can be consolidated into one symbol. In addition, there are two process symbols that instruct the user to wait for an outside entity to do something; this is certainly not an activity worthy of mention! There is also a form-signing decision symbol that only has a "no" flowline coming out of it (apparently there is no reason why a "yes" instance would occur!). There are also three cases where documents are listed as sources of information or forms for data entry by employees—these can be safely removed. An overall problem is that the flowchart winds about the page in a manner reminiscent of the Mississippi River; a straighter, top-down reconfiguration would be much more understandable. The result, the much cleaner version shown in Exhibit 3.7, imparts the same information, but does so with approximately half the symbols.

(e) Proper Use of Flowlines

Of particular interest is the use of flowlines within a flowchart. Flowlines are the lines that connect symbols within a flowchart and reveal the direction of process flow. If handled

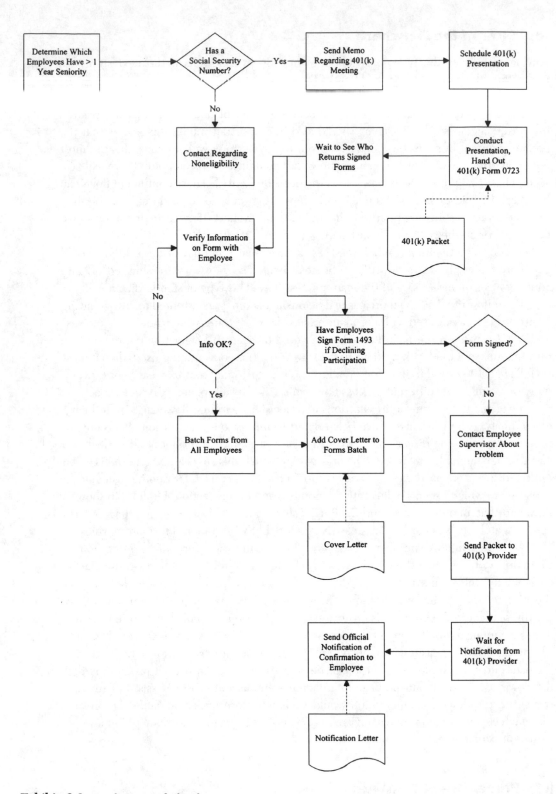

Exhibit 3.6 Poorly Designed Flowchart

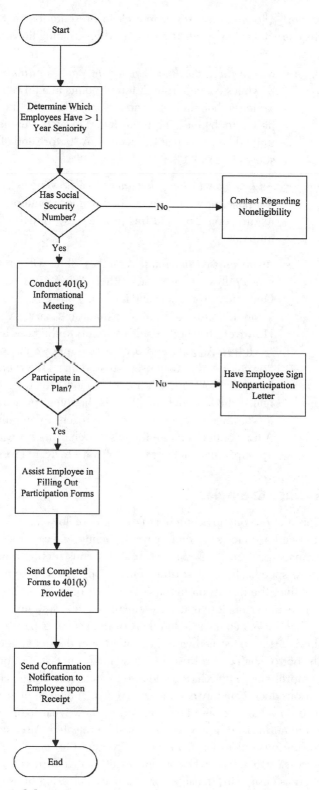

Exhibit 3.7 Properly Formatted Flowchart

properly, flowlines can result in a clean presentation that does not confuse the reader. Here are a few key points to focus on when creating flowlines:

- *Merge those flowlines having the same destination.* If there are a number of flowlines coming from different points in a flowchart, all of which connect to the same symbol, then one can greatly reduce the number of lines appearing on the flowchart by merging them together at the earliest point so that only a single unified line arrives at the symbol. A "before and after" example of this concept is shown in Exhibit 3.8.

- *Add arrows to long flowlines.* If a flowline is so long that it extends beyond the page, or wraps around one or more symbols, a reader may not understand its direction. To avoid this problem, overlay the flowline with arrows at regular intervals.

- *Avoid crossed flowlines.* A process flow will be barely discernible if flowlines repeatedly cross over each other. There are several ways to avoid this problem. One is to use outgoing and incoming off-page connector symbols on either side of a potential cross-over point so that users can see where the flow is supposed to go. However, this method adds symbols to the flowchart, increasing the overall level of clutter. Another approach is to duplicate process steps in different parts of a flowchart, rather than use a crossed line. However, this also results in an increase in symbols. A third solution is to allow the cross-over, but to use a "bubble" that makes the flowline look like it is "hopping" over the underlying flowline. Though less aesthetically pleasing, this approach is generally understandable to the reader. A final option is to see if one's flowcharting software has a rearrange feature that attempts to reconfigure the software to avoid crossed flowlines.

(f)   Flowcharted Procedure Examples

This section contains a number of examples of flowcharts for the more common accounting transactions, such as accounts payable, billing, and cash receipts. These are vastly simplified formats, but can be used as the basis for constructing more detailed flowcharts that will more specifically apply to the transactions in one's own accounting system. Wherever possible, the discussion for each flowchart notes those areas that can be expanded upon when converting it to match a company's actual systems.

Exhibit 3.9 contains a flowchart of the accounts payable function. The top half of the flowchart is concerned with the matching of documentation related to a purchase, while the bottom half covers the printing, signing, and distribution of checks to suppliers. A more comprehensive flowchart could also include an off-page connector that shows where the various documents are coming from that are being compared during the matching process. The flowchart can also be expanded to show what happens if an invoice is received but is not authorized by anyone and must be rejected. Also, steps can be added that relate to the various types of signature levels required for checks of different sizes. It may also be necessary to describe the handling of alternative forms of payment and their authorization, such as cash, wire transfers, or automated clearing house (ACH) payments. All of these additions will result in a much larger flowchart, so it may be useful to split it up into numerous smaller flowcharts that are linked with off-page connectors.

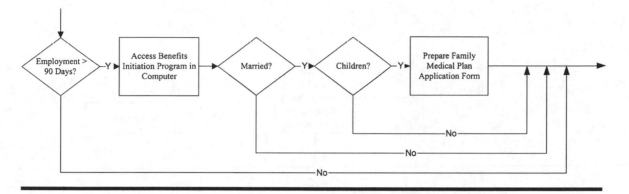

Example of Merged Flowlines:

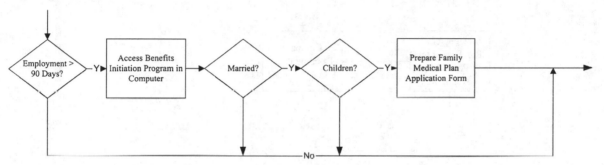

Exhibit 3.8 How to Merge Multiple Flowlines

Exhibit 3.10 describes a typical billing transaction. Its top half describes the process of verifying invoice information, while the bottom half describes how this information is converted into an invoice. A more detailed version should also include some discussion of the approval process for unusual pricing that has been granted to a customer, as well as alternative forms of invoicing, such as electronic data interchange (EDI) or creating invoices at the point of delivery.

Exhibit 3.11 describes a simplified cash receipts procedure that assumes all cash is received either in the form of checks or ACH transfers. In reality, there are several other types of cash receipt, such as over-the-counter cash, credit card payments, lock box receipts, or wire transfers that should also be described. Also, since this is an area in which theft is always a possibility, there may be a need for some additional steps that describe extra control points.

The next flowchart (Exhibit 3.12) is unique, for it shows the applicability of using parallel activities during the financial statement closing process. Notice how the many closing steps can be greatly compressed by splitting them into separate streams of activities and allowing them to run side by side. In only one case, where accounts payable information feeds into the fixed assets activities, is there any dependence between separate sets of activities. This is a clear-cut case in which the use of a flowchart makes the overall comprehension of a series of processes much easier to understand.

Purchasing is a lengthy process that includes many steps, some of which can be added to Exhibit 3.13 to arrive at a more comprehensive presentation. The existing flowchart shows the general flow of requisitions to the purchasing staff, which puts large items out for bid

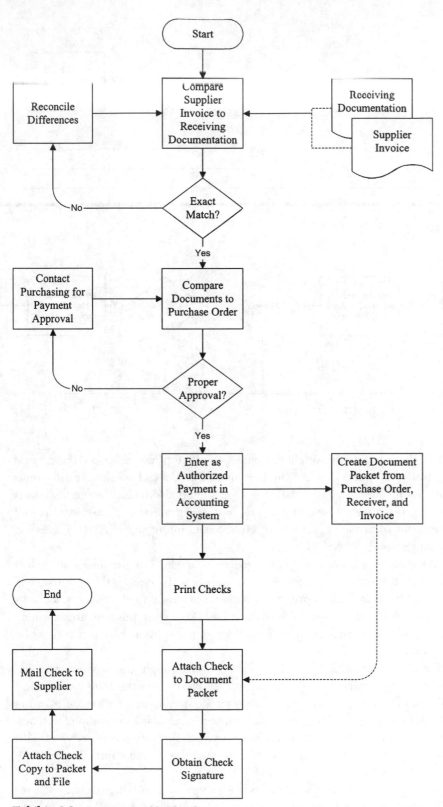

Exhibit 3.9 Accounts Payable Flowchart

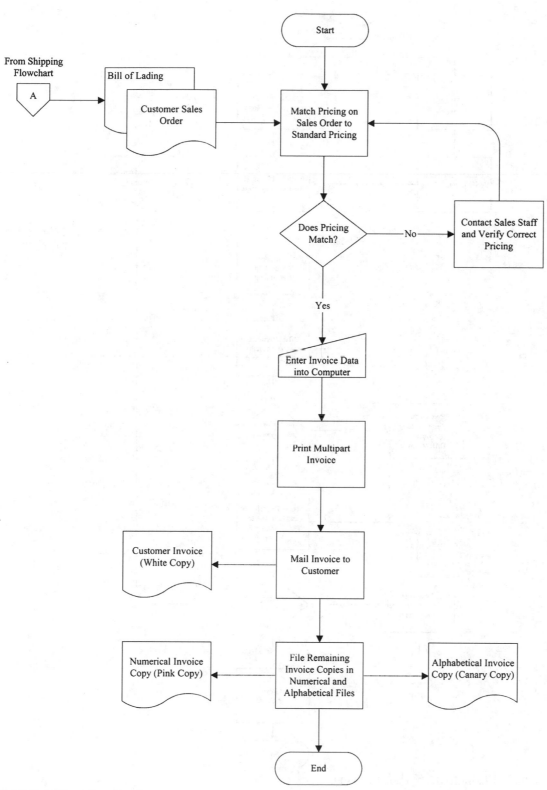

Exhibit 3.10 Billing Flowchart

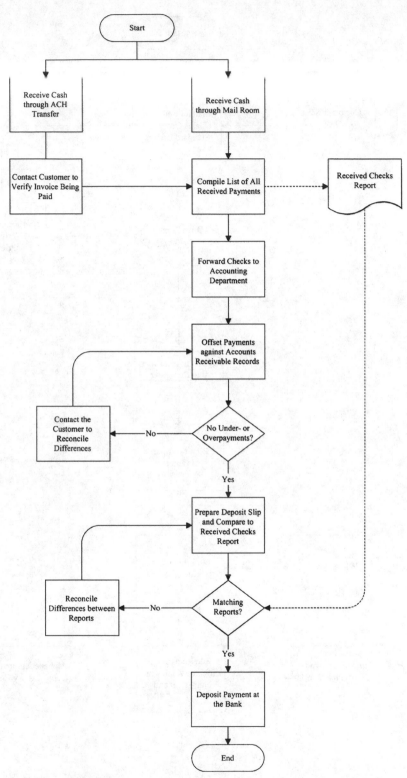

Exhibit 3.11 Cash Receipts Flowchart

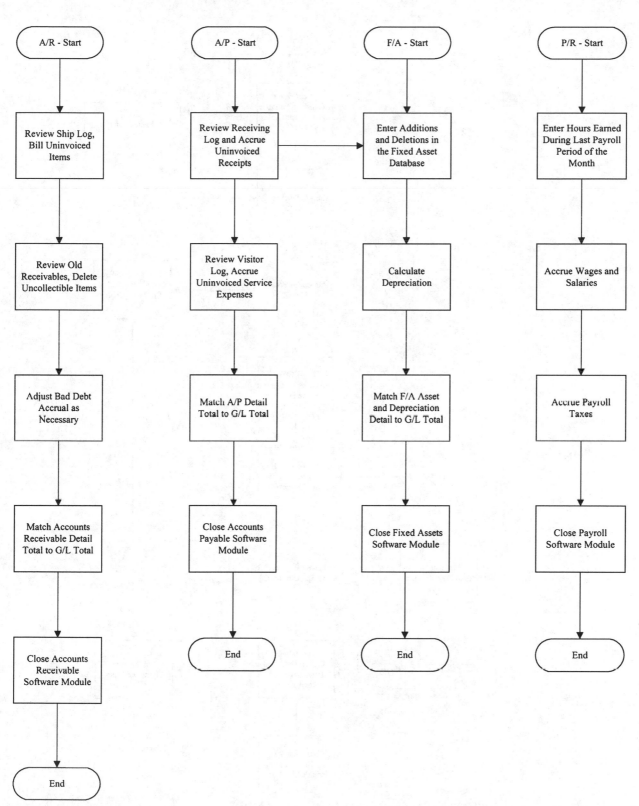

Exhibit 3.12 Financial Statement Closing Flowchart

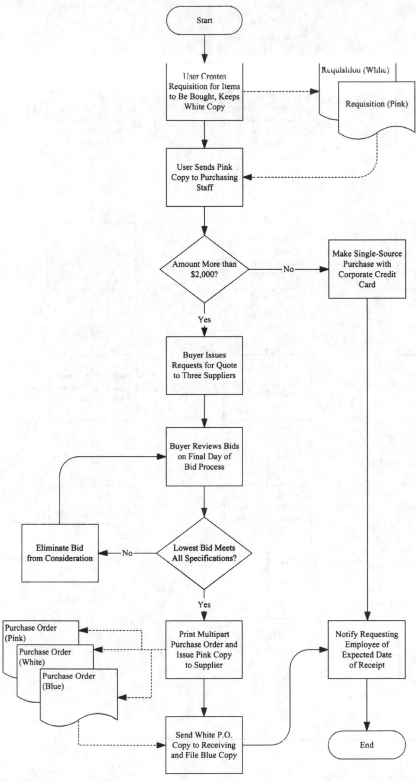

Exhibit 3.13 Purchasing Flowchart

and then places an order. Other tasks that can be added include the approval process for requisitions, the use of online catalogs to bypass many of the purchasing steps, and the use of procurement cards, plus the different process flow used for blanket purchase orders, not to mention the transmission of purchase orders by EDI. Given the large number of additions to this flowchart, it is generally presented in a multilayered format, with a multitude of off-page connector symbols linking the assemblage together.

3.5 FORMAT OF THE PROCEDURE

A procedure should follow a standard format to the greatest extent possible so that the same set of ancillary information—such as retrieval numbers and issue dates—can be uniformly included in all documents. This makes it easier to update procedures. A standard procedure format is shown in Exhibit 3.14. This layout shows a logo block where a company's logo should be copied into the document, as well as a header block in the upper right corner that contains a standard set of identification information. The main text area contains a brief header describing the procedure subject, as well as the detailed procedure (or instructions for completing a form) and some additional information.

Within the format shown in Exhibit 3.14, a procedure is laid out as a series of consecutively numbered tasks that accomplish a specific function. A procedure documents the flow of data and what each described work area does to that data to process it and pass it forward to the next work area. It is not a job description, job outline, policy, or form description.

The first part of the procedure is the header section, which includes a standard set of identification information. An example of a header is shown in Exhibit 3.15, where we see listed a company logo, retrieval number, page number, issue date, and the retrieval number of any document being superseded.

The narrative portion of a procedure begins immediately below the header block. Although the format of this section can vary considerably, the general narrative pattern for a procedure is an opening paragraph on the background of the subject and the intent of the procedure. This first paragraph may be labeled Background or Present Procedure. This paragraph is followed by a detailed itemization of the new procedure. If the user may require additional information, the bottom of the procedure can include a contact name or phone number to call. If there is an attachment to the procedure, such as a flow-chart or form, it is described at the end of the procedure, and is identified using the exact header name used for the attachment. One can also include a distribution list that identifies the departments or positions to which the procedure should be sent.

The following four examples illustrate how general policies and procedures are developed, in what order the information is presented, and the probable distribution of each one; they also illustrate the considerable versatility of this system.

Example 1: Sales Department Reorganization

A company sells products to original equipment manufacturers (OEMs), to wholesale distributors, and to large retailers. This information is presented as background material at the beginning of the procedure narrative.

3-Hole
Punched

1" Margin

Policy/Procedure Statement

| LOGO |

L. O. GRANT ORGANIZATION, INC.

- RETRIEVAL NO. (Assigned when released)
- PAGE   (Style 1 of, 2 of, ...)
- ISSUE DATE   (Month, day, year)
- ORIGINATOR   (Person or Unit)
- SUPERSEDES   (Retrieval No. of
                 replaced statement, if
                 applicable)

SUBJECT: (All capital letters) (Used for Indexing)

Background or Problem

Narrative explaining cause of problem and need for revision.

1" Margin

Revised Policy or Procedure

Narrative explanation, effective date, and enforcement.

Revised or New Form (If Applicable)

Uses of the form and general instructions.

Completing the Form (If Applicable)

Detailed instructions for completing each area of the form.

Summary

Name, address, telephone number where assistance can be obtained.

Attachments: (Use exact name of attachments)

Distribution: (Optional)

Exhibit 3.14   Standard Procedure Layout Specifications

Policy/Procedure Statement	Retrieval No.:	10-150
	Page:	1 of 3
	Issue Date:	3/15/0X
Brasto Publishing	Supersedes:	10-148
Subject: Monthly Journal Entry Review		

Exhibit 3.15. Standard Procedure Header Format

Sales have fallen off. The next section of the procedure describes what actions will be taken to deal with this problem, and how it will be implemented. This includes setting up separate sales teams for each customer type, which will require a different supporting management structure and account code system to record transactions. The procedure can also list the types of internal reports that will be generated to track this new system, and to whom the reports will be distributed (probably the executive officers, the entire sales force, and accounts payable manager).

Example 2: New Corporate Committee

The policy and procedure format is used to describe the creation of a new budgeting committee. The subject line would read *New Budget Committee.* The opening paragraph states the purpose of the committee and any expected benefits of having it.

The body of the document will describe how the committee is formed, what positions serve on it, the frequency and location of meetings, and its expected output. Distribution would be to all executive officers and department managers. This approach is quite useful in larger organizations where several committees function on a regular basis.

Example 3: Release of Financial Information

An organization may receive requests from outside entities, such as the press or credit reporting agencies, for financial information. Sometimes the person receiving the request is not fully qualified to give such information. The problem can be resolved by the use of a policy statement that defines the rules for release of such information and that also names the positions qualified to release such information.

The subject *Release of Financial Information* would define the contents of the policy. The opening paragraph would explain the problem and how it may adversely impact the organization. The second paragraph, which might be labeled *Policy for Release of Financial Information,* would set up a procedure under which any employee receiving a request for financial information would forward it to one of the authorized personnel noted in the procedure. There may be further information regarding specific restrictions on certain types of information, and under what circumstances legal counsel should be involved.

Example 4: New Receiving Report

A potential receiving problem has been discovered, so a new receiving procedure must be issued to address the problem. The company issuing the procedure buys large quantities of steel bars and rolls of sheet steel. Raw material inventories have been consistently short, and a review of existing procedures reveals that the receiving department always records

Policy/Procedure Statement	Retrieval No.:	Index
	Page:	1 of 1
	Issue Date:	12/31/0X
Brasto Publishing	Supersedes:	N/A
Subject: Cumulative Index through December 31, 2008		

Retrieval Number	Date	Distribution	Subject
10-000	3/15/02	Cash Clerk	Authorize a wire transfer payment
10-001	3/15/02	Cash Clerk	Process cash receipts
10-002	3/15/02	Cash Clerk	Process credit card payments
10-003	3/15/02	Cash Clerk	Process credit card refunds
10-004	3/15/02	Cash Clerk	Reconcile bank statement to book balance
10-005	3/15/02	Cash Clerk	Reconcile petty cash
10-101	4/30/02	Ledger Clerk	Accrue for earned vacation time
10-102	4/30/02	Ledger Clerk	Accrue for income taxes payable
10-103	4/30/02	Ledger Clerk	Accrue for unpaid wages
10-104	4/30/02	Ledger Clerk	Accrue for warranty expenses
10-105	4/30/02	Ledger Clerk	Calculate earnings per share
10-106	4/30/02	Ledger Clerk	Create journal entries
10-107	4/30/02	Ledger Clerk	Create the budget
10-108	4/30/02	Ledger Clerk	Calculate accruals
10-201	5/31/02	Treasury	Conduct a daily cash sweep
10-202	5/31/02	Treasury	Create borrowing base certificate
10-203	5/31/02	Treasury	Issue capital stock
10-204	5/31/02	Treasury	Issue dividends
10-205	5/31/02	Treasury	Pay for outstanding debt
10-206	5/31/02	Treasury	Prepare a cash forecast
10-207	5/31/02	Treasury	Process a letter of credit
10-301	6/30/02	Assets Clerk	Calculate depreciation on fixed assets
10-302	6/30/02	Assets Clerk	Conduct inventory of fixed assets
10-303	6/30/02	Assets Clerk	Enter fixed asset payments
10-304	6/30/02	Assets Clerk	Evaluate capital purchase proposals
10-305	6/30/02	Assets Clerk	Record gain/loss on sale of an asset
10-401	7/31/02	Inventory Clerk	Cycle count inventory
10-402	7/31/02	Inventory Clerk	Physical count inventory
10-403	7/31/02	Inventory Clerk	Track scrap transactions
10-501	8/31/02	Payroll Clerk	Calculate excess life insurance payments
10-502	8/31/02	Payroll Clerk	Calculate payroll taxes
10-503	8/31/02	Payroll Clerk	Calculate profit sharing
10-504	8/31/02	Payroll Clerk	Process payroll transactions
10-505	8/31/02	Payroll Clerk	Summarize timesheets

Exhibit 3.16.   Procedures Index

the weights from the supplier-affixed mill tags on each roll received. The solution is to install scales at the receiving dock, weigh each item received, and enter both the mill tag weight and measured weight on the receiving report.

The background paragraph should explain the underlying problem of raw material shortages and the probable cause, and the next section would describe the revised weighing and reporting procedure, as well as the form alteration that creates space to report on actual received weights. Distribution would be to all accountants involved in inventory control, and the entire receiving department.

Once a set of procedures has been created, one should categorize them in a master index procedure so that one can easily determine what procedures are available, when they were created, where they can be located, and to whom they are issued. An example of such an index is shown in Exhibit 3.16.

3.6 WORK STEPS FOR CONSTRUCTING A PROCEDURES MANUAL

Constructing a procedures manual is a major project for all but the smallest organizations. These steps are designed to provide structure to the process and create boundaries over the number of procedures being produced, which will keep the organization from getting bogged down in an endless cycle of procedure creation and updating.

1. *Define the project.* The largest single problem with the construction of a procedures manual is that no one knows when to stop. Instead, new procedures keep pouring in from all parts of the company for the most mundane and inconsequential items, resulting in a massive manual that is never truly finished and is never issued. To avoid this, it is very important to define immediately the company functions for which procedures will (and will not) be written, as well as make a rough guess at the total number of procedures that will be generated. This keeps the project within boundaries that give it a reasonable expectation of completion.

2. *Obtain a project sponsor.* No project of any size is ever completed unless there is someone in upper management who believes strongly enough in the project to support it through budget battles and the allocation of other scarce corporate resources. The positions that are generally most interested in a procedures manual are the chief financial officer and chief operating officer, so these people should be approached first. If they are not interested, the controller is also acceptable, though this person tends to have less influence over other parts of the company, which may result in a manual that covers only the accounting and finance areas.

3. *Determine the size of the project team.* The only other item needed prior to making a budget request for funds is to determine the size of the project team, because the main expense is labor. To do so, take the previously estimated total number of procedures, multiply them by a generous estimated number of hours each, and factor in an overage percentage, resulting in an approximate number of man-hours for the work. Then determine the average pay rate per person, and multiply this amount by the total number of estimated hours to determine the total labor expense. It may also be necessary to budget for some travel to outlying company locations, as well as for office space for the team and the production and distribution costs of the manual.

4. *Obtain an approved budget.* Present the proposed budget through the usual budget process, using the project sponsor to obtain approvals when needed. If the approved budget level is inadequate, scale back the number of procedures to be written to reflect the number of paid hours available. If reduction is needed, give feedback to the project sponsor regarding the pared-down size of the manual so that there will be no surprises when it is eventually issued.

5. *Determine the number of procedures to be written.* A general estimate of the total number of procedures to be added to the manual was done initially, but now it is time to develop a master list of procedures. To do so, each department should be contacted and asked for a full list of the procedures they would like to have. List all these procedures together and determine the total number in the list. It is almost always far more than the budgeted number. Then work with the department managers to throw out the least important procedures. This can be a time-consuming process; some managers will insist on having more than their share of procedures, so the project sponsor must intervene to decide which departments will be given more or less than their fair share of procedures. When complete, there should be a master list of procedures that the project team uses as its basis for all future planning.

6. *Prioritize the procedures.* Once the master list of procedures is complete, it is necessary to determine which are the most important. Though all of them may be completed, one should always complete a core set of procedures first, in case funds are cut off before the project is finished or a need arises for an advance release of the procedures before they have all been completed. The criteria for establishing importance can vary considerably, such as ranking one department over another if the department's work is considered more critical. Another method is to complete all of the procedures related to a specific process cycle, such as order fulfillment or purchasing, so that those activities are completely documented. The common approach is a political one, whereby each department receives an allocation of procedures; though not necessarily the best way to prioritize procedures, this method does allow all departments to participate in the process at about the same time, which increases the degree of user buy-in to the project and gives it a better overall chance of success.

7. *Establish a time line.* A set of due dates and milestones should be assigned to the project, to establish boundaries for when work is expected to be completed. For example, there should be regularly scheduled review dates to ensure that progress on procedures is acceptable. There should also be milestones for the completion of specific groups of procedures (usually for easily grouped clusters, such as by department or process cycle).

8. *Issue requests for existing procedures.* Based on the master list of prioritized procedures, send out requests to all department managers, asking for any existing documentation of targeted procedures. The returned information may include paper-based or electronic procedure formats, and may be in text or graphical mode. Whatever the format, it is wise to collect as much existing procedural information as possible, as this forms a foundation for subsequent interviews and, in many cases, also provides such complete information that there is little additional work to do, except for reformatting the material into a standard procedure layout.

9. *Undertake initial interviews.* Using any previously collected documentation, go to the departments that need procedures and obtain additional information through interviews. This should include multiple interviews whenever possible so that

one cannot only verify information with different people, but also have the same interviewees review the interviewer's written notes for accuracy. As a general rule, the first interview *will* result in erroneous procedural information, so follow-up interviews are necessary to increase the level of information accuracy.

10. *Send out preliminary procedures for review.* Once the procedures have been completed, send them out to the department managers for review. These people will probably pass along the documents to the experts within their organisations who are most able to determine if there are any inaccuracies in the information. It is helpful to determine in advance if other employees should also review the preliminary procedures. This is a key point for procedures that are used by multiple departments—simply having one of the users review them does not cover the full range of possible users. Also, when sending procedures out for review, it is helpful to attach a review form to them, explaining how to review a procedure, as well as how to note changes to the document. There should also be a control document for tracking when procedures are sent for review, as well as when they were received back and who reviewed them. This document is most useful for determining which reviewers have not returned documents so that timely follow-up to complete the review process can be done.

11. *Update preliminary procedures.* Once the procedures have been reviewed and returned, input the changes into the procedures database. This step should include an independent review of the updated documents by an experienced editor who can verify that all required changes were made, as well as ensure that the documents use correct grammatical conventions. There should also be a control document for this stage of work, because procedure updates may be performed over a long period of time (depending on how long it takes to recover documents that are out for review), and some updates may be missed. By regularly examining the control document, on which are noted the procedures that have been updated, it is an easy matter to track down and update those still requiring this work.

12. *Approve procedures.* Approvals should be kept to a minimum. If only accounting information is released, a three-step preparation and approval system generally works best. The system consists of origination, editing for accuracy and consistency, and officer approval. Origination is done best at the unit level, such as by the manager of payroll, payables, budgeting, and so forth. The controller should then review the proposed release for consistency and accuracy. Finally, the chief financial officer's staff should review the proposed release for possible legal conflicts, as well as conflicts with the procedures of other company segments. If approved, the procedure is released for general distribution.

13. *Assemble procedures manuals.* Once the procedures have been approved, they must be formatted properly. The typical format includes a company logo, the date of the procedure, the page number, the version number, and the index number. Once the procedures are formatted, the publisher must be notified of how many copies to print, which is based on the distribution list (see next item). Also, the type of binder must be determined, which may include inserts on the spine and cover itemizing the contents. Finally, depending on the size of the volume, it may be useful to include index tabs that delineate the procedures of each department. There are a wide range of prices, depending on the layouts, types of binders, inserts, and use of color, so try to match the budget to the options selected.

14. *Determine procedures distribution list.* Once the procedures writing is completed, it is time to determine who should receive the resulting manuals. This can be as

simple as issuing a fixed number of manuals to each department head and giving them the responsibility for handing out the books. However, this tends to result in an uneven distribution of valuable documents, so it is generally best to determine, with the assistance of the department managers and the human resources coordinator, what job titles should receive a procedures manual. This approach makes it a simple matter to distribute manuals based on the job descriptions listed in the human resources database. It is also necessary to determine which parts of the manual go to each recipient. For a very large manual, possibly encompassing a multitude of binders, it can be cost-prohibitive to distribute all of it to everyone, especially those who do not need it. Accordingly, the list of position titles to whom the manual should go must also include a description of exactly what part of the manual is to be sent.

15. *Distribute procedures manuals.* Once the procedures binders arrive from the printer, it becomes a simple matter to use the distribution list to send out procedures manuals to recipients, either through interoffice mail (if there is one location) or the postal service (if there are many locations). If there are multiple locations, it may be necessary to update the distribution list (see the preceding step) with mailing addresses for each recipient. All mailings should include a note asking the receiving organization to return the binder if the recipient no longer works for the company so that these expensive documents can be used elsewhere.

16. *Determine frequency of review.* Once the initial procedures documentation work is completed, it is time to determine how frequently the process should be repeated. Integral to the frequency question are the funds available, the likely need for additional new procedures (especially common if businesses are being added that are unrelated to existing ones), and the need for rapid updates. This last factor is most important if a company uses its procedures manual as a training tool for employees—if the actual procedure is no longer correctly reflected in the written procedures, the binder is of no further use as a training tool. A typical review cycle is once a year, with more frequent updates only if the department needing the update designates it as being on a rush basis (which can be limited by charging the rush update work back to the requesting department!).

17. *Obtain approval of budget continuations.* Once the frequency of procedures updates has been determined, one must make estimates of the continuing staff time and distribution costs that will be needed. Because these are the two main cost drivers for the process, it is then a simple matter to compile a budget request for the upcoming year that should encompass the project requirements. The main variables that may require an increase in funding are requests for a number of new procedures, more recipients of the expensive procedures binders, or the addition of new subsidiaries that also require new procedures writing.

18. *Write a project review.* Once the project is complete and the budget request has been submitted for the upcoming year, there is one step remaining—to review the entire process with participants to see whether any problems with the process came up that could be corrected the next time around. This is a frequently ignored step, as everyone involved wants to move on to other work. However, this is a critical step for reducing the work required to produce quality procedures when valuable staff time can be used elsewhere, and costs can be lowered in the future. In short, a carefully reviewed and documented project review is an excellent way to leave recommendations for the next project team assigned to updating procedures, making the process easier and less expensive in the future.

The exact process used to create or update a procedures manual will vary from company to company. Some businesses are so small that many of the preceding steps are unnecessary—a few people can gather a sufficient amount of information in a short time to rapidly assemble a reputable procedures manual. Other companies have so many far-flung divisions that the procedures writing chore becomes massive, with a full-time team to research and write procedures and an ongoing staff to handle updates. In this environment, the preceding process steps are clearly not sufficient for timely and successful completion of the project. Instead, these steps are designed to serve the needs of the majority of small- to medium-sized businesses with enough departments and procedures to require a formal documentation process.

3.7 SUGGESTED LIST OF PROCEDURES

The exact procedures chosen will depend on their criticality within a specific business, as well as how much they are needed as control points. Also important are the amount of resources consumed by them and the proportion of total time taken by an employee to complete them. Thus, the procedures chosen for inclusion in a procedures manual will vary considerably by company. A short list of the more common procedures can be used as the basis for a procedures manual:

Cash

- Authorize a wire transfer payment.
- Process cash receipts.
- Process credit card payments.
- Process credit card refunds.
- Reconcile bank statement to book balance.
- Reconcile petty cash.

Financial Statements

- Accrue for earned vacation time.
- Accrue for income taxes payable.
- Accrue for unpaid wages.
- Accrue for warranty expenses.
- Calculate earnings per share.
- Calculate overhead costs and application thereof.
- Create journal entries.
- Create the budget.
- Calculate accruals.
- Enter the budget into the financial statement report.

Financing

- Conduct a daily cash sweep.
- Create borrowing base certificate.
- Issue capital stock.
- Issue dividends.
- Pay for outstanding debt.
- Prepare a cash forecast.
- Process a letter of credit.
- Request additional debt from a revolving credit line.

Fixed Assets

- Calculate depreciation on fixed assets.
- Conduct inventory of fixed assets.
- Enter fixed asset payments.
- Evaluate capital purchase proposals.
- Record gain/loss on sale of an asset.

Inventory and Purchasing

- Cycle count inventory.
- Physical count inventory.
- Purchase under economic order quantity calculations.
- Purchase small tools and supplies.
- Receive deliveries from unqualified suppliers.
- Receive deliveries from qualified suppliers.
- Track scrap transactions.

Payroll

- Calculate excess life insurance payments.
- Calculate payroll taxes.
- Calculate profit sharing.
- Process payroll transactions.
- Summarize timesheets.

Payments

- Calculate commissions.

- Calculate royalties.

- Calculate sales taxes.

- Match receiving, purchasing, and supplier documents.

- Obtain authorization for non–purchase order acquisitions.

- Print 1099 forms.

- Process manual check payments.

- Review expense reimbursements.

- Void checks.

Sales

- Authorization of bad debts.

- Billings to employees.

- Calculation of allowance for bad debt reserve.

- Collection of overdue accounts.

- Create customer invoices.

- Issue credit to customers.

- Record sales returns.

- Record scrap sales.

Other

- Conduct due diligence review of an acquisition.

The preceding list is meant for just the accounting department, but the accountant may also be called upon to prepare procedures for other departments. Unfortunately, this project encompasses so many functional areas that it is difficult to determine where to start. The following is a sample listing, sorted by functional area, of the most common procedures that may be needed in a procedures manual for most companies. These are just the core procedures; additional procedures will be needed based on the special requirements of each company, which are determined mainly by the structure of the organization and the industry in which it is located.

Administration

- Copier and fax repairs

- Ordering office supplies

- Reception management

- Voice mail setup

Computer Systems

- Daily batch processing
- Database maintenance
- Database purging
- E-mail setup
- Password maintenance
- Programming request processing
- Restore from backup
- System backup
- System security maintenance
- Time clock backup

Engineering

- Bill of materials creation
- Changing standard costs
- Effectivity date changes
- Engineering change notices
- Engineering document numbering
- Engineering document storage
- Project prioritization
- Project tracking
- Work order routing

Human Resources

- 401 (k) change processing
- Birthday notifications
- Cafeteria plan change processing
- Forklift training
- Injury reports
- Last pay increase/review notification
- Life insurance change processing

- Medical insurance change processing
- Safety training
- Security review
- Training request

Logistics

- Capacity planning
- Cycle counting
- Floor stock location maintenance
- Master schedule maintenance
- Master scheduling
- Material returns to suppliers
- Opening, reviewing, and closing orders
- Order entry
- Order picking
- Physical inventory count
- Product recall receipts
- Production scheduling
- Purchase orders
- Purchasing for prototypes
- Receiving
- Resolving scheduling conflicts
- Returns to suppliers
- Running material requirements reports
- Scrap reporting
- Shipping
- Supplier master records, adding
- Staging
- Weekly planning meeting

Production

- Lock out/tag out

- Machine calibration
- Machine maintenance requests
- Machine preventive maintenance
- Machine shutdown check-off list
- Machine startup check-off list
- Maintenance on-call procedure
- Scrap reporting

Quality Assurance

- Corrective action reports
- First and last piece inspection
- Inspection equipment calibration
- Inspection equipment control
- Nonconforming material control
- Placing production on hold status
- Quality records maintenance
- Receiving returned goods
- Sample retention
- Temporary deviation

Sales

- Forecast management
- Price book maintenance
- Pricing changes
- Quoting
- Recall notifications
- Sales forecasting
- Special services quotes

3.8 OTHER USES FOR PROCEDURES MANUALS

The accounting department is not the only company function that can profit from the use of a properly created and maintained procedures manual. It is also useful in any situation where a department's operations can benefit from a set of consistently performed procedures. Examples of such areas are the Management Information Systems department (which needs a data processing manual to cover such issues as system backups, disaster recovery planning, and the timely production of scheduled reports) and the Human Resources department (which needs a manual dealing with all employee-related benefits, safety issues, and disciplinary concerns). Examples of procedure manuals for these two departments are included in later chapters of this book.

Chapter 4

MAINTAINING AND DISTRIBUTING ACCOUNTING MANUALS

4.1 INTRODUCTION

The process of creating an accounting manual does not end with the creation of policies and procedures, for even the best manual will be of no use if it is not properly organized and distributed in a manner that makes it thoroughly readable and instructive. In this chapter, we will explain why a master copy of the manual must be kept, even for years after it has been superseded. Also, we will review the mechanics of physically assembling the accounting manual, determining the best possible members for the distribution list, and ensuring that everyone receives and understands it. This can be a very complex process, especially in a multilocation organization. By the end of this chapter, it will become apparent that the distribution task is crucial to the overall success of an accounting manual.

The greatest innovation to come to the field of accounting manual design and maintenance in many years is the conversion of manuals to an electronic format. In this chapter, we will explore the various types and combinations of formats that can be used, as well as discuss why these changes are beneficial and how to create electronic manuals. The reader may be interested in overhauling the entire current system of accounting manual presentation to take advantage of current innovations.

4.2 MAINTAINING ACCOUNTING MANUALS

As soon as a new manual has been released, maintenance is not far behind. Accounting manual changes consist of adding or deleting something, changing a record, account, or procedure, or clarifying a previous release. Maintenance of documentation can vary considerably, from a minor change that may affect only a few people to a massive change such as the installation of new systems or major overhaul of existing systems.

There are three levels of change and several ways to announce or publish changes. Minor changes—such as adding or deleting one or a few account numbers, income or expense codes, or approval authorizations—can be reported by interoffice correspondence or memoranda to those departments or employees affected by the change. The memorandum would specify the change and the reason for it; the change would be related to a specific manual or prior release with enough information to enable the recipient to enter the change in his or her copy of the proper manual.

Intermediate changes, such as the replacement of a significant portion of a manual, the introduction of a new form, a significant change in an existing form, or a policy or procedural change that may affect most operations within the company, are disclosed through the policy/procedure statement (P/PS) system, possibly in conjunction with replacement sections of the manual as attachments.

A major change, such as a new accounting system, a new data processing system affecting users, or a replacement of several action or transaction forms, would require the rewriting and reissuance of the manual, or major sections thereof if the changed affected only one or two separate sections of a manual. These types of changes are noted in Exhibit 4.1 in relation to how they are used for each of the various manuals. In all cases, the determination that maintenance is required and the level of reporting changes are both subjective and judgmental. The person or group most closely related to each manual is probably the best source for determining the impact of an addition, deletion, or other change to that manual.

Each of the manuals discussed in this book require the levels and methods of reporting changes related to typical maintenance items:

General Accounting Manual

Typical minor changes consist of adding or deleting a few account codes, or a change in a form. In most cases, changes of this type only affect one or two employees or departments, so the logical method of reporting the change is a memorandum to the affected users.

The introduction of a new form or replacement of an existing form, changes in many account numbers, or changes in organizational structure with little impact on the general accounting procedures are best reported through the P/PS system. It is here that the background information can be reported, the changes can be described in any amount of detail desired, and the distribution can be handled in an effective manner. However, if several P/PS statements are issued over a short time period, you should consider reissuing the manual or major subsections—a major change.

A major change in the general accounting manual would be the introduction of many new accounts, a new general accounting system or major subsystem, a reorganization of a significant portion of the operations of the company, or substantial changes in data entry processing or processing methods and reports.

General Accounting Manual
- *Minor change.* Use memorandum to user departments.
- *Intermediate change.* Use policy/procedure statement.
- *Major change.* Reissue manual or major sections thereof.

Corporate Policies
- *Any change.* Reissue manual or major sections thereof.

Procedure Statements
- *Any change.* Issue new P/PS and supersede old P/PS if appropriate.

Purchasing Card Manual
- *Any change.* Use policy/procedure statement.

Accounting Controls Manual
- *Any change.* Reissue manual or major sections thereof.

Period-End Manual
- *Any change.* Revise and publish new manual.

Budgeting Manual
- *Any change.* Revise and publish new manual.

Property Accounting Manual
- *Minor change.* Use memorandum to user departments.
- *Intermediate change.* Use policy/procedure statement.
- *Major change.* Reissue manual or major sections thereof.

Forms Manual
- *Minor change.* Use memorandum to user departments.
- *Intermediate change.* Use policy/procedure statement.
- *Major change.* Reissue manual or major sections thereof.

Document Management Manual
- *Any change.* Use policy/procedure statement.

*User Manual
- *Minor and intermediate changes.* Use memorandum to department users.
- *Major change.* Reissue manual annually or if substantial changes, such as a new accounting system, have been implemented.

*Information Technology Manual
- *Minor change.* Use memorandum to user departments.
- *Intermediate change.* Use policy/procedure statement.
- *Major change.* Reissue Manual or major sections thereof.

*Human Resources Manual
- *Any change.* Revise and publish new manual.

Exhibit 4.1   Maintenance Methods for Accounting Manuals

* Please see http://www.wiley.com/go/manual for these Chapters and more related content.

Policy and Procedure Statements

Policy and procedure statements are never updated; they are superseded and a new P/PS released. The heading of the new P/PS would indicate the retrieval number of the one superseded; the body of the new P/PS would only mention the superseded one in the background information section in general terms.

Purchasing Card Manual

The purchasing card manual is relatively short, and should require minimal changes on an ongoing basis. Thus, changes to it should be released only as part of an entirely new manual. This is doubly important because the manual is used as a training document for new users of corporate purchasing cards.

Accounting Controls Manual

The contents of the accounting controls manual will likely change every few months, as changes to systems and transactions require alterations to the underlying control systems. Since controls are usually interconnected, it is best to issue a new controls document for an entire transactional area whenever control modifications are made within that area.

Period-End Manual

The period-end manual should be in a constant state of revision, because part of the closing procedure is to review completed tasks and see if increased efficiencies can be obtained by revising the timing or work instructions in the manual. Consequently, this manual should be incrementally revised and released in its entirety following most month-end closings, and completely overhauled at least once a year.

Budgeting Manual

The budgeting manual is typically updated just once a year and released as a new version as part of the budgeting process, usually toward the end of the current fiscal year. At this time, all older versions of the budgeting manual should be collected and destroyed so that no one uses budgeting procedures from an out-of-date version.

Property Accounting Manual

The property accounting manual is essentially a highly specific subset of the forms manual, relating strictly to the recording of transactions for fixed assets. As such, the same rules relating to the forms manual apply to the property accounting manual.

Forms Manual

The forms manual is a series of forms and instructions for completing accounting forms. Updating usually consists of replacing the instructions or the form, or both. The procedure is an exception to the rule that asking the user to update a manual by removing and replacing pages is to be avoided. If the forms manual has a known sequence, such as a form number or official title, inserting new pages is not burdensome. When issuing a new form or a replacement form, the covering memorandum should explain its purpose and location in the forms manual. If deleting a form from the accounting system, the interoffice memorandum is the only method available for informing holders of the forms manual of the deletion. If the forms manual has a published index, it should be reissued after two or three changes have been made to the contents of the manual.

Document Management Manual

The document management manual rarely changes. Also, since this is a relatively low-risk area, it is generally safe to let changes to the manual accumulate, and issue a new manual only at relatively lengthy intervals, such as once a year.

* User Manual

The user manual is a periodic-release type of manual, essentially to inform new employees following a period of employee turnover. However, if the manual remains substantially unchanged, maintenance is handled in the same manner as for the general accounting manual. Minor maintenance need not be reported because the people affected are informed through a memorandum or letter. If a new or replacement form included in the user manual is being issued, the holders of the user manual should be informed by memo or through the P/PS system. If the change is major—such as a new accounting system or substantial changes thereto, or a major policy change negates a large portion of the manual—then a new manual should be written and published and the holders notified to destroy the old manual. User manuals should be dated so that, if a user makes an inquiry to accounting, both parties would be referring to the same publication.

If newly hired employees need the user manual, they should receive the latest manual with updates noted or copies of the change letters or memos included. If the manual is used as the basis of a training session for new employees, the changes would be discussed as part of the instruction.

* Information Technology Manual

Portions of this manual resemble the forms manual in style and content. Changes in record layouts, batch input or processing forms, and output report layouts are handled by asking each recipient of the manual to remove existing pages and insert record or report layouts. If there are many changes, or the system is being drastically altered or replaced, then a new manual should be compiled and issued, along with instructions to destroy the old manual.

* Human Resources Manual

This manual contains a number of policies that directly impact the manner in which the company deals with its employees. For this reason, changes in the polices over time will have an impact on the benefits, pay, and hiring policies of the company, which will have a direct monetary impact on employees. Consequently, the human resources manual can be used as the basis for lawsuits by employees against the company when company actions deviate from the policies outlined in the manual. For this reason, it is very important to incorporate all suggested changes into the manual at one time, and then release the new manual to all recipients at the same time, being careful to collect and destroy all old manuals being replaced. Given the risk of lawsuits, at least one copy of each older version of the manual should be stored in a locked and fireproof location. Also, recipients should

---

* Please see http://www.wiley.com/go/manual for these Chapters and more related content.

sign a document stating that they have received the new manual and turned in the old version so there is no chance of having old manuals treated as current ones.

Updating manuals is highly judgmental. Indications of the need for the release of new information to the holders of any manuals include an increase in transaction errors, a sudden disregard of company policy or procedure, or consistently faulty transaction coding indicating the preparer has not been informed of a change in the coding structure.

The preparer of the manuals or systems documentation should maintain a record of the distribution of each type of release if updates and new releases are to be distributed to the original recipients in an orderly manner. The minimum amount of information contained in a distribution record should be:

- Name of the released document

- Date published

- Retrieval number (if any)

- Distribution list

For small-issue releases, such as the general accounting manual, specific names and titles may be recorded. For larger, more general releases, the general name of the employee group may be listed. For example, if a P/PS were released to supervisors, department heads, and senior management, names would not be needed because the next release, even if it is an update of a previous publication, would be addressed the same way.

Large lists of names are difficult to maintain because of employee turnover in most organizations. At all times, the primary objective of releasing information is to get the information to the right department or designated level of personnel. The distribution list should be fairly definitive. For example, if a P/PS is used to announce a special change in the retirement plan for employees over 60 years old, the distribution list should have that description. Maintaining specific names is not important because it is unlikely that a similar release will be issued to exactly the same employees. Thus, designated group names become an important part of the distribution system.

4.3 RESPONSIBILITY FOR MAINTENANCE OF MANUALS

The person selected to document an accounting system should have a fairly comprehensive knowledge of modern accounting practices, some knowledge of the organization, and a strong desire to complete the assignment. In a very large organization, a specialist may be employed in a staff position, reporting to the controller or chief financial officer. This person should be given as much authority as an internal auditor, with full access to the officers and department managers, documents, and the current procedures in use. The position title should indicate the span of authority, such as Director of Systems Documentation.

Two specific employee types immediately come to mind: the recent college graduate with a major or minor in accounting, or an older person within two or three years of retirement—an excellent use of an experienced person with prior management-level experience in the accounting function.

In many organizations, the task of documenting accounting systems can be assigned to the controller, who can assign specific areas or tasks to knowledgeable supervisors reporting to him or her. The controller then becomes the editor, approver, and publisher of accounting manuals. In any case, the assignment should be closely allied with and monitored by the controller's office, for it is here, at the highest level of knowledge, that the working accounting procedures are controlled, changed when necessary, and maintained appropriately.

The following is a brief summary of the most appropriate documenters for each of the accounting manuals:

General Accounting Manual

The controller is the logical choice to develop this manual. Department or functional supervisors of payroll, payables, cash receipts, investments, cost accounting, fixed assets, and so on can be assigned specific documentation tasks related to their operation or to the general operations of accounting. The controller would supervise the editing, printing, and publishing. In a large organization, a staff position could be added to handle these tasks.

Policy Statements

Policy statements should be changed only by senior management, sometimes requiring approval by the board of directors. Consequently, the chief financial officer or controller should be responsible for updates to this manual, with approvals being properly documented and stored for later audit review.

Procedure Statements

Because policy and procedure statements are the heart of an ongoing accounting operation, these should be under the controller's jurisdiction. Most P/PS statements are originated in departments, and the system of bringing the policy or procedure to the controller with the request to publish it is a most satisfactory solution.

Purchasing Card Manual

The manager of the purchasing card program is responsible for maintenance of the purchasing card manual. This person generally falls within the jurisdiction of the purchasing or materials management departments. In the absence of such a person, the responsibility can devolve upon the accounts payable manager.

Accounting Controls Manual

Accounting controls are a critical part of a company's risk management system, and so should be the responsibility of the chief financial officer (who is also responsible for risk management). Under no circumstances should this responsibility be shifted too low in the organization, to the transaction-level supervisors, since they would be tempted to eliminate controls in favor of creating more streamlined systems.

Period-End Manual

The logical preparer of the period-end manual is the assistant controller in charge of financial statement preparation, working in conjunction with the director of internal audit or a knowledgeable audit manager, particularly if the person works closely with the external auditors to facilitate a speedy, effective financial audit of the organization. The audit specialist should be able to write effective programs of examination for specific audit functions. Effectively handled, a comprehensive pre-audit review and a detailed period-end manual can reduce the cost of an independent audit significantly.

Budgeting Manual

The budgeting manual is essentially the work instructions for the area over which the budgeting manager has full responsibility; accordingly, this person should be responsible for the manual. If a company is too small to employ a budgeting manager, then responsibility for the manual should shift back to the controller.

Property Accounting Manual

Property accounting forms and related instructions fall completely within the responsibility area of the fixed assets accountant, so this position should have responsibility for this manual. If there is no fixed assets accountant, then responsibility should shift back to the controller.

Forms Manual

Again, the controller is selected to centralize the accumulation of forms and forms descriptions. A small working task force can be organized to bring all current forms up to date and then describe how each form is to be completed and used. Once the total forms manual is in place, it is not difficult to make additions or deletions for the relatively infrequent changes in operating forms.

Document Management Manual

Responsibility for the document management manual can be placed on a variety of positions, but is generally assigned to an assistant controller or similar mid-level accounting position. The key requirement for this position is a current knowledge of legal requirements for record storage.

* User Manual

This manual is ideally suited to be a cooperative department or functional project, headed by the controller or a staff assistant to the controller. Each department or functional area knows the forms in use, the proper data to be included, the approvals, and the related problems based on prior outside user questions and complaints. Each preliminary writer should be instructed to write only what is necessary for the user to know. It is not necessary to describe all the inner workings, controls, or procedures employed to edit, enter, summarize, and report the data or produce a final output report; this manual only covers basic input forms and procedures related to user-provided information required by forms.

* Information Technology Manual

The writer of this manual should have some knowledge of basic business data processing. However, much of the required manual contents can be determined with extensive interviews of user personnel and computer analysts and programmers. Suppliers of packaged accounting systems should provide user documentation. In most cases, this user documentation must be customized to an organization's specific methods and procedures.

---

* Please see http://www.wiley.com/go/manual for these Chapters and more related content.

*** Human Resources Manual**

The bulk of the policies, procedures, and forms itemized in this manual will be compiled by the human resources staff, with the exception of a few instructions that may be generated in conjunction with the payroll function of the accounting department. Accordingly, responsibility for this manual will largely fall upon the human resources manager, in conjunction with some assistance from the payroll staff.

The following is a job description showing the traits desirable in an employee who will be assigned the writing and compiling tasks, and the criteria for selecting an outside consultant who may be employed to produce specific accounting manuals.

Documenter Job Description

- Degree in accounting

- Large-company business experience

- Knowledge of internal accounting controls

- Good writing ability (style)

- Desire to spend several years in this job

- Good interviewing techniques

Consultant Selection Criteria

- Significant experience in writing documentation for accounting, data processing, or similar operations

- Well-designed plan to use internal employees as much as possible for start-up materials

- Good, readable writing style. (Review several recent reports or actual documentation prepared by the consultant who will be assigned to the job).

- Full understanding of the exact requirements of the specific manuals that he or she will complete.

Outside consultants may require that office space, photocopying, and printing services be provided.

4.4 PHYSICAL CONSTRUCTION OF THE MANUAL'S BINDER

Before issuing an accounting manual, the subset of policies, procedures, forms, and flowcharts that have previously been developed must be assembled into a cohesive whole. We will address this task as two parts: the binder and the contents.

The first part seems simple enough—just buy a boxful of binders. However, there are some subtleties to the purchase of a binder that should be considered:

---

* Please see http://www.wiley.com/go/manual for these Chapters and more related content.

- *Use a loose-leaf binder.* Any accounting manual will start to go out of date the moment it is released for general use, just because a company's systems are always changing to reflect alterations in the business. Accordingly, the accounting manual should be stored in a binder that can be easily opened so that pages can be inserted or removed at any time in the future.

- *Buy the slant-ring version of the binder.* If there is a choice, it is better to purchase binders in the slant-ring style. This is because the slant-ring version holds more pages than the standard circular rings, and also tends to result in less page jamming. These features easily outweigh its slight increase in cost.

- *Buy binders that are too large.* When first creating an accounting manual, it is quite likely that the number of documents created will not cover all possible topics, if only because there will be pressure to release some sort of document to help the accounting department as soon as possible. The trouble is that the binder purchased for this first release may not be sufficiently large to encompass the additional pages that will be added during future releases. Accordingly, the binder purchased should be much wider than the size needed to hold the pages produced for the first release.

- *Base binder size on the ring width.* Less-expensive binders are likely to cost less because their manufacturer has scrimped on the size of the ring within the binder, while still creating a binder that has an impressively wide spine. A purchaser of such a binder will find that the binder will hold fewer pages than expected. A much better way to predict the page capacity of a binder is to base it on the inside diameter of the ring; one inch of ring diameter will hold roughly 200 pages of paper (though this will vary if heavier-weight paper types are used).

- *Buy a stiff binder.* A stiff binder cover is preferred, because this type of binder is more likely to be stood up on end for storage, and so will be more visible to the user. Alternatively, a soft binder is more likely to be stored horizontally, and so may be buried under a stack of other papers, which makes it invisible to the user, and so less likely to be used.

- *Buy binders with plastic overlay covers.* It is not acceptable to issue an accounting manual that is completely unidentified by any type of marking; it will certainly be shuffled in with other user binders that are similarly unmarked, and will never be used at all. Instead, there should be plastic overlay covers on the front, back, and spine. The exact type of identification sheets used within these overlays is up to the manual development team; a suggestion is to use a different color insert for different types of binders. For example, the accounting manual may have a blue cover, and the human resources manual may be red. This makes it easier for the manual development team to differentiate the manuals as it prepares them for delivery to recipients.

- *Use clearly visible index tabs.* Avoid index tabs that are flush with the edge of a page, for these will not be clearly visible to the user. Instead, any type of index tab that stands out clearly is preferred. Some users may prefer a particular type that is color-coded by topic, but users will probably not understand the color scheme if there are many topics (which require many colors).

- *Reference procedure numbers on index tabs.* It is very common to group procedures by department or function on index tabs. However, this approach may not work if department names or processes change over time, which will require the distribution of new tabs, and possibly a heavily reorganized manual. Instead, the tabs should identify clusters of procedures by the range of their identifying numbers.

Though a seemingly minor topic, this section included eight points that primarily targeted the type of binder to use for an accounting manual. These are subtle items, but can make the difference between a professional-looking and heavily used manual and one that is undistinguished and rarely used.

4.5　CREATION AND STORAGE OF THE MASTER MANUAL COPY

With all binders completed, it is now necessary to create a complete master document for this issue of the accounting manual. There are several reasons for doing so. One is that the distribution process may take place over several weeks or months, depending on how the roll-out plan has been developed (such as providing training alongside a new manual, which tends to result in a much slower, though more thorough, roll-out). When there is a long interval between the first and last mailing, there is some danger that the later recipients will receive documents that contain newer changes than those that were sent to the earlier recipients; this can result in differences in transactional processing throughout the company. Another problem is that the company may choose to bring suit against an employee for improperly completing a procedure or following a policy. If so, the employee may use the defense of having relied on an earlier or later version of the manual. It is difficult to counteract this defense unless there is a master copy of the manual on hand that relates to the period under discussion.

Given these points, one should address the following steps to create a master copy of the manual:

1. *Assign the same release date to all documents.* All new pages that are to be inserted in the manual should be given the expected release date for the manual, rather than the earlier date when they were actually created. This avoids the contention that some other date on a document indicates that there was a separate, earlier release of documents.

2. *Update the revision history.* If the manual contains a list of dates when each document was updated, be sure to include any new revision dates on this list. This is especially useful for legal reasons, allowing a company to prove a complete history of when new documents were issued to employees.

3. *Verify that old page versions are replaced.* If new versions of documents have been created for this most recent master copy, then verify (several times) that the old pages have been taken out of the manual and replaced with the new ones. It is not acceptable to send out the manual with duplicate or missing pages because this confuses readers.

4. *Create multiple tables of contents.* Once all of the pages have been inserted or deleted, create two tables of contents for the manual. One should be in order by the subject topic, as shown in Exhibit 4.2. A reader can look up a topic in this

C	Document Number
Cash, Petty	0307
Cash, Receipts	0329
Cash, Reconciliation	0305
Cash, Deposits	0300
Cash, Electronic Funds Transfer	0372
Cash, Wire Transfer	0399
D	
Deposits, Cash	0300

Exhibit 4.2 Table of Contents Sorted Alphabetically by Subject Topic

Document Number	Procedure Description
0300	Cash, Deposits
0305	Cash, Reconciliation
0307	Cash, Petty
0329	Cash, Receipts
0372	Cash, Electronic Funds Transfer
0399	Cash, Wire Transfer
0423	Billing, to Service Customers
0569	Collections
0721	Finance Charge Deductions

Exhibit 4.3 Table of Contents Sorted Numerically by Subject Identifier

table, then use the related document number to find it within the manual. This is the table of contents that will be used most heavily, and so should be the first of the two tables. The second of the tables should itemize the manual's contents by sequential document number. An example is shown in Exhibit 4.3. This table reflects the actual order in which the manual is organized; this may be of some use to employees who are already familiar with the general grouping of documents within the manual, allowing them to find documents more readily with this type of presentation.

5. *Update the existing tables of contents.* If the manual already exists and is only being updated, then the previous step can be eliminated. Instead, the document design team only needs to verify that all of the latest document changes have been properly reflected in the two tables of contents.

6. *Lock up the master copy.* Once the set of documents is complete, the primary issue remaining is to ensure that no one changes its contents without formal approval. The physical copy should be locked up, preferably in a fireproof safe. The electronic copy of the manual should be given password protection in the computer system so that only authorized personnel can change it. This does not mean that the

preceding master copy should be thrown out when the new one is completed. On the contrary, and as noted at the beginning of this section, there are legal reasons for keeping older copies of the manual. Accordingly, older master copies should be clearly labeled with their dates of completion, and kept in storage. The legal department should notify the manuals team of the dates on which these older copies can be safely destroyed.

4.6 CREATION AND MAINTENANCE OF THE DISTRIBUTION MAILING LIST

The most expensive way to distribute a manual is to do a bulk mailing to every employee in the organization. This can be prohibitively expensive if there are many employees. It also does not make much sense from the perspective of subsequently updating the information contained within it, as many employees cannot be bothered with replacing pages in their manuals. As noted in the last section, updating a manual is also an issue from a legal perspective, because there is a risk that employees will base their actions on old versions of a manual. A better and much less expensive approach is to create a list of positions within the company that are most likely to use the manual, and which will be responsible for making its contents available to other employees. This usually means that supervisors are the ones most likely to be on the mailing list for a manual.

Once the mailing list has been determined, it can be converted into a matrix, such as the one shown in Exhibit 4.4. This one has converted the names of recipients to their job titles, because employee departures and hires would otherwise render the mailing list obsolete very rapidly. The matrix also lists the type of manual that each person should receive. By subdividing the total number of manuals into subsets for each recipient, a company can reduce the cost of creating an excessive number of manuals. Of particular note is that there is a date listed in the matrix for each manual that has been sent to each person on the mailing list. This is the date of the most recent update sent, and is of great value to the manuals design team in determining who has not yet received the most recent update to a manual.

With this mailing list matrix in hand, a company can easily determine what manual has been issued to a specific job position, as well as the last date on which it was updated, which greatly aids in the process of sending out updated information.

4.7 PHYSICAL DISTRIBUTION PROCESS

With all of the distribution materials now ready, as well as the list to recipients, how do we go about actually distributing the manuals? The first step is to create a cover letter that goes with the manual, describing why the manual is being sent out and what changes have been made to it since the last release. Some time should go into writing this part of the letter: A vivid description of key changes is the best way to get the reader to immediately review the attached materials. If only a partial release is being issued, then the letter should also include a detailed listing of exactly what pages in the old manual are being replaced. If training classes related to the manual have been developed at this time, the letter should also include a list of training dates and locations. In addition, it should also list the name

Recipient Job Title	Accounting Manual	Budgeting Manual	Human Resources Manual	Information Technology Manual	Period-End Close Manual
Assistant Controller	11/08				04/08
Budget Manager	11/08	03/08			04/08
CFO	11/08	03/08	08/07	07/07	04/08
CIO		03/08	08/07	07/07	
Controller	11/08	03/08	08/07		04/08
Development Manager				07/07	
Engineering Manager		03/08	08/07		
H/R Manager		03/08	08/07		
Production Manager		03/08	08/07		

Exhibit 4.4 Mailing List Matrix

and phone number of a person on the manuals development team who can be called if the recipient thinks there is a problem with it. This letter should be mail merged with the distribution list to personalize it with the names of recipients.

The manual development team has now completed all of the materials needed to distribute the manuals. At this point it can shift the physical distribution process to the company mailroom, which is better equipped to handle the distribution task. However, many smaller organizations do not have a mailroom, so the development team must handle this chore as well. If so, the following steps should be followed:

1. *Match cover letters to manuals.* If there are several different manuals, such as an accounting manual and a human resources manual, then the staff must match up the cover letter for each person to the correct types of manuals. This may require double checking to avoid mistakes.

2. *Securely package manuals.* Internal deliveries may require minimal packaging, especially if the sturdiest possible binders have already been obtained to hold manual documents. However, anything designated for external delivery may receive rough handling, and should be packaged accordingly.

3. *Route local deliveries through internal mail stops.* If there is an internal company delivery system, then the development team should determine the correct mail stop for each recipient, address the packages to be delivered, and send them on their way.

4. *Route external deliveries through a delivery verification service.* If any documents are being sent outside the company delivery system, then the development team will want to verify that they were received by the person to whom they were sent. This requires mailing through a service, such as Federal Express (FedEx) or United Parcel Service (UPS), that will record the name of the person to whom a package was delivered. An alternative is to contact all recipients a few days after the mailing date to verify receipt of the package.

Manuals are primarily being sent to people in management positions, so it is critical that they share this information with their staff. Some managers are not good at this task, which results in a group of employees who are not well versed in the most current procedures. There are several ways in which the manuals development team can go straight to the employees to notify them that a new manual has been issued, and that they should see their supervisors to review it. One approach is to include this information in a bulletin that can be posted on company bulletin boards and other public places. Another alternative is to include a notice in the company newsletter, such as this:

> **Human Resources Employees:** A new human resources manual was issued to all managers in the Human Resources department on October 3rd. Since this manual contains extensive updates to existing policies, procedures, and forms, we strongly recommend that you talk to your supervisor about reviewing it.

Another alternative is to maintain a copy of the most recent version of the manual in a public place, such as the copy room (convenient for making copies of the most pertinent pages) or the cafeteria. The only problem with this approach is that the manuals can suffer from extensive use and will need to be replaced with great frequency.

4.8 ISSUANCES TO NEW EMPLOYEES

New employees may be hired at any time, and it is most unlikely that they will arrive on precisely the same dates when new manuals are released. Consequently, they may be left without any knowledge of a company's policies and procedures for quite some time. There are several ways to avoid this problem.

One approach is to create a form for use by the human resources department, which it forwards to the manuals development group whenever a new employee is hired. This should serve as sufficient notification that a manual should be sent to that person, who should also be added to the ongoing mail list for future updates.

Another approach is to have the human resources staff send a notification to the new employee's supervisor as a reminder to go over the supervisor's copy of the manual. A further step may be to require the supervisor to sign a document attesting to the completion of such training, and to send it back for inclusion in the employee's file.

Yet another approach is to schedule all new employees for training in the use and contents of company manuals as part of their new employee indoctrination. This may include the scheduling of later classes that cover the manuals in greater detail. If this approach is used, then the human resources staff should also maintain a database that lists who has attended these classes, in case reminder messages must be sent out.

4.9 MANUAL RETRIEVAL

Some companies go to great lengths to determine the location of manuals that have been left behind by departing employees, even going to the extreme of withholding final paychecks until the manuals are turned in or deducting their cost from final paychecks. The reasons given are that the company manual is a confidential document that should not be revealed to outsiders, and that it is a valuable document that is difficult to reproduce.

One should seriously discount both of these arguments. If an employee wants to disseminate the contents of a manual to all possible competitors, all that is needed is an hour on the local copier—and there is very little that a company can do to stop this sort of behavior. As for retrieving valuable manuals for later use, how would an incoming employee feel about being given a hand-me-down accounting manual that is laced with notes and scribbles? It is better to throw out all "pre-owned" manuals and issue new ones, even if there is a modest attendant cost.

The only reason why a manual should be retrieved when an employee leaves is that it is less likely to be maintained with new document updates, and so will eventually contain less-than-accurate information. Consequently, there should be a notation in the exit interview form that reminds the interviewer to inquire if the manual has been turned in. This is a much more reasonable approach than forcing departing employees to pay for unreturned manuals.

4.10   BENEFITS OF USING ELECTRONIC MANUALS

Why switch to an electronic manual? Among the excellent reasons for doing so are reductions in the costs of preparing, updating, and (especially) distributing accounting manual information to users. In addition, and perhaps most importantly, a properly designed mix of electronic presentations can make it much easier for users to find the procedural information that they need, which will greatly enhance the overall comprehension and usage of the information contained within the accounting manual. Some of the main benefits are:

- *Cannot lose the manual.* In a large accounting department where there are many potential users of a set of accounting manuals, it is more the rule than the exception for some of the manuals to be missing as people take them for reference purposes. This is a problem for anyone who needs a quick answer to a procedural problem. However, by using an electronic manual, all users can access the same data all of the time, and the manual cannot be lost.

- *Faster access to desired information.* A traditional accounting manual will contain a table of contents, and in rare cases an index too. These forms of reference may not be sufficient for allowing a user to rapidly locate the precise procedural information needed within a short period of time. An electronic document, on the other hand, may include pull-down help screens that contain needed information, or indexes of related information that can be accessed throughout the document, or imbedded hypertext that can be clicked to shift a user to related information. It may also be possible to conduct searches of the entire document based on a few key words. Given all of these alternatives for accessing information, it is much easier for a user to find specific information with an electronic manual than it is with a paper-based one.

- *Greater frequency of updates.* A traditional system for updating documentation will require that changes be gradually accumulated until there are enough to justify the cost of sending out replacement pages to the existing manuals. It may be a number of months before this takes place, so all procedural changes that have been requested in the meantime will be put on hold. By switching to electronic manuals, this issue is eliminated and incremental adjustments can be made to the documents at once; revised documents can be posted for electronic distribution. The only issue here is that users may not know that changes have been made to the electronic documents unless a notification, such as an e-mail, is sent to them that describes the change; they can then access the relevant text within the electronic documents and print or download the changes that they need.

- *Instant data access.* When using an electronic manual, the speed with which data can be accessed will usually be an improvement over the use of a paper-based manual. A few clicks of a mouse will bring the relevant text to a user's computer, whereas the user of a traditional manual takes substantially more time to locate it in the manual, refer to its table of contents, and then access the appropriate information. A side benefit of having instant data access is that users will be more inclined to access the information in the manual when they are not certain about a particular procedure, rather than guessing at the correct approach. Thus, greater adherence to corporate policies and procedures becomes more likely.

- *Provides an additional help capability.* A traditional accounting manual tends to be a rather dry collection of policies, procedures, and forms. However, when an electronic manual is used, it is also possible to employ drop-down menus that provide access to help information, as well as hypertext that can send a user to definitions or examples that are tied directly to the information currently being reviewed. Though adding this feature to an electronic document certainly increases the time required to create it, the resulting presentation will result in a much higher degree of user comprehension.

- *Reduced cost of distribution.* If documents can be made available for downloading by users, they can be accessed when needed without any need for expensive shipping and handling charges. The only case where there would still be some cost of distribution is in acquiring equipment for employees who must access the information but do not currently have any computer access.

- *Reduced documentation tracking cost.* When a set of expensive paper-based manuals are issued to a user, the issuing entity must keep track of who has received them so that it can issue revision documents at regular intervals. If there are many such recipients, this can become an administrative hassle, because over time the recipients will change their locations within the company, and probably will not always contact the manuals development group to inform them of this fact. By switching to electronic manuals, one can avoid the necessity for tracking mailing addresses. Nonetheless, one should still trace the e-mail addresses of clusters of probable users so that notices can be sent out when changes are made to the electronic documents. This does not mean that the e-mail addresses *of specific* individuals must be tracked, but rather that the e-mail addresses of all likely users of a manual can be clumped together for a group notification; for example, all accounts receivable personnel should receive notification if a portion of the manual that applies to them is altered, but not any other members of the organization.

- *Send comments to the maintainer of the manual.* Anyone can send a memo back to the documentation design team in regard to suggestions for improve ments to the accounting manual—however, it takes time to write a memo and post it through the interoffice mail or postal service. Given the effort required, most design teams do not hear back from users of its manuals. However, when an e-mail button is added to the presentation of an electronic manual, it is a simple matter for a user to fire off a request for changes. The result is a stream of productive comments from users back to the design team.

Many of the advantages listed here are related to logistics—how to get the most recent production (e.g., product updates) to customers (e.g., users of the manuals) with the lowest possible distribution cost. The basic work of collecting information about a process flow and writing procedures about it does not change at all, just the compilation, presentation, and distribution of the resulting information (unless help facilities are added to the basic text).

4.11 DISADVANTAGES OF USING ELECTRONIC MANUALS

Though the just-noted advantages of using electronic manuals are powerful ones, there are also several problems that one should be aware of. In some instances, these may be sufficiently important to curtail the use of electronic manuals:

- *Cost of reprinting electronic documents.* Though the manuals development staff may save a significant amount of money from no longer having to print accounting manuals, this does not mean that paper costs are completely eliminated. On the contrary, every user of an electronic manual may feel compelled to print it out, either due to a greater comfort level with paper-based documents or because access to the electronic manual is relatively limited. This may result in a greater reprinting cost on a company-wide basis than was previously the case for the manuals development staff.

- *Duplicate use of both paper-based and electronic manuals.* There may be cases where some continued use of the existing paper-based manuals must continue, in addition to the use of electronic manuals. One reason for this situation is when long-term employees who use the old manuals are unwilling to try some thing new. Another reason is that some employees may not have ready computer access to the electronic documentation. Whatever the reason may be, this situation will call for the retention of most existing systems (and costs) required to create, distribute, and update the paper-based manuals, as well as new systems (and costs) for the electronic versions.

- *More complex formatting requirements.* There are a variety of ways in which an electronic manual can be formatted—frequently calling for more than one format at the same time. For example, it may be necessary to in sert some procedures into the "Help" fields attached to the company account ing software, as well as a separate version that is formatted to be downloaded and printed out by users, while yet a third version is set up with interactive links and online demonstrations, with the intention of being used more frequently by first-time users. All of the formats have a different use, and may greatly increase the utility of the electronic manual, but they also call for a much greater formatting effort on the part of the manuals development staff.

- *Methods of electronic access required.* Though it is increasingly unlikely in today's interconnected world, some potential users of electronic manuals may not have ready access to the computers or intranet/Internet connections that they need to gain access to electronic manuals. If this is a problem, the cost of properly equipping these employees may greatly exceed any benefits that might otherwise be gained from the use of electronic manuals. On the other hand, this may just be one more reason to give computer access to these employees, and tip the scales in favor of doing so.

- *No access if the computer system is down.* Though greater computer reliability makes system outages an increasingly small problem, there are times when a glitch in the network or in a computer will keep users from accessing electronic manuals. The likelihood of this issue can be further reduced with the use of battery backups for all computers and network servers, as well as fiber optic cabling in environments where manufacturing emissions can interrupt the flow of data through cables. If problems remain, then it may be necessary to add a paper-based manual to the mix of options available to users.

One of the key problems noted here is that electronic documents may not completely replace the existing paper-based manuals for a variety of reasons. As a result, a separate system is used to maintain the electronic manual, as well as its predecessor. This will result in greater costs than was previously the case, so a manager should carefully analyze the impact of this conversion to determine if costs will indeed rise as a result of the changeover.

4.12   BASIC ELECTRONIC MANUAL

In its most basic form, what is an online accounting manual? It is essentially a direct restatement of the existing paper-based manual, with no enhancements such as interactive tutorials, help menus, or sound or video clips. Despite the lack of these additional features, a basic online accounting manual can be quite an attractive option, because it requires limited skill to transfer documents to the online format. The files are either posted directly to the company intranet, or else they are incorporated into the help screens used in the corporate accounting software. By using this approach, a company can have its manuals available to the company as a whole with very little effort.

In these formats, a user is expected to either download the necessary files and review them on his or her computer, or review them on the screen when accessed through the accounting system. Though this is a reasonable approach to accessing the necessary information, and will present information that is similar to what users have come to expect, it does not result in an enhanced learning environment where new tools are added to the basic manual files. Consequently, the most rudimentary online manual should be treated as a jumping-off point, from which many other features can be added to make the electronic manual a real pleasure for users to access and browse through. These additional features are described in some of the following sections.

4.13 ACCOUNTING MANUAL ON AN INTRANET, EXTRANET, OR THE INTERNET

One may have heard of a number of different terms that relate to the centralized storage and dissemination of information (for our purposes, the accounting manual)—the Internet, intranet, and extranet. What are they, and how can they be used as a storage medium for the electronic manual?

The Internet is based on the use of hypertext, which allows anyone with access to an Internet browser to jump between information links on many different computers, located anywhere on the planet. It is an extraordinarily open form of communication, but can subject a user to a potential overflow of information, as there may be millions of possible locations in which data is stored.

An intranet is essentially the same thing as the Internet, in that hypertext is used and browser software is sufficient for general access. However, outside users are restricted from access by a corporate firewall. Also, incoming files may be rejected (or at least screened for viruses) by the firewall software. Thus, a company has a much greater ability to control the type and volume of information flowing through an intranet. It is on an intranet that most electronic manuals will be found, rather than being posted for general access on the Internet. The reason for this restricted level of access is partially because outsiders have no real need to see an accounting manual, and also some information contained within the manual may be considered confidential.

An extranet is simply a collection of intranets that are mutually accessible to users, though the amount of access may be restricted between the intranets. Users are also generally given access from the extranet to the Internet. This concept is most commonly used for sharing information with business partners (either customers or suppliers). There is some limited applicability for electronic manuals within an extranet, but only for those policies, procedures, and forms that must be accessed by business partners to understand how to conduct transactions with a corporation.

For the purposes of the discussion in the following sections, we will assume that a company has installed its electronic manual on the corporate intranet, as this is the most likely location for it to be positioned.

4.14 ELECTRONIC MANUAL WITH EMBEDDED HYPERTEXT

One of the chief advantages of creating an electronic manual is the use of embedded hypertext. This is text located anywhere within a document that contains linkages to other parts of the document, such as help screens and tutorials. By clicking on hypertext, a user can be shifted instantly to related information that is crucial to his or her understanding of the information being reviewed. This greatly enhances the speed with which a user can access the most relevant information pertaining to the issue at hand.

An alternative use for hypertext is to send a user to an e-mail screen so that he or she can send a message directly to the manuals development staff in regard to any issues that should be fixed in the electronic manual. This greatly improves the speed with which feedback about problems will be given to preparers.

Another use for hypertext is to send a user to an area of the manual that contains explanations of highly technical information contained within a procedure. For example, the content from a relevant FASB (Financial Accounting Standards Board) pronouncement related to the proper treatment of foreign exchange rates for month-end reporting can be linked via hypertext to a procedure that deals with this issue. It is even possible to have some outside expert maintain the section of the manual that deals with technical issues, and store it on a Web server at some other physical location—the hypertext links will still access the relevant data. This approach is particularly useful in those cases where a company cannot afford to pay for its own staff of in-house experts, instead providing linkages to the data provided by an outside entity.

The sample text shown in Exhibit 4.5 contains a series of hypertext links, which are noted in bold and underlined. Key words that require explanatory definitions are provided with hypertext links, as are technical topics. At the bottom of the text, the user is also provided with hypertext links to several related topics, plus links that will send the user to an e-mail feedback form or to an interactive tutorial regarding the current topic.

There are several key issues related to the text in Exhibit 4.5. First, though the topic of inventory valuation is quite a long and complex one, we have reduced it into a very small and readable snippet that provides just a brief overview of the process. By doing so, a reader can easily access the key information related to the topic without having to scroll down beyond a single computer screen of information. Second, the additional information that makes up this topic is accessed through hyperlinks; by using this formatting method, we allow the user to go directly to those related topics that are of most importance while by-passing all other topics that are of less relevance. Finally, by adding a series of related topics at the bottom, we prevent the user from having to guess at what other information might be available in the electronic manual—instead, the linkages are made available for the easiest possible access.

The hypertext linkages noted in Exhibit 4.5 are recreated in graphical form in Exhibit 4.6, where we see that the hypertext links allow a user to switch between several different files—including files for forms, definitions, procedures, tutorials, and accounting rules. To improve the readability of the presentation, not all linkages are traced to related databases. Based on the number of files shown in Exhibit 4.6, it is evident that hypertext linkages can be an effective way to cross-reference information from a wide variety of information sources.

Unfortunately, it is also possible to misuse links—which adds to a user's confusion. For example, an excessive proliferation of links will give a user so many choices for where to go for extra information that it takes an excessively long time to explore every possible item of related information. Also, links to only slightly related topics will not assist user comprehension of a topic. This later issue is best resolved through clear writing skills so that only the most relevant information is included in a manual. The most common problem with hypertext linkages is when they are not adjusted to reflect ongoing changes in the documentation. For example, a new definition that is added to the definitions database will not be of much use to readers if it is not referenced anywhere with hypertext links, because no one will be aware of its presence. Similarly, if information is deleted but the related hypertext links are not, users can become confused. Thus, constant maintenance of hypertext links to reflect changes in related information sources is mandatory.

Inventory Valuation Overview

To value inventory, one must establish a clear **period-end cut-off** so that transactions occurring after the cut-off are not mistakenly included within the valuation calculation. To aid in this effort, all items on the receiving or shipping docks should be clearly identified as being either included within or excluded from the counting process. Next, **counting procedures** must be created for use by counting teams that make use of specific prenumbered **forms**. The **count teams** must be selected from a group of employees who are knowledgeable in the characteristics of the inventory. The teams must then be educated in the use of count procedures, and then set to count specific sections within the inventory area. Once the count is complete and audited, the **count sheets** are entered into the computer system and costed using the existing **LIFO** cost database. Next, the inventory valuation is sorted by total dollar amount and checked to see if any obvious **costing anomalies** are present; if so, the unit quantities, units of measure, and costs for these items are reviewed and corrected, if necessary. Next, the inventory is reviewed for **obsolescence** issues, with the cost of obsolete items being eliminated from the inventory valuation. Finally, **lower of cost or market** rules are applied to the inventory to further reduce the valuation, if necessary.

Related Topics:

Average Costing

- **Consignment inventory**

FIFO

- **Generally accepted accounting principles**

- **Inventory controls**

- **Perpetual inventory system**

- **Valuation of supplies**

Other Items:

- **Access the Inventory Valuation Tutorial**

- **Contact the Manuals Development Team**

Exhibit 4.5   Embedded Hypertext

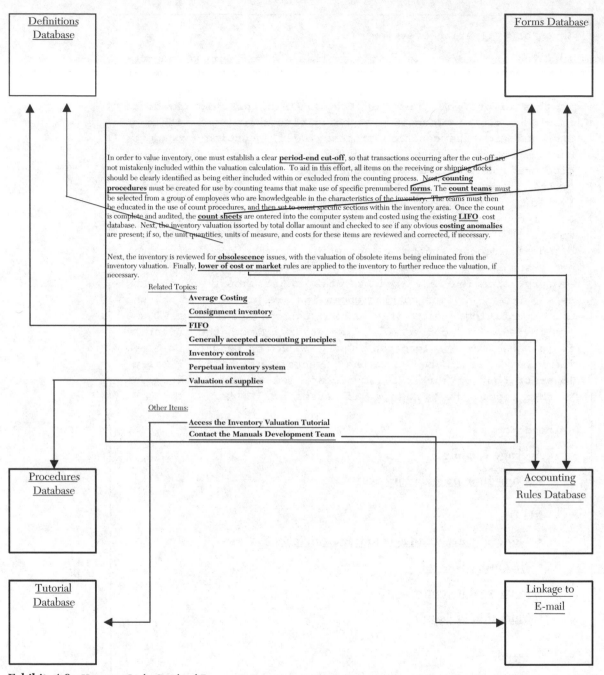

Exhibit 4.6   Hypertext Links Graphical Representation

4.15 ELECTRONIC MANUAL WITH ADVANCED INDEXING FEATURES

A standard paper-based manual will assist the reader in finding information by listing the names of all policies, procedures, and forms in the table of contents—and that is all. A more advanced manual may also list the names of related procedures as part of a cross-references section. However, this may not be sufficient for a user who is trying to find the

- Accounts Payable Processing

- Billing Processing

- Cash Receipts Processing

- Financial Statement Preparation

- Inventory Valuation

Exhibit 4.7   Traditional Table of Contents for an Accounting Procedures Manual

usage for a particular word, or whose concept of a topic is different from the title already given to it.

These problems can be avoided through the use of more advanced alphabetical indexes. When used with an electronic manual, there is no reason to create an abbreviated table of contents that may only include a few dozen items. Instead, we can create a much larger version with hundreds of entries. For example, Exhibit 4.7 lists a traditional table of contents for a portion of an accounting manual.

These are obviously highly aggregated topics that do not give a user much information about the precise types of information that he or she is searching for. However, an electronic manual can be outfitted with a multilevel table of contents that allows for a much greater level of detail. By clicking on one of the major category headings, an additional set of more detailed topics will be revealed beneath it—and even more levels of detail, if necessary. As an example, Exhibit 4.8 shows sublevels of contents for just the "Accounts Payable Processing" category of the table of contents.

The above list does not have to appear in a massive pull-down table of contents listing on a computer screen. Instead, it is much easier to only have the main categories appear, and then click on each one to "drill down" to greater levels of detail. Another approach is to set up a search feature that allows a user to type in a few key phrases. The system will respond with a short list of topical entries, possibly drawn from several different parts of the table of contents. For example, an entry of "Documentation Matching" in such a search field would result in a list of topics from the policies, procedures, *and* tutorials sections of the table of contents. The search feature is especially useful when a user finds that information could be listed under myriad similar headings, and does not want to spend the time manually combing through all of them.

The multilayered table of contents, when combined with a data search field, allows users to locate relevant information much more rapidly in an electronic manual than can be managed with an identical paper-based manual.

4.16 ELECTRONIC MANUAL WITH BUILT-IN HELP INFORMATION

A traditional paper-based accounting manual does not hold out much hope for a user who reads through the standard policy and procedures formats, but simply does not "get it." They usually have to consult with a more experienced employee who can assist them with

Accounts Payable Processing

- Definitions
  - Discount
  - Electronic Funds Transfer
  - Matching
  - Receiving Documentation
  - Routing Number
  - Vendor
  - Voucher
  - Wire Transfer
- Flowcharts
  - The Accounts Payable Process Flow
- Forms
  - Check Request
  - Purchase Order
  - Requisition
  - Three-Way Matching Verification
  - Voucher
- Policies
  - Early Payment
  - Cash Payment
  - Approvals
  - Check Signing
  - Documentation Matching
- Procedures
  - Cash Payment
  - Check Payment
  - Credit Memo Processing
  - Documentation Matching
  - Electronic Funds Payment
  - Supplier Invoice Cancellation
  - Supplier Invoice Data Entry
- Tutorials
  - Documentation Matching
  - Payment Methods
  - Supplier Invoice Data Entry

Billing Processing . . .

Exhibit 4.8 Expanded Table of Contents

overcoming information that is not sufficiently clearly presented or for which they do not possess enough background information. However, this can require a significant amount of employee time. A better approach is to use some of the help features of an electronic manual.

Hypertext itself, as discussed in the last section, is a tremendous improvement over traditional manuals in that it provides a reader with a multitude of information sources. Simply by making use of all possible hypertext links, a user will be much more likely to find the answers to most issues.

Another approach is to install a list of frequently asked questions (FAQ) that is linked to each topic in the database. The linkage is through a hypertext connection, and will reference a reader to a separate file that is constantly being updated with the answers to questions that have repeatedly cropped up in the past. This file may be updated by the in-house training staff. Or a linkage can be to an Internet Web site maintained by the provider of whatever software packages that a company may be using; the provider can update the FAQ based on queries that their customer service staff has received. The use of an online FAQ list is highly recommended, for it will cover the vast majority of user comprehension problems that continually arise. Only a small minority of other user questions will then have to be answered by other means.

Another help feature is a comprehensive database of explanations that can be accessed at any time from the menu of the electronic manual. This database can include either a search feature or detailed table of contents, as long as it brings a user straight to an explanation of the current problem area. Much of the information contained within this help database will duplicate the information contained within a well-designed electronic manual with a plethora of hypertext links, so many companies will prefer to avoid the expense of creating this feature and will instead focus their efforts on ensuring that this help information is more fully integrated into the basic manual. This is a valid response, since the creation of a full-blown help database is a significant effort; realistically, only the minority of employees whose questions have not already been answered by the FAQ section of the database will use it.

A final feature can be added for those users whose questions are not answered through any other feature of the electronic manual. These are usually the most difficult questions that either cannot be anticipated or represent such a small minority of issues that it is not worth adding explanatory information to the electronic manual that will address them. In these instances, the manual can include a phone number to the company help desk (or to the company expert on a specific informational area), an e-mail message box that will send the request to an appropriate party, or an e-mail message box that will page the company help desk staff and require them to call the user back at once. Any of these options will allow for a relatively rapid response to the most difficult employee questions.

The additional help options noted here will result in an electronic manual that is much more likely to provide users with the explanations they need to increase their comprehension of the information contained within an accounting manual. Even better, it means that users are much more likely to use the manual, because they will come to realize that it is the most complete resource of accounting information for them. This in turn leads to more wide-ranging acceptance of the policies and procedures contained within it, and therefore fewer transactional exceptions.

4.17 ELECTRONIC MANUAL WITH BUILT-IN TUTORIALS

A beginning user of a procedure will have a much higher degree of comprehension if the electronic manual goes beyond the typically dry listing of steps to follow, and additionally contains a tutorial that shows exactly how to create a transaction. This requires the addition of a button to the existing layout that takes the user to a separate tutorials database where he or she can peruse a multiscreen, step-by-step procedure. Such a tutorial should include exact representations of the computer screens that will be used to create each transaction, as well as added notes that discuss key features of each step in the process. The user should be able to shift backward and forward in the tutorial at will to find the steps that are most critical to comprehension.

The amount of effort required to create a tutorial is considerable, so they should be limited only to the most important processes that will be needed by a number of users. If a process is only to be used by a small number of people, then it will be more cost-effective to give them personalized training, rather than spend far more time creating a computer-based training environment for them.

There are software packages available that also allow one to create interactive question-and-answer sessions with users, as well as final quizzes to test user comprehension. Given their added cost, these packages are generally not appropriate for smaller corporations. Another alternative is the computer-based training movie; this is created by software that replicates on-screen the actions of someone who is walking through a standard set of activities while explaining each action through a microphone. The resulting movie will show a user exactly what is being done to process a transaction (or some other activity) while the accompanying voice recording explains what is going on. Just as is the case with a movie that is inserted into a video cassette recorder, this movie format contains on-screen buttons for rewind, pause, play, and fast forward. Each movie is easily created—just plot out the steps to be followed during the movie, practice them a few times, then press the "record" button and start recording the movie. The audio portion of the movie can be added concurrently or at a later time. The required software is generally in the $50 to $150 range, and may require a download to individual computers where the software will be resident. The software that is currently available for making computer-based movies includes ScreenCam by Lotus (www.lotus.com), HyperCam by Hyperionics (www.hyperionics.com), Camtasia Recorder and Producer by TechSmith (www.techsmith.com), and CameraMan by MotionWorks (www.mwg.com).

The key point to remember for online tutorials is to create them only for high-volume applications, given the significant labor time required to develop them.

4.18 WRITING TIPS FOR ELECTRONIC MANUALS

The writing format for a traditional paper-based accounting manual does not work well for an electronic manual, because the size of the reading area (the computer screen) is considerably smaller than the printed page. Also, the paper-based format does not take advantage of the many features that can be added to an electronic document, as have been described over the past few sections of this chapter. Instead, some of the following writing tips should be used:

- *Use a consistent format.* There are a great many features that can be added to an electronic manual, such as help buttons, hypertext, references to a glossary, access buttons to send an e-mail to a procedure writer, tutorials, and so on. However, the trouble with this feature-rich environment is that the screen can become excessively cluttered. To avoid this problem, the design team should determine a standardized format that it will use for all screens in the electronic manual, so a user will always find the same reference points at the same spot on any screen being viewed. This does not mean that some good potential features must be left out of the standard format, but that the format should be constructed in such a way that they are compressed into a readable format that does not excessively clutter the screen. This is a sufficiently important topic that the design team should consult with users to see what potential formats yield the greatest benefit to them.

- *Keep the message short.* The electronic manual is ideally suited for delivering short snippets of information to the user—preferably within a single computer screen so that a minimum amount of scrolling is needed. If the text is excessively long, users will tend to jump around through the presented material and will not absorb it as well. Accordingly, the anticipated documentation should be carefully structured in advance so that topics are kept short; and heavy use should be made of hypertext so that users can easily jump to related topics. This can be a difficult transition for a procedure writer to make, and requires a great deal more structure to one's writing than was previously the case. A good way to truncate the length of presented text is to divide it into segments, each of which only deals with a single main idea. If a secondary idea is also contained within the text, then split it off and cross-reference it with hypertext.

- *Cross-reference heavily.* One of the main writing tips for the electronic manual is to break down information into a large number of small text messages, so it makes sense to spend a great deal of time ensuring that a reader is able to easily collect a sufficient amount of information about a topic through the use of hypertext links. By creating many cross-references, related topics can be easily clustered together for rapid perusal. This is a major part of the work required to create an online manual, and is worth the extra effort of having users verify that the cross-references used in the manual are sufficiently comprehensive.

- *Continually review references to new text.* When any new information is entered into an electronic manual, no one will know that it is now available until it is added to the online help screen, table of contents, and hypertext linkages of the manual. It is essentially invisible, inaccessible knowledge until these changes take place. Consequently, a great deal of attention must be paid to these reference sources.

- *Avoid dangling hypertext links.* Information may be deleted from a manual when it is out of date, no longer relevant, or attached to a process that is no longer in use. When this happens, the manual design team should verify that all hypertext linkages to it have been eliminated so that users will not attempt to access information that is no longer provided.

• *Reinforce topics with glossaries and tutorials.* Whenever there is the slightest doubt that a reader may not understand the content of a message, add hyper text links to an online glossary that explains key words or provide links to online tutorials that will walk an employee through a particularly important transaction. Because these tools are available, use them to the greatest possible extent.

The writing tips noted here will result in an electronic document that requires more preplanning of the final document than had previously been the case for a paper-based manual. The accounting topic will now be broken down into a much larger number of small topics, which must then be carefully reassembled into a highly readable presentation structure. This does not mean that the chore of assembling an electronic manual is meant to be a daunting one—only that extra effort in this area will result in a vastly more rewarding experience for anyone using it, much more so than would be the case for even the most perfectly designed paper-based manual.

4.19   EXAMPLE OF COMPREHENSIVE ELECTRONIC MANUAL FEATURES

A number of features have been mentioned in this chapter that can be added to an electronic manual. The exact layout and content of the resulting electronic manual is entirely up to the discretion of the manual development team. Nonetheless, an example of a fully developed format is noted in Exhibit 4.9, more to provide a starting point for further development than as the best possible layout. The exhibit contains the text from Exhibit 4.5 but goes on to surround it with additional linkages to other features of the electronic manual.

In Exhibit 4.9, a sidebar has been added that contains a number of links to various types of information, such as the help desk, the table of contents, and a tutorial. They are itemized in order, so the most commonly used ones are listed at the top. An alternative approach is to list these items in alphabetical order and let users scan through the list to find what they need. It is also possible to include this information in a top bar that contains drop-down menus. The worst place to itemize these linkages is at the bottom of the text, because users may not realize that they must scroll down some distance to gain access to the links and so may not realize they are available at all.

If a particular screen does not contain all of the linkages used in the master layout (e.g., there is no tutorial available), then the format should remain the same, for two reasons. First, users should become used to having information available to them in the exact same spots on the screen, every time. Second, there may eventually be a need to include a linkage in the missing location; leaving it initially blank will allow the development staff to more easily fill in the linkage at a later date.

4.20   USING THE PDF FORMAT FOR ELECTRONIC FILES

One problem with the use of electronic files for the distribution of manuals is that users may not have the required type of software to read them. This problem has been avoided by Adobe with its Adobe Acrobat software by making the reader version a free download (available at its www.adobe.com site). One must only pay for the software if it is to be used

---

Inventory Valuation Overview

Keyword Search

Table of Contents

Glossary

Help

Tutorial

Contact Help Desk

To value inventory, one must establish a clear **period-end cut-off** so that transactions occurring after the cut-off are not mistakenly included within the valuation calculation. To aid in this effort, all items on the receiving or shipping docks should be clearly identified as being either included within or excluded from the counting process. Next, **counting procedures** must be created for use by counting teams that make use of specific prenumbered **forms**. The **count teams** must be selected from a group of employees who are knowledgeable in the characteristics of the inventory. The teams must then be educated in the use of count procedures, and then set to count specific sections within the inventory area. Once the count is complete and audited, the **count sheets** are entered into the computer system and costed using the existing **LIFO** cost database. Next, the inventory valuation is sorted by total dollar amount and checked to see if any obvious **costing anomalies** are present; if so, the unit quantities, units of measure, and costs for these items are reviewed and corrected, if necessary. Next, the inventory is reviewed for **obsolescence** issues, with the cost of obsolete items being eliminated from the inventory valuation. Finally, **lower of cost or market** rules are applied to the inventory to further reduce the valuation, if necessary.

Exhibit 4.9 Inventory Valuation Overview: Full Electronic Format

to *create* documents. The resulting portable document file (PDF) file format has become extremely popular.

- A document can be created in one's favorite file format and then be converted into the PDF format with no loss of formatting.

- Web pages in the PDF format look exactly line Web pages with the latest Web technology, such as cascading style sheets and javascript.

- Text stored in the PDF format can be saved to the rich text format (RTF) for later importing into word processing software for further editing and formatting.

- PDF files can be opened in the Windows, Mac OS, and UNIX operating environments.

- A PDF file is compact in size, so it can be quickly downloaded, frequently faster than the document formats in which a file was originally designed.

- Such features as text boxes, check boxes, list boxes, radio buttons, digital signature fields, and more can be added to a document within Acrobat.

- Acrobat allows one to develop PDF forms containing fields that can change depending upon user input. Users can use this feature to fill in information on a PDF form and then submit it electronically.

- Reviewers can add comments and position them at the location of the requested changes. Many types of changes can be added, such as electronic sticky notes, text, audio, stamps, graphic or text markups, and attached files. Also, comments from multiple reviewers can be merged into a single, consolidated PDF file to facilitate the review process.

- A PDF file can also be set to allow no changes by users to the document.

- Any links on PDF file pages are active, so additional Web pages can be downloaded as needed without returning to a Web browser.

- A variety of navigational elements allow readers to locate specific information more quickly within a PDF document, such as thumbnails (automatically generated miniature page previews), bookmarks, links, and full-text indexes.

This wide array of benefits has made Acrobat the preferred software for the development of any document that will be widely distributed electronically.

4.21 MAINTAINING AN ELECTRONIC MANUAL

There are several key differences between the maintenance of a paper-based manual and one that is constantly accessed electronically by employees:

- *Constant maintenance.* A traditional procedure maintenance system uses batch processing of procedural changes—that is, changes are accumulated until the pile reaches an impressive height, and then all the changes are incorporated at once, resulting in a small number of procedure distributions per year. With an electronic manual, there is no need to wait to make changes, as there is no distribution cost. Accordingly, changes are made to the manual as soon as they are received. This calls for more daily attention to the task, rather than a short-term project orientation.

- *Additional training.* A small amount of additional training is needed to access the online procedure database and alter existing information. Though this is not a major item, some training is required for everyone associated with ongoing procedure maintenance.

- *Less review time.* Because changes can be made to the database at any time, there is some pressure to make immediate changes to the database, though this can result in incorrect procedures. This is different from the traditional approach, which involves a mass mailing of proposed changes to users, who can comment on them for some time before they are incorporated into the existing manual.

- *Stratified review system.* Given the high speed of procedure updating, there is an increased need for a stratified review system, whereby minor changes or any changes to minor procedures can bypass the traditional lengthy review process; larger changes should still be screened before permanent alterations are made.

- *Database access issues.* The procedures staff finds itself dealing with complaints from users regarding their access to the database. Though the procedures staff has no control over who gets access to the computer network, it will nonetheless find itself in the midst of user requests for more access, which it must forward to the computer system department for action, perhaps with recommendations regarding the real need of each applicant for the desired computer workstation.

Thus, the administrator of an online procedures manual will find that changes are made to procedures more frequently. More training and review systems are needed to ensure that the changes are the correct ones and that they are entered correctly. Though it may not seem to be in this person's job description, issues surrounding user access to the database will occupy a portion of his or her time.

Chapter 5

CORPORATE POLICIES MANUAL[1]

5.1 INTRODUCTION

The corporate policies manual may include only a few policies tied to key control problems that the company has encountered in the past, or it can take the approach of providing policies for control over a wider range of functional areas on a prospective basis. Either approach works, though the latter can better assist in maintaining an acceptable degree of corporate risk management, and is recommended.

The following list of corporate policies and explanatory comments covers a broad range of areas, including cash, hedges, barter transactions, inventory valuation, intangible assets, research and development costs, investments, debt extinguishment, warrants, lease terminations, dividends, options, and foreign currency translations. Though not all will apply to any company's specific circumstances, a number of them can be copied directly into one's corporate policy manual, depending on the structure of the company and its manner of doing business.

Accounts Payable

- *When paying from a copy of a supplier invoice, the additional approval of the controller must be obtained prior to payment.* This policy reduces the risk of duplicate payment.

---

[1] Adapted with permission from Chapters 2–12 of Bragg, *GAAP Implementation Guide*, John Wiley & Sons, 2004.

- *There shall be a standard naming convention to create supplier names in the vendor master file.* This policy reduces the incidence of multiple records for the same supplier.

Billing

- *The billing and collection functions shall be segregated.* This policy makes it more difficult for collections personnel to intercept incoming customer payments and alter the related invoices to hide the missing funds.

- *All invoices must be issued within one day of shipment or completion of service delivery.* This policy accelerates cash flow by avoiding billing delays.

- *A single revenue recognition method shall be used for all installment sales.* This policy prevents the manipulation of reported profitability levels by switching between the installment and cost recovery methods of revenue recognition.

- *The company shall not use bill and hold transactions.* This policy avoids use of a revenue recognition method that is easily subject to abuse.

- *Access to the billing software shall be restricted to authorized users.* This policy keeps unauthorized employees from issuing credit memos, which can hide the theft of incoming cash from customers.

Capital Stock

- *Stock issuance costs shall include only certificate printing, security registration, and legal and underwriting fees.* This policy is designed to strictly limit the types of expenses that can be charged against the proceeds from a stock offering. By doing so, there is little room for extraneous expenses to be netted against a stock sale.

Cash Disbursements

- *No accounts payable personnel shall be authorized to sign checks or approve money transfers.* This policy is designed to separate the preparation of accounts payable documents from their approval, thereby keeping a single person from falsely creating a payable and authorizing its payment to himself.

- *All check or money transfers exceeding $_____ shall be countersigned by the _____ position.* This policy provides for a second review of very large payments to ensure that they are appropriate, and to reduce the incidence of fraudulent transfers. Unfortunately, many banks do not review the existence of a second signature on a check, making this a less effective policy.

- *All check signers shall be adequately bonded.* This policy requires a company to retain an adequate level of bonding on its check signers to ensure that it will suffer no loss if a signer commits fraud. Bonding companies usually conduct a background review on check signers before agreeing to provide bond, which may give a company warning of previously unknown fraudulent employee activities, thereby allowing it to remove check-signing authority from someone before she has the opportunity to commit fraud again.

- *The check signer will not sign blank checks under any circumstances*. All checks signed must first have a payment date, payee, and payment amount listed on them in ink.

- *The checking account will be funded only in an amount sufficient to match outstanding checks*. This policy keeps a large fraudulent check from resulting in a large cash loss.

- *All check stock shall include security features, such as watermarks and "Void" pantographs*. This policy reduces the risk of check forgery.

- *There shall be no more than two authorized check signers*. One check signer shall be designated as the primary signer to whom all checks are routed, and the other is a backup who signs checks only when the primary check signer is not available. This policy reduces the risk that checks will be routed to the check signer least likely to question the payment.

- *No check signers will have access to any accounting functions*. This policy maintains check signer independence from the accounting function.

- *Anyone conducting the bank reconciliation will have no access to other disbursement functions*. This policy keeps the reconciliation person independent from the accounting function.

- *Signature plates and signature stamps shall be stored in a locked safe at all times other than when check printing is being conducted*. This policy reduces the risk of checks being fraudulently signed.

- *A manual signature is required on all checks exceeding a dollar value of $____*. This policy allows for the use of signature plates for smaller checks, but imposes an additional review on larger payments.

- *Electronic payments shall be the preferred method of payment*. This policy reduces a variety of control problems associated with check payments.

- *The company shall use "positive pay," whereby it sends a list of issued checks to its bank, which the bank shall use as the basis for accepting checks*. This policy eliminates the acceptance of fraudulent checks.

- *All checks shall include printed security features, such as the use of a different font size and type for each printed character*. This policy reduces the risk of check forgery.

- *Password access shall be required for software used to initiate electronic payments*. This policy reduces the risk of fraudulent transfers initiated from the software.

- *A signed approval document is required for all manually initiated electronic payments as well as for the initial setup of supplier accounts for electronic payments. Electronic payments exceeding $____ require a second approval by the [position]*. This policy increases the level of control over new suppliers, large payments, and any payments falling outside the normal purchasing system.

- *All company bank accounts will have an automated clearinghouse (ACH) debit filter installed, with debits allowed only on an individual approval basis*. This policy prevents unauthorized transfers of funds from the company's bank accounts.

- *All suppliers who are allowed ACH debit access to a company bank account must have daily cumulative debit limits*. This policy reduces the risk of large unauthorized ACH debits being made against company funds.

- *All electronic payments shall be issued from a single account that is not automatically replenished*. This policy reduces the risk of large fraudulent transfers of company funds.

Cash Receipts

- *The cash application staff must take the full amount of their earned vacation time each year*. This policy improves the chances of detecting lapping schemes being run by cash application employees.

- *The check handling and cash disbursement functions shall be segregated*. This policy reduces the risk that employees will double pay a supplier and then intercept a refund check from the supplier.

- *Cash withdrawal privileges shall be assigned by the Board of Directors*. This policy restricts access to deposited funds to authorized personnel.

- *Checks shall be posted within one day of receipt*. This policy accelerates the availability of cash and also ensures that problem checks are addressed as soon as possible.

- *Access to the cash receipts software shall be restricted*. This policy reduces the risk that cash receipt records will be altered in order to hide the theft of cash.

- *Customers shall be periodically asked to remit electronic payments*. This policy eliminates a number of control problems related to the receipt and processing of paper checks.

- *Cash shall be deposited daily*. This policy reduces the risk of on-site cash theft, while also accelerating the use of cash.

- *The unapplied cash account shall be reviewed daily*. This policy ensures that the unapplied cash account is reviewed constantly, so that unapplied cash problems are resolved as soon as possible.

- *The company will offer a free ____ to each customer who is not offered a receipt at the point of sale*. This policy allows customers to review the sale transaction to verify its accuracy.

- *Each sales clerk is responsible for the contents of a specific cash register*. This policy links specific employees to specific cash registers, so that missing cash can be more easily traced.

- *Cash refunds must be authorized by a supervisor*. This policy prevents sales clerks from recording a refund on their cash register and then pocketing the cash.

- *All cash will be stored in the company safe during non-work hours.* This policy improves the storage security of on-site cash.

- *The corporate safe will be located in a visible position.* This policy makes it more difficult for someone to break into the safe.

- *The combination to the safe shall be changed at least once a year, or when anyone knowing the combination leaves the company.* This policy makes it more difficult for someone to break into the safe.

- *Surveillance systems shall monitor all cash registers.* This policy deters fraud by sales clerks, who are aware of the monitoring.

Construction Contracts, Long-Term

- *Construction contract revenue shall be calculated using the percentage of completion method.* This policy allows a company to calculate all construction revenues using a consistent methodology, so there is no question of using one method over another to gain a short-term advantage in reporting the amount of revenue.

- *Accounts used in overhead pools shall be reviewed annually and altered only with management approval.* This policy keeps the accounting staff from arbitrarily altering the contents of overhead cost pools. Overhead pool alterations are a classic approach for shifting expenses out of the current period and into construction-in-progress asset accounts.

Credit Card Receipts

- *All customer credit card information shall be shredded once payment transactions have been completed.* This policy reduces the risk of customer credit information being fraudulently used.

- *All employees having access to customer credit card information shall be bonded.* This policy mitigates the risk that the company will suffer losses due to the theft of credit card information by its employees.

- *A background check shall be conducted on all employees having access to customer credit card information.* This policy increases the chance that unqualified employees will be kept away from customer credit card information.

- *Access to computer files containing customer credit card information shall be strictly limited to authorized personnel.* This policy reduces the risk that credit card information can be fraudulently accessed.

Credit Management

- *The credit manager will create and enforce the use of a credit policy that defines how to calculate a credit limit, information required of customers in order to determine a credit limit, standard terms of sale, and collection techniques to be employed.* This policy introduces consistency into the credit management process.

- *Customers must complete a new credit application once every _____ years if their annualized order quantity exceeds $_____.* This policy allows the company to spot changes in the financial condition of its customers and adjust its credit limits accordingly.

- *The credit manager will conduct periodic training of the credit staff in credit procedures.* This policy reduces the risk that high-risk customers will be granted credit.

- *No shipments are allowed without prior approval by the credit department.* This policy reduces the risk of default by customers on outstanding receivables.

- *The credit department will review the credit of all customer orders for which the order amount exceeds $____.* This policy reduces the risk of default by customers on outstanding receivables.

- *The credit manager must approve all increases in customer credit limits.* This policy reduces the risk that employees will approve significant credit increases without prior review.

- *The credit manager will store the credit approval stamp in a locked location when it is not in use.* This policy reduces the risk that a sales order will be fraudulently approved.

- *Any customer whose check payment is returned due to not sufficient funds (NSF) must complete a new credit application.* This policy improves the credit staff's ability to spot reductions in the financial condition of its customers and adjust credit limits accordingly.

- *Customers must complete a new credit application if their newest order exceeds $____ and they have not placed an order in at least ____ year(s).* This policy detects changes in the financial condition of sporadic customers.

- *The credit department will review the credit status of the top 20% of customers each year, as measured by sales volume.* This policy detects changes in the financial condition of the company's largest customers.

- *The credit department will review the credit status of any customers who skip payments.* This policy increases the credit staff's ability to spot customers whose financial condition is deteriorating, and adjust their credit limits accordingly.

- *The credit department will review the credit levels of customers who stop taking early payment discounts.* This policy increases the credit staff's ability to spot customers whose financial condition is deteriorating, and adjust their credit limits accordingly.

- *The credit manager shall arrange for electronic credit rating change notifications for all major customers.* This policy provides rapid warning of changes in the financial condition of customers.

Credit Memos

- *The collections and credit memo recording functions shall be segregated.* This policy prevents a collections person from fraudulently intercepting customer payments and offsetting the related invoices with credit memos.

- *Credit memos require prior supervisory approval.* This policy prevents employees from intercepting incoming customer payments and then issuing credit memos to cancel the related customer receivable.

Current Liabilities

- *There shall be no carryforward of sick time past the current year.* A common problem is for employees to build up massive reserves of unearned sick time, for which they must be paid when they eventually leave the company. This policy is designed to eliminate all unused sick time at the end of each calendar year, thereby keeping accrued sick time expense to a minimum.

- *The number of hours of vacation time carried forward past the current year is capped at _____ hours.* Some employees have a habit of not taking vacation time, resulting in large vacation accruals that can grow for years. Not only does this represent a significant current liability, but it also presents a control problem, since employees who do not take vacation may be staying on the job in order to hide fraudulent activities. This policy is designed to resolve both problems by allowing only a modest carryforward of earned vacation time.

- *The vacation accrual shall be based on the maximum year-end carryforward amount of vacation hours.* The accrual of vacation time is subject to a great deal of interpretation, since it can be based on the current amount of vacation time existing, the maximum available for the year, the maximum carryforward amount, or an estimate of the carryforward amount. By switching between various estimation methods, one can easily modify the vacation accrual to alter reported financial results. This policy requires one to use just one estimation method, thereby removing the variability from the calculation method.

Debt, Convertible

- *Debt conversions to equity shall always be recorded using the book value method.* This policy keeps the accounting staff from switching between the book value and market value methods, whereby they could use the market value method to recognize gains and the book value method to avoid losses.

- *Debt conversion calculations shall always be verified by the audit staff.* This policy is designed to ensure that any expenses associated with debt conversions to stock shall be correctly calculated. Either internal or external auditors can be used; the main point is to require independent verification of all journal entries related to debt conversions.

Debt Extinguishment

- *Debt shall not be extinguished early if the primary aim is to report a gain or loss on the extinguishment.* If a company buys back its bonds when the stated interest rate on the debt is lower than the current market interest rate, it will recognize a gain on the transaction, but must refinance the purchase with more expensive debt at current market rates. Thus, this policy is designed to keep company management from creating transactions that appear to increase profits when the underlying results worsen the company's financial situation.

- *When interest rates allow, the company shall repurchase its debt with less expensive debt.* Though it sounds obvious, this policy is designed to force management to make the correct decision to always use less expensive debt, even though this will result in the recognition of a loss when the older, more expensive debt is eliminated from the company records.

Debt Issued with Stock Warrants

- *Debt issuance calculations incorporating attached stock warrants shall always be verified by the audit staff.* This policy ensures that a separate party comprised of either internal or external auditors reviews the allocation of value between issued bonds and warrants, since the allocation is critical to the amount of bond discount that must be subsequently amortized.

Dividends

- *The Board of Directors shall not time property dividend declarations in order to influence reported earning levels from gains or losses recognized on property to be distributed.* A gain or loss on assets must be recognized on the date of a dividend declaration if there is a difference between the fair market and book values of the assets. This can give rise to deliberate timing of dividend declarations in order to recognize gains or losses in specific reporting periods. This policy points out to directors that such behavior is not acceptable.

- *The Board of Directors shall not time scrip dividend declarations to influence reported levels of indebtedness.* A scrip dividend is a note payable issued to shareholders in place of cash, and is generally a bad idea unless there is an immediate expectation of cash receipts to pay off the resulting notes. Further, a Board could time a scrip dividend declaration to immediately follow the issuance of year-end financial statements, so that readers of the statements will not be aware of the sudden increase in indebtedness until the next financial statements are released. This policy is designed to bring the potential reporting issue to the attention of the Board, though it still has the ability to override the policy.

Employee Stock Ownership Plan (ESOP)

- *The Board of Directors shall not time dividend declarations in order to influence the recognition of a compensation expense for unallocated ESOP shares.* When shares held in an ESOP have not yet been allocated to employees, a declared dividend on those shares is charged to compensation expense in the current period. Since this may represent a significant alteration in reported profit levels, there can be a temptation to time the dividend declaration in order to avoid reporting a profit reduction. This policy is designed to bring the potential reporting issue to the attention of the Board, though it still has the ability to override the policy.

- *Periodic accruals of ESOP compensation costs shall be based on the fair market value of company stock at the end of the current reporting period.* It is common practice for a company to allocate shares from its ESOP to plan participants only at the end of each year, at which point compensation expense is recognized for the fair market value of the allocated shares. The amount of this compensation expense should be estimated and partially accrued in each month of the year leading up to the actual allocation. A problem can arise in estimating what the fair market value of the stock will be at the end of the year, since this can result in significant variances in estimates from month to month, with wildly fluctuating compensation expense accruals based on these estimates. The best approach is to use this policy to create the accrual based on the assumption that the actual fair market value at the end of the current reporting period shall match the year-end fair market value, thereby removing valuation estimates from the calculation.

Evaluated Receipts System

- *Purchase orders shall be required for the purchase of all items exceeding $____.* This policy requires suppliers to have a purchase order number prior to shipping goods to the company; this is needed to approve receipts as part of the evaluated receipts program.

- *Suppliers must attach the company-issued purchase order number to all shipments to the company.* This policy ensures that the proper identification number is attached to every supplier delivery.

- *All supplier deliveries will be rejected at the receiving dock if they do not contain an authorizing purchase order number.* This policy prevents the receipt of items that cannot be identified for payment through the evaluated receipts system.

- *The evaluated receipts system will automatically reject supplier deliveries if the purchase order unit balance is less than the delivered quantity.* This policy prevents the receipt of excessively large deliveries.

- *The evaluated receipts system will automatically flag any packing slip units of measure that do not match the purchase order units of measure.* This policy reduces the risk that incorrect quantities are received.

- *Access to the purchase order system shall be restricted to approved users.* This policy reduces the risk that purchase orders will be improperly issued.

Fixed Assets

- *Management must approve all asset additions through a formal review process.* This policy requires the management team to follow a formal review process that requires both the use of cash flow analysis and a hierarchy of approvals depending on the size of the proposed expenditure.

- *All assets with a purchase price exceeding $1,000 shall be recorded as fixed assets.* This policy reduces the amount of paperwork associated with fixed asset tracking by shifting smaller assets into the expense category.

- *The capitalization limit shall be reviewed annually.* This policy requires the controller to verify that the existing capitalization limit represents a reasonable balance of minimized record keeping for fixed assets and not an excessive amount of charges to expense for lower-cost assets.

- *Capital investment results shall be reviewed annually.* This policy requires a company to compare the actual results of a capital investment to what was predicted in its capital investment proposal form. The intent is to highlight incorrect assumptions that may still be used for other capital investment proposals, which can then be corrected to ensure better ongoing capital investment decisions.

- *Conduct an annual inventory of all fixed assets.* This policy requires the accounting staff to compare the record of fixed assets to their actual locations, typically resulting in not only adjustments to their recorded locations, but also a determination of the need to dispose of selected assets.

- *A detailed record shall be maintained of each fixed asset acquired.* This policy forces one to centralize the record-keeping for each asset, making it much easier to identify, locate, cost, and determine the warranty provisions associated with each one.

- *All asset valuations associated with dissimilar asset exchanges shall be reviewed by an outside appraiser.* This policy prevents the accounting staff from intentionally creating gains or losses on asset exchange transactions by assuming incorrect asset fair values.

- *Copies of property records shall be maintained in an off-site location.* This policy reduces the risk of lost records by requiring a periodic shifting of record copies to a secure outside location.

- *All asset transfers and disposals require management approval.* This policy brings any asset movements to the attention of the accounting department, which can then record the revised asset locations in the accounting records. The policy also allows one to review the proposed prices to be obtained from the sale or disposal of assets.

- *Periodically review all fixed assets for impairment.* This policy ensures that the accounting staff will regularly compare the book value of all fixed assets to their fair value, and write down the book value to the fair value if this is the lower amount.

- *Responsibility for the following fixed asset functions will be segregated:*
  - Fixed asset acquisition
  - Fixed asset transaction recording
  - Custody of the fixed asset
  - Fixed asset disposal
  - Reconciliation of physical assets to accounting records

- *Access to the fixed asset master file shall be restricted to authorized personnel.* This policy keeps baseline fixed asset information from being altered.

- *Fixed assets that are lost or stolen must be replaced with funds from the responsible department.* This policy is designed to firmly affix responsibility for each asset to a specific department manager.

Foreign Currency Financial Statements, Translation Of

- *Periodically review the status of highly inflationary economies where subsidiaries are located.* This policy is designed to determine the date when a local economy either becomes highly inflationary or is no longer defined as such under accounting rules. This is of importance in determining what type of translation method to use.

Foreign Currency Transactions, Translation Of

- *Maintain or have access to a database of daily exchange rates for all currencies in which the company conducts transactions.* This policy allows the accounting staff to have ready access to exchange rates for its translation and currency transaction activities.

Funds Investment

- *At least $____ shall be invested in overnight investments and in negotiable marketable obligations of major U.S. issuers.* This policy forces the treasury staff to attain a minimum level of liquidity. The fixed dollar amount used in the policy should be regularly reviewed to match upcoming budgeted working capital requirements.

- *No more than ____% of the total portfolio shall be invested in time deposits or other investments with a lack of liquidity.* This policy is similar to the preceding one, except that it ignores a fixed liquidity requirement, focusing instead on a maximum proportion of the total portfolio that must be retained for short-term requirements. This policy tends to require less periodic updating.

- *The average maturity of the investment portfolio shall be limited to ____ years.* This policy is designed to keep a company from investing in excessively long maturities. The policy can be broken down into more specific maturity limitations for different types of investments, such as 5 years for any U.S. government obligations, 1 year for bank certificates of deposit, and 270 days for commercial paper.

- *Investments in foreign commercial paper shall be limited to those unconditionally guaranteed by a prime U.S. issuer and fully hedged.* This policy is designed to lower the risk of default on investments in securities issued by foreign entities.

- *Investments in commercial paper shall be limited to those of companies having long-term senior debt ratings of Aa or better.* This policy is designed to limit the risk of default on commercial paper investments by focusing investments on only the highest-grade commercial paper.

- *Investments in bank certificates of deposit shall be limited to those banks with capital accounts exceeding $1 billion.* This policy is designed to limit the risk of default on certificates of deposit, on the assumption that large capital accounts equate to minimal risk of bank failure.

- *Investments shall be made only in investments backed by U.S. government debt obligations.* This policy can be used in place of the preceding ones that specify allowable investments in nongovernment investments. This policy tends to be used by highly risk-averse companies who place less emphasis on the return generated from their investments.

- *Securities physically held by the company shall be stored with an accredited third party.* This policy improves the physical control over securities.

- *If an employee is responsible for the physical security of securities held by the company, then this person cannot also be responsible for recording the securities in the accounting records.* This policy prevents an employee from removing securities and then eliminating evidence of the securities from the accounting records.

Goods in Transit

- *Revenue shall be recognized on goods in transit based on the point when the company no longer has title to the goods.* This policy ensures that there is a consistent cutoff of the point at which a company records revenue on shipments of finished goods to customers.

- *Incoming inventory shall be recorded after it has been received and inspected.* This policy ensures that the quantity and quality of incoming inventory has been verified prior to recording it in the inventory database, thereby avoiding later problems with having incorrect usable quantities on hand.

- *Goods received on consignment shall be identified and stored separately from company-owned inventory.* This policy keeps a company from artificially inflating its inventory by the amount of incoming consignment inventory, which would otherwise increase reported profits.

- *Consignment inventory shipped to reseller locations shall be clearly identified as such in both the shipping log and the inventory tracking system.* This policy keeps a company from inflating its sales through the recognition of shipments sent to resellers that are actually still owned by the company.

- *The company will not be responsible for in-transit inventory from suppliers.* This policy requires the use of standard shipping terms on purchase orders that clearly shift responsibility to suppliers or third-party delivery entities.

Hedges

- *The determination of hedge effectiveness shall always use the same method for similar types of hedges.* Generally accepted accounting principles (GAAP) allows one to use different assessment techniques in determining whether a hedge is highly effective. However, changing methods, even when justified, allows the accounting staff room to alter effectiveness designations, which can yield variations in the level of reported earnings. Consequently, creating and consistently using a standard assessment method for each type of hedge eliminates the risk of assessment manipulation.

- *A hedge shall be considered highly effective if the fair values of the hedging instrument and hedged item are at least ____% offset.* GAAP does not quantitatively specify what constitutes a highly effective hedge, so a company should create a policy defining the number. Different hedging ranges can be used for different types of hedges.

Intangible Assets

- *All transactions involving the recording of intangible assets must be approved by the external auditors in advance.* Intangible assets are subject to a considerable degree of scrutiny by auditors. By gaining advance approval of these transactions, it is much less likely that there will be significant audit adjustments related to them after the end of the fiscal year.

- *Periodically review all intangible assets for impairment.* This policy ensures that the accounting staff will regularly compare the book value of all intangible assets to their fair value, and write down the book value to the fair value if this is the lower amount.

Inventory Accounting

- *A complete physical inventory count shall be conducted at the end of each reporting period.* This policy ensures that an accurate record of the inventory is used as the basis for a cost-of-goods-sold calculation.

- *The materials manager is responsible for inventory accuracy.* This policy centralizes control over inventory accuracy, thereby increasing the odds of it being kept at a high level.

- *Cycle counters shall continually review inventory accuracy and identify related problems.* This policy is intended for perpetual inventory systems, and results in a much higher level of inventory accuracy and attention to the underlying problems that cause inventory errors.

- *No access to the inventory is allowed by unauthorized personnel.* This policy generally leads to the lockdown of the warehouse, yielding much greater control over the accurate recording of inventory issuance transactions.

- *No inventory transaction shall occur without being immediately recorded in the perpetual inventory database.* This policy keeps the inventory database accurate at all times, preventing errors from arising when employees adjust the database on the incorrect assumption that the current record is correct.

- *Only designated personnel shall have access to the inventory database and item master file.* This policy ensures not only that only trained employees adjust inventory records, but also that the responsibility for their accuracy can be traced to designated people.

- *Employees receiving inventory from another location or department must affirm the quantity, identity, and unit of measure of the inventory being received.* This policy reduces the risk that inventory will be misidentified or fraudulently removed at the transfer point.

- *The company's warehouse locations shall not be publicized.* This policy reduces the risk of inventory theft by people outside the company.

Inventory Tracking

- *The warehouse staff is not allowed to record inventory transactions in the perpetual inventory card file.* This policy reduces the risk that the warehouse staff will remove items from stock and record a transaction to eliminate the inventory.

- *Access to the perpetual inventory card file shall be restricted to the warehouse clerk.* This policy reduces the risk that inventory records will be fraudulently modified.

- *All inventory transactions shall be entered in the inventory database within ____ minutes of the transaction occurring.* This policy reduces the risk that cycle counting errors will be caused by late transaction entries.

- *Access to the inventory database shall be restricted to authorized personnel.* This policy reduces the risk that the database can be manipulated to hide evidence of inventory theft.

- *The warehouse staff is not allowed to record specialty inventory transactions in the inventory database.* This policy reduces the risk that specialty transactions will be incorrectly entered in the database.

- *Specific character lengths shall be required for bar code scanner data entry fields.* This policy reduces the risk that entries for other fields will be entered into the wrong database fields.

- *The warehouse staff will upload data from their portable scanners at every scheduled work break.* This policy improves the speed with which the inventory database is updated.

Inventory Valuation

- *ABC classification.* The warehouse manager shall review the ABC classification of all items in stock at least once a year, and rearrange inventory storage within the warehouse based upon this revised classification.

- *Bill of materials.* Only the engineering department shall make changes to the bill of materials database.

- *Changes in product components shall be immediately reflected in the associated bills of materials.* This policy ensures that the costs assigned to a product through a bill of materials accurately reflect the current product configuration as designed by the engineering staff.

- *Changes in production processes shall be immediately reflected in labor routings.* This policy ensures that the costs assigned to products through labor routings accurately reflect the actual production process, equipment usage, and production staffing.

- *Delivery.* The company shall deliver completed customer orders no later than two days following receipt of those orders.

- *Drop shipping.* The company shall endeavor to have suppliers drop ship items directly to customers whenever possible.

- *Engineering changes.* The engineering department shall implement an engineering change order only after the proposed change has been formally reviewed and approved by the cost accounting, production, and manufacturing departments.

- *Formal inventory obsolescence reviews shall be conducted at least annually.* This policy requires an inventory review team to periodically scan the inventory for obsolete items, which not only removes the cost of such items from stock, but also gives management a chance to profitably dispose of older inventory items before they become worthless.

- *Hedge inventory.* The company shall not invest in hedge inventories for such events as possible strikes or supplier disputes without prior approval by senior management.

- *Lower of cost or market calculations shall be conducted at least annually.* This policy ensures that excessively high inventory costs are stripped out of the inventory before they can become an excessively large proportion of it. This policy may be modified to require more frequent reviews, based on the variability of market rates for various inventory items.

- *Management shall actively seek out, identify, and dispose of scrap as soon as possible.* This policy requires the production team to remove scrap from the manufacturing process immediately, thereby keeping it from being recorded in the inventory records and artificially inflating profits.

- *Obsolescence.* Inventory parts shall be designated obsolete once the products of which they are components have been withdrawn from production and there is no recent evidence of service or repair requirements.

- *Only designated personnel shall have access to the labor routing and bill of materials databases.* This policy ensures that untrained employees are kept away from the critical computer files needed to value inventory quantities.

- *Putaway.* Inventory items shall be put away immediately after receipt.

- *Standard cost records shall be updated at least annually.* This policy ensures that standard costs used in inventory valuations do not stray too far from actual costs.

- *Supplies reordering.* Supplies not tracked through the inventory system shall be visually reviewed at least daily for reordering purposes.

- *Impacted inventory will be drawn down prior to the implementation of engineering change orders, with the exception of change orders related to product safety.* This policy reduces the risk of inventory obsolescence due to engineering change orders.

Investment, Equity Method of Accounting

- *The CFO shall regularly review with the Board of Directors the existing assumptions of significant influence over all entities the voting common stock of which the company owns between 20 and 50%.* Evidence of significant influence requires a company to use the equity method in reporting the financial results of an investee, whereas a lack of influence would require it to record the investment in an investment portfolio category. Regularly reviewing the level of influence over an investee will ensure that the appropriate accounting treatment is used.

- *The tax rate used to recognize taxes under equity method gains shall be the higher of the rates paid on dividend income or sale of the investment.* The income tax rate used to record equity method transactions can be either the tax rate on dividends or from sale of the investment, depending on the investor's intent to eventually dispose of the method. Always using the higher tax rate goes against GAAP to some extent, but keeps the accounting staff from inflating income by using the more conservative tax rate.

Investment in Debt Securities Accounting

- *The unrecognized amount of gains or losses on held-to-maturity securities shall be regularly reported to the Board of Directors.* Management may designate poor-performing debt securities as held-to-maturity, in which case any changes in their fair value will not be recognized. This policy is designed to reveal any gains or losses that would be recognized if these securities were to have any other portfolio designation, so the Board is aware of any "hanging" gains or losses.

- *Debt securities shall not be classified as held-to-maturity unless sufficient investments are already on hand to cover all budgeted short-term cash requirements.* GAAP already requires that debt securities not be classified as held-to-maturity if a company does not have the ability to hold the securities for the required time period—this policy is more specific in stating that all anticipated cash flows be fully covered by other investments before any debt securities receive the held-to-maturity classification. The policy makes it more likely that a company will not be forced to prematurely liquidate its held to-maturity debt portfolio.

Investment Portfolios, Transfer Between

- *The Board of Directors shall be notified of the reasons for any significant shift in the designation of securities between the held-to-maturity, available-for-sale, and trading portfolios, and the approximate impact on different categories of income.* This policy is designed to require management to justify its actions in shifting securities between portfolios, which is likely to reduce the amount of shifting, while also keeping the Board informed of any likely movements of gains or losses between the Operating Income and Other Comprehensive Income parts of the income statement.

Investment Portfolios, Transfer of Debt Securities Among

- *The Board of Directors must authorize all shifts in investment designation out of the held-to-maturity portfolio.* There are specific accounting instances where the transfer of securities out of the held-to-maturity portfolio will preclude a company's subsequent use of the held-to-maturity portfolio. Accordingly, the Board of Directors should be notified of the reasons for such a designation and give its formal approval before the designation change can be made.

Just-in-Time Manufacturing Systems

- *All suppliers needed for the just-in-time system shall have their product quality and delivery reliability certified by the company.* This policy improves the company's ability to have incoming goods shipped directly to the production lines without any receiving inspection.

- *No workstation operator shall process work without an authorization to create a specific quantity of inventory (e.g., a kanban).* This policy reduces the risk that excessive quantities of inventory will be produced.

- *Standard container sizes shall be used to move, store, and count inventory in the production process.* This policy makes it easier to track inventory quantities.

Lease Terminations

- *Only the Board can approve lease termination agreements.* GAAP requires that the expenses associated with lease terminations be recognized on the date when the lease termination notice is issued to the lessor. Since the expenses recognized can be substantial, there can be a tendency by management to time the termination notice to alter reported financial results. By requiring the Board to issue final approval of such agreements during its regularly scheduled meetings, management is less likely to intentionally alter financial results through the use of lease termination agreements. The policy is even more effective if the Board is informed of the amount of any lease expense to be recognized as part of the termination notification.

Lessee Accounting

- *Lease termination dates shall be regularly reviewed.* It is extremely common for lease agreements to require a written notice of lease cancellation near the end of the lease term. If no written notice is received by the lessor, then the lease payments are contractually required to be continued for some predetermined number of months, which usually is detrimental to the lessee. This policy is designed to ensure a periodic review of lease termination dates, so that lease cancellation notices can be sent in a timely manner.

- *No company leases shall include a guaranteed residual value clause.* A company can negotiate smaller periodic lease payments by guaranteeing the lessor a significant residual value at the end of the lease, which typically calls for a large cash payment back to the lessor. Though such a clause can assist in reducing up-front cash payments, it can also result in an unacceptably high cash liability in the future.

- *The legal department shall send a copy of each signed lease document to the accounting department.* The accounting department must be aware of the amount and timing of all lease payments, so the legal department should be required to provide it this information via copies of all signed leases. For larger companies, this policy would require that leases be sent to the finance department instead of accounting, since the finance staff would be more concerned with cash forecasting.

Manufacturing Resources Planning System (MRP II)

- *A minimum level of inventory record accuracy of 95% shall be maintained.* This policy supports the minimum inventory record accuracy level for an MRP II system.

- *A minimum labor routing record accuracy of 95% shall be maintained.* This policy supports the minimum labor routing record accuracy level needed for an MRP II system.

- *A minimum level of bill of materials record accuracy of 98% shall be maintained.* This policy supports the minimum bill of materials record accuracy level needed for an MRP II system.

- *Changes in product components shall be immediately reflected in the associated bills of materials.* This policy ensures that the costs assigned to a product through a bill of materials accurately reflect the current product configuration as designed by the engineering staff.

- *Changes in production processes shall be immediately reflected in labor routings.* This policy ensures that the costs assigned to products through labor routings accurately reflect the actual production process, equipment usage, and production staffing.

- *Access to the inventory item master file shall be restricted to authorized personnel.* This policy reduces the risk of MRP II logic errors caused by incorrect record changes.

- *Purchased quantities shall be based on specific production requirements.* This policy reduces the placement of large-quantity orders that have lower per-unit purchase costs.

Marketable Equity Securities Accounting

- *All securities purchases shall be designated as trading securities at the time of purchase.* This policy is intended to avoid the designation of an investment as "available for sale," which would allow management to avoid recording short-term changes in the fair value of the investment in reported earnings. The policy removes the ability of management to alter financial results by shifting the designation of an investment.

- *All losses on securities designated as available-for-sale shall be considered permanent.* Accounting rules allow one to avoid recognizing losses on available-for-sale securities by assuming that the losses are temporary. By using this policy to require an immediate write-down on all losses, management no longer has the ability to manipulate earnings by making assumptions that losses are temporary in nature.

- *Available-for-sale securities shall not be sold solely to recognize related gains in their fair market value.* Accounting rules do not allow ongoing recognition of gains in the value of available-for-sale securities in earnings until they have been sold, so there is a natural temptation to manage earnings by timing their sale. This policy is designed to set an ethical standard for management to prevent such actions from taking place. In reality, this is a difficult policy to enforce, since management can find reasonable excuses for selling securities when their unrecognized gains are needed for bookkeeping purposes.

Notes and Bonds

- *All notes and bonds shall be issued only subsequent to approval by the Board of Directors.* This policy gives the Board control over any new debt liabilities. In reality, anyone lending money to the company will require a Board motion, so this policy is likely to be imposed by the lender even if it does not exist internally.

- *Debt sinking funds shall be fully funded on scheduled dates.* This policy is designed to force the treasury staff to plan for the timely accumulation of funds needed to pay off scheduled principal payments on debt, thereby avoiding any last-minute funding crises.

- *Recognition of unearned revenue for attached rights shall match offsetting discount amortization as closely as possible.* This policy is designed to avoid the manipulation of revenue recognition for attached rights. For example, if a value is assigned to an attached right, the debit will be to a discount account that will be ratably recognized as interest expense over the term of the debt; however, the credit will be to an unearned revenue account for which the potential exists to recognize revenue much sooner, thereby creating a split in the timing of revenue and expense recognition. Though this split may be valid in some cases, an effort should be made to avoid any significant disparities, thereby avoiding any surges in profits.

- *The fair market interest rate shall be used to value debt transactions where property is being obtained.* This policy is designed to prevent any manipulation of the value assigned to an acquired asset as part of a debt-for-property transaction. By always using the fair market rate, there is no possibility of using an excessively high or low interest rate to artificially alter the cost at which the acquired property is recorded on the company books.

- *Debt shall always be issued at stated rates as close to the market interest rate as possible.* Though there are valid reasons for issuing debt at rates significantly different from the market rate, this causes a problem with determining the market rate to be applied to debt present value calculations, which has a significant impact on the amount of interest expense recognized. Instead, this policy avoids the problem by requiring debt issuances to have stated interest rates so close to the market rate that there is no possibility of a significant debt valuation issue.

Order Entry

- *Extended rights of return shall not be allowed.* This policy limits the ability of the sales staff to engage in channel stuffing and sales declines in subsequent periods.

- *Special sale discounts shall not be allowed without senior management approval.* This policy prevents short-term sales bubbles that result in channel stuffing and sales declines in subsequent periods.

Payroll

- *Employees can carry a maximum of ____ hours of unused vacation time forward into the next calendar year.* This policy greatly reduces the effort required to calculate the year-end vacation expense accrual, and also keeps employees from building up large unused vacation balances.

- *The company does not make purchases on behalf of employees.* This policy keeps the payroll staff from having to track a series of period deductions from employee pay in order to cover the cost of items purchased by the company for employees.

- *The company does not issue advances on company pay.* This policy keeps the payroll staff from having to manually enter pay deductions into the payroll system to offset pay advances.

- *The company will provide access to computer kiosks for all employees.* This policy assists the payroll department in requiring employees to switch to electronic pay stubs and W-2 forms, so the company no longer has to manually distribute these documents.

- *All employees shall be paid by direct deposit or payroll card.* This policy is useful for switching 100% of employees to electronic payments, either through a bank account (with direct deposit) or to a payroll debit card.

- *Commissions shall be paid based only on cash received.* This policy enhances the intensity of a company's collection efforts by indirectly involving the sales staff in collection efforts if they wish to be paid a commission.

- *Final commissions for terminated sales staff shall be based on cash received from shipments made up until the termination date.* This policy requires that actual cash receipts data be used as the basis for final commissions, thereby eliminating the risk of a commission overpayment that would otherwise not be recoverable.

- *The chief financial officer (CFO) must approve all off-cycle payrolls.* This policy tends to reduce the number of time-consuming additional payrolls, on the assumption that few employees will want to make this request of the CFO.

- *Employees are responsible for removing ineligible family members from the company health plan.* This policy allows the company to extract reimbursement from employees if it is discovered that they have incorrectly placed ineligible family members on their insurance applications.

- *No employee can be responsible for both processing payroll and distributing pay.* This policy ensures that proper segregation of duties keeps anyone from creating a paycheck, recording it, and then pocketing the funds.

- *All pay advances require the written approval of the employee's immediate supervisor, department manager, and controller.* This policy introduces a sufficient number of approvals to discourage the use of pay advances.

- *All negative deductions must be approved by the payroll manager.* This policy reduces the risk that employees will fraudulently receive additional pay through the use of negative deductions.

- *Hourly employees must submit an approved timesheet by the designated date and time in order to be paid as part of the regular payroll cycle.* This policy puts the burden of timesheet submission on individual employees, rather than the payroll staff.

- *Absent employees must be given a signed authorization to another employee to obtain the employee's paycheck on their behalf.* This policy reduces the company's liability in case another employee diverts funds from the employee's paycheck.

- *The paymaster has no other payroll-related responsibilities than distributing paychecks.* This policy reduces the risk that an employee will create paychecks for ghost employees and then retain the checks.

- *Payroll taxes shall be remitted in full on a timely basis.* This policy makes it clear to the payroll manager that taxes must be remitted in the full amount and on time, with no exceptions.

- *Pay authorization documents shall be centrally stored.* This policy ensures that access to all pay-related authorizations can be easily restricted, while also reducing the likelihood that authorization documents can be lost.

- *Access to the payroll system and employee master file shall be restricted to authorized personnel.* This policy reduces the risk of fraudulent payroll transactions.

- *Access to the employee master file shall be segregated from other payroll activities.* This policy makes it more difficult to both create and pay a ghost employee.

- *Any change to an employee's direct deposit information requires the employee's signature and formal identification.* This policy reduces the risk that payroll payments will be diverted to the wrong party.

- *Employees accessing online payroll remittance and W-2 information must set up user identification and password information to access their accounts.* This policy keeps unauthorized parties from accessing confidential payroll information.

Petty Cash

- *Reimbursements from petty cash are authorized for expenditures of up to $____ per transaction.* This policy keeps employees from obtaining large payments from petty cash funds that would otherwise have required supervisory approval prior to payment.

- *Petty cash may not be used for advances, or the reimbursement of gifts, personal loans, traffic citations, personal expenses, or interest charges.* This policy prevents petty cash payments for expenditures that would not normally be approved for payment.

- *The petty cash fund shall be small enough to require replenishment about twice per month.* This policy establishes a rough guideline for establishing the size of a fund.

- *Petty cash should be kept in a locked box within a locked drawer when the custodian is absent.* This policy recognizes the ease with which petty cash can be stolen, and so requires double locking of the storage location.

- *A petty cash contact alarm shall be installed under every petty cash box.* This policy results in an alarm when a petty cash box is physically removed.

Procurement Cards

- *All procurement card users will follow a standard monthly reconciliation checklist to ensure that all card liabilities for which there are no receipts are reported, and that card liabilities are rejected if there are sufficient grounds for doing so.* This policy reduces the risk that expenditures will be incorrectly charged or incurred.

- *The managers of all departments to which procurement card expenses are charged must approve those expenses.* This policy reduces the risk that expenses will be improperly incurred or incorrectly charged.

- *Procurement card users shall not use their cards to acquire materials normally ordered through the MRP II system.* This policy keeps purchases from occurring outside the automated purchasing system of the MRP II system.

- *Cash advances shall be prohibited for all procurement cards, unless the cards are specifically intended for travel-related expenditures.* This policy reduces the risk of fraudulent access to and use of cash.

- *Department managers must approve all changes in procurement card spending limits, which shall be restricted to suppliers having a certain SIC code, daily purchasing limits, and monthly purchasing limits.* This policy reduces the risk of overspending or fraudulent purchases.

- *Procurement cards shall be restricted to the smallest possible number of authorized users.* This policy prevents the proliferation of procurement cards to users who have less control over their spending habits.

- *Procurement card users must sign an agreement with the company, detailing their responsibilities in using the card, and clearly stating the consequences of misuse.* This policy acts as a deterrent to anyone who might otherwise be tempted to misuse a card.

Purchasing

- *A purchase order must be issued for all requisitions exceeding $____.* This ensures that all requisitions are first reviewed by the purchasing department for correct pricing, sourcing, quality, and payment terms prior to ordering.

- *Employees authorized to create a record in the vendor master file shall be barred from approving payments to suppliers.* This policy reduces the risk that an individual will create a fake supplier and then approve payments to it.

- *Password access shall be required to make changes to the vendor master file.* This policy reduces the risk that fraudulent or incorrect payments will be made.

- *A tracking log shall record all changes made to the vendor master file.* This policy reduces the risk that fraudulent or incorrect payments will be made.

- *A person outside of the purchasing or payables departments shall regularly review all changes made to the vendor master file, which shall be traced with a tracking log.* This policy reduces the risk that fraudulent or incorrect payments will be made.

- *The vendor master file shall be purged of duplicate and noncurrent supplier records at least once a year.* This policy reduces the risk of having multiple supplier accounts.

- *Access to the purchase order system shall be restricted to approved users.* This policy reduces the risk that purchase orders will be improperly issued.

- *Requisition responsibility shall be assigned to one person for specific areas of the warehouse.* This policy reduces the risk of duplicate requisitioning by different warehouse employees.

- *The purchasing and receiving functions shall be segregated.* This policy keeps employees from initiating orders and removing the received items from the company.

- *The purchasing manager will regularly notify suppliers of the names of company employees who are allowed to issue purchase orders for specific commodity groups.* This policy reduces the risk of fraudulent orders being placed.

- *The purchasing manager will regularly notify suppliers that the company does not consider verbal purchase authorizations to be a purchasing commitment.* This policy provides a deterrent to the issuance of verbal purchase orders by employees.

- *The purchasing manager must countersign all purchase orders exceeding $____.* This policy provides additional oversight of large purchasing commitments.

- *The warehouse manager will conduct a daily review of inventory, using a visual reordering system, to determine reordering needs, and communicate this information to the purchasing department.* This policy reduces the risk of inventory stockouts.

- *Minimum order quantities shall be used when cost-effective.* This policy enforces the acquisition of goods in the smallest possible minimum order quantities, so there is less inventory on hand.

Receiving

- *All supplier deliveries will be rejected at the receiving dock unless there is an authorizing purchase order with a sufficient quantity open to cover the unit quantity of the delivery.* This policy reduces the risk that unauthorized deliveries will be received.

- *Incoming inventory shall be recorded after it has been inspected.* This policy ensures that the quantity and quality of incoming inventory has been verified prior to recording it in the inventory database, thereby avoiding later problems with having incorrect usable quantities on hand.

- *In cross-docking situations, the data entry of receiving documents shall be replaced by advance shipping notices.* This policy automates the entry of receiving information.

Research and Development Costs

- *All research and development (R&D) costs must be recorded under unique general ledger account codes.* Because GAAP requires that all R&D costs be charged to expense in the current period, it is imperative that these costs be segregated for easy review. Otherwise, it is likely that the costs will be mixed into other general ledger accounts and possibly capitalized, thereby incorrectly increasing reported profits.

Revenue, Barter

- *The company shall not engage in barter transactions whose sole purpose is the creation of revenue.* This policy informs the accounting staff that it is unacceptable to create barter swap transactions whose sole purpose is to create additional revenue without the presence of any economic reason for the transaction.

- *All expenses associated with barter transactions shall be recognized in the same proportions as related revenues.* This policy is designed to keep expenses associated with barter swap transactions from being significantly delayed while revenues are recognized up front. The policy will keep profits from being incorrectly recorded in advance.

Revenue, General

- *Preliminary revenue summaries shall be issued no later than one day following the close of an accounting period.* This policy is designed to prevent the accounting staff from artificially keeping the books open past the end of the reporting period, since it must commit to a specific revenue figure within a day of closing.

- *Extended rights of return shall not be allowed.* This policy limits the ability of the sales staff to engage in "channel stuffing," since it cannot offer special rights of return to customers in exchange for early sales. The policy keeps a company from gyrating between large swings in sales caused by channel stuffing.

- *Special sale discounts shall not be allowed without senior management approval.* This policy prevents large bursts in sales caused by special price discounts that can stuff a company's distribution channels, causing rapid sales declines in subsequent periods.

- *The company shall not use bill and hold transactions.* Though bill and hold transactions are allowable under clearly defined and closely restricted circumstances, they are subject to abuse, and so should generally be avoided. This policy ensures that bill and hold transactions would require Board approval before being used.

- *Estimated profits on service contracts shall be reviewed monthly.* This policy ensures that estimated losses on service contracts are identified and recognized promptly, rather than being delayed until the contracts are closed.

Revenue Recognition When Collection Is Uncertain

- *A single revenue recognition method shall be used for all installment sales.* This policy keeps an accounting department from switching back and forth between the installment method and cost recovery method for recognizing this type of revenue, which would otherwise allow it to manipulate reported levels of profitability.

Revenue Recognition When Right of Return Exists

- *A sales return allowance shall be maintained for all goods sold with a right of return.* This policy ensures that profits are not initially overstated by the amount of any potential returns by requiring an initial reserve to be established.

Shipping

- *No order will be shipped unless its sales order has been approved by the credit department.* This policy reduces the risk that unapproved orders will be inadvertently shipped.

- *Consignment inventory shipped to reseller locations shall be clearly identified as such in both the shipping log and the inventory tracking system.* This policy reduces the risk that off-site inventory will not be accounted for.

Stock Appreciation Rights

- *Vesting periods for stock appreciation rights (SAR) shall not exceed the standard vesting period used for other stock grants.* Since the gradual increases in the value of a SAR grant must be charged to expense in the period when the increases occur, a company could delay this expense recognition by lengthening the service period required before the SAR is earned by an employee. This policy is designed to require the use of a standard vesting period for all types of stock grants, thereby avoiding extremely long SAR vesting periods.

Stock Options

- *The current dividend yield shall be used for all option valuation assumptions.* When a company uses the popular Black-Scholes option pricing formula to determine the compensation expense associated with its options, it can reduce the amount of expense recorded by assuming an increased dividend yield in the future. This policy is designed to freeze the dividend assumption, thereby nullifying the risk of deliberate expense modifications in this area.

- *The expected term of all options shall be based on the results of the last ____ years.* When a company uses SFAS 123 guidelines to record compensation expense, part of the calculation is an estimate of the time period over which options are expected to be held by recipients. If this assumed period is shortened, the value of the options is reduced, resulting in a lower compensation expense. Consequently, there is a tendency to assume shorter expected terms. This policy is designed to force the accounting staff to always use a historical basis for the calculation of expected terms, so there is no way to modify the assumption.

- *Option-based compensation expense shall be adjusted at regular intervals for the forfeiture of options.* An estimate of option forfeitures should be made at the time when option compensation expenses are first made under SFAS 123. If actual experience with option forfeitures varies from expectations, the difference must be recognized as a change in accounting estimate in the current period. The trouble is that accountants can ignore the changes for some time and record them only in accounting periods where their impact is most useful to the accountant. This policy is designed to avoid the timing of adjustments by requiring regular adjustments at set intervals. Including this action item in the month-end closing procedure is a good way to ensure compliance with the policy.

- *Option vesting periods shall be identical for all option and stock grants.* When a company reduces the vesting period for its options, it can reasonably justify using a shorter option life if it expenses its stock options using the Black-Scholes model. This policy discourages the Board of Directors from shortening vesting periods by making it necessary to also shorten all types of stock grants at the same time, thereby also introducing some vesting consistency to the complete range of corporate stock grants.

- *Compensation expenses shall be recognized for both new option grants and those still outstanding from prior years.* When a company elects to charge its option grants to expense, a common practice is to ignore outstanding options issued in prior years, and instead charge only new options to expense. This underreports the prospective compensation expense. This policy is designed to force full disclosure of the expense associated with all option grants.

- *The minimum value model shall be used to calculate compensation expense for option grants as long as the company is privately held.* When a company is privately held, it can still use the fair value method promulgated under SFAS 123. The problem is that the fair value method requires the use of a stock volatility measure as part of the calculation, which is entirely a matter of opinion when shares are not publicly traded. To avoid the potential manipulation associated with volatility calculations under this scenario, the policy recommends the use of the minimum value model, which is the same as the fair value method, minus the stock volatility calculation.

Stock Subscriptions

- *Stock subscription plans for employees must be approved by the Board of Directors.* This policy requires the Board to authorize the number of shares that may be sold to employees, as well as any discounts on those purchases. By requiring ongoing approval of additions to the number of shares authorized for distribution, the Board can maintain effective control over this program.

Stock, Treasury

- *The initial sale price of all stock shall be recorded by stock certificate number.* When stock is repurchased into the treasury, it is possible that the original sale price of each share repurchased must be backed out of the stock account, depending on the accounting method used. This policy requires that sufficient records be kept to allow such future treasury stock transactions to be properly recorded.

- *The circumstances of any greenmail stock repurchases shall be fully documented.* This policy is designed to provide proper documentation of the amount of any stock repurchased under the threat of a corporate takeover. By doing so, one can more easily determine the price under which shares were repurchased, as well as the market price of the stock on that date. This is critical information for the recognition of expenses related to excessively high repurchase costs, which can have a major negative impact on reported earnings levels.

Chapter 6

ACCOUNTING PROCEDURES

6.1 INTRODUCTION

This chapter begins with a series of 10 process flowcharts, which itemize all the procedures that a typical accounting department can expect to be involved with; there are even additional procedures listed for the purchasing, shipping, and receiving departments, because these three areas initiate paperwork that eventually flows to the accounting department. By creating flowcharts first, one can identify all activities and thereby ensure that a procedure is written for each one. Also, each box in the flowcharts contains an identifying index number for each procedure, which is later listed as the procedure number in the header for each procedure. Thus, one can first refer to a process flowchart for the specific procedure needed, then trace the index number to the detailed procedure (which is also listed here, sorted in order by process flowchart designation). The process flowcharts are:

- Acquisitions (Exhibit 6.1)
- Billing (Exhibit 6.2)
- Budget (Exhibit 6.3)
- Credit (Exhibit 6.4)
- Financial Statements (Exhibit 6.5)
- Fixed Assets (Exhibit 6.6)
- Funds Management (Exhibit 6.7)
- Internal Audit (Exhibit 6.8)
- Inventory (Exhibit 6.9)

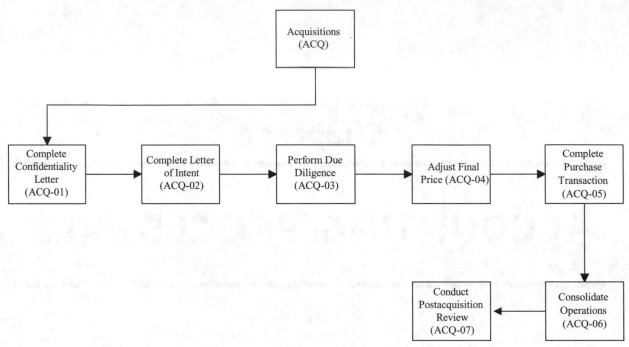

Exhibit 6.1 Acquisitions Flowchart

- Payroll (Exhibit 6.10)

- Purchasing Cycle (Exhibit 6.11)

Some organizations may want to fill out these procedures with additional sections pertaining to the definition of any technical terms included in the procedure, as well as references to related documents or policies.

The exact procedures used here are designed for specific software packages and company procedures, and so are not meant for exact copying by a user. Instead, it is best to review the general layout and terminology used in each procedure, and then use this information to design a customized set of procedures for one's own specific circumstances. The following procedures are included in this chapter:

1. **Acquisitions (ACQ)**
   - Complete confidentiality letter (ACQ-01)
   - Complete letter of intent (ACQ-02)
   - Perform due diligence (ACQ-03)
   - Adjust final price (ACQ-04)
   - Complete purchase transaction (ACQ-05)
   - Consolidate operations (ACQ-06)
   - Conduct postacquisition review (ACQ-07)

2. **Billing (BIL)**
   - Ship to customer (BIL-01)
   - Drop ship inventory (BIL-02)
   - Enter billing in computer (BIL-03)

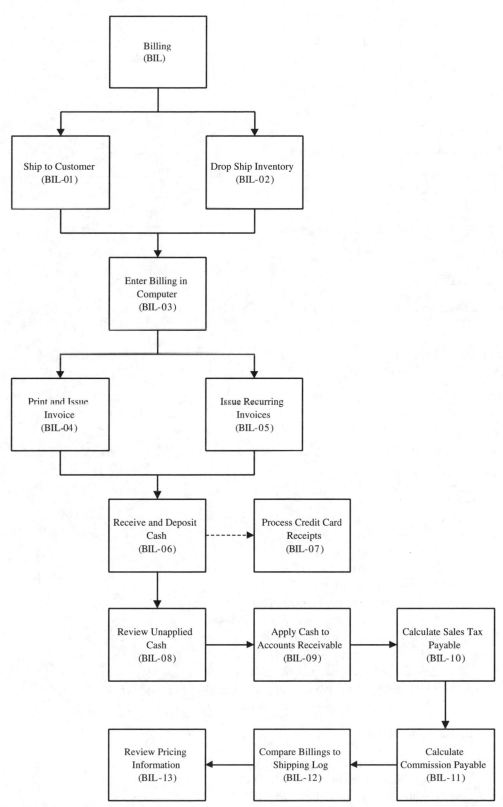

Exhibit 6.2 Billing Flowchart

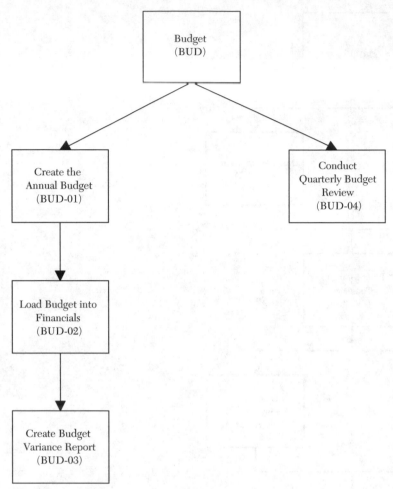

Exhibit 6.3   Budget Flowchart

- Issue recurring in voices (BIL-04)
- Print and issue invoice (BIL-05)
- Receive and deposit cash (BIL-06)
- Process credit card receipts (BIL-07)
- Apply cash to accounts receivable (BIL-08)
- Review unapplied cash (BIL-09)
- Calculate sales tax payable (BIL-10)
- Calculate commission payable (BIL-11)
- Track exceptions between shipping log and sales journal (BIL-12)
- Review pricing information (BIL-13)

3. Budget (BUD)

- Create the annual budget (BUD-01)
- Load budget into financials (BUD-02)
- Create budget variance report (BUD-03)
- Conduct quarterly budget review (BUD-04)

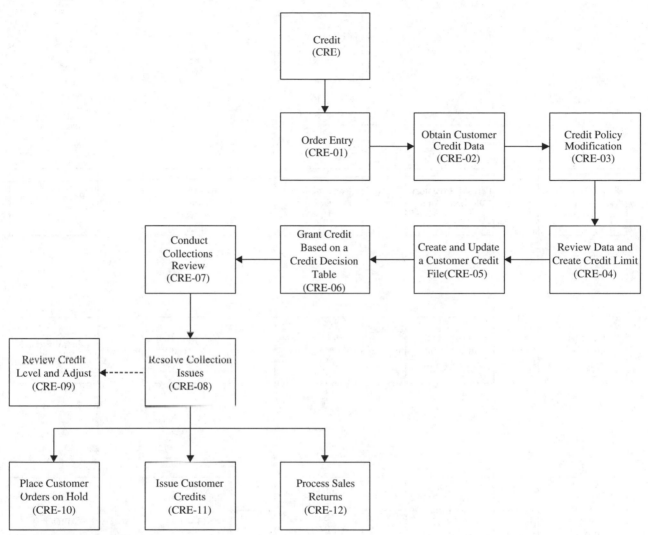

Exhibit 6.4 Credit Flowchart

4. Credit (CRE)

- Order entry (CRE-01)
- Obtain customer credit data (CRE-02)
- Credit policy modification (CRE-03)
- Review data and create credit limit (CRE-04)
- Create and update a customer credit file (CRE-05)
- Grant credit based on a credit decision table (CRE-06)
- Conduct collections review (CRE-07)
- Resolve collections issues (CRE-08)
- Issue customer credits (CRE-09)
- Process sales returns (CRE-10)
- Place customer orders on hold (CRE-11)
- Review credit level and adjust (CRE-12)

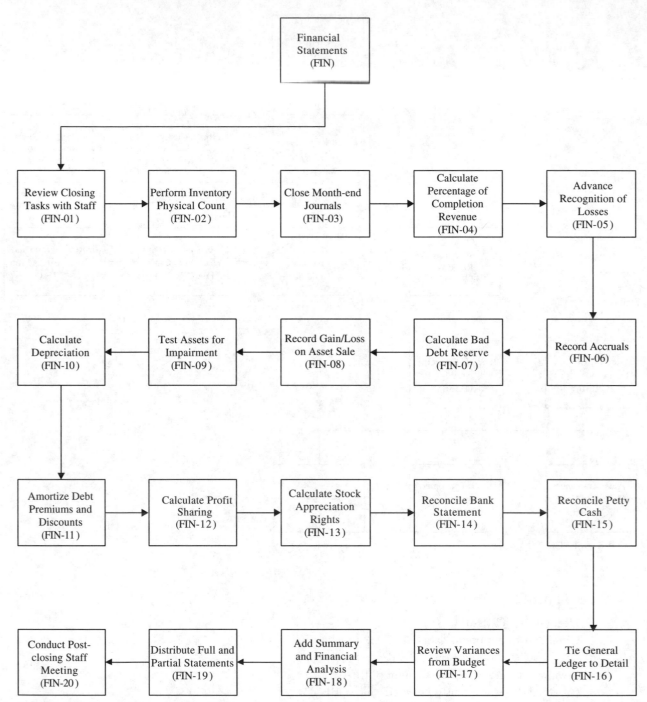

Exhibit 6.5   Financial Statements Flowchart

5. Financial Statements (FIN)

- ○ Review closing tasks with staff (FIN-01)
- ○ Perform physical inventory count (FIN-02)
- ○ Inventory count tag, front and back (FIN-03)

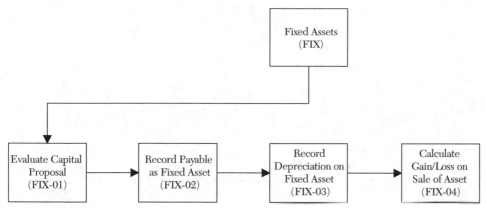

Exhibit 6.6 Fixed Assets Flowchart

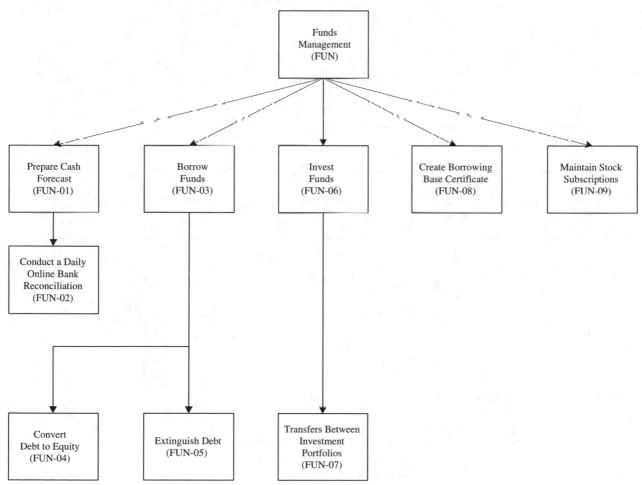

Exhibit 6.7 Funds Management Flowchart

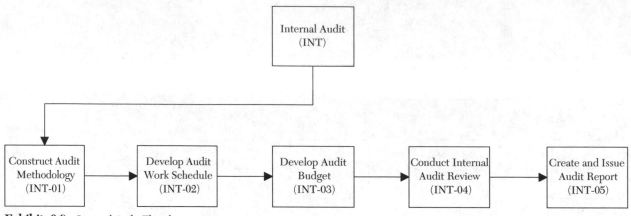

Exhibit 6.8 Internal Audit Flowchart

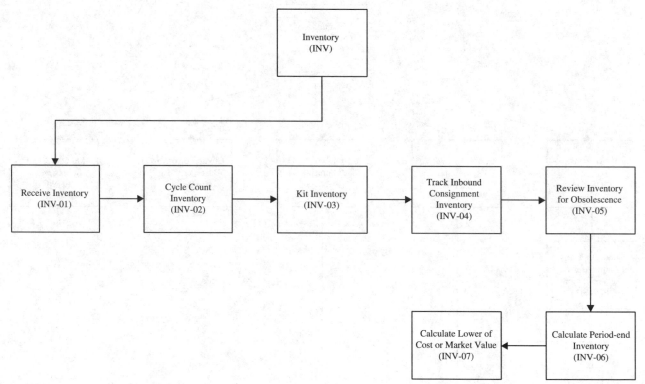

Exhibit 6.9 Inventory Flowchart

- Calculate percentage of completion revenue (FIN-04)
- Advance recognition of losses (FIN-05)
- Record accruals (FIN-06)
- Calculate bad debt reserve (FIN-07)
- Record gain/loss on asset sale (FIN-08)
- Test assets for impairment (FIN-09)
- Calculate depreciation (FIN-10)
- Amortize debt premium & discounts (FIN-11)

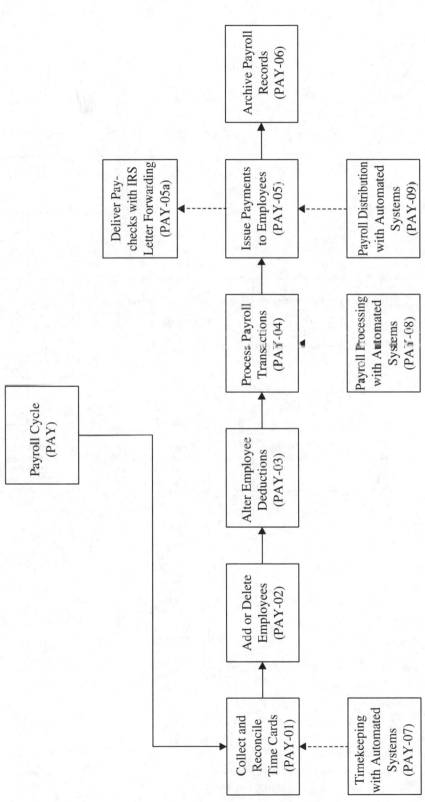

Exhibit 6.10 Payroll Flowchart

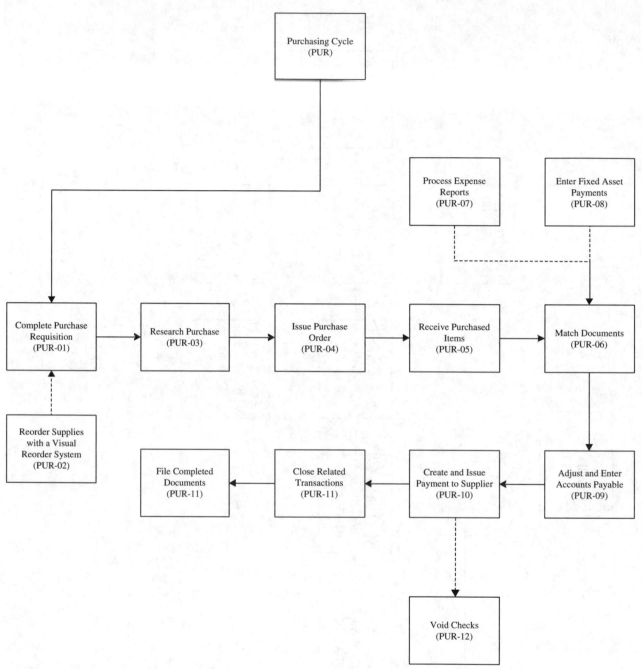

Exhibit 6.11 Purchasing Cycle Flowchart

- ◦ Calculate profit sharing (FIN-12)
- ◦ Calculate stock appreciation rights (FIN-13)
- ◦ Reconcile bank statement (FIN-14)
- ◦ Reconcile petty cash (FIN-15)
- ◦ Tie general ledger to detail (FIN-16)
- ◦ Review variances from budget (FIN-17)

- Add summary and financial analysis (FIN-18)
- Distribute full and partial statements (FIN-19)
- Conduct postclosing staff meeting (FIN-20)

6. Fixed Assets (FIX)

- Evaluate capital proposal (FIX-01)
- Record payable as fixed asset (FIX-02)
- Record depreciation on fixed asset (FIX-03)
- Calculate gain/loss on sale of asset (FIX-04)

7. Funds Management (FUN)

- Prepare cash forecast (FUN-01)
- Conduct a daily on-line bank reconciliation (FUN-02)
- Borrow funds (FUN-03)
- Extinguish debt (FUN-04)
- Convert debt to equity (FUN-05)
- Invest funds (FUN-06)
- Transfers between investment portfolios (FUN-07)
- Create borrowing base certificate (FUN-08)
- Maintain stock subscriptions (FUN-09)

8. Internal Audit (INT)

- Construct audit methodology (INT-01)
- Develop audit work schedule (INT-02)
- Develop audit budget (INT-03)
- Conduct internal audit review (INT-04)
- Create and issue audit report (INT-05)

9. Inventory (INV)

- Receive inventory (INV-01)
- Cycle count inventory (INV-02)
- Kit inventory (INV-03)
- Track internal consignment inventory (INV-04)
- Review inventory for absolescence (INV-05)
- Calculate period-end inventory (INV-06)
- Calculate lower of cost or market value (INV-07)

10. Payroll (PAY)

- Collect and reconcile time cards (PAY-01)
- Add or delete employees (PAY-02)
- Alter employee deductions (PAY-03)
- Process payroll transactions (PAY-04)
- Issue payments to employees (PAY-05)
- Deliver paychecks with IAS letter forwarding (PAY-06)
- Archive payroll records (PAY-07)
- Timekeeping with automated systems (PAY-08)
- Payroll processing with automated systems (PAY-09)
- Payroll distribution with automated systems (PAY-10)

11. Purchasing Cycle (PUR)

- ○ Complete purchase requisition (PUR-01)
- ○ Reorder supplies with a visual reorder system (PUR-02)
- ○ Research purchase (PUR-03)
- ○ Issue purchase order (PUR-04)
- ○ Receive purchased items (PUR-05)
- ○ Match documents (PUR-06)
- ○ Process expense reports (PUR-07)
- ○ Enter fixed asset payments (PUR-08)
- ○ Adjust and enter accounts payable (PUR-09)
- ○ Create and issue payment to supplier (PUR-10)
- ○ Close related transactions (PUR-11)
- ○ File completed documents (PUR-12)
- ○ Void checks (PUR-13)

Though budgeting procedures are included in this chapter to provide a complete set of accounting procedures, they are also dealt with again in Chapter 10, which is solely concerned with that topic.

Policy/Procedure Statement	Retrieval No.:	ACQ-01
Brasto Publishing	Page:	1 of 1
	Issue Date:	10/28/0X
	Supersedes:	N/A
Subject: Complete Confidentiality Agreement		

1.	**PURPOSE AND SCOPE**	
	This procedure is used by the chief financial officer to complete the confidentiality letter that must be signed by both parties prior to taking additional steps to complete an acquisition.	
2.	**RESPONSIBILITIES**	
	CFO	**Chief Financial Officer**
3.	**PROCEDURES**	
3.1	CFO	**Locate Boilerplate Letter Format**
		1. Call up the confidentiality letter format.
		2. Print the letter.
		3. Forward the letter to corporate counsel and schedule a meeting to go over special confidentiality issues related to the target company.
3.2	CFO	**Alter Letter to Match Current Situation**
		1. Alter the format of the confidentiality letter.
		2. Have the altered letter reviewed by corporate counsel.
		3. Reprint extra copies and send to president for signature.

3.3	CFO	**Have Letter Signed** 1. Have president sign all copies of confidentiality letter. 2. Store one copy of letter in acquisitions file. 3. Forward all other copies to president of target company by traceable express delivery.
3.4	CFO	**File Letter** Upon receipt of signed copies from target company, store them in the acquisition file, replacing the earlier, unsigned, copy.

Complete Confidentiality Agreement

Policy/Procedure Statement	Procedure No.:	ACQ-02
Brasto Publishing	Page:	1 of 1
	Issue Date:	10/28/0X
	Supersedes:	N/A
Subject: Complete Letter of Intent		

1. **PURPOSE AND SCOPE**

    This procedure is used by the chief financial officer to ensure the completion of the letter of intent that is used to notify the management of a target company that the acquiring company is making a bid.

2. **RESPONSIBILITIES**

    CFO   **Chief Financial Officer**

3. **PROCEDURES**

    3.1   CFO   **Locate Boilerplate Letter Format**
    1. Call up the letter of intent format.
    2. Print the letter of intent.
    3. Update the letter based on the preliminary purchase terms already discussed with the target company.
    4. Forward the letter to corporate counsel and schedule a meeting to go over legal issues related to the letter of intent.

    3.2   CFO   **Have Letter Signed**
    1. Schedule a meeting with the president to review the terms of the letter.
    2. Obtain the signature of the president on two copies of the letter of intent.

    3.3   CFO   **Issue and File Letter Copies**
    1. Put an unsigned copy of the letter of intent in the acquisitions file.
    2. Send the other two (signed) copies to the president of the target company by traceable express mail.
    3. Upon receipt of the signed copy from the target company, replace the unsigned copy in the acquisitions file with the signed copy.

Complete Letter of Intent

Policy/Procedure Statement	Retrieval No.:	ACQ-03
Brasto Publishing	Page:	1 of 1
	Issue Date:	10/28/0X
	Supersedes:	N/A
Subject: Perform Due Diligence		

1. **PURPOSE AND SCOPE**

   This procedure helps outline the general business fundamentals of a potential acquisition target. This procedure is used by the controller.

2. **RESPONSIBILITIES**

   CONTROLLER   **Controller**

3. **PROCEDURES**

3.1 CONTROLLER   **Review Sales and Marketing**
- What is the current customer concentration?
- What is the profitability by customer?
- Does the typical customer purchase the complete product line?
- What are sales by geographic region?
- Which of the various lines have resulted in the greatest market penetration?
- What is the seasonally of sales?
- Has the target received any requests to expand its market geographically? Who has asked, and what product lines were requested?
- What is the organizational structure of the sales and marketing team?
- What types of outside sales representative relationship(s) do they have?
- What is the commission structure?
- What was the unit sales volume by product for last year, and current projections for the upcoming year?
- What types of agreements exist with customers in regard to price changes in response to changes in raw material prices?
- What customer agreements "lock in" pricing for fixed time periods?
- What is the return merchandise history for the last 18 months across all product lines?
- Have there been any recent product recalls?

3.2 CONTROLLER   **Review the Competition**
- Who are the primary competitors?
- What is their share of the market?
- What information is available on competitors in regard to sales volume, distribution, and products?

3.3 CONTROLLER   **Review New Products**
- What new products are being developed? What is the time line for the introduction of these products?

		• What products have been introduced in the past year? What is their sales performance so far?
		• What proportion of sales are from products that have been on the market for at least five years?
3.4	CONTROLLER	**Review Product Designs**
		• Which organization has been responsible for product development? What are the skills and composition of the staff?
		• What kind of design software do they use?
		• Are there any existing patents for design or function on existing products? When are they due to expire?
		• Have existing design patents within the industry affected product options?
3.5	CONTROLLER	**Review Finance and Accounting**
		• What transfer costs are used between subsidiaries?
		• Review the accounts receivable aging for old items and investigate.
		• Review the accounts payable aging and investigate old unpaid items.
		• Are operations matching budgeted performance levels?
		• What depreciation schedule do they use for major assets?
		• What leases are current?
		• How long does the facility lease run? Is there an option to renew it?
		• Obtain a copy of the building lease.
		• Obtain a copy of the asset list.
		• Obtain detailed financial statements for the last two years.
		• Obtain a list of all loans, as well as the detailed agreements for them.
		• Obtain a copy of the current business plan and financial projections.
		• Obtain the most current credit report. What are the average payable days?
		• Obtain a listing of the inventory. What proportion of the inventory has not been used recently? Are there any clearly obsolete items?
		• What are the percentages of the cost of goods sold attributable to direct labor, materials, and overhead?
		• What costs comprise the overhead expense?
		• What costs go into the overhead allocation calculation?
		• Are expenses being sufficiently accrued for?
		• Are liabilities (such as pensions, taxes, warranties, insurance, litigation, and environmental remediation claims) underfunded?
		• Does the company's bank want to continue funding any existing debt?
3.6	CONTROLLER	**Review Legal and Tax Issues**
		• Are there any outstanding legal issues? Has there been a history of legal problems?
		• What type of corporation structure is involved (partnership, Sub S, or C)?
		• Are there any carryover tax credits?

		• Obtain a list of all stockholders, and their proportions of ownership.

• Obtain a list of all stockholders, and their proportions of ownership.
• Are there any potential environmental problems?
• Has OSHA recently reviewed the facility? What was the result?
• Is the facility unionized?

3.7   CONTROLLER   **Review Computer Systems Issues**
• What type of software is used for accounting and manufacturing activities?
• Describe the network layout.
• Does the company use electronic data interchange?
• Obtain a list of all computers currently in use, including model numbers and age.

3.8   CONTROLLER   **Review General Management Issues**
• Obtain a copy of the current organization chart.
• Obtain a listing of salaries and employment agreements for key employees.
• Obtain a copy of the current benefit plan.

3.9   CONTROLLER   **Review Logistics Issues**
• What mode of transport do they use? Is there any in-house freight delivery service?
• What shipping range do they believe is competitive for their products?
• Are there any long-term supply contracts that the company is locked into that have unfavorable rates?

3.10 CONTROLLER   **Review Manufacturing Issues**
• What products are currently being produced?
• What types of manufacturing automation are in use?
• What percentage of machines are currently used?
• What percentage of the facility square footage is currently used?
• What brand and age of machines are being used? How soon before they need replacement?
• Do they use machine monitoring systems? What kind are used?
• Is there an active preventive maintenance system in place?

Perform Due Diligence

Policy/Procedure Statement	Procedure No.:	ACQ-04
	Page:	1 of 1
	Issue Date:	10/28/0X
Brasto Publishing	Supersedes:	N/A
Subject: Adjust Final Price		

1. PURPOSE AND SCOPE

This procedure is used by the chief financial officer as a set of guidelines that covers the maximum price to which the company will adjust its bid based on due diligence findings.

2. RESPONSIBILITIES

CFO **Chief Financial Officer**

3. PROCEDURES

3.1 CFO **Review Policy for Maximum Price Guidelines**
1. Summarize the controller's due diligence report and note all areas in which purchase price adjustments are necessary, based on variances from the original information on which the original letter of intent was based.
2. Refer to the company policy on maximum pricing guidelines, in case any pricing requires upward adjustment.
3. Document all downward pricing adjustments, along with exact calculations, and store this information in the acquisitions file.

3.2 CFO **Calculate Final Price Based on Due Diligence Results**
1. Summarize all pricing adjustments in a standard report format.
2. Schedule a meeting with the president to review all pricing adjustments and the final price.
3. Obtain the president's approval of the final pricing offer.

3.3 CFO **Communicate Price to Target Company**
1. Create a cover letter to the president of the target company, explaining all pricing adjustments. Include the pricing adjustment summary sheet. Include an offer termination date in the cover letter.
2. Copy the packet and store it in the acquisitions file.
3. Send the packet to the target company by traceable express mail.

Adjust Final Price

Policy/Procedure Statement	Retrieval No.:	ACQ-05
	Page:	1 of 1
Brasto Publishing	Issue Date:	10/28/0X
	Supersedes:	N/A
Subject: Complete Purchase Transaction		

1. **PURPOSE AND SCOPE**
   This procedure is used by the chief financial officer to ensure that all legal and financial documentation has been completed for an acquisition.

2. **RESPONSIBILITIES**
   CFO   **Chief Financial Officer**

3. **PROCEDURES**

3.1   CFO   **Review Checklist of All Purchase Documentation**
Access the standard checklist of purchase documentation.

3.2   CFO   **Verify That All Checklist Items Have Been Completed**
1. Ensure that the environmental testing report has been completed and reviewed for problems.
2. Verify that there are no legal attachments to any target company assets.
3. Ensure that all property taxes have been paid by the target company or put in escrow through the date of the acquisition.
4. Verify that bridge loans for the acquisition have been approved by lenders.
5. Ensure that the auditors have completed their investigative audit of the target company.
6. Verify that the appraised value of all assets matches the summary total against which the original price was based.

3.3   CFO   **Follow Up on Missing Checklist Items**
1. Draft a list of all checklist issues that have not yet been completed.
2. Assign responsibility for all tasks, and schedule due dates.
3. Follow up to ensure that all checklist items are complete.

3.4   CFO   **Complete Purchase Transaction**
1. Prepare all purchase documentation and submit it to all parties for review.
2. Incorporate any final changes into the documentation.
3. Schedule a meeting with representatives from the target company, as well as all legal advisors, to sign the purchase documentation.

Complete Purchase Transaction

Policy/Procedure Statement	Procedure No.:	ACQ-06
Brasto Publishing	Page:	1 of 1
	Issue Date:	10/28/0X
	Supersedes:	N/A
Subject: Consolidate Operations		

1. **PURPOSE AND SCOPE**

    This procedure is used by the chief financial officer to ensure that the proper steps are followed in consolidating the operations of an acquired entity into those of the company.

2. **RESPONSIBILITIES**

    CFO   **Chief Financial Officer**

3. **PROCEDURES**

3.1   CFO   **Assign Consolidation Project Team**

1. Determine the available staff and management group available for assignment to the consolidation project team.
2. Select the team from this group, based on past experience and management skill.
3. Meet with the team leader to determine the dates and locations for the consolidation project.

3.2   CFO   **Setup Consolidation Guidelines and Deadlines**

1. Review the team leader's recommendations for deadlines and revise as necessary.
2. Review with the team leader the standard set of consolidation activities and revise it as necessary, depending on the conditions at the target company.
3. Create a list of milestone dates and meetings to review progress.
4. Meet with the entire consolidation team to review the project plans.

3.3   CFO   **Conduct Milestone Progress Reviews**

1. Meet with the consolidation team on the previously specified dates to review progress.
2. Address the need for changes in the composition of the team to ensure that due dates are met, or else modify the due dates.
3. Issue a written communication to the team leader regarding expectations for the next milestone meeting.

Consolidate Operations

Policy/Procedure Statement	Retrieval No.:	ACQ-07
Brasto Publishing	Page:	1 of 1
	Issue Date:	10/28/0X
	Supersedes:	N/A
Subject: Conduct Postacquisition Review		

1. **PURPOSE AND SCOPE**
   This procedure is used by the chief financial officer to ensure that solutions are found to any problems encountered during the acquisition process.

2. **RESPONSIBILITIES**
   CFO **Chief Financial Officer**

3. **PROCEDURES**

3.1 CFO **Conduct Postacquisition Review**
   1. Schedule a review meeting with members of the consolidation team.
   2. Issue an agenda of discussion items in advance of the meeting.
   3. Review all issues that arose during the latest consolidation that related to increased costs or delayed deadlines, as well as new initiatives for correcting both problems, plus concerns raised by team members.

3.2 CFO **Assign Responsibilities for Resulting Projects**
   1. Specify who is responsible for projects that will improve the consolidation process the next time. Set up deadlines and precisely define expectations.
   2. Agree to the date and subject matter for a follow-up meeting regarding these issues.

Conduct Postacquisition Review

Policy/Procedure Statement		Procedure No.:	BIL-01
Brasto Publishing		Page:	1 of 1
		Issue Date:	10/28/0X
		Supersedes:	N/A
Subject: Ship to Customer			

1. **PURPOSE AND SCOPE**

   This procedure is used by the shipping supervisor to ensure that the proper paperwork and computer transactions are completed when product is shipped to a customer.

2. **RESPONSIBILITIES**

   SHIPPING   **Shipping Supervisor**

3. **PROCEDURES**

   3.1   SHIPPING   **Print Daily Shipping List**

   Go to the REPORTS screen in the computer system and access the Shipping List report. Enter today's date and press ENTER. The report will print.

   3.2   SHIPPING   **Verify That all Shipments Are Available**
   1. Go to the INVENTORY menu and select the ON HAND screen. Verify that all finished goods listed on the shipping list are also noted on the screen as being on hand and available for ship ment.
   2. If the required quantities are not available, contact the customer service staff to ascertain customer wishes regarding partial orders, or contact the production scheduling staff to ensure that the production department will complete the missing products as soon as possible.
   3. Mark all other items on the shipping list as being ready for delivery.

   3.3   SHIPPING   **Prepare Shipments**
   1. Using the shipping list, remove all targeted items from the warehouse bins and relocate them to the sllipping area.
   2. Contact freight carriers regarding pickup times.
   3. Prepare bills of lading and packing slips for all shipments.
   4. Load shipments on trucks for delivery.

   3.4   SHIPPING   **Complete Related Paperwork**
   1. Complete the shipping log.
   2. Send copies of the bills of lading and packing slips to the accounting department by interoffice mail. Include a copy of the day's shipping log, which should match all other documentation sent.

   3.5   SHIPPING   **Complete Related Computer Transactions**

   Go to the INVENTORY menu in the computer system. Access the SHIP screen and enter the customer, ship date, part number, and quantity shipped for each shipment sent out that day.

Policy/Procedure Statement	Retrieval No.:	BIL-02
	Page:	1 of 1
	Issue Date:	10/28/0X
	Supersedes:	N/A

Brasto Publishing

Subject: Drop Ship Inventory

1. **PURPOSE AND SCOPE**
   This procedure is used by the order entry and accounting staffs to ensure that products are shipped directly to customers from suppliers, and that the company properly invoices customers for these deliveries.

2. **RESPONSIBILITIES**
   ACC STAFF   **Accounting Staff**
   OE STAFF   **Order Entry Staff**

3. **PROCEDURES**

   3.1   OE STAFF   **Relay Customer Order for Drop Shipment**
   1. If a customer order arrives through an automated Web order entry system, the order entry system automatically flags an item as a drop shipment from a supplier to the customer, and sends an electronic data interchange or e-mail message to the supplier, containing all relevant shipment information. The order entry system or staff then verifies a return receipt message from the supplier.
   2. If a customer order is entered manually by the order entry staff, they enter it in the order entry database in the usual manner. The logistics staff identifies the ordered item as a drop shipment, and notifies the supplier of all shipment information; either by fax, e-mail, or electronic data interchange. The logistics staff then verifies a return receipt message from the supplier.

   3.2   ACC STAFF   **Invoice Customer for Drop Shipment**
   1. Upon shipment of the order, the supplier sends to the company accounting department a shipping notification, identifying the customer, date of shipment, and items and quantities shipped.
   2. The accounting staff prepares two copies of an invoice and sends one to the customer.
   3. The accounting staff makes two copies of the shipping notification, attaches the original to the retained invoice, and files it in the customer file. It retains the first copy of the shipping notification until the supplier bills the company for the shipped goods, at which point the accounts payable staff attaches the notification to the supplier invoice as proof of delivery and processes the invoice for payment.
   4. The accounting staff sends the remaining copy of the shipping notification to the order entry staff, which logs the shipment into the order entry system, thereby completing the order in the system. If the supplier's delivery only partially fills an order, the order entry staff contacts the supplier to discuss the delivery date for any backlogged items.

3.3	OE STAFF	**Verify Drop Shipment Delivery**
		1. The accounting staff periodically investigates all supplier invoices for which no shipping notification has been received. This involves contacting the supplier for a copy of the shipping notification and then billing the customer based on the information in the shipping notification.
		2. The order entry staff periodically investigates all customer orders for which no supplier shipping notification has been received. This involves sending a summary list of all unfilled orders from the order entry system to the supplier, verifying receipt of the list, and discussing shipment options.

Drop Ship Inventory

Policy/Procedure Statement	Retrieval No.:	BIL-03
	Page:	1 of 1
Brasto Publishing	Issue Date:	10/28/0X
	Supersedes:	N/A
Subject: Enter Billing in Computer		

1. **PURPOSE AND SCOPE**
    This procedure is used by the accounts receivable clerk to complete daily billings to customers.

2. **RESPONSIBILITIES**
    ACC RECV   **Accounts Receivable Clerk**

3. **PROCEDURES**

3.1 ACC RECV **Shipping Paperwork**
Find the shipping paperwork in the "shippers" box in the mail room. The paperwork should include a handwritten shipping log, as well as white and green copies of the bills of lading. Separate these documents into different piles.

3.2 ACC RECV **Verify Bills of Lading**
Verify that there is a bill of lading for every order listed on the shipping log, and also that all bills of lading are listed on the log. Then put the bills of lading in order, first by customer number and then by order number (if there is more than one order per customer). Next, check the "carrier" column of the shipping log. Most orders will have "Customer Pickup" listed next to them. Any accompanying freight sheet is filled out by the shipping department. These are usually turned in ahead of time and kept in a file. Pull out the appropriate sheets, because they are needed for invoicing.

3.3	ACC RECV	**Review Freight Sheets**
		Review the freight sheets. If the bill of lading reads "Packing List" on the top, the order has already been picked by the shipping department. If it reads "Customer Order Picklist" and the shipment quantities are handwritten in the blanks, the order still must be picked. To pick an order, go to SHIP in the software, enter the issue type, and then enter the customer number. If the quantity showing on the screen for an item matches the quantity handwritten in the bill of lading, press ENTER to pick that item. If the quantities differ, type the handwritten quantity into the order and press ENTER. Pick all of the items on the order, and then proceed to the next order.
3.4	ACC RECV	**List All Picked Orders**
		List all picked orders. The resulting list should include all the orders in the stack, plus any orders shipped out today. In this step, go through the list and choose only those orders that were shipped the previous day and for which there are bills of lading. It may be difficult to determine the order numbers for some shipments, because there may be more than one sequence number for the same customer order number. You may need to look at all of the orders with a particular order number to find the correct one. To pick one, make sure the item numbers and quantities match the bill of lading.
3.5	ACC RECV	**Check Pricing**
		Check the pricing for each order and verify that there is a charge for pallets and shipping. Enter the customer order number and sequence number to check prices. Each customer has a price sheet in the price book that lists current prices for all of the items it orders. The price sheet will also tell you whether or not to charge that customer for pallets. This is also where the freight sheet is used. Check the freight code on the order and make sure that it matches what the shipping department has written on the freight sheet. If the code is "prepaid," do not charge the customer for freight. If it is "prepay and add," you must add the amount on the freight sheet to the invoice. If the order was sent collect, there will be no freight sheet, because the customer is arranging and paying for its own freight.

Enter Billing in Computer

Policy/Procedure Statement	Retrieval No.:	BIL-04
Brasto Publishing	Page:	1 of 1
	Issue Date:	10/28/0X
	Supersedes:	N/A
Subject: Issue Recurring Invoices		

1. **PURPOSE AND SCOPE**

   This procedure is used by the billing staff to issue recurring invoices near month-end, for goods or services provided during the following month.

2. **RESPONSIBILITIES**

ACC RECV	**Accounts Receivable Clerk**
PRICING	**Pricing Clerk**
SALES	**Sales Staff**

3. **PROCEDURES**

   3.1 ACC RECV **Print Billing Report**
   1. Two weeks prior to month-end, print two copies of the Recurring Invoices report for the following month.
   2. Forward a copy to the sales manager and pricing clerk, with a request for them to note any corrections directly on the report and then return it to the accounts receivable clerk.

   3.2 PRICING **Verify Pricing**
   1. Verify the accuracy of all product or service prices listed on the report. Note changes directly on the report.
   2. Return the report to the accounts receivable clerk.

   3.3 SALES **Verify Contact Information**
   1. Verify the accuracy of all contact information listed on the report. Note changes directly on the report.
   2. Note changes to recurring goods or services on the report. If a customer has canceled further activity, cross out the customer.
   3. Return the report to the accounts receivable clerk.

   3.4 ACC RECV **Correct and Issue Invoices**
   1. Upon receipt of the corrected reports, enter all changes noted by the pricing clerk and sales staff in the computer system.
   2. Reprint the Recurring Invoices report and verify that all corrections have been made.
   3. Reset the date of the accounting software to the first day of the following month.
   4. Use Procedure BIL-05 to create invoices based on the Recurring Invoices report.
   5. When completed, reset the date of the accounting software back to the current date.
   6. Issue the resulting invoices to customers at once.

Issue Recurring Invoices

Policy/Procedure Statement	Retrieval No.:	BIL-05
	Page:	1 of 1
Brasto Publishing	Issue Date:	10/28/0X
	Supersedes:	N/A
Subject: Print and Issue Invoice		

1. **PURPOSE AND SCOPE**
   This procedure is used by the accounts receivable clerk to print and issue invoices to customers as well as to file.

2. **RESPONSIBILITIES**
   ACC RECV   **Accounts Receivable Clerk**

3. **PROCEDURES**
   3.1   ACC RECV   **Create Electronic Invoice**
   1. Install the latest version of Adobe Acrobat software.
   2. Go to the Create Invoice screen in the accounting software. Enter all information for the new invoice. When complete, print a test invoice. Verify that the following information on the invoice is correct:

      - Accounting department contact information
      - Contact information for a credit card payment
      - The payment due date
      - The early payment discount date

   3. Print the invoice to the "Adobe PDF" printer that will appear in the list of available printers. Use the invoice number as the file name.
   4. Send the invoice to a customer by linking it to an e-mail message as a file attachment.

   3.2   ACC RECV   **Create Paper Invoice**
   1. Go to the Create Invoice screen in the accounting software. Enter all information for the new invoice. When complete, print a test invoice as noted in section 3.1.
   2. Go to the Billing Batch screen and select all unprinted invoices.
   3. Turn on the printer and verify that the continuous-feed invoice stock is correctly positioned in it.
   4. Print a sample invoice to ensure that the line settings are correct.
   5. Verify that the continuous-feed invoice stock has not been burst.
   6. Print the complete batch of invoices.
   7. Scan the invoices to ensure that they were correctly printed. Have a second person independently review all large-dollar invoices to ensure that the correct quantities, prices, extensions, and sales taxes were used.
   8. If there are no errors, check off the flag in the accounting software asking if the print run was successful.

3.3	ACC RECV	**Prepare and Send Invoices**

3.3　ACC RECV　**Prepare and Send Invoices**
1. Burst all invoices, with the white copies going to the CUSTOMER bin, the goldenrod copies to the ALPHABETICAL FILE bin, and the pink copies to the NUMERICAL FILE bin.
2. Stuff envelopes with the white invoice copies.
3. Stamp "Address Correction Requested" on every envelope.
4. Affix postage to the envelopes and put them in the interoffice mail, marked for outside delivery.

3.4　ACC RECV　**File Invoice Copies**
1. Attach the pink invoice copies to the billing of lading and packing slip copies, and file by customer.
2. File the goldenrod copies in numerical order.

Print and Issue Invoice

Policy/Procedure Statement	Retrieval No.:	BIL-06
	Page:	1 of 1
Brasto Publishing	Issue Date:	10/28/0X
	Supersedes:	N/A
Subject: Receive and Deposit Cash		

1. **PURPOSE AND SCOPE**
   This procedure is used by the mailroom and cash clerk to receive cash from a variety of sources and deposit it into the company bank account.

2. **RESPONSIBILITIES**
   CASH   **Cash Clerk**
   MAIL   **Mailroom Staff**

3. **PROCEDURES**

   3.1   MAIL   **Receive Checks and Cash Through Mail**
   1. Enter today's date on a new copy of the Mailroom Remittance Sheet (see Exhibit 6.12).
   2. Enter on the Sheet for each check received the check number, customer name, the city and state from which the payment was sent, and the amount paid. If cash is received, enter this amount in the "Source if not check" column. Enter the grand total of all checks and cash received at the bottom of the Sheet. Sign and date the Sheet.
   3. Insert all checks and cash received, along with the completed Sheet and a remittance copy, in a locking interoffice mail pouch and have it couriered to the Cash Clerk.
   4. When the courier returns with an initialed copy of the Sheet, showing evidence of receipt by the Cash Clerk, file it by date in a locking cabinet in the mailroom.

   3.2   CASH   **Total and Record Cash**
   1. Open the interoffice mail pouch from the mailroom containing the daily checks and cash receipts. Initial the enclosed copy of the Mailroom Remittance Sheet and return it by courier to the mailroom.
   2. Summarize all cash and checks received on an adding machine tape.
   3. Enter all checks received on a deposit slip, as well as cash receipts in a lump sum. Verify that the deposit slip total and the adding machine tape total are the same. If not, recount the cash and checks.

   3.3   CASH   **Prepare and Issue Deposit**
   1. Give the deposit slip and attached checks and cash to the second cash clerk, who compares the check total to the Mailroom remittance Sheet forwarded from the mailroom. Reconcile any differences.
   2. Split all remittance advices from the checks, and copy all checks that have invoice numbers written on them. Verify that this packet of information matches the total that is to be sent to the bank in the deposit.
   3. Send the completed deposit to the bank by courier.

   3.4   CASH   **Forward Information**
   Send the remittance advice packet to the accounts receivable staff, which will apply it to outstanding accounts receivable.

Receive and Deposit Cash

Company Name
Mailroom Remittance Sheet
Receipts of [Month/Day/Year]

Check Number	Source if Not Check	Sender	City and State	Amount
1602		The Rush Airplane Company	Scranton, PA	$ 126.12
	Cash	Rental Air Service	Stamford, CT	$ 19.50
2402		Automatic Service Company	Los Angeles, CA	$ 316.00
1613		Voe Parts Dealer	Toledo, OH	$ 2.90
9865		Brush Electric Company	Chicago, IL	$ 25.50
2915		Ajax Manufacturing Company	Cleveland, OH	$ 1,002.60
8512		Apex Machine Tool Co.	New York, NY	$ 18.60

Total Receipts $ 1,511.22

Prepared by: _____
Date: _____

Exhibit 6.12   Mailroom Remittance Sheet

Policy/Procedure Statement	Retrieval No.:	BIL-07
	Page:	1 of 1
Brasto Publishing	Issue Date:	10/28/0X
	Supersedes:	N/A
Subject: Process Credit Card Receipts		

1.   PURPOSE AND SCOPE
This procedure is used by the cash clerk to process credit card payments through an Internet-based processing site.

2.   RESPONSIBILITIES
CASH   **Cash Clerk**

3.   PROCEDURES
3.1   CASH   **Collect Credit Card Information**
Verify that the customer has supplied all information required for the credit card processing: name on the card, credit card number, expiration date, and billing address. Also retain the customer's phone number in case the payment is not accepted, so corrected information can be obtained.

3.2   CASH   **Enter Credit Card Transaction**
1. Access the Internet credit card processing site and log in.
2. Enter all customer-supplied information on the Web screen, as well as the invoice number, amount to be billed, and a brief description of the billing.
3. If the transaction is not accepted, call the customer and review all supplied information to determine its accuracy. As an alternative, obtain information for a different credit card from the customer.
4. If the transaction is accepted, go to the accounting computer system and log in the cash receipt associated with the transaction. Date the transaction one day forward, since this more closely corresponds to the settlement date and corresponding receipt of cash.

3.3   CASH   **Complete Related Paperwork**
1. Stamp the invoice with a "Paid in Full" stamp, initial the stamp, and make a copy of it.
2. Mail one copy of the stamped invoice to the person whose name was on the credit card (*not* the person listed on the invoice, if any), since this person will need it as a receipt.
3. Enter the cash receipt in the computer system, labeling it as a credit card receipt, and file the remaining copy in the customer file by date.

Process Credit Card Receipts

Policy/Procedure Statement	Retrieval No.:	BIL-08
	Page:	1 of 1
Brasto Publishing	Issue Date:	10/28/0X
	Supersedes:	N/A
Subject: Apply Cash to Accounts Receivable		

1. **PURPOSE AND SCOPE**

   This procedure is used by the accounts receivable clerk to apply cash received from customers to open accounts receivable balances.

2. **RESPONSIBILITIES**

   ACC RECV   **Accounts Receivable Clerk**

3. **PROCEDURES**

   3.1   ACC RECV   **Summarize Cash Receipts**

   Add up all daily cash receipts and match the paper tape of the summarization to the individual payments to ensure that the total is correct.

   3.2   ACC RECV   **Enter Total Cash Amount**

   Go to the accounting software and enter the APPLY screen. At the top of the screen, enter today's date and the total amount to be applied.

   3.3   ACC RECV   **Apply Individual Payment Amounts**

   1. For each customer payment, enter the customer number, individual check amount, the check number and date, and then TAB to the detail section of the screen. If the check is from a customer not listed in the Customer Master File, then manually enter the customer name in the Customer Name field.
   2. The list of all open invoices for each customer will appear. Click on each invoice being paid and enter any discounts taken.
   3. If some portion of the check is for an invoice not currently unpaid, then credit the payment to the Other Liabilities account, and note any supporting information in the Details field.
   4. After identifying all invoices paid by each customer, click on the "Next Payment" button at the bottom of the screen. Continue in this fashion until all receipts have been entered.

   3.4   ACC RECV   **Notify Collections Staff of Incomplete Payments**

   1. If a customer has made an incomplete payment, print the Cash Receipts Report for the day when the payment was recorded.
   2. Highlight all partial payments on the report, and make additional notations as necessary.
   3. Forward the report to the credit manager.

   3.5   CREDIT   **Thank Customers for Timely Payment**

   1. Print the Customer Ledger Report. Scan through the report and select ten customers at random who have paid for invoices in a timely manner.
   2. Access the Customer Master File and locate the contact information for each of the selected customer's accounts payable managers.
   3. Call each accounts payable manager and thank him or her for the timely payment.

   3.6   ACC RECV   **File Receipt Documentation**

   Staple the cash receipts report to the daily cash receipts, and file the set of documents in the applied cash filing cabinet.

Apply Cash to Accounts Receivable

Policy/Procedure Statement	Retrieval No.:	BIL-09
Brasto Publishing	Page:	1 of 1
	Issue Date:	10/28/0X
	Supersedes:	N/A
Subject: Review Unapplied Cash		

1. **PURPOSE AND SCOPE**

    This procedure is used by the cash application staff to disposition all cash receipts that cannot be applied to open accounts receivable.

2. **RESPONSIBILITIES**

    ACC RECV   **Accounts Receivable Clerk**

3. **PROCEDURES**

    3.1 ACC RECV   **Print Unapplied Cash Report**

    Go to the accounting software and print the Unapplied Cash Report. If there is no such report, go to the General Ledger Report and select only the Unapplied Cash general ledger account, and print the detail.

    3.2 ACC RECV   **Investigate Discounted Payments**

    1. Examine the remittance advice accompanying each unapplied check payment and compare the indicated invoice number to the same invoice number in the Accounts Receivable Aging Report.
    2. Contact the customer's accounts payable staff and determine why the payment was discounted from the original invoice amount. Document the answer.
    3. Discuss the reasons for discounts taken with the credit manager or controller. If the reason is acceptable, apply the payment to the invoice and process a credit (see procedure CRE-09) for the remaining balance. Apply the credit against the remaining balance.
    4. If the reason for the discount taken relates to an operational issue within the company, document the problem and send it to the Chief Operating Officer for action. Also enter the following information about the discount in the corporate deduction tracking database:

        *   Customer name
        *   Date deduction taken
        *   Amount of deduction taken
        *   Invoice number on which deduction taken
        *   Reason given for deduction
        *   Customer contact information

    5. If the reason for the discount taken is not acceptable, send a letter to the customer, signed by the controller, that explains the company's position relative to the discount, and reminding the customer that it still owes the open balance.
    6. Copy the letter to the credit manager, and store another copy in the customer's file.

3.3 ACC RECV	**Return Overpayments** 1. If investigation reveals that the customer has overpaid or double paid an invoice, apply the payment to the Other Liabilities general ledger account. 2. Create a manual check to the customer for the amount of the overpayment (thereby avoiding creating a new vendor account in the computer system). 3. Apply the manual check to the Other Liabilities general ledger account to eliminate the liability. 4. Make a photocopy of the customer's check and remittance advice, and include it in a mailing to the customer with the repayment check, as well as a note describing the reason for the payment. 5. File the company copy of the remittance advice and any supporting documentation in the accounts payable files.

Review Unapplied Cash

Policy/Procedure Statement	Procedure No.:	BIL-10
	Page:	1 of 1
Brasto Publishing	Issue Date:	10/28/0X
	Supersedes:	N/A
Subject: Calculate Sales Tax Payable		

1.   PURPOSE AND SCOPE

This procedure is used by the assistant controller to calculate state and local sales taxes on monthly sales.

2.   RESPONSIBILITIES

ASST CNTLR	**Assistant Controller**
ACCT PAY	**Accounts Payable Clerk**
CONTROLLER	**Controller**

3.   PROCEDURES

3.1   ASST CNTLR   **Print Invoice Register**

Go to the "Accounts Receivable Reports" screen in the accounting software. Print out the Sales Tax Register for the preceding month. This report itemizes invoices by the state in which items were sold.

3.2   ASST CNTLR   **Summarize Invoice Totals by Taxing Region**

The report is subtotaled for each state. Extract these subtotals from the report and list the amounts on a separate sheet of paper.

3.3   ASST CNTLR   **Insert Invoice Summary Totals into Tax Documents**

Go to the tax forms file and remove a sales tax reporting form for each state in which the company recorded a sale in the previous month. Transfer the sales totals to these documents and fill out all other required fields on the forms.

3.4   CONTROLLER   **Obtain Independent Review of Tax Filings**

Take the completed sales tax forms and invoice registers to the controller, who should verify that the correct amounts have been transferred from the registers to the forms, and that all other information on the forms is correct. The controller should then sign the forms and return everything to the assistant controller.

3.5   ACCT PAY   **Obtain Check Payment for Tax Filings**

Attach a payment request form to each tax form and take them to the accounts payable clerk. This person enters the requests into the computer system for inclusion in the next check run.

3.6   ASST CNTLR   **Issue Tax Payment**

Once the check run is complete, the accounts payable clerk removes the sales tax payments from the run, attaches them to the tax forms, and mails them to the appropriate taxation authorities.

3.7   ASST CNTLR   **File Tax Records**

File the company's copy of each tax return in the sales tax files, along with the invoice register that provides backup information for each return.

Calculate Sales Tax Payable

Policy/Procedure Statement	Retrieval No.:	BIL-11
Brasto Publishing	Page:	1 of 1
	Issue Date:	10/28/0X
	Supersedes:	N/A
Subject: Calculate Commission Payable		

1. **PURPOSE AND SCOPE**

   This procedure is used by the accounts payable clerk to calculate monthly commission payments. The accounting department is responsible for this procedure.

2. **RESPONSIBILITIES**

   ACCT PAY   **Accounts Payable Clerk**
   CONTROLLER   **Controller**

3. **PROCEDURES**

   3.1 CONTROLLER **Access the Commissions Report**

   The controller prints out the commissions report that lists sales by customer detail and gives it to the accounts payable clerk. To print this report, go to the ACCOUNTS RECEIVABLE REPORTS menu and access the "Sales by Salesperson" report. Select the dates for the month for which commissions are being calculated. Then click the "Printer" icon to generate the report.

   3.2 ACCT PAY **Calculate Commissions**

   1. If paying commissions based on billings, print the Sales Journal for the commission calculation period.
   2. If paying commissions based on cash receipts, print the Cash Receipts Journal for the commission calculation period.
   3. Access the Commissions spreadsheet in Excel for each salesperson, which should be recorded in a new workbook for each month.
   4. In each commission spreadsheet, note the invoice date, number, and invoice total (net of sales tax) of invoices transferred from either the Sales Journal or Cash Receipts Journal (depending on the commission payment method). Multiply each invoice line item by the appropriate commission percentage, and calculate a commission total at the bottom of the report.

   3.3 ACCT PAY **Print the Commissions Report**

   Print a copy of the commission report for each salesperson and e-mail it to them for review. Also submit a master copy to the controller for review and approval. Following approval, print commission checks for the sales staff, staple a copy of the commission report to each check receipt, and issue the checks. File the calculations and reports in the commissions file.

3.4	AUDIT STAFF	**Audit Commissions**
		1. Determine the commission period for which commissions are to be reviewed.
		2. Obtain the approved commission plans for all sales personnel.
		3. Obtain the commission statements for all sales staff for the test period.
		4. Obtain the sales journal for the test period.
		5. Trace all commission, bonus, override, and split percentages back to the commission plans, noting any variances from the plans.
		6. Trace all invoice amounts shown on the commission statements back to the sales journal. Investigate any invoice amounts listed on the commission reports that do not match the totals shown on the sales journal. Also investigate any invoices shown on the sales journal which are not included in any of the commission statements.
		7. Verify that each statement contains an approval signature.
		8. Prepare a report of all exceptions found, along with recommendations. Forward it to the audit committee and formally review it with the controller.
		9. Schedule a date in the audit department activities calendar to return and verify that recommended changes have been implemented.

Calculate Commission Payable

Policy/Procedure Statement	Retrieval No.:	BIL-12
Brasto Publishing	Page:	1 of 1
	Issue Date:	10/28/0X
	Supersedes:	N/A
Subject: Track Exceptions Between the Shipping Log and Sales Journal		

1. **PURPOSE AND SCOPE**

   This procedure is used by the billing staff to verify that all items shipped have been properly invoiced.

2. **RESPONSIBILITIES**

   ACC RECV   **Accounts Receivable Clerk**

3. **PROCEDURES**

   3.1   ACC RECV   **Print Comparison Documents**
   1. Go to the Accounts Receivable section of the accounting software and print the Sales Journal report for the comparison period, which lists the line items on each invoice.
   2. If the Shipping Log is computerized, print it for the comparison period. Otherwise, photocopy the manual version kept in the shipping department.

   3.2   ACC RECV   **Conduct Comparison**
   1. For each invoice, trace the quantity shipped back to the shipping log for each line item, crossing off matching items on each document. Circle any items on the invoice register that do no match shipped quantities, and vice versa.
   2. Once the comparison is complete, circle all items in the Shipping Log that are not found in the Sales Journal. Also, circle all items in the Sales Journal that are not found in the Shipping Log.
   3. If there were shipped items on the Shipping Log from the immediately preceding comparison period that had not been reflected in the Sales Journal, compare the preceding period's Shipping Log to the current Sales Journal to see if they were invoiced late.
   4. Enter all exception items in the table shown in Exhibit 6.13.

   3.3   ACC RECV   **Investigate and Correct Problems Found**
   1. Review all cases on the exceptions table for which the invoiced quantity does not match the shipped quantity, and interview all applicable employees to determine the reason for the difference.
   2. Review the cases on the exceptions table for which there was no invoice to match the shipped quantity, and interview all applicable employees to determine the reason for the difference.
   3. Review the cases on the exceptions table for which there was no recorded shipment to match the invoiced quantity, and interview all applicable employees to determine the reason for the difference.

4. Compare problems found to the documentation of issues noted during the previous comparison period, and make note of ongoing repetitive problems that have not been fixed from the previous period.

5. Implement corrective invoicing where necessary with the billing staff.

6. Enter recommendations to correct problems in the exceptions table shown in Exhibit 6.13.

Track Exceptions Between the Shipping Log and Sales Journal

Per Sales Journal				Per Shipping Log			Variance	Recommended
Date	Invoice No.	Item No.	Quantity	Date	Item No.	Quantity	Reason	Improvement

Exhibit 6.13   Shipping Log/Sales Journal Exceptions Table

Policy/Procedure Statement	Retrieval No.:	BIL-13
	Page:	1 of 1
Brasto Publishing	Issue Date:	10/28/0X
	Supersedes:	N/A
Subject: Review Pricing Information		

1. **PURPOSE AND SCOPE**

   This procedure is used by the Accounts Receivable Clerk to locate all invoice pricing errors occurring during a fixed time period, determine underlying problems, and report on the results to management.

2. **RESPONSIBILITIES**

   ACC RECV   **Accounts Receivable Clerk**

3. **PROCEDURES**

   3.1   ACC RECV   **Locate Invoice Pricing Errors**
   1. Go to the accounting software and access the invoice register for the past month.
   2. Convert the invoice register to an Excel file. Open the Excel file and sort the invoice list by dollar order. Delete all invoices from the list that do not have a credit balance.
   3. Search the description field for each credit for wording regarding corrections of pricing errors. Retain these records and delete all others. Print the spreadsheet.

   3.2   ACC RECV   **Investigate Pricing Variances**
   1. Transfer the following information to a separate spreadsheet report: credit number, credit amount, customer name, correct price, actual price charged, the quantity of product to which the correction applies, the grand total pricing error, and the initials of the customer service person who processed the credit.
   2. Go to the customer service person who processed the credit and determine the cause of the pricing error. Include this information on the spreadsheet.

   3.3   ACC RECV   **Report on Pricing Variances**
   1. Print the spreadsheet and distribute it to the sales manager, controller, and chief operating officer.
   2. Enter the total number of pricing errors and the total dollar error in the monthly corporate statistics report.

Review Prioing Information

Policy/Procedure Statement		Procedure No.:	BUD-01
		Page:	1 of 1
Brasto Publishing		Issue Date:	10/28/0X
		Supersedes:	N/A
Subject: Create the Annual Budget			

1. **PURPOSE AND SCOPE**
   This procedure is used by the controller to guide the process of updating the annual budget.

2. **RESPONSIBILITIES**
   CONTROLLER   **Controller**

3. **PROCEDURES**

3.1   CONTROLLER   **Update Budget Assumptions**
   1. Review the assumptions listed on the assumptions page of the budget with senior management, and revise as necessary.
   2. Define the capacity levels of all bottleneck operations in the company, as well as the maximum capacity of key production lines and facilities. If capacity levels are expected to be significantly altered due to known downtime during the budget period, note the estimated downtime in the assumptions section of the budget.
   3. Verify that the criteria used for ranking capital budget proposals remain the same, and adjust as necessary. This should include an adjustment of the corporate and incremental cost of capital to reflect current funding conditions.
   4. Discuss with the CFO the maximum amount of funding that is likely to be available for both working capital and capital budgeting purposes during the budget period, and enter these amounts in the assumptions section of the budget.
   5. Review with senior management the step costing points at which significant new investments must be made in the company's capacity structure in all departmental areas. Note in the assumptions section the capacity levels at which these step costs will be triggered (e.g., reaching 85% production capacity on the ABC production line will require an additional $2.8 million for a supplemental production line).

3.2   CONTROLLER   **Update Expenses**
   As of mid-November, issue to each department of listing of its expenses that are annualized based on actual expenses through October of the current year. The listing should include the personnel in each department and their current pay levels. Request a return date of 10 days in the future for this information, which should include estimated changes in expenses.

3.3	CONTROLLER	**Update Revenue** As of mid-November, issue to the sales manager a listing of revenue by month by business unit, through October of the current year. Request a return date of 10 days in the future for this information, which should include estimated changes in revenues.
3.4	CONTROLLER	**Update Capital Expenditures** As of mid-November, issue a form to all department heads, requesting information about the cost and timing of capital expenditures for the upcoming year. Request a return date of 10 days in the future for this information.
3.5	CONTROLLER	**Update Automation** As of mid-November, issue a form to the manager of automation, requesting estimates of the timing and size of reductions in headcount in the upcoming year that are due to automation efforts. Request a return date of 10 days in the future for this information. Be sure to compare scheduled headcount reductions to the timing of capital expenditures, as they should track closely.
3.6	CONTROLLER	**Update the Budget Model** This task should be completed by the end of November.

- Update the numbers already listed in the budget with information as it is received from the various managers. This may involve changing "hard-coded" dollar amounts or flex budget percentages. Be sure to keep a checklist of who has returned information so you can follow up with those who have not.
- Update the "Last Year" cells on the right side of the budget model, using annualized figures.
- Verify that the indirect overhead allocation percentages shown on the budgeted factory overhead page are accurate.
- Verify that the FUTA, SUTA, FICA, medical, and workers' compensation amounts listed at the top of the staffing budget page are still accurate.
- Add job titles and staffing levels to the staffing page as needed, along with new average pay rates based on projected pay levels made by department managers.
- Run a depreciation report for the upcoming year, add the expected depreciation for new capital expenditures, and add this amount to the budget.
- Revise the loan detail budget based on projected borrowings through the end of the year.
- Verify that the groups of staff positions used to summarize payroll expenses continue to reflect the pay structure of the company. If not, create new groupings or alter existing ones to more accurately summarize payroll expenses.
- Review the summarized budget model with attached dashboard that is used by senior management. Adjust the model as necessary to reflect the needs of the senior management team.

		• Meet with the human resources (HR) manager to determine how the budget model is to be incorporated into the company's system of performance measurements and rewards, and determine what data feeds are needed from the budget model by the HR manager to accomplish this.
		• Review the general ledger accounts referenced in the budget. Eliminate any accounts for which the budgeted amounts are likely to be excessively small, merge related accounts together, add accounts for new operations, and delete accounts for operations that have been eliminated.
		• Conduct a general review of the budget model to see if it can be simplified in any way, both in terms of a reduction in the information presented and the complexity of the underlying model.
3.6	CONTROLLER	**Review the Budget** Print out the budget and circle any budgeted expenses or revenues that are significantly different from the annualized amounts for the current year. Go over the questionable items with the managers who are responsible for those items.
3.7	CONTROLLER	**Revise the Budget** Revise the budget, print it again, and review it with senior management. Incorporate any additional changes.
3.8	CONTROLLER	**Issue the Budget** Bind the budget and issue it to the management team.

Create the Annual Budget

Policy/Procedure Statement	Procedure No.:	BUD-02
Brasto Publishing	Page:	1 of 1
	Issue Date:	10/28/0X
	Supersedes:	N/A
Subject: Load Budget into Financials		

1. **PURPOSE AND SCOPE**

   This procedure is used by the controller to enter all data from the budget model into the financial statement database in the computer system.

2. **RESPONSIBILITIES**

   CONTROLLER   **Controller**

3. **PROCEDURES**

   3.1   CONTROLLER   **Locate Budget Model**
   1. Call up the completed budget model.
   2. Print the budget.
   3. Verify that there is a valid account number for every budget line item in the budget model.
   4. Highlight the budget numbers that must be input into the financial statement database.

   3.2   CONTROLLER   **Access Computer Input Screen**
   1. Call up the accounting software package, and access the BUDGET menu. Then access the INPUT BUDGET screen from that menu.
   2. Enter the appropriate budget year to be entered, as well as the budget version.

   3.3   CONTROLLER   **Enter Budget Information**
   1. Enter the account number for each budget line item.
   2. Enter the budget in each month on the screen for that account number.
   3. Verify that the months entered and the amounts are correct, and then press ENTER.
   4. Repeat for all account numbers.

   3.4   CONTROLLER   **Verify Entered Information**
   1. Go to the BUDGET menu and access the REPORTS screen.
   2. Select the BUDGET report and enter the correct budget year and version. Print the report.
   3. Compare the entered amounts to the amounts listed on the budget model. Go back to step 3.3 to correct any incorrectly entered budget numbers.

Load Budget into Financials

Policy/Procedure Statement	Retrieval No.:	BUD-03
	Page:	1 of 1
	Issue Date:	10/28/0X
Brasto Publishing	Supersedes:	N/A
Subject: Create Budget Variance Report		

1. PURPOSE AND SCOPE

This procedure is used by the financial analyst to calculate and report on the extent of actual financial results from budgeted expectations.

2. RESPONSIBILITIES

FINL ANALYST   **Financial Analyst**

3. PROCEDURES

3.1   FINL ANALYST   **Locate Budget Variance Spreadsheet**

Call up the budget variance spreadsheet.

3.2   FINL ANALYST   **Enter New Year Budget**

1. Enter all expense line items from the budget model into the variance model.
2. Verify that the same managers listed in the variance report from last year are still responsible for expense line items this year.
3. Send the preliminary variance report to the controller to verify the accuracy of the format and numbers.

3.3   FINL ANALYST   **Enter Year-to-Date Actual Amounts**

1. Enter both year-to-date and last month actual expenses in the report.
2. Verify that the expense totals match the numbers in the financial statements.
3. Sort the report by responsible manager and subdivide the report so that each manager only receives the listing of accounts for which they are responsible.

3.4   FINL ANALYST   **Issue Variance Report**

1. Schedule meetings with all department managers who are receiving the report.
2. Go over all negative variance items, and record their responses regarding actions to take to correct problems.
3. Include manager comments in the final variance report, and issue it to senior management.

Create Budget Variance Report

Policy/Procedure Statement	Procedure No.:	BUD-04
	Page:	1 of 1
Brasto Publishing	Issue Date:	10/28/0X
	Supersedes:	N/A
Subject: Conduct Quarterly Budget Review		

1. **PURPOSE AND SCOPE**

   This procedure is used by the controller to review with other department managers the comparison of actual to budgeted financial results for their departments for the last quarter.

2. **RESPONSIBILITIES**

   CONTROLLER   **Controller**

3. **PROCEDURES**

   3.1   CONTROLLER   **Prepare Quarterly Budget Report**
   1. Extract the most recent budget variance report.
   2. Print copies of the report and issue it to those managers who are listed as being responsible for expense line items.

   3.2   CONTROLLER   **Conduct Manager Interviews**
   1. Meet with managers to verify their intentions regarding currently negative variances.
   2. Record these comments on the report.
   3. Supply managers with any additional requested information, such as added detail regarding expenses, or copies of actual supplier invoices.

   3.3   CONTROLLER   **Report Results to General Manager**
   1. Highlight all negative variances on the budget report, and sort it by the names of responsible managers.
   2. Issue the completed budget variance report to the general manager.

Conduct Quarterly Budget Review

Policy/Procedure Statement	Retrieval No.:	CRE-01
	Page:	1 of 1
Brasto Publishing	Issue Date:	10/28/0X
	Supersedes:	N/A
Subject: Order Entry		

1.   PURPOSE AND SCOPE

This procedure is used by the order entry staff to process customer orders.

2.   RESPONSIBILITIES

ORDER   **Order Entry Staff**

3.   PROCEDURES

3.1   ORDER   **Review Electronic Orders**

1. Call up the Electronic Order screen, which contains all electronic orders received from customers.
2. If the dollar value of the order exceeds $___ contact the customer and request a formal, signed purchase order in addition to the regular electronic order.
3. If the computer system indicates that an ordered item is out of stock, e-mail the customer and indicate both an estimated shipment date and suggest a replacement item that is currently in stock.
4. Scan all customer orders for which credit limits have been established and where credit limits have not been exceeded. E-mail the credit manager to review the credit limits of any existing customers whose total receivables outstanding are over 80% of their credit limits.
5. Access only those orders for which the computer system has no record of an established level of customer credit. Accept the order if the total amount is less than $___. Otherwise, e-mail the customer with a link to an electronic form for a customer application, and put the order on hold until the customer forwards a completed form.
6. Access only those orders for which the customer has an established line of credit, but has placed no order in at least one year. Accept the order if the total amount is less than $___. Otherwise, e-mail the customer with a link to an electronic form for a customer application with a note explaining that a periodic resubmission is necessary. Put the order on hold until the customer forwards a completed form.
7. Access only those orders for which the credit limit has been exceeded. E-mail the customer with a link to an electronic form for a customer application with a note explaining that a new credit application is required whenever the credit limit is exceeded. Put the order on hold until the customer forwards a completed form. Also notify the credit manager of the situation.

3.2	ORDER	**Forward New Credit Applications to Credit Department**
		1. Call up the Completed Credit Application screen each day and access all applications completed since the last review date.
		2. Verify that all information requested on the form has been completed. If not, send the electronic form back to the customer with a request to enter information in the incomplete field(s). If fields are repeatedly not completed or done so incorrectly, e-mail the information technology staff with a request to redesign the electronic form, so that the system will not accept a form until all fields are completed within certain delimited ranges.
		3. Forward the completed credit application information to the credit manager for further disposition.
3.3	ORDER	**Review Confirming Purchase Orders**
		1. Upon receipt of a confirming purchase order, call up the original order in the computer system and compare all terms and conditions between the two documents.
		2. If there are significant adverse conditions imposed by the confirming purchase order, notify the credit manager of the situation and forward to him or her a copy of the confirming purchase order. Place the order on hold until notified by the credit manager.

Order Entry

Policy/Procedure Statement	Retrieval No.:	CRE-02
Brasto Publishing	Page:	1 of 1
	Issue Date:	10/28/0X
	Supersedes:	N/A
Subject: Obtain Customer Credit Data		

1. PURPOSE AND SCOPE

This procedure is used by the credit clerk to obtain credit information about prospective customers and determine an initial credit limit.

2. RESPONSIBILITIES

CREDIT   **Credit Clerk**

3. PROCEDURES

3.1   CREDIT   **Obtain Credit References**
1. Pull the Customer Credit Application form (Exhibit 6.14) from the forms cabinet.
2. Fax the form to the customer who is requesting credit.
3. If the customer requests the form by e-mail, copy if from the Forms subdirectory and attach it to an e-mail.

3.2   CREDIT   **Contact Credit References**
1. Verify with each customer reference listed on the form the maximum and average amounts of credit granted and used, as well as any issues with slow payment.
2. Obtain the names of other credit references from these references, if possible, and record the answers to the same questions from them.
3. Contact the bank reference listed on the form and verify the existence and duration of the applicant's activity with the bank.
4. Document all information obtained and attach it to the completed Customer Credit Application form.

3.3   CREDIT   **Obtain Credit Information from Other Sources**
1. Contact Dun & Bradstreet's automated online credit reporting system, enter the customer's address, and specify that you want to receive the Business Information Report.
2. Print the Business Report and attach it to the completed Customer Credit Application form.

3.4   CREDIT   **Assign Credit Limit to Customer**
1. Assign the standard initial company credit limit of $___ to the customer. If the initial customer order size is larger than the standard initial credit limit or if the application or credit report indicate some danger of not being paid, review the credit limit with the Controller.
2. Enter the credit limit in the "For Company Use" part of the Customer Credit Application, as well as the customer number as assigned by the computer system, and sign and date this entry.
3. Enter the approved initial credit limit in the computer system.
4. File the completed Customer Credit Application in alphabetical order by customer name.

Obtain Customer Credit Data

Customer Credit Application

Contact

Company Name: _____

For Company Use

Customer No:	
Credit Limit:	
Date Approved:	
Approved By:	

Address: _____

Address: _____

City: _____ State: ____ Zip: _____

Date Started: _____ State of Incorporation: _____

Parent Company Name and Address: _____

Contact Name: _____ Phone: _____

Web Site: _____ Fax: _____

Credit

Credit Requested: $_____ Annual Sales: $_____

Annual Profit: $_____ Total Cash: $_____

Total Debt: $_____ Retained Earnings: $_____

Bank Name: _____ Bank Contact: _____

Bank Address: _____

Checking Account Number: _____ Savings Account Number: _____

References

Reference Name: _____ Phone: _____

Reference Address: _____

Reference Name: _____ Phone: _____

Reference Address: _____

Reference Name: _____ Phone: _____

Reference Address: _____

I hereby authorize the above-referenced bank and trading partners to release credit information to the Company for use in reviewing this credit application.

Officer Signature: _____

Print Officer Name: _____ Officer Title: _____

Return to The Company
Address
City State, Zip Code

Exhibit 6.14 Customer Credit Application

Policy/Procedure Statement	Retrieval No.:	CRE-03
	Page:	1 of 1
Brasto Publishing	Issue Date:	10/28/0X
	Supersedes:	N/A
Subject: Credit Policy Modification		

1. PURPOSE AND SCOPE
This procedure is used by the credit manager to modify credit levels granted based on various internal and external conditions.

2. RESPONSIBILITIES
CREDIT MGR   **Credit Manager**

3. PROCEDURES

3.1   CREDIT MGR   **Credit Modification Based on Product Margins**

1. Create a Gross Margin Report listing all products, with their associated gross margins, and sorted by gross margin percentage. Establish the weighted average gross margin for all products listed in the report, with the weighting based on sales volume.
2. Establish a credit multiplier for higher product margins above the weighted average, and the reverse for product margins lower than the weighted average. For example, if the gross margin on product Alpha is 40% and the weighted average is 25%, then allow a credit multiplier of 1.15 for sales of Alpha.
3. Organize a quarterly meeting involving the sales manager, cost accountant, and credit staff to review changes in product-based credit multipliers.
4. During the meeting, distribute the latest Gross Margin report with associated credit multipliers to the credit staff and roll play how the multipliers are to be used if customers request credit for a purchase.

3.2   CREDIT MGR   **Credit Modification Based on Economic Conditions**

1. Organize a quarterly meeting involving the sales manager, credit manager, and chief operating officer to discuss trends in economic conditions that are affecting the company.
2. Using relevant leading indicators and anecdotal evidence, determine if there is sufficient evidence of economic changes within the industry to warrant a change in the corporate credit policy. For example, a general expansion in the economy may warrant the introduction of a multiplier into the credit scoring model of 1.2, so that all credit scores are automatically increased by 20%, allowing customers 20% higher credit limits.
3. Document the reasons for the credit multiplier change and send it as a memo to all meeting participants for sign-off.
4. Send an authorization to the credit clerk to access the credit scoring software and alter the economic conditions multiplier.

		5. If the multiplier has been reduced, print the Available Credit Report, showing the total credit allowed for each customer and the net credit available, to see if the multiplier reduction has resulted in any customers exceeding their credit limits. If so, meet with the credit staff to determine strategies for bringing these customers into compliance with the revised credit level.
		6. If the multiplier has been increased, print the Available Credit Report and send it to the sales manager, who can use it to target more sales to customers with newly available credit.
3.3	CREDIT MGR	**Credit Modification Based on Product Obsolescence**
		1. Obtain the monthly report of inventory items declared obsolete by the Materials Review Board.
		2. Review the list with the purchasing staff to determine which obsolete items on the list can be successfully disposed of at reduced margins, and cross them off the report. This should leave nothing on the report but items expected to be scrapped.
		3. Issue the reduced obsolete inventory list to the sales staff and credit department, with instructions that there is no credit requirement on sales of these items.

Credit Policy Modification

Policy/Procedure Statement	Retrieval No.:	CRE-04
Brasto Publishing	Page:	1 of 1
	Issue Date:	10/20/0X
	Supersedes:	N/A
Subject: Review Data and Create Credit Limit		

1. **PURPOSE AND SCOPE**
   This procedure is used by the Controller to adjust customer credit limits on an ongoing and regularly scheduled basis.

2. **RESPONSIBILITIES**
   CONTROLLER   **Controller**

3. **PROCEDURES**

3.1   CONTROLLER   **Access the Customer Account**
       Access the Customer file in the computer system and extract the customer name, account code, credit limit, standard payment terms, and sales for the year-to-date to an electronic spreadsheet.

3.2   CONTROLLER   **Annualize the Sales Report**
       Annualize the year-to-date sales figure extracted from the Customer file, so it shows the projected full-year sale level for each customer. Review the sales figure for each customer and adjust it for any seasonal variations that would result in significant changes to the computed annualized sales figure.

3.3   CONTROLLER   **Enter Bad Debt Information**
       Add to the spreadsheet the total amount of any bad debts incurred by the company for each customer.

3.4   CONTROLLER   **Enter Overdue Receivable Balances**
       Enter in separate columns in the spreadsheet the current amount of receivables due from customers that are more than 45 days old and more than 90 days old.

3.5   CONTROLLER   **Determine Modified Credit Limits**
       1. In the spreadsheet, divide the annualized sales for each customer by its standard payment terms, yielding an estimated credit limit.
       2. Sort the spreadsheet by bad debts and overdue receivable balances to highlight problem customers, and review and manually modify the estimated credit limits for them.
       3. Ignore any calculated changes modifying the existing credit limit by no more than ten percent.
       4. Using the revised spreadsheet, discuss significant changes to the existing credit limits with the Controller and obtain his or her approval of the changes.

3.6   CONTROLLER   **Enter Changes**
       Round the calculated changes in the estimated customer credit limits from the spreadsheet to the nearest $___. Enter the calculated credit limit changes in the accounting database for each customer.

Review Data and Create Credit Limit

Policy/Procedure Statement	Retrieval No.:	CRE-05
	Page:	1 of 1
Brasto Publishing	Issue Date:	10/28/0X
	Supersedes:	N/A
Subject: Create and Update a Customer Credit File		

1. **PURPOSE AND SCOPE**
   This procedure is used by the credit staff to set up and update customer credit files.

2. **RESPONSIBILITIES**
   CR STAFF   **Credit Staff**

3. **PROCEDURES**
   3.1   CR STAFF   **Create Credit File**
   1. Access the customer master file and determine if a new applicant has purchased from the company in the past. If not listed online, also access digitized records or the paper-based customer records to see if a record exists.
   2. If there is no existing record, create a new customer index number using the first five characters of the customer's corporate name, followed by the first unused sequential three digit number. For example, if there were four existing companies beginning with the name SMITH, the index number for the next company whose name begins with SMITH will be SMITH005.
   3. Using the completed credit application as the source document, create a record in the customer master file, using the index number created in the preceding step.
   4. If a document imaging system is available, scan the credit application and accompanying information, such as personal guarantees and financial statements, into the system.
   5. If paper files are used to store customer records, create a label containing both the customer index number and customer name, and affix it to the file. Add a standard checklist of credit information required for the file to the inside cover of the file. An example is shown in Exhibit 6.15. Collect all records shown on the checklist, and note the date of each document on the checklist.

   3.2   CR STAFF   **Update Credit File**
   1. Once a year, export the Active Customer report, which lists sales volume by customer for the past year, to an electronic spreadsheet. Sort the report by sales volume in declining order. Print the report for all customers whose annual purchases from the company exceeded $____.
   2. For all customers whose sales exceed the limit noted in the preceding step, require new financial statements and print a new Dun & Bradstreet credit report.
   3. Once this information is received, calculate a new credit score for each customer, and require a detailed review by the credit manager.
   4. Once the credit review is complete, insert the new documents in the customer folder or digitize them and include them in the document management system.

Create and Update a Customer Credit File

DOCUMENT NEEDED		DOCUMENT DATE	INITIALS
Credit application	√	January 12, 20X7	SRB
	√	*February 01, 20X8*	*ATW*
Credit report	√	January 14, 20X7	SRB
	√	*February 06, 20X8*	*ATW*
Credit change document	√	January 18, 20X7	SRB
Customer contact information	√	January 11, 20X7	SRB
	√	*February 03, 20X8*	*ATW*
Financial statements	√	January 19, 20X7	SRB
	√	*February 10, 20X8*	*ATW*
Personal guarantee	√	January 27, 20X7	SRB

Exhibit 6.15 Customer File Checklist

Policy/Procedure Statement	Retrieval No.:	CRE-06
	Page:	1 of 1
	Issue Date:	10/28/0X
Brasto Publishing	Supersedes:	N/A
Subject: Grant Credit Based on a Credit Decision Table		

1. **PURPOSE AND SCOPE**
   This procedure is used by the credit staff to grant on-the-spot credit based on a simplified scoring system.

2. **RESPONSIBILITIES**
   CREDIT   **Credit Staff**

3. **PROCEDURES**
   3.1 CREDIT   **Grant Credit with Decision Table**
   1. If the initial order is for less than $1,000, grant credit without further review.

2. If the initial order is for between $1,000 and $10,000, require a completed credit application and financial statements. Grant credit of no more than 10% of the customer's net worth, not to exceed the amount of the initial order.

3. If the initial order is for more than $10,000, require a completed credit application and audited or reviewed financial statements. If the customer is profitable, create a credit limit of 10% of the customer's net worth. Reduce the credit limit by 10% for every percent of customer loss reported.

4. If the order is from an existing customer and there is no history of credit problems, increase the credit limit by 20% no more frequently than once every three months.

5. If the order is from an existing customer and the order exceeds the credit limit by more than 20%, or there is a history of payment problems, forward the credit request to the credit manager for review.

6. If the order is from an existing customer who has an unpaid invoice more than 60 days old, freeze the order until payment is received on the open invoice.

Grant Credit Based on a Credit Decision Table

Policy/Procedure Statement	Retrieval No.:	CRE-07
	Page:	1 of 1
Brasto Publishing	Issue Date:	10/28/0X
	Supersedes:	N/A
Subject: Conduct Collections Review		

1. PURPOSE AND SCOPE

This procedure is used by the accounts receivable clerk to manage the collections process.

2. RESPONSIBILITIES

ACC RECV   **Accounts Receivable Clerk**

3. PROCEDURES

3.1 ACC RECV   **Print Accounts Receivable Aging**

Go to the accounting software and access the ACCOUNTS RECEIVABLE screen. Print the accounts receivable aging, making sure that the aging date buckets are set at 10, 30, and 60 days. This bucket configuration will separate out all invoices that are 40 days old and older, which is the primary grouping of invoices that require collections activity.

3.2 ACC RECV   **Distribute Accounts Receivable Aging to Sales Staff**

1. Access the Accounts Receivable Aging Report (ARA Report). Using the field selection function, list the salesperson name for each invoice in the report.
2. Export the file to an Excel electronic spreadsheet.
3. Sort the ARA Report by salesperson, and then extract each salesperson's report section to a different spreadsheet. Save each spreadsheet using the name of the targeted salesperson.
4. E-mail each spreadsheet to the targeted salesperson, with an attached note regarding any collection problems.

3.3 ACC RECV   **Highlight Receivable Problems**

1. Review the ARA Report and identify all large invoices that will be due for payment within the next__days. Issue payment notification letters and copies of the invoices to these customers. Note on the ARA Report the dates on which letters were sent.
2. Review the ARA Report and circle or highlight all invoices that are more than 40 days old. These are the invoices requiring collection activity.
3. Compare the Cash Receipts Journal to the ARA Report, looking for any customers who skip large payments, only paying smaller invoices instead. Make note of this issue in the customer file, and also forward the information to the credit manager.
4. Compare the Discounts Taken Report to the ARA Report, looking for any customers who have stopped taking early payment discounts. Make note of this issue in the customer file, and also forward the information to the credit manager.

3.4	ACC RECV	**Contact Customers**

1. Stratify the customers listed on the ARA Report in declining order by total dollars overdue, using a different color highlighter to note those customers requiring the most immediate attention.
2. Print the Customer Contact Report, which contains a list of all customers, their main accounts payable contacts, e-mail addresses, phone numbers, and fax numbers. Using this information, note on the ARA Report the states in which customers are located, so calls can be placed at the correct time within the time zone of each customer.
3. Use the Customer Contact Report and the stratified version of the ARA Report to contact customers and determine why payment has not been made. If a customer states that a payment is being processed or is in the mail, verify exactly which invoices are being paid and additionally inquire about any overdue invoices not included in the incoming payment.

3.5	ACC RECV	**Maintain Contact Log**

Go to the customer contact log book and write down in it, for each customer, the date of contact, who was contacted, and what information was gained. Use this information as a reference whenever calling the customer again in the future. Also if there is new customer contact information as a result of the day's calls, update the "Customer Master Report" with this information.

3.6	ACC RECV	**Review Accounts with Credit Department**

If, as a result of the day's phone calls, it is necessary to alter a customer's credit status to more properly reflect his or her ability to pay, then go to the credit department and review the customer's credit situation with the credit manager. If new credit terms are decided upon, contact the customer to let him or her know about the revised situation.

3.7	ACC RECV	**Select Collection Tactics**

Based on the customer's payment history, the status of its latest credit report, on-site visits (if any), and the size of overdue invoices, select a mix of collection tactics from the following list, which is sorted in increasing order of severity:

- Stamp a reminder notice on late invoices
- Send invoice by certified mail
- Issue dunning letters
- Issue dunning letters by e-mail
- Issue dunning letters to managers outside the accounts payable staff
- Issue attorney letters
- Call on a regular basis
- Visit the customer
- Have a senior manager contact a counterpart at the customer
- Accept a merchandise return
- Set up a periodic payment schedule
- Convert a receivable into a promissory note
- Send a completed small claims court complaint form
- Sue customer in small claims court
- File an involuntary bankruptcy petition for the customer

Conduct Collections Review

Policy/Procedure Statement	Retrieval No.:	CRE-08
	Page:	1 of 1
	Issue Date:	10/28/0X
Brasto Publishing	Supersedes:	N/A
Subject: Resolve Collection Issues		

1. PURPOSE AND SCOPE

This procedure is used by the collections clerk to determine the causes of collection problems and find solutions to them.

2. RESPONSIBILITIES

COLLECT   **Collections Clerk**

3. PROCEDURES

3.1   COLLECT   **Summarize Collection Issues**

1. Contact the customer regarding why it has not paid each invoice on time. Note the reasons in the collections contact log (see Exhibit 3.16).
2. Based on the previous history of reasons given by the customer, ascertain if there is a correctable internal problem causing the collection issue, or if the problem lies with the customer.

3.2   COLLECT   **Correct Internal Problems**

1. Summarize all internal problems for all collection customers to determine which problems recur the most frequently. Sort the list in declining order of frequency.
2. Meet with the assistant controller to determine what actions to take internally that will correct these problems.
3. The internal controller meets with the controller regarding these issues, who meets with other department heads to determine a course of action.
4. The controller regularly follows up on these issues and consults with the collections staff to see if problem areas are declining in frequency.

3.3   COLLECT   **Increase Collection Activities**

If the problem is deemed to be with the customer, then meet with the assistant controller to determine the best course of action, which can include a reduction in credit terms for future orders, an increased number of collection calls, dunning letters, or referral to an attorney or collection agency.

Resolve Collection Issues

COLLECTIONS CONTACT	CUSTOMER	INVOICE NUMBER	AMOUNT	NEXT CONTACT DATE	COMMENTS
Jones	Alpha Labs	5418	$500.25	5/04	Waiting on controller approval
Jones	Blue Moon	5009	250.00	5/09	Sent bill of lading
Jones	White Ice	5200	375.15	5/03	Sent replacement part
Jones	Zora Inc.	5302	1,005.00	5/12	Meeting in person to discuss
Smith	Chai Tea	5400	2,709.15	5/01	Issued credit for price change
Smith	Deal Time	5417	5,010.00	5/13	Sent claim to bankruptcy court
Smith	Energy Ltd.	5304	128.45	5/08	Faxed new invoice copy
Smith	Foo & Sons	5215	495.31	5/07	Waiting for callback
Smith	Green Way	5450	95.97	5/05	Offered 25% discount to pay

Exhibit 6.16 Collections Contact Log

Policy/Procedure Statement	Retrieval No.:	CRE-09
Brasto Publishing	Page:	1 of 1
	Issue Date:	10/28/0X
	Supersedes:	N/A
Subject: Issue Customer Credits		

1. **PURPOSE AND SCOPE**

   This procedure is used by the accounts receivable clerk to determine the correct method for processing a credit memo.

2. **RESPONSIBILITIES**

   ACC RECV   **Accounts Receivable Clerk**

3. **PROCEDURES**

   3.1 ACC RECV   **Receive Request for Credit Memo**

   1. A credit memo request must be made using the Bad Debt Write-Off Approval Form (see Exhibit 6.17). If someone requests this information without the proper form, give that person a blank Bad Debt Write-Off Approval Form along with a sample form and request that it be filled out completely.
   2. Upon receipt of a completed form, file it in the "To Do" box until the end of the week, when the credit memos are batched for further processing.

3.2	ACC RECV	**Obtain Approval for Credit**

3.2   ACC RECV   **Obtain Approval for Credit**

1. Take the batch of credit memos to the Controller for approval. The Controller signs each one if they are approved. If not, send the credit memos back to the requestors with a note explaining why they cannot be granted. If more information is needed on the form, make the recipient aware of the need for more information.

2. If the "Customer unable to pay" field was checked on the form, send a copy to the Credit Clerk. If the "Damaged Goods" field was checked, send a copy to the Shipping Manager. If the "Incorrect pricing" field was checked, send a copy to the Billing Manager. If the "Incorrect shipment quantity" field was checked, send a copy to the Shipping Manager. If the "Product quality not acceptable" field was checked, send a copy to the Quality Assurance Manager.

3.3   ACC RECV   **Create Credit Memo**

In the accounting computer system, enter a new invoice for each credit granted, using a negative balance equaling the amount of the requested credit. Be sure to enter an explanation on the invoice, noting whether this is a credit to be issued to the customer or an internal credit to be filed away. Print the credit memos during the daily printout of invoices.

3.4   ACC RECV   **Distribute Credit Memo**

When bursting the invoices after the print run is complete, separate the credit memos and put them in a separate stack. If they are marked as *internal* invoices, file all copies in the customer folders and do not send any documentation to the customers. If they are marked as *external* credit memos, send one copy to the customer, put another copy in the customer's file, and put the final copy in the credit memos file.

Issue Customer Credits

Company Name
Bad Debt Write-Off Approval Form

Customer Name: _____   Invoice Number: _____

Customer Code: _____   Invoice Amount: _____

Reason for Write-Off

☐ Customer unable to pay

☐ Damaged goods

☐ Incorrect pricing

☐ Incorrect shipment quantity

☐ Product quality not acceptable

Other nonstandard reasons for a write-off: _____

_____

_____

Requested Write-off Amount: _____

Name of Requesting Clerk:_____

Signature of Requesting Clerk: _____   Date: _____

Name of Approving Manager: _____

Signature of Approving Manager: _____   Date: _____

Exhibit 6.17   Bad Debt Write-Off Approval Form

Policy/Procedure Statement	Retrieval No.:	CRE-10
	Page:	1 of 1
Brasto Publishing	Issue Date:	10/28/0X
	Supersedes:	N/A
Subject: **Process Sales Returns**		

1. **PURPOSE AND SCOPE**
   This procedure is used by the accounts receivable clerk calculate the correct amount of credit to apply to a sales return.

2. **RESPONSIBILITIES**
ACC RECV	**Accounts Receivable Clerk**
RECEIVING	**Receiving Clerk**
QUALITY	**Quality Assurance Clerk**

3. **PROCEDURES**

   3.1 ACC RECV **Assign Sales Return Authorization Number**
   Upon receipt of a sales return inquiry from a customer, assign the customer a unique sales return authorization number. Enter this number on the Sales Return Authorization Form (see Exhibit 6.18), as well as quantity, product number, and description of the items being returned. In addition, enter one of the standard reason codes on the form into the "Reason for Return" field. Store a copy of the form in the sales return file, sorted by date. Send another copy to the receiving department.

   3.2 RECEIVING **Accept Sales Return**
   1. When a product is returned by a customer to the receiving dock, compare the sales return authorization number listed on the package to the list of open sales return authorization numbers. Accept the delivery if there is a numerical match and the product quantity and type is the same. If the number does not exist, or the product type is incorrect, or the quantity is too large, reject the order.
   2. If the order is acceptable, log it into the inventory database into the "Requires Review by Quality Assurance" category. Notify quality assurance that it needs to inspect returned product. Forward the shipping information attached to the delivery to the accounting department, and enter the receipt into the receiving log.

   3.3 QUALITY **Determine Damage Credit**
   Upon receipt of notification from the receiving staff, the quality assurance clerk must inspect the returned goods, verifying the condition of the packaging, documentation, and product. If any of these items require replacement, complete a Product Repair Ticket and attach it to the returned goods. Send a copy of the Ticket to the accounting department.

3.4	ACC RECV	**Calculate Sales Return Credit**

1. Upon receipt of the shipping information attached to the sales return, the accounts receivable clerk uses the Sales Return Credit Calculation Form (see Exhibit 6.19) to determine the correct amount of credit to be granted to the customer.
2. Enter the product number, quantity returned, product description, unit price, and extended price for each item returned on the form.
3. Calculate the amount of damage credit to enter on the form by multiplying the required product repairs listed on the Product Repair Ticket by the standard product cost listed in the computer system for each item.
4. Reduce the amount of credit by a __% restocking fee, and also subtract a $__ transaction fee.
5. Calculate the net credit granted.
6. Sign and date the form.
7. File one copy of the form in the customer file, sorted by date. Forward another copy to the clerk who processes credits (see the Issue Customer Credits procedure).

Process Sales Returns

Company Name
Sales Return Authorization Form

Customer Name: _____　　Date. _____

Sales Return Authorization Number: _____ **(Required)**

	Product Being Returned		Reason for
Number	Quantity	Description	Return
_____	_____	_____	_____
_____	_____	_____	_____
_____	_____	_____	_____
_____	_____	_____	_____

Standard Reason Codes:
　1 = Product damaged in transit
　2 = Product quality below required level
　3 = Incorrect product shipped
　4 = Incorrect quantity shipped
　5 = Shipment made to wrong location
　6 = Other (describe below)

Other reasons for return: _____

_____

_____

Exhibit 6.18　Sales Return Authorization Form

Company Name
Sales Return Credit Calculation Form

Customer Name: _____   Date: _____

Sales Return Authorization Number: _____

Product Number	Quantity	Description	Unit Price	Extended Price	Damage Credit
_____	_____	_____	_____	_____	_____
_____	_____	_____	_____	_____	_____
_____	_____	_____	_____	_____	_____
_____	_____	_____	_____	_____	_____
_____	_____	_____	_____	_____	_____

Totals _____ _____

Less:

   20% Restocking Fee _____

   Total Damage Credit _____

   $25 Transaction Fee $ 25

Net Credit Granted _____

_____   _____
   Clerk Signature   Clerk Name

Exhibit 6.19 Sales Return Credit Calculation Form

Policy/Procedure Statement	Retrieval No.:	CRE-11
	Page:	1 of 1
Brasto Publishing	Issue Date:	10/28/0X
	Supersedes:	N/A
Subject: Place Customer Orders on Hold		

1. PURPOSE AND SCOPE

This procedure is used by the collections clerk to freeze customer orders currently active in the computer system that have not yet been shipped.

2. RESPONSIBILITIES

COLLECT   **Collections Clerk**

3. PROCEDURES

3.1   COLLECT   **Create Hold Transaction**

Go to the ORDERS menu in the computer system, and access the CUSTOMER screen. Set the customer status to "hold delivery."

3.2   COLLECT   **Notify Customer and Employees of Hold Status**

1. Issue an e-mail to the customer service representative and the sales manager to inform them that the customer is on Hold status.
2. Call the accounts payable person at the customer and inform him or her of the change in ship ment status.

Place Customer Orders on Hold

Policy/Procedure Statement	Retrieval No.:	CRE-12
	Page:	1 of 1
Brasto Publishing	Issue Date:	10/28/0X
	Supersedes:	N/A
Subject: Review Credit Level and Adjust		

1.   **PURPOSE AND SCOPE**
     This procedure is used by the credit clerk to revise credit levels based on internal collection experience, and to adjust those levels based on this information.

2.   **RESPONSIBILITIES**
     CREDIT   **Credit Clerk**

3.   **PROCEDURES**

3.1   CREDIT   **Summarize Internal Collection Experience**
                      1.   Obtain all collections contact information about a specific customer from the collections clerk.
                      2.   Compare this information to externally obtained credit data.
                      3.   Obtain additional verbal information from the collections clerk, such as that person's opinion of the correct credit level.

3.2   CREDIT   **Determine New Credit Level**
                      Using the credit setting policy as the chief guideline, alter the customer's credit level. However, because this policy is based on historical information, the credit clerk should also base the decision on forward-looking information, such as information from other creditors regarding a general inability to pay, or a prospective bankruptcy filing.

3.3   CREDIT   **Adjust Credit Level in Computer System**
                      1.   Go to the ORDERS menu in the computer system and access the CUSTOMER screen. Alter the dollar amount in the "Credit" field.
                      2.   Contact the sales and customer service staffs to inform them of this change.

Review Credit Level and Adjust

Policy/Procedure Statement	Retrieval No.:	FIN-01
	Page:	1 of 1
	Issue Date:	10/28/0X
Brasto Publishing	Supersedes.	N/A
Subject: Review Closing Tasks with Staff		

1. **PURPOSE AND SCOPE**
   This procedure is used by the controller to assign closing responsibilities to various members of the accounting staff.

2. **RESPONSIBILITIES**
   CONTROLLER   **Controller**

3. **PROCEDURES**
3.1   CONTROLLER   **Schedule Staff Meeting**
      1. Schedule a meeting with all accounting staff who are involved in the month-end closingprocess, specifying a time and place.
      2. Issue an agenda to this group prior to the meeting.
3.2   CONTROLLER   **Hold Meeting**
      Review with this group the order in which tasks will be completed, as well as who is responsible for completing each one. Emphasize changes to the schedule that were agreed on at the end of the last month's closing process.

Review Closing Tasks with Staff

Policy/Procedure Statement	Retrieval No.:	FIN-02
Brasto Publishing	Page:	1 of 1
	Issue Date:	10/28/0X
	Supersedes:	N/A
Subject: Perform Physical Inventory Count		

1.   PURPOSE AND SCOPE
This procedure is used to create a structured approach to a physical inventory count.

2.   RESPONSIBILITIES
  CONTROLLER   **Controller**

3.   PROCEDURES
3.1   CONTROLLER   **Preparation for the Count**
Take the following steps one week before the physical count:
1. Contact the printing company and order a sufficient number of sequentially numbered count tags. The first tag number should always be "1000." The tags should include fields for the product number, description, quantity count, location, and the counter's signature.
2. Review the inventory and mark all items lacking a part number with a brightly colored piece of paper. Inform the warehouse manager that these items must be marked with a proper part number immediately
3. Clearly mark the quantity on all sealed packages.
4. Count all partial packages, seal them, and mark the quantity on the tape.
5. Prepare "Do Not Inventory" tags and use them to mark all items that should not be in cluded in the physical inventory count.
6. Issue a list of count team members, with a notice regarding where and when they should appear for the inventory count.

3.2   CONTROLLER   **One Day before the Count**
1. Remind all participants that they are expected to be counting the next day.
2. Notify the warehouse manager that all items received during the two days of physical counts must be segregated and marked with "Do Not Inventory" tags.
3. Notify the manager that no shipments are allowed for the duration of the physical count.
4. Notify the warehouse manager that all shipments for which the paperwork has not been sent to accounting by that evening will be included in the inventory count on the following day.
5. Notify the warehouse manager that all shipping and receiving documentation from the day before the count must be forwarded to the accounting department that day, for immediate data entry. Likewise, any pick information must be forwarded at the same time.
6. Notify all outside storage locations to fax in their inventory counts.

3.3	CONTROLLER	**Morning of the Physical Inventory Count**

1. Enter all transactions from the previous day.
2. Assemble the count teams. Issue counting instructions to them, as well as blocks of tags, for which they must sign Give each team a map of the warehouse with a section highlighted on it that they are responsible for counting. Those teams with forklift experience will be assigned to count the top racks; those without this experience will be assigned the lower racks.
3. Call all outside storage warehouses and ask them to fax in their counts of company-owned inventory.
4. The count supervisor assigns additional count areas to those teams that finish counting their areas first.
5. The tag coordinator assigns blocks of tags to those count teams that run out of tags, tracks the receipt of tags, and follows up on missing tags. All tags should be accounted for by the end of the day.
6. The data entry person enters the information on the tags into a spreadsheet, and then summarizes the quantities for each item and pencils the totals into the cycle count report that was run earlier in the day.
7. The count supervisor reviews any unusual variances with the count teams to ensure that the correct amounts were entered.
8. Review the test count with an auditor, if necessary. Give the auditor a complete printout of all tags, as well as the cycle counting spreadsheet, showing all variances.

3.4	CONTROLLER	**Job Descriptions**

- The *count supervisor* is responsible for supervising the count, which includes assigning count teams to specific areas and ensuring that all areas have been counted and tagged. This person also waits until all count tags have been compared to the quantities listed in the computer, and then checks the counts on any items that appear to be incorrect.
- The *tag coordinator* is responsible for tracking the blocks of count tags that have been issued, as well as for accounting for all tags that have been returned. When distributing tags, mark down the beginning and ending numbers of each block of tags on a tracking sheet, and obtain the signature of the person who receives the tags. When the tags are returned, put them in numerical order and verify that all tags are accounted for. Once the verification is complete, check off the tags on the tracking sheet as having been received. Once returned tags have been properly accounted for, forward them to the extension calculation clerk.
- The *extension calculation clerk* is responsible for summarizing the amounts on the tags (if there are multiple quantities listed) to arrive at a total quantity count on each tag. This person also compares the part numbers and descriptions on each tag to see if there are any potential identification problems. This person forwards all completed tags to the data entry person.

- The *data entry person* is responsible for entering the information on all count tags into the computer spreadsheet. When doing so, enter all the information on each tag into a spread sheet. Once a group of tags has been entered, stamp them as having been entered, clip them together, and store them separately. Once all tags are entered in the spreadsheet, sort the data by part number. Print out the spreadsheet and summarize the quantities by part number. Transfer the total quantities by part number to the cycle count report. If there are any significant variances between the counted and cycle count quantities, bring them to the attention of the count supervisor for review.

3.5	CONTROLLER	**Time and Place**

The count begins at 7:30 AM and ends at 4:30 PM on the first day of the count. If the count continues to a second day, it will begin at the same time, and count teams will be released whenever the counts have been completed. On both days, all count teams should meet at the warehouse gate.

3.6	CONTROLLER	**Counting Responsibility**

1. Count the bin locations assigned to you. These will be marked on a map of the warehouse with a highlighter. When you have counted all of the items in your assigned area, return to the count supervisor, who will assign additional count areas to you.

2. For each item counted in a separate bin location, enter the product code and date on the part of the inventory tag that is labeled "Pallet" and tape it to the inventory item. Rip off the other part of the tag (see Exhibit 6.20) and mark on it the product code, description, location, and quantity counted. Also initial the tag or list the number of your count team. Keep this part of the tag and return it to the tag coordinator when you run out of tags. This person will ensure that all of the tags assigned to you have been returned. If some are missing, you must locate and return them to the tag coordinator.

3. If there are many boxes of the same item to count, list the individual amounts on a tag, and an extensions calculation person will add them up for you. For example, if there are 18 boxes of 300 and a partial box of 12, just enter $(18 \times 300) + 12$ on the tag.

3.7	CONTROLLER	**General Information**

- Do not count any item that has a "Do Not Inventory" tag on it.
- Scales will be provided to all count teams. The warehouse supervisor is available for training in the use of scales.
- Use a pen (not a pencil) to enter information on count tags. To make a quantity correction, put a line through the old quantity, write the new quantity next to it, and initial the change.
- ALL tags must be accounted for! If you do not use some, return them to the tag coordinator.

Perform Physical Inventory Count

```
        ╭────⬭────╮                    ╭────⬭────╮
        │ Tag: 2024 │                  │          │
        │ Part No. _____ Unit ___      │          │
        │ Description _____       │          │
        │ Quantity _____         │          │
        ├ ─ ─ ─ ─ ─ ─ ─ ─ ─ ─ ─        ├ ─ ─ ─ ─ ─ ─ ─ ─ ─
```

Tag: 2024		
Part No. _____ Unit ___		
Description _____		
Quantity _____		

2024

	After Count	
	Part No. _____	
Description _____		
Unit _____		
Quantity _____		
Location _____		
Counter _____		
Checker _____		

	After Count	
Date	Issued	Rcvd

(Front)   (Reverse)

Exhibit 6.20   Inventory Count Tag, Front and Back

Policy/Procedure Statement	Retrieval No.:	FIN-03
	Page:	1 of 1
Brasto Publishing	Issue Date:	10/28/0X
	Supersedes:	N/A
Subject: Complete Closing Tasks Prior to Month-End		

1. **PURPOSE AND SCOPE**
   This procedure is used by the closing staff to complete a variety of closing activities prior to month-end.

2. **RESPONSIBILITIES**
   GL ACCT   **General Ledger Accountant**

3. **PROCEDURES**

   3.1   GL ACCT   **Conduct Error Review (three days before close)**
   1. Print the financial statements, including statements for subsidiaries, and review them for possible errors, such as negative balances or amounts that vary significantly from the budget.
   2. For a possible error, access the detailed information in the general ledger and determine its cause. If necessary, post a correcting journal entry.
   3. If investigation reveals that the information is accurate but represents a significant variance, then create a footnote explaining the situation, for later inclusion in the financial statements.

3.2	GL ACCT	**Determine Inventory Accuracy (three days before close)**

1. Print the Inventory Location Report (inventory sorted by location) and randomly select 20 items on the report for review.
2. Trace all 20 items from the report to their actual locations, and trace an additional 20 items from storage bins back to the report. Record them as correct if they are in the correct location, have quantities within 5% of the recorded value, and have the correct part numbers.
3. Divide the number of correct items by the total number of counts made. If the inventory accuracy percentage is less than 95%, authorize a physical count immediately following month end.

3.3	GL ACCT	**Adjust Obsolescence Reserve (three days before close)**

1. Meet with the Materials Review Board (MRB) to discuss the status of inventory designated as obsolete.
2. Print the Obsolete Inventory Report and determine the estimated disposition values of all items on it.
3. Calculate the obsolescence reserve by subtracting the total disposition value from the book value of the items on the report.
4. Adjust the booked obsolescence reserve to match the calculated obsolescence reserve.

3.4	GL ACCT	**Update Vacation Expense Accrual (three days before close)**

1. Access the Vacation Accrual spreadsheet, which lists the accrued vacation that will be available for all employees as of year-end.
2. For any employee whose accrued vacation is lower than the carryforward cap of __hours, transfer the lower accrual amount to the Vacation Accrual spreadsheet.
3. Verify that the salary and annualized wage levels shown on the Vacation Accrual spreadsheet are correct, and adjust as necessary.
4. Change the accrued vacation listed in the general ledger liability account to the total shown on the spreadsheet.

3.5	GL ACCT	**Complete Allocation Bases (two days before close)**

1. Access the allocation base spreadsheet and load in the most recent activity information for the allocation base, using activity information from the immediately preceding month.
2. Access the expense allocation spreadsheet and enter the revised allocation bases.

3.6	GL ACCT	**Issue Notifications (two days before close)**

1. Notify the receiving staff that all receipts through month-end must be input into the computer system no later than the end of business on the last day of the month.
2. Notify the shipping staff that all shipments through month-end must be input into the computer system no later than the end of business on the last day of the month.
3. Notify all employees that expense reports must be submitted no later than the morning of the first day of the following month.

3.7	GL ACCT	**Calculate Preliminary Commissions (two days before close)**

1. Print the sales journal.
2. Transfer from the sales journal the commissionable billed invoice amounts (net of sales taxes and billed reimbursable expenses) to the commission calculation spreadsheets for each sales person.
3. Verify the accuracy of the commission percentages listed on the commission calculation spreadsheets.

3.8	GL ACCT	**Accrue Interest Expense (two days before close)**

1. Access the electronic spreadsheet containing current debt levels.
2. Update the spreadsheet for any debt additions or repayments during the month, as well as for any changes in the interest rate paid. Also update the spreadsheet for any late changes in debt levels during the previous month, after the spreadsheet was previously updated.
3. Calculate the interest expense for the current month, and record it with a journal entry.

3.9	GL ACCT	**Adjust Bad Debt Reserve (two days before close)**

1. Print the Accounts Receivable Aging Report (ARA Report).
2. Review the report with the credit manager to determine which receivables are most likely to not be collected.
3. Calculate the likely amount of bad debts on the ARA Report by multiply the total receivables in the 0 to 30, 31 to 60, 61 to 90, and 90+ day time buckets by historical bad debt rates for each category.
4. Use the greater of the figures derived in steps two and three as the bad debt reserve to be used. Adjust the existing bad debt reserve in the general ledger to match this figure.

3.10	GL ACCT	**Complete Online Bank Reconciliation (one day before close)**

1. Access the bank's online records of the company's bank transactions, and print the complete set of transactions for the month. Also record the bank's ending account balance as of the current date.
2. Call up in another window the bank reconciliation module of the accounting software, and use the printout of bank records to reconcile the book and bank records.
3. Use journal entries to adjust the book records to match the bank records, as necessary.

3.11	GL ACCT	**Accrue Unpaid Wages (one day before close)**

1. Access the timekeeping records for all hourly employees since the last pay date. Compile the total hours recorded in the time system during that period, and extrapolate this amount through month-end.
2. Access the Wage Accrual electronic spreadsheet and enter the extrapolated unpaid wages of all hourly employees in the spreadsheet.
3. Verify that the wage rates listed in the spreadsheet for each employee are current, and adjust as necessary.
4. Transfer the total wage accrual on the spreadsheet to the wage accrual journal entry.

3.12	GL ACCT	**Review Billable Hours (one day before close)**

1. Print the Summary Timesheet report for the current month.
2. Review the report for the following items:
   - All employees have charged at least 40 hours during every week of the month.
   - All employees have charged billable hours to jobs on which they actually worked.
   - All employees have charged time off to a vacation or holiday charge code and not to a billable code.
   - All employees have charged billable time to billable charge codes, not administrative charge codes.
   - All employee time charged to overtime was approved in advance of the overtime hours being worked.
3. Have employees adjust their timesheets for any problems found during this review.

3.13	GL ACCT	**Review Rebillable Expenses (one day before close)**

Review all rebillable expense reports for the following items:
- They are being charged to the correct customer jobs.
- They have been assigned the correct job codes in the accounting software.
- All expenses are preapproved by customers.
- If for federal government work, that they meet the Federal Acquisition Regulation guidelines.
- All expenses are listed in the correct categories on expense reports.
- All expense report totals correctly summarize detailed expenditures.
- There are supporting receipts that match all expenses listed on the lead page of the expense reports.

3.14	GL ACCT	**Update Fixed Asset Changes (one day before close)**

1. Print the fixed asset general ledger account for the current month, as well as for the last day of the preceding month (if fixed assets were closed one day early in the preceding month).
2. Verify that all items listed exceed the corporate capitalization limit. If not, create a journal entry to charge them to expense.
3. Load all remaining items into the fixed assets module.
4. Photocopy all supporting documentation for items entered in the fixed assets module, and store it in a fixed assets binder, sorted by fixed asset type.
5. Print the depreciation report in the fixed assets module for the current month, and update the recurring depreciation entry with this information.

3.15	GL ACCT	**Accrue Unbilled Expenses (one day before close)**

1. At the close of business on the last day of the month, print the Unbilled Receipts Report, showing all items for which a purchase order has been issued, but for which no supplier invoice has been received.
2. Create an expense accrual for all items on the report. Be sure to set up the accrual to automatically reverse in the following period.

		3. Also accrue for any recurring expenses for which an invoice has not yet been received, and for which no purchase order exists. This typically includes the following items:

- Electricity
- Gas
- Telephones
- Waste pickup and disposal
- Water

| 3.16 | GL ACCT | **Complete Some Financial Reports (one day before close)** |

1. Update all footnotes to and commentary on the financial statements.
2. Update any operational and statistical information in the financial reporting package that is available prior to month-end.

Complete Closing Tasks Prior to Month-End

Policy/Procedure Statement	Retrieval No.:	FIN-04
	Page:	1 of 1
Brasto Publishing	Issue Date:	10/28/0X
	Supersedes:	N/A
Subject: Calculate Percentage of Completion Revenue		

1. **PURPOSE AND SCOPE**
   This procedure is used by the General Ledger Accountant to determine the amount of revenue to be recognized on a construction project.

2. **RESPONSIBILITIES**
   GEN LEDGER   **General Ledger Accountant**

3. **PROCEDURES**

3.1   GEN LEDGER   **Collect Project Costing Information**
   1. Access the approved project bid file and determine the estimated gross profit percentage for the project.
   2. Discuss the estimated gross margin with the project manager to verify that the percentage is still valid. If not, use the project manager's revised estimate.
   3. Access the general ledger and note the total amount of expenses accumulated to date in the project's construction-in-progress account.

3.2   GEN LEDGER   **Calculate Percentage of Completion**
   1. Divide the total project expenses by one minus the estimated gross profit percentage to arrive at total expenses plus the estimated gross profit.
   2. Access the project billing records and determine the total amount of billings made to the customer thus far.

3.3   GEN LEDGER   **Record Change in Percentage of Completion**
   Subtract the total expenses and estimated gross profit from the billings figure. If the amount of expenses and gross profits is larger than the billed amount, debit the Unbilled Contract Receivables account and credit the Contract Revenues Earned account for the difference. If the amount of expenses and gross profits is less than the billed amount, debit the Contract Revenues Earned account and credit the Billings Exceeding Project Costs and Margin account for the difference.

Calculate Percentage of Completion Revenue

Policy/Procedure Statement	Retrieval No.:	FIN-05
	Page:	1 of 1
	Issue Date:	10/28/0X
	Supersedes:	N/A
Subject: Advance Recognition of Losses		

Brasto Publishing

1. PURPOSE AND SCOPE

This procedure is used by the General Ledger Accountant to periodically review service contracts to determine the existence of any projected contract losses.

2. RESPONSIBILITIES

GEN LEDGER **General Ledger Accountant**

3. PROCEDURES

3.1 GEN LEDGER **Collect Project Costing Information**

Summarize all project-to-date direct costs from the relevant general ledger account.

3.2 GEN LEDGER **Calculate Percentage of Completion**

1. Go to the project manager and review the amount of estimated costs yet to be incurred on the project. Compare this amount to the estimated completion cost from the last review to see if there are any unusual changes, and discuss the differences. Also verify the cost estimated against any project planning database, such as a Gantt or Critical Path Method chart.
2. Summarize all project billings to date, and verify the amount of remaining billings, adjusted for any contract modifications.
3. Combine the actual and estimated costs and subtract them from the total expected project revenues. If the costs exceed revenues, notify the controller of the difference with a memo, outlining the reasons for the loss.

3.3 GEN LEDGER **Record Change in Percentage of Completion**

Debit the Loss on Contracts account for the amount of the estimated loss. Use the offsetting credit to eliminate any unrecognized costs stored in an asset account, and credit the remaining loss to the Estimated Loss on Service Contracts account.

Advance Recognition of Losses

Policy/Procedure Statement	Retrieval No.:	FIN-06
	Page:	1 of 1
Brasto Publishing	Issue Date:	10/28/0X
	Supersedes:	N/A
Subject: Record Accruals		

1. **PURPOSE AND SCOPE**
   This procedure is used by the general ledger clerk to record standard accruals in for the current reporting period.

2. **RESPONSIBILITIES**
   GL CLERK   **General Ledger Clerk**

3. **PROCEDURES**
3.1   GL CLERK   **Locate List of Standard Accruals**
   1. Obtain the list of standard accruals, a copy of which is listed in the journal entries folder.
   2. Verify that explanations and completion dates are included in the file for each accrual.

3.2   GL CLERK   **Calculate Accruals**
   1. *Commissions.* Access the Commissions electronic spreadsheet and create a new page for the current month. Copy forward formulas from the last month. Print the sales journal and transfer all sales from it to the Commissions spreadsheet, including the invoice date, number, amount, customer name, product sold commission type, and commission rate for each sale. Send a copy of the completed commission spreadsheet to the salesperson, sales manager, and controller for verification. Then send it to the payroll manager for entry into the payroll system.
   2. *Royalties.* Access the Royalties electronic spreadsheet and create a new page for the current month. Copy forward formulas from the last month. Transfer to the report the general ledger balance for sales related to the specific product for which a royalty is owed. Calculate the royalty percentage. Send the report to an authorized signer, and then send the report to the accounts payable staff for payment.
   3. *Vacations.* Access the Vacations electronic spreadsheet. Update the annualized salary for each person in the report, and add or subtract employees based on personnel activity during the past month. Verify with the human resources staff the maximum carryforward vacation hours for each person in the report, and update the report accordingly. Enter from the general ledger the currently accrued vacation balance. When completed, send the report to the general ledger accountant, who will enter any adjustments in the general ledger.

		4. *Wages.* Access the Wage Accrual electronic spreadsheet and create a new page for the current month. Copy forward formulas from the last month. Transfer to the report from the payroll system the number of unpaid hours for all employees, as well as their current pay rates. Verify that all hourly employees are included in the report. When completed, send the report to the general ledger accountant, who will enter any adjustments in the general ledger.
3.3	GL CLERK	**Verify Accruals** 1. Meet with the assistant controller and review each accrual, verifying that each one is still needed. 2. Review the journal entry records from the last reporting period to see if additional recurring entries should be made. 3. Compare accrual amounts to actual expenses to see if the amounts accrued are still valid. 4. Make any alterations to the accruals file.
3.4	GL CLERK	**Enter Accruals in Computer System** 1. In the accounting computer system, enter the standard accrual number for each entry, which brings up the standard accounts and dollar amounts on the screen. 2. Verify the amounts and press ENTER to accept each accrual for the new reporting period. 3. For new accruals, clear the screen and enter the account numbers, amounts, and the number of periods over which to repeat the entry, and press ENTER.

Record Accruals

Policy/Procedure Statement	Retrieval No.:	FIN-07
Brasto Publishing	Page:	1 of 1
	Issue Date:	10/28/0X
	Supersedes:	N/A
Subject: Calculate Bad Debt Reserve		

1. **PURPOSE AND SCOPE**

   This procedure is used by the collections clerk to alter the bad debt reserve to reflect new billing and bad debt activity in a reporting period.

2. **RESPONSIBILITIES**

   COLLECT   **Collections Clerk**

3. **PROCEDURES**

   3.1   COLLECT   **Identify Bad Debts**
   1. Print the accounts receivable aging report and review all invoices on the report that are at least 60 days old with the collections staff.
   2. If the collections staff deems a reviewed invoice to be uncollectible, complete a bad debt authorization form for it and charge it off to the bad debt reserve account.

   3.2   COLLECT   **Calculate Bad Debt Reserve**
   1. Once all receivables designated as bad debts have been cleared from the aging report, summarize the total amount written off during the reporting period, which can be obtained from the list of written-off invoices listed in the bad debt reserve account in the general ledger.
   2. Enter the period's bad debt total as a running balance in an electronic spreadsheet alongside the remaining accounts receivable balance for the reporting period. Calculate the rolling three-month bad debt percentage of accounts receivable on this spreadsheet.
   3. Multiply the rolling three-month bad debt percentage calculated from the spreadsheet by the remaining accounts receivable balance to determine the estimated amount of bad debt reserve required.
   4. If the amount of estimated bad debt reserve is greater than the actual amount listed in the general ledger, make an entry crediting the bad debt reserve account for the difference, with the offsetting debit going to the bad debt expense account.

Calculate Bad Debt Reserve

Policy/Procedure Statement	Retrieval No.:	FIN-08
	Page:	1 of 1
Brasto Publishing	Issue Date:	10/28/0X
	Supersedes:	N/A
Subject: Record Gain/Loss on Sale of an Asset		

1. **PURPOSE AND SCOPE**
   This procedure is used by the Fixed Assets Clerk to calculate and record the gain or loss on any asset sales.

2. **RESPONSIBILITIES**
   F/A CLERK   **Fixed Assets Clerk**
   GEN LEDGER   **General Ledger Accountant**

3. **PROCEDURES**

3.1 F/A Clerk   **Summarize Asset Sale Information**
   1. Receive documentation from the purchasing department regarding the sale of assets. This should include a signed Asset Disposition form that authorized someone to sell an asset. If the document is not signed by an authorized person, return it with a note asking for the appropriate signature. The document should be accompanied by a copy of the bill of sale, and a copy of the check or other document that shows proof of the amount paid.
   2. Once the sale documentation is complete, go to the fixed asset database and call up the record for the asset being sold. The easiest way is to conduct a search based on the name of the asset, though the documentation may contain the asset number, which can also be used to find the correct record.
   3. Write down the original asset cost and total accumulated depreciation, which is located in the record in the fixed asset database.

3.2 F/A Clerk   **Calculate Gain or Loss on Sale**
   1. Subtract the sale amount and accumulated depreciation from the original asset cost. If there is a positive amount left over, this is a loss on the sale of the asset. If there is a negative amount left over, this is a gain on the sale of the asset.
   2. Obtain a journal entry form and complete it for the gain or loss transaction. The asset's original cost goes in the "Credit Column," while the accumulated depreciation amount goes in the "Debit Column." The sale amount is a debit to cash. If there is a gain, this is recorded as a credit. A loss is recorded as a debit.
   3. Forward the journal entry form to the general ledger accountant.

3.3	GEN LEDGER	**Update Accounting Records**
		1. Use the completed journal entry form to enter a journal entry in the accounting database.
		2. Access the fixed asset database and record the sale of the asset. Print the fixed asset database after this transaction is recorded and compare the total for the account to the general ledger, to ensure that the information is recorded in the same amounts in both locations.
		3. File a copy of the gain or loss calculation in the journal entry book, and also in the permanent file documenting the addition or removal of fixed assets.

Record Gain/Loss on Sale of an Asset

Policy/Procedure Statement	Retrieval No.:	FIN-09
	Page:	1 of 1
	Issue Date:	10/28/0X
Brasto Publishing	Supersedes:	N/A
Subject: Test Assets for Impairment		

1. **PURPOSE AND SCOPE**

   This procedure is used by the Fixed Assets Clerk to determine if the fair value of a fixed asset has dropped below its book value, and to adjust the book value down to the fair value if this is the case. Most assets have book values clustered near the corporate capitalization limit, and therefore are so small that impairment testing would not result in significant asset valuation changes. Accordingly, this procedure is designed to test the values of only the largest assets.

2. **RESPONSIBILITIES**

   F/A CLERK   **Fixed Assets Clerk**
   GEN LEDGER   **General Ledger Accountant**

3. **PROCEDURES**

   3.1   F/A Clerk   **Select Assets for Testing**
   1. Sort the fixed asset register by declining net book value (e.g., original purchase price less accumulated depreciation).
   2. Select for impairment testing those 20% of the listed assets containing 80% of the total book value of the asset register.

   3.2   F/A Clerk   **Determine Level of Impairment**
   1. Determine the total undiscounted cash flows expected to be generated from each of the selected assets (including net salvage value) and list this amount next to their net book values.
   2. Compare the net book value figure to the undiscounted cash flow figure and highlight those assets for which the book value is higher.
   3. For the highlighted assets, determine the amount of the variance between the net book value and the undiscounted cash flow figure. Send the variance to the general ledger accountant.

   3.3   GEN LEDGER   **Update Accounting Records**
   1. Enter in the general ledger the reduction in value of the impaired assets.
   2. Reduce the net book values of all adjusted assets in the fixed asset register to match the amount of their undiscounted cash flows.

   3.4   F/A Clerk   **Revise Depreciation Calculations**
   Calculate depreciation based on the new reduced book value figures and adjust any recurring depreciation journal entries to include these changes.

Test Assets for Impairment

Policy/Procedure Statement	Retrieval No.:	FIN-10
	Page:	1 of 1
Brasto Publishing	Issue Date:	10/28/0X
	Supersedes:	N/A
Subject: Calculate Depreciation		

1. **PURPOSE AND SCOPE**
   This procedure is used by the General Ledger Accountant to ensure that the correct depreciation type and period is used for each capitalized asset.

2. **RESPONSIBILITIES**
   GEN LEDGER   **General Ledger Accountant**

3. **PROCEDURES**

   3.1   GEN LEDGER   **Determine and Record Asset Type**
   1. Compare the type of asset to the company policy statement on asset types in the accounting policy manual.
   2. Go to the fixed assets register in the computer database and enter the asset under the correct asset category.

   3.2   GEN LEDGER   **Set Depreciation Parameters**
   1. When adding the asset to the database, set the number of years of depreciation in accordance with the standard listed in the company policy statement on asset types.
   2. Set the first-year depreciation at the half-year convention.
   3. Set the depreciation method as the _____ method.

   3.3   GEN LEDGER   **Print and Store Depreciation Information**
   1. Print the transaction and store it in the fixed assets records manual.
   2. Print the depreciation register and verify that the system has correctly calculated the depreciation expense for the newly added asset.

Calculate Depreciation

Policy/Procedure Statement	Retrieval No.:	FIN-11
Brasto Publishing	Page:	1 of 1
	Issue Date:	10/28/0X
	Supersedes:	N/A
Subject: Amortize Debt Premiums and Discounts		

1.   **PURPOSE AND SCOPE**
     This procedure is used by the General Ledger Accountant to determine the amount of discount or premium to amortize in a given accounting period.

2.   **RESPONSIBILITIES**
     GEN LEDGER   **General Ledger Accountant**

3.   **PROCEDURES**
3.1 GEN LEDGER   **Calculate Discount or Premium Amortization**
     1. Determine the present value of the outstanding bond at the beginning of the calculation period. To do this, determine the present value of all interest payments for the bond instrument, as well as the present value of the principal payment at the end of the borrowing period, using the market rate of interest as the basis for the discount factor.
     2. Calculate the interest expense in the reporting period by multiplying the market interest rate by the bond's present value for the number of days in the accounting period.
     3. Subtract from the calculated interest expense the actual cash payment made for interest expense to the bondholders, which is based on the stated interest rate rather than the market interest rate. Using the difference between the two numbers, create a journal entry offsetting the outstanding discount or premium.
     4. Add this interest rate difference to the outstanding present value of the bond if there is a discount, or subtract it from the bond if there is an outstanding premium.
     5. Store the new balance of the bond present value, as well as the newly reduced discount or premium, which will be used as the basis for the effective interest calculation in the next reporting period.

Amortize Debt Premiums and Discounts

Policy/Procedure Statement	Procedure No.:	FIN-12
	Page:	1 of 1
	Issue Date:	10/28/0X
	Supersedes:	N/A
Brasto Publishing		
Subject: Calculate Profit Sharing		

1. **PURPOSE AND SCOPE**

   This procedure is used by the assistant controller to calculate the correct amount of profit-sharing expense accrual to be charged to the financial statements each month.

2. **RESPONSIBILITIES**

   ASST CNTLR   **Assistant Controller**

3. **PROCEDURES**

   3.1   ASST CNTLR   **Determine Estimated Monthly Profit**

   Complete the preliminary financial statements. This should include all adjustments and accruals in all revenue and expense areas, as well as comparisons of budgeted amounts to actual.

   3.2   ASST CNTLR   **Locate Profit Sharing Calculation**

   Go to the formula page of the procedures manual and locate the formula for profit sharing. In brief, it requires an accrual of 10% of pretax profits for the compensation of the management team, and 10% of the after-tax profits for the compensation of everyone else in the company.

   3.3   ASST CNTLR   **Determine Profit-Sharing Accrual**

   Calculate the profits for the management team first, which will reduce the overall profit level for the second calculation, which is after-tax profits for the other employees.

   3.4   ASST CNTLR   **Record Profit-Sharing Accrual**

   Record the profit-sharing calculation in the general ledger, with the expense being debited to the "Profit Sharing" account and the credit to "Accrued Expenses."

   3.5   ASST CNTLR   **File the Profit-Sharing Calculation**

   Insert the profit-sharing calculation into the journal entries book, alongside the related entry.

Calculate Profit Sharing

Policy/Procedure Statement	Retrieval No.:	FIN-13
	Page:	1 of 1
Brasto Publishing	Issue Date:	10/28/0X
	Supersedes:	N/A
Subject: Calculate Stock Appreciation Rights		

1. PURPOSE AND SCOPE

This procedure is used by the Treasurer to calculate incremental changes in any stock appreciation rights, and to record the related compensation expense.

2. RESPONSIBILITIES

TREASURER	**Treasurer**
GEN LEDGER	**General Ledger Accountant**

3. PROCEDURES

3.1   TREASURER   Determine Company Valuation

1. Collect the most recent public sector revenue valuation multiple from a reputable investment banking firm. Insert the multiple for each business segment into the "Public Sector Valuation Multiple" field in the Stock Appreciation Rights report (see Exhibit 6.21).

2. Enter in the "Segment Revenue" field the most recent annualized revenue for each company business segment for which a public sector valuation multiple can be determined.

3.2   TREASURER   Determine Share Valuation

1. Update the "Number of Shares" field in the Share Valuation portion of the report for each stock type with the most recent share total, updated for any stock transactions having occurred since the last report was completed.

2. Update the "Participation Percentage" field for each stock type, if stock rights have change since the last report was completed. Also add any new stock types that may have been issued.

3.3   TREASURER   Determine Compensation Expense

1. Update the number of stock appreciate rights (SAR) issued in the "Number of Shares" field in the SAR Compensation Expense portion of the report, as well as the date of issuance and the price at which the rights were issued.

2. Enter in the report the amount of SAR compensation expense previously recorded in the general ledger.

3. Print the report and send a copy to the General Ledger Accountant.

3.4   GEN LEDGER   Record Compensation Expense

Upon receipt of the most recent Stock Appreciation Rights report, enter the amount listed in the "SAR Compensation Expense Accrual" field in the general ledger as an adjustment to the compensation expense account.

Calculate Stock Appreciation Rights

Stock Appreciation Rights
Standard Calculation Form

Company Valuation:

Business Segment	Segment Revenue	Public Sector Valuation Multiple	Estimated Company Valuation
Outdoor advertising	$4,500,000	1.2	$5,400,000
Publishing	$12,250,000	1.7	$20,825,000
Rentals	$8,050,000	1.0	$8,050,000
	$24,800,000		$34,275,000

Share Valuation:

Stock Type	Number of Shares	Participation Percentage	Estimated Value per Share
Common	12,000,000	100%	$ 2.2624
Preferred Series A	1,500,000	200%	$ 4.5248
Stock Appreciation Rights	150,000	100%	$ 2.2624
	13,650,000		

SAR Compensation Expense:

Date of SAR Issuance	Number of Shares	Issuance Price	Compensation Expense
5/15/2005	50,000	$ 1.10	$ 58,119
8/21/2005	80,000	$ 1.38	$ 70,590
11/3/2005	20,000	$ 1.75	$ 10,248
	150,000		$ 138,956

SAR compensation already recognized: $ 120,000

SAR compensation expense accrual: $ 18,956

Exhibit 6.21 Stock Appreciation Rights Calculation Form

Policy/Procedure Statement	Retrieval No.:	FIN-14
	Page:	1 of 1
Brasto Publishing	Issue Date:	10/28/0X
	Supersedes:	N/A
Subject: Reconcile Bank Statement		

1. **PURPOSE AND SCOPE**
    This procedure helps the accounts payable clerk compare his or her internal cash records to those of the bank and reconcile any differences between the two.

2. **RESPONSIBILITIES**

    ACC PAY   **Accounts Payable Clerk**

3. **PROCEDURES**

    3.1   ACC PAY   **Entries**
    During the month, enter each lockbox or deposit amount in its entirety, print the batch total, and store the batch total report with the lockbox or deposit record. Take the following steps to apply cash:
    - Go to the accounting computer system's cash application module. Call up the account of the customer for whom a payment has been received.
    - Log in the amount received, the date of the payment, and the identifying number of the check. Repeat the process until all cash has been applied for all the invoices paid by each customer.
    - Use a journal entry to record cash receipts for items not related to invoices.

    3.2   ACC PAY   **Manual Checks**
    During the month, enter manual checks into the computer system as soon as they are issued.

    3.3   ACC PAY   **Journal Entries**
    1. Make a journal entry to record all expenditures associated with each payroll as soon as the payroll is generated.
    2. Make a separate journal entry for each wire transfer noted on the bank statement, unless these cash flows are already accounted for through the accounts payable or accounts receivable systems.

    3.4   ACC PAY   **Reconcile the General Ledger Balance**
    1. Once the month-end bank statement arrives, reconcile the general ledger to the bank balance with the following steps:
    2. Go to the accounting computer system and access the bank reconciliation module.
    3. Check off all issued checks listed in the bank reconciliation module that are listed as having cleared the bank on the bank statement. If any check amounts listed by the bank differ from the amounts listed in the module, make a journal entry to correct to the bank balance.

4. Check off all deposits listed in the bank reconciliation module that are listed has having been received by the bank on the bank statement. If any deposit amounts listed by the bank differ from the amounts listed in the module, make a journal entry to correct to the bank balance.
5. Make a separate journal entry for each special expense or revenue item on the bank statement, such as a monthly account processing fee.
6. Record in the accounting system any manual checks not previously recorded, but which are listed on the bank statement as having cleared the bank.
7. If all items reconcile and the bank statement still does not match, then the only remaining possible solution is that the beginning bank reconciliation was incorrect.
8. When the reconciliation is complete, print the Bank Reconciliation (see Exhibit 6.22) and store it with the bank statement in a bank statement file for the current year, sorted by month.

Reconcile Bank Statement

Company Name
Bank Reconciliation

Bank: _____ Account No: _____

As of _____

	Balance 11/30/xx	Receipts	Disburse-ments	Balance 12/31/xx
Per bank....................	$ 126,312.50	$ 92,420.00	$ 85,119.00	$ 133,613.50
Add:				
Deposits in transit				
11/30 per book	$ 5,600.00	$ (5,600.00)		
12/31 per book		$ 12,500.00		$ 12,500.00
Deduct:				
Outstanding checks				
November (see list)	$ 4,320.00		$ (4,115.00)	$ 205.00
December (see list)			$ 6,110.00	$ 6,110.00
Other Items:				
Bank charges not recorded			–5.01	5.01
Per books.....................	$ 127,592.50	$ 99,320.00	$ 87,108.99	$ 139,803.51

Prepared by _____
Date _____

Exhibit 6.22 Bank Reconciliation

Policy/Procedure Statement	Retrieval No.:	FIN-15
	Page:	1 of 1
Brastu Publishing	Issue Date:	10/28/0X
	Supersedes:	N/A
Subject: Reconcile Petty Cash		

1. **PURPOSE AND SCOPE**
   This procedure is used by the cash clerk to conduct a manual reconciliation of the petty cash balance in any petty cash box.

2. **RESPONSIBILITIES**
   CASH   **Cash Clerk**

3. **PROCEDURES**

   3.1   CASH   **Determine Book Balance**
                           Access the general ledger account for the petty cash box and determine the amount of cash it should contain as of the last reconciliation.

   3.2   CASH   **Reconcile Petty Cash Box**
                           1. Go to the petty cash box and add up all cash contained in the box. Subtract this amount from the box balance as of the last reconciliation and add any amounts deposited into the box during the interval since the last reconciliation. This calculation reveals the amount of missing cash that should be accounted for by expense vouchers.
                           2. Add up all vouchers in the box and compare this amount to the predetermined amount of missing cash. If they do not match, review petty cash procedures with the person responsible for it.
                           3. Create a journal entry summarizing the expenses represented by all vouchers in the box, as well as the amount of any shortfalls or overages. Staple the vouchers to this journal entry and give the packet to the general ledger accountant for entry into the general ledger.

   3.3   CASH   **Replenish Petty Cash Box**
                           Calculate the amount of cash that should be added to the petty cash box, based on usage levels, and recommend to the assistant controller in charge of accounts payable that this amount of cash be forwarded to the person responsible for the petty cash box.

Reconcile Petty Cash

Policy/Procedure Statement	Retrieval No.:	FIN-16
	Page:	1 of 1
Brasto Publishing	Issue Date:	10/28/0X
	Supersedes:	N/A
Subject: Tie General Ledger to Detail		

1. **PURPOSE AND SCOPE**

   This procedure is used by the general ledger clerk to verify that general ledger summary balances equal the totals for subsidiary journals.

2. **RESPONSIBILITIES**

   GL CLERK   **General Ledger Clerk**

3. **PROCEDURES**

   3.1   GL CLERK   **Locate Summary Balances in General Ledger**

   1. Print the summary level general ledger report, using the GL option in the REPORTS screen.
   2. Highlight any balance sheet accounts with an ending balance.

   3.2   GL CLERK   **Compare to Subsidiary Journal Totals**

   1. For all account balances exceeding $1,000, compare the general ledger ending balance to the amount shown in the subsidiary-level journal.
   2. If there is no journal, then compare the balance to the manually maintained listing.

   3.3   GL CLERK   **Investigate Variances**

   1. For any accounts for which the general ledger balance does not match the supporting detail, print out the detail level general ledger for those accounts, using the GL DETAIL option in the REPORTS screen.
   2. Compare the detail in the general ledger to the detail in the subsidiary journal to find any differing items.
   3. Investigate the reasons for these variances, and make correcting journal entries if necessary.

Tie General Ledger to Detail

Policy/Procedure Statement	Procedure No.:	FIN-17
	Page:	1 of 1
Brasto Publishing	Issue Date:	10/28/0X
	Supersedes:	N/A
Subject: Review Variances from Budget		

1. **PURPOSE AND SCOPE**
   This procedure is used by the financial analyst to determine the amount and reason for actual revenue and expense variances from budgeted levels.

2. **RESPONSIBILITIES**
   FINL ANALYST   **Financial Analyst**

3. **PROCEDURES**

   3.1   FINL ANALYST   **Print Budget versus Actual Financial Statements**
   Print the financial statements.

   3.2   FINL ANALYST   **Identify Key Variances**
   1. Review the complete set of financial statements and circle all items for which there is a negative variance between the budget and actual expenses of at least $1,000 for the month, or $1,000 per month (cumulatively) for the year-to-date.
   2. Note the name of the responsible manager next to these negative variances.

   3.3   FINL ANALYST   **Investigate Key Variances**
   1. Review the circled variances with the responsible managers to determine the reasons for their occurrence.
   2. If necessary, also print out the detailed list of transactions that created the ending expense totals, and investigate the largest ones to ascertain their nature.

   3.4   FINL ANALYST   **Report on Key Variances**
   1. Prepare a report that identifies the reasons for the largest negative variances.
   2. Meet with the controller to go over this variance information.
   3. Revise the report as necessary and forward it to the assistant controller, who will include it in the financial statements.

Review Variances from Budget

Policy/Procedure Statement	Retrieval No.:	FIN-18
	Page:	1 of 1
Brasto Publishing	Issue Date:	10/28/0X
	Supersedes:	N/A
Subject: Add Summary and Financial Analysis		

1. **PURPOSE AND SCOPE**

   This procedure is used by the assistant controller to ensure that all standard notes and analyses are included in the financial statement package.

2. **RESPONSIBILITIES**

ASST CNTLR	**Assistant Controller**
CONTROLLER	**Controller**

3. **PROCEDURES**

   3.1   ASST CNTLR   **Compile Footnotes to Financial Statements**

   Go to the footnotes file from the last set of financial statements, and update them based on any subsequent changes. Most of this information is boilerplate and requires no changes, but any text in red is intended for monthly updates.

   3.2   ASST CNTLR   **Compile Numerical Notes to Financial Statements**

   1. Update the numerical notes to the financial statements.
   2. The updates should include the historical year-to-year comparison, the monthly balance sheet and income statement, ratios, and breakeven analysis. These are all located on separate worksheets within the same spreadsheet.

   3.3   ASST CNTLR   **Compile Written Commentary on Financial Statements**

   Based on the variance and numerical analyses already completed, update the written commentary from the previous month's financial statements.

   3.4   CONTROLLER   **Review Completed Financial Statements**

   1. Using the previous month's financial statements as a guide, assemble them for the newest month in the same order, being sure to number all pages and refer to them in the table of contents.
   2. Create separate financial statements for individual departments, which are to be released to department managers. Refer to the distribution list from the previous month to see who gets which pages of the financial statements.

   3.5   ASST CNTLR   **Assemble Financial Statements**

   Copy and bind the financial statements.

Add Summary and Financial Analysis

Policy/Procedure Statement	Procedure No.:	FIN-19
Brasto Publishing	Page:	1 of 1
	Issue Date:	10/28/0X
	Supersedes:	N/A
Subject: Distribute Full and Partial Statements		

1. **PURPOSE AND SCOPE**

   This procedure is used by the controller to ensure that the correct full and partial monthly financial reports are issued to the standard list of recipients.

2. **RESPONSIBILITIES**

   CONTROLLER   **Controller**

3. **PROCEDURES**

   3.1   CONTROLLER   **Determine Report Distribution**

   Mark the cover of each financial statement with the name of the person to whom it is being released, using the distribution list from the previous month.

   3.2   CONTROLLER   **Distribute Financial Reports**

   1. Distribute the financial statements to the appropriate individuals.
   2. If the financial statements are considered confidential, then have each recipient sign for his or her copy.
   3. Send statement copies to external entities via registered mail or traceable express mail.

Distribute Full and Partial Statements

Policy/Procedure Statement	Retrieval No.:	FIN-20
	Page:	1 of 1
Brasto Publishing	Issue Date:	10/28/0X
	Supersedes:	N/A
Subject: Conduct Postclosing Staff Meeting		

1. **PURPOSE AND SCOPE**
   This procedure is used by the controller to ensure that the standard set of topics are covered during the postclosing review of all closing activities.

2. **RESPONSIBILITIES**
   CONTROLLER   **Controller**

3. **PROCEDURES**
   3.1   CONTROLLER   **Schedule Staff Meeting**
   1. Schedule a staff meeting with all personnel involved in the closing process.
   2. Issue an agenda to all participants prior to the meeting.

   3.2   CONTROLLER   **Hold Meeting**
   1. Review with the closing team the results of the most recent closing, as well as problems encountered.
   2. Discuss areas for potential improvement, which may include items from the following checklist:
      - Complete work on closing activities prior to month-end.
      - Defer minor closing activities until after the core closing period.
      - Locate and correct transaction errors in advance.
      - Move the reporting of operating data from the financial statements to other reports.
      - Restrict the number of reports issued.
      - Standardize the reports issued.
      - Complete financial statement footnotes in advance.
      - Improve the accuracy of inventory counts.
      - Eliminate journal entries.
      - Automate journal entries.
      - Defer routine work not related to the close.
      - Centralize closing tasks with a smaller number of people.
      - Automate additional closing activities.
   3. Assign responsibilities for all resulting projects, as well as due dates.
   4. Issue a follow-up memo confirming responsibilities and due dates.

Conduct Postclosing Staff Meeting

Policy/Procedure Statement	Retrieval No.:	FIX-01
Brasto Publishing	Page:	1 of 1
	Issue Date:	10/28/0X
	Supersedes:	N/A
Subject: Evaluate Capital Proposal		

1. **PURPOSE AND SCOPE**
    This procedure is used by the financial analyst to verify the assumptions, cash flows, and net present value of all capital proposals.

2. **RESPONSIBILITIES**
    FINL ANALYST   **Financial Analyst**

3. **PROCEDURES**

3.1   FINL ANALYST   **Verify Assumptions**
1. Review each submitted Capital Investment Proposal Form (see Exhibit 6.23) to ensure that all fields have been completed. If not, return the form to the sender, with a note regarding the missing information.
2. Review all assumptions with the person submitting the form. If they vary significantly from assumptions used for previous approved capital budgets, or if there are reasonable grounds for doubt, modify the underlying numerical data.

3.2   FINL ANALYST   **Verify Cash Flows**
1. Review all itemized cash flows listed in the form, including expenditures for equipment, working capital, and maintenance with the project manager, purchasing staff, sales staff, and anyone else with a reasonable degree of knowledge regarding the amount or timing of the cash flows.
2. Adjust the amount or timing of cash flows in the capital expenditure analysis based on the preceding cash flow review.

3.3   FINL ANALYST   **Calculate Net Present Value**
1. Obtain the cost of capital from the Controller, and use it to discount the stream of cash flows listed in the Capital Investment Proposal Form. Verify the calculation against the net present value listed in the form.
2. If the project seems unusually risky, also recalculate the net present value using a higher discount rate, to be determined by the Controller.

3.4   FINL ANALYST   **Issue Recommendation**
1. If the net present value is positive, then issue a favorable project recommendation to the Controller and project sponsor.
2. If the net present value is negative, but the type of project listed on the Capital Investment Proposal Form is listed as a "Legal requirement" or "Safety issue," issue a favorable project recommendation to the Controller and project sponsor.
3. If the net present value is negative and the type of project listed on the Capital Investment Proposal Form is listed as "New product-related," "Old product extension," or "Repair/replacement," issue an unfavorable project recommendation to the Controller and project sponsor.

Evaluate Capital Proposal

Name of Project Sponsor: *H. Henderson*   **Submission Date:**   *[Date]*

Investment Description:

Additional press for newsprint.

Cash Flows:

Year	Equipment	Working Capital	Maintenance	Tax Effect of Annual Depreciation	Salvage Value	Revenue	Taxes	Total
0	−5,000,000	−400,000		800,000				−5,400,000
1			−100,000	320,000		1,650,000	−700,000	1,170,000
2			−100,000	320,000		1,650,000	−700,000	1,170,000
3			−100,000	320,000		1,650,000	−700,000	1,170,000
4			−100,000	320,000		1,650,000	−700,000	1,170,000
5		400,000	−100,000	320,000	1,000,000	1,650,000	−700,000	2,570,000
Totals	−5,000,000	0	−500,000	2,400,000	1,000,000	8,250,000		1,850,000

Tax Rate:	**40%**
Hurdle Rate:	**10%**
Payback Period:	4.28
Net Present Value:	(86,809)
Internal Rate of Return:	9.4%

Type of Project (check one):

Legal requirement	
New product-related	
Old product extension	Yes
Repair/replacement	
Safety issue	

Approvals:

Amount	Approver	Signature
<$5,000	Supervisor	
$5–19,999	General Mgr	
$20–49,999	President	
$50,000+	Board	

Exhibit 6.23   Capital Investment Proposal Form

Policy/Procedure Statement	Retrieval No.:	FIX-02
	Page:	1 of 1
Brasto Publishing	Issue Date:	10/28/0X
	Supersedes:	N/A
Subject: Record Payable as Fixed Asset		

1. **PURPOSE AND SCOPE**

   This procedure is used to process fixed asset transactions by the accounts payable clerk.

2. **RESPONSIBILITIES**

   ACC PAY   **Accounts Payable Clerk**

3. **PROCEDURES**

   3.1   ACC PAY   **Add Assets**

   Go to the EDIT menu and choose "Add Assets." Enter information in the "General Information" section: you must use an asset number to add an asset. Then click on the bottom half of the screen to enter information about the cost basis. To save the new asset, go to the menu and choose "Save Asset."

   3.2   ACC PAY   **Delete Assets**

   Select the Asset you want to delete. From the EDIT menu, choose "Delete Asset" and then confirm the deletion.

   3.3   ACC PAY   **Edit Assets**

   Select an asset in the schedule folder and then go to the VIEW menu and choose "Asset Detail." Click on the field to make any changes. From the EDIT menu, choose "Save Asset."

   3.4   ACC PAY   **Find an Asset**

   From the EDIT menu, pick "Find Asset." Enter the asset number and press ENTER. Then, depending on your search criteria, pick either "Next Asset," "Previous Asset," "First Asset," or "Last Asset" from the EDIT menu.

   3.5   ACC PAY   **Print a Report**

   From the TOOLS menu, choose "Reports." Select a report from the list and click OK.

   3.6   ACC PAY   **Sell an Asset**

   Select the asset for which you want to record sales information and click the "Disposal" tab. Click on the "Disposal" check box to enter information for this asset. Enter the asset number. Use the 'TAB' key to move to the "Disposal Date" field. Then enter the disposal date, followed by the sale price.

Record Payable as Fixed Asset

Policy/Procedure Statement	Procedure No.:	FIX-03
	Page:	1 of 1
Brasto Publishing	Issue Date:	10/28/0X
	Supersedes:	N/A
Subject: Record Depreciation as Fixed Asset		

1. **PURPOSE AND SCOPE**
   This procedure is used by the general ledger accountant to ensure that the correct depreciation type and period is used for each capitalized asset.

2. **RESPONSIBILITIES**
   GL ACCT **General Ledger Accountant**

3. **PROCEDURES**

   3.1 GL ACCT **Determine Type of Asset**
   1. Compare the type of asset to the company policy statement on asset types in the accounting policy manual.
   2. Go to the fixed assets register and enter the asset under the correct asset category, using the ADD ASSET screen.

   3.2 GL ACCT **Determine Type and Length of Depreciation Method**
   1. In the ADD ASSET screen, set the number of years of depreciation in accordance with the standard listed in the company policy statement on asset types.
   2. Set the first-year depreciation at the half-year convention.
   3. Set the depreciation method as the sum-of-years-digits, which is standard for all depreciation for all assets.
   4. Use the PRINT option at the bottom of the screen to verify this entry.

   3.3 GL ACCT **Calculate Depreciation**
   Print the depreciation register from the REPORTS screen and verify the system has calculated the depreciation expense for the newly added asset correctly.

Record Depreciation as Fixed Asset

Policy/Procedure Statement	Retrieval No.:	FIX-04
Brasto Publishing	Page:	1 of 1
	Issue Date:	10/28/0X
	Supersedes:	N/A
Subject: Calculate Gain/Loss on Sale of Asset		

1.   PURPOSE AND SCOPE

This procedure is used by the assistant controller to calculate the gain or loss on the sale or disposal of any capital assets.

2.   RESPONSIBILITIES

ASST CNTLR   **Assistant Controller**

3.   PROCEDURES

3.1   ASST CNTLR   **Determine Which Assets Are Being Disposed Of**

Receive documentation from the purchasing department regarding the sale of assets. This should include a signed Asset Disposition form that authorized someone to sell an asset. If the document is not signed by an authorized person, return it with a note asking for the appropriate signature. The document should be accompanied by a copy of the bill of sale, and a copy of the check or other document that shows proof of the amount paid.

3.2   ASST CNTLR   **Find Assets in Fixed Assets Listing**

Once the sale documentation is complete, go to the fixed asset database and call up the record for the asset being sold. The easiest way is to conduct a search based on the name of the asset, though the documentation may contain the asset number, which can also be used to find the correct record.

3.3   ASST CNTLR   **Extract Cost and Depreciation Figures**

Write down the original asset cost and total accumulated depreciation, which is located in the record in the fixed asset database.

3.4   ASST CNTLR   **Determine Gain or Loss**

Subtract the sale amount and accumulated depreciation from the original asset cost. If there is a positive amount left over, this is a loss on the sale of the asset. If there is a negative amount left over, this is a gain on the sale of the asset.

3.5   ASST CNTLR   **Record Journal Entry**

Obtain a journal entry form and complete it for the gain or loss transaction. The asset's original cost goes in the "Credit" column, while the accumulated depreciation amount goes in the "Debit" column. The sale amount is a debit to cash. If there is a gain, this is recorded as a credit. A loss is recorded as a debit.

3.6   ASST CNTLR   **Record Change in Fixed Asset Database**

Access the fixed asset database and record the sale of the asset. Print the fixed asset database after this transaction is recorded and compare the total for the account to the general ledger to ensure that the information is recorded in the same amounts in both locations.

3.7   ASST CNTLR   **File the Gain or Loss Calculation**

File a copy of the gain or loss calculation in the journal entry book, and also in the permanent file documenting the addition or removal of fixed assets.

Calculate Gain/Loss on Sale of Asset

Policy/Procedure Statement	Retrieval No.:	FUN-01
Brasto Publishing	Page:	1 of 1
	Issue Date:	10/28/0X
	Supersedes:	N/A
Subject: Prepare Cash Forecast		

1.   **PURPOSE AND SCOPE**

The accounting department uses this procedure to allow the accounts payable clerk to access information on the current day's cash balances and to recommend changes to the disposition of cash.

2.   **RESPONSIBILITIES**

ACC PAY   **Accounts Payable Clerk**

3.   **PROCEDURES**

3.1   ACC PAY   **Access the Cash Spreadsheet**

Access the Cash Forecast (see Exhibit 6.24) electronic spreadsheet.

3.2   ACC PAY   **Update the Cash Forecast**

1.   Enter the current date in the "Date Last Updated" field in the Cash Forecast spreadsheet.
2.   Determine the current cash balance from the general ledger and enter this information in the Beginning Cash Balance spreadsheet.
3.   Discuss likely sales prospects with the sales manager and enter only the most likely sales in the "Receipts from Sales Projections" section of the spreadsheet. The week in which a cash projection is made should reflect the anticipated cash receipt date from a sale, not the date on which a sale is initially made.
4.   Print the accounts receivable aging report and enter the expected receipt dates for all invoices with balances exceeding $_____. Summarize the expected cash receipt dates for smaller invoices and enter them in the "Cash, Minor Invoices" line.
5.   Enter expected cash expenditures in the "Cash Out" section.
6.   Move the cells containing the "Budgeted Cash Balance" at the bottom of the spreadsheet to correspond to the week-ending dates matching the month-end dates for which budgeted cash information is available, and enter in those cells the budgeted month-end cash balance for each month.

3.3   ACC PAY   **Recommend Cash Transfers**

E-mail the Cash Forecast spreadsheet to the Controller, noting any time periods when incoming cash flows will be insufficient to cover expected cash outflows. Recommend cash movements based on the following rules:

- Any excess in the collected balance over $_____ should be transferred back to the line of credit, unless there is a payroll due within the next three days or if accounts payable checks are due for collection within three days.
- Any shortfall in cash should be transferred to the checking account from the line of credit if accounts payable checks have been floating for five days, or if payroll is due the next day.
- All recommendations for transfers in or out are in increments of $1,000.

Prepare Cash Forecast

Cash Forecast

Date Last Updated: 3/9/2008

	3/9/2008	3/16/2008	3/23/2008	3/30/2008	4/6/2008	4/13/2008	4/20/2008	4/27/2008	5/4/2008	May-2008 (partial)	Jun-2008	Jul-2008
					For the Week Beginning on							
Beginning Cash Balance	$ 1,037,191	$ 1,034,369	$ 968,336	$ 967,918	$ 918,082	$ 932,850	$ 918,747	$ 829,959	$ 834,924	$ 754,124	$ 809,592	$ 798,554
Receipts from Sales Projections:												
Coal Bed Drilling Corp.										$ 16,937		$ 174,525
Oil Patch Kids Corp.										48,521		28,775
Overfault & Sons Inc.								12,965			$ 125,000	
Platte River Drillers									2,500	53,000		
Powder River Supplies Inc.									3,000		15,000	14,500
Submersible Drillers Ltd.									8,700	2,500	16,250	16,250
Commercial, Various											25,000	25,000
Uncollected Invoices:												
Canadian Drillers Ltd.			$ 9,975									
Coastal Mudlogging Co.			6,686									
Dept. of the Interior	$ 1,823			11,629		$ 2,897						
Drill Tip Repair Corp.				5,575						$ 18,510		
Overfault & Sons Inc.			9,229									
Submersible Drillers Ltd.				4,245								
U.S. Forest Service		2,967	812	8,715								
Cash, Minor Invoices	2,355	-	3,668		21,768							
Total Cash In	$ 4,178	$ 2,967	$ 30,370	$ 30,164	$ 21,768	$ 2,897	$ -	$ 12,965	$ 14,200	$ 139,468	$ 185,750	$ 259,050
Cash Out:												
Payroll + Payroll Taxes		$ 62,000		$ 65,000			$ 68,000		$ 71,000	71,000	$ 138,000	138,000
Commissions				7,000					7,000		9,000	9,000
Rent			10,788				10,788				10,788	10,788
Capital Purchases			10,000						10,000		10,000	10,000
Other Expenses	7,000	7,000	10,000	8,000	7,000	7,000	10,000	8,000	7,000	14,000	32,000	32,000
Total Cash Out:	$ 7,000	$ 69,000	$ 30,788	$ 80,000	$ 7,000	$ 17,000	$ 88,788	$ 8,000	$ 95,000	$ 85,000	$ 199,788	$ 199,788
Net Change in Cash	$ (2,822)	$ (66,033)	$ (418)	$ (49,836)	$ 14,768	$ (14,103)	$ (88,788)	$ 4,965	$ (80,800)	$ 54,468	$ (10,038)	$ 59,262
Ending Cash:	$ 1,034,369	$ 968,336	$ 967,918	$ 918,082	$ 932,850	$ 918,747	$ 829,959	$ 834,924	$ 754,124	$ 808,592	$ 799,554	$ 857,816
Budgeted Cash Balance:				897,636				833,352		800,439	815,040	857,113

Exhibit 6.24 Cash Forecast

Policy/Procedure Statement	Retrieval No.:	FUN-02
Brasto Publishing	Page:	1 of 1
	Issue Date:	10/28/0X
	Supersedes:	N/A
Subject: Conduct a Daily Online Bank Reconciliation		

1. **PURPOSE AND SCOPE**

   This procedure is used by the general ledger clerk to reconcile each bank account on a daily basis over the Internet.

2. **RESPONSIBILITIES**

   GL ACCT   **General Ledger Accountant**

3. **PROCEDURES**

   3.1   GL ACCT   **Activate Screens**

   1.   Access the Internet. Then click on the relevant bank account bookmarked under the Favorites section of Internet Explorer.
   2.   Enter the corporate user ID and password for the account number to enter the bank account records, and access the detail records screen for the bank account.
   3.   Minimize the window.
   4.   Access the corporate accounting software. Enter the software's bank reconciliation screen and call up the account number for the bank account currently open on the other screen.

   3.2   ACC RECV   **Conduct Daily Reconciliation**

   1.   Maximize the bank's reconciliation window.
   2.   Set the transaction range for the bank record detail to the previous day, and print the resulting page(s) of results. Minimize the screen.
   3.   Using a ruler, move down the transaction printout report and check off each cleared check on the accounting software's reconciliation screen. Scratch off each item on the report that has been checked off on the screen.
   4.   Using a ruler, move down the transaction printout report and check off each cleared deposit on the accounting software's reconciliation screen. Scratch off each item on the report that has been checked off on the screen.
   5.   Use the accounting software's transaction adjustment feature to record any remaining items listed on the bank reconciliation report.
   6.   Maximize the bank's reconciliation window. Switch to the bank statement summary screen. Copy down the ending balance for the account. Minimize the screen.
   7.   Enter the account's ending balance in the software's bank reconciliation screen. If the adjusted book balance matches the bank balance, maximize the bank's reconciliation window and log out. If not, review the daily entries and those of prior days (as necessary) to determine the location of the reconciliation error.
   8.   Log out of the bank's reconciliation window and exit the Internet. Return to the accounting software and save the bank reconciliation entries.

Conduct a Daily On-Line Bank Reconciliation

Policy/Procedure Statement	Retrieval No.:	FUN-03
Brasto Publishing	Page:	1 of 1
	Issue Date:	10/28/0X
	Supersedes:	N/A
Subject: Borrow Funds		

1. **PURPOSE AND SCOPE**

   This procedure is used by the chief financial officer to borrow funds from the line of credit.

2. **RESPONSIBILITIES**

   CFO   **Chief Financial Officer**
   GL ACCT   **General Ledger Accountant**

3. **PROCEDURES**

   3.1 CFO   **Determine Required Borrowing Level**
   1. Review the short-term cash forecast and determine the immediate cash need from that report.
   2. Verify that there is a sufficient amount left on the line of credit to borrow.
   3. Verify that the current borrowing base is sufficient to fund an increase in the line of credit.
   4. Verify that no bond investments are being liquidated in time to relieve the cash shortfall, as indicated on the Bond Status report (see Exhibit 6.25).

   3.2 CFO   **Complete Borrowing Forms**
   1. Extract a copy of the Loan Borrowing/Paydown Form (see Exhibit 6.26) from the forms cabinet and fill it out, entering the amount determined in the first step. Check the "Borrow box on the form, list the loan number against which the funds will be charged, and note the company account number into which the funds are to be shifted. Also circle the "From" wording to the left of the loan number and the "To" wording to the left of the company account number to indicate the direction of funds flow.
   2. Have an authorized signer sign the borrowing form.
   3. Enter on the form the company phone number the lender should call to verify the amount of loaned funds.

   3.3 CFO   **Borrow Funds**
   1. Fax the form to the bank.
   2. Call the bank to verify receipt of the fax.
   3. Send the borrowing form to the general ledger accountant for proper recording in the general ledger.

   3.4 GL ACCT   **Record Borrowing Information**
   1. Enter the amount of the loan in the appropriate general ledger accounts.
   2. File the Loan Borrowing/Paydown Form in the banking transactions file, sorted by date.

Borrow Funds

Company Name
Bond Status Report

Beginning Serial Number	Ending Serial Number	Sale Price	Face Value	Stated Rate	1st Interest Payment Date	2nd Interest Payment Date	Principal Payment Date	Total Principal	Conversion Date	Conversion Price
00001	01000	$950	$1,000	9.375%	15-Mar	5-Sep	15-Sep-2015	$1,000,000	15-Sep-2020	$50
01001	02000	$975	$1,000	9.375%	15-Mar	5-Sep	10-Oct-2015	$1,000,000	10-Oct-2020	$50
02001	03000	$990	$1,000	9.375%	15-Mar	5-Sep	20-Nov-2015	$1,000,000	20-Nov-2020	$50
10000	12000	$850	$1,000	9.100%	15-Feb	15-Aug	15-Feb-2018	$2,000,000	15-Feb-2023	$52
12001	14000	$860	$1,000	9.100%	15-Feb	15-Aug	31-Mar-2018	$2,000,000	31-Mar-2023	$52
14001	16000	$845	$1,000	9.100%	15-Feb	15-Aug	20-Apr-2018	$2,000,000	20-Apr-2023	$52
20000	25000	$910	$1,000	9.250%	1-May	1-Nov	5-May-2020	$5,000,000	5-May-2025	$55
30000	34000	$935	$1,000	9.850%	1-Apr	1-Aug	10-Apr-2021	$4,000,000	10-Apr-2026	$56
40000	48000	$980	$1,000	9.950%	1-Jun	1-Dec	5-Jun-2022	$8,000,000	5-Jun-2027	$60
50000	56000	$942	$1,000	9.450%	1-Jun	1-Dec	11-Jul-2023	$6,000,000	11-Jul-2028	$62
								$32,000,000		

Exhibit 6.25 Bond Status Report

Loan Borrowing/Paydown Form
for [Company Name]

<u>To the attention of:</u>
    Lending officer name
    Lending entity name
    Lending entity address

<u>Borrow</u>	<u>Paydown</u>	<u>Dollar Amount</u>		<u>Loan Number</u>		<u>Company Account Number</u>
☐	☐	$ _____	From To	_____	From To	_____
☐	☐	$ _____	From To	_____	From To	_____
☐	☐	$ _____	From To	_____	From To	_____
☐	☐	$ _____	From To	_____	From To	_____
☐	☐	$ _____	From To	_____	From To	_____

<u>Authorization:</u>

_____   _____   _____
       Signature   Printed Name   Title/Date

_____
   Confirmation Phone Number

Exhibit 6.26 Loan Borrowing/Paydown Form

Policy/Procedure Statement	Retrieval No.:	FUN-04
	Page:	1 of 1
Brasto Publishing	Issue Date:	10/28/0X
	Supersedes:	N/A
Subject: Extinguish Debt		

1. **PURPOSE AND SCOPE**
   This procedure is used by the chief financial officer to process the repurchase of debt by the issuer.

2. **RESPONSIBILITIES**
   CFO   **Chief Financial Officer**
   GEN LEDGER   **General Ledger Accountant**

3. **PROCEDURES**
   3.1 CFO **Obtain Approval of Debt Extinguishment**
   1. Examine the bond documentation to determine the amount of any extra fees required to extinguish debt early, such as termination fees or premium payments. Calculate the full extinguishment cost including these factors, and compare it to the cost of replacement financing to see if the proposed extinguishment will result in increased cash flow for the company.
   2. Obtain written approval from the Board of Directors to retire the debt, and include this document in the corporate minute book.
   3. If there is a trustee managing bondholder transactions, notify the trustee of the proposed extinguishment.

   3.2 CFO **Notify Bondholders of Extinguishment**
   Notify bondholders of the date on which conversion shall occur, and the price they will receive for each bond held. If required by the bond document, this information may require publication to the general public well in advance of the extinguishment date.

   3.3 GEN LEDGER **Summarize and Record Transaction**
   1. If the original record of the bond issuance included recognition of the intrinsic value of its equity portion, this recognition must be reversed. To do so, determine the number of shares that could have been converted on the retirement date. Then calculate the difference between the strike price and the fair market value of the stock on that date, and multiply it by the number of shares that could have been converted. Debit the result to the Additional Paid-In Capital account.
   2. If bond issuance costs were incurred and capitalized, then any remaining unamortized amounts left in the asset account as of the date of the debt extinguishment must be recognized as expense.
   3. If there is any unamortized discount or premium related to the original bond issuance, recognize that portion of the remaining amount that equates to the proportion of debt being retired.
   4. If any premium is being paid to retire the debt, charge this premium to expense at the time of the retirement.
   5. On the retirement date, issue settlement funding to the bondholder trustee to retire the bonds.

Extinguish Debt

Policy/Procedure Statement	Retrieval No.:	FUN-05
	Page:	1 of 1
Brasto Publishing	Issue Date:	10/28/0X
	Supersedes.	N/A
Subject: Convert Debt to Equity		

1. **PURPOSE AND SCOPE**

   This procedure is used by the chief financial officer to process a request by a bondholder to convert that entity's bond holdings to company stock.

2. **RESPONSIBILITIES**

   CFO   **Chief Financial Officer**

   GEN LEDGER   **General Ledger Accountant**

3. **PROCEDURES**

   3.1   CFO   **Verify Available Number of Shares**

   Verify that a sufficient number of shares are authorized and available to fulfill the request by the bondholder.

   3.2   GEN LEDGER   **Record Debt Conversion to Equity**

   1. Send documentation of the request to the general ledger accountant, who records any accrued but unpaid interest expense on the bond, debiting it to expense and crediting the capital account (if the bondholder forfeits the interest). The general ledger accountant should initial the step to signify its completion.

   2. If the market value method is used to record the conversion transaction, the general ledger accountant should also note in the procedure the date of the conversion, the market price of the stock on that date, and initial next to this information.

   3.3   CFO   **Retire Bonds and Issue Stock**

   1. Update the bond ledger by recording the retirement of the bond serial number.

   2. Create a stock certificate for the bondholder and obtain valid signatures authorizing the certificate. Issue the certificate to the former bondholder by registered mail.

   3. Update the stock ledger by recording the stock certificate number and the number of shares issued.

Convert Debt to Equity

Policy/Procedure Statement		Retrieval No.:	FUN-06
		Page:	1 of 1
Brasto Publishing		Issue Date:	10/28/0X
		Supersedes:	N/A
Subject: Invest Funds			

1.   PURPOSE AND SCOPE

This procedure is used by the chief financial officer to invest funds in accordance with the corporate investment policy.

2.   RESPONSIBILITIES

CFO   **Chief Financial Officer**

GEN LEDGER   **General Ledger Accountant**

3.   PROCEDURES

3.1   CFO   **Determine Amount of Funds to Invest**

1. Review the short-term cash forecast with the financial analyst and determine the amount of funds that are not immediately needed for operations.
2. Adjust the forecast based on unusual cash flows not noted in the standard report format.

3.2   CFO   **Determine Appropriate Investment Instrument**

Using the corporate investing policy and the size of the investable cash amount as guidelines, select the appropriate investment vehicle. For the short-term cash investments, select the most liquid investments on the investing policy.

3.3   CFO   **Invest Funds**

1. Extract a copy of the investment form from the forms cabinet and fill it out, entering the amount determined in the first step.
2. Have an authorized signer sign the investment form.
3. Fax this form to the company's investment firm.
4. Call the firm to verify receipt of the fax.
5. Send the investment form to the general ledger accountant.

3.4   GEN LEDGER   **Record Investment**

1. Upon receipt of the investment form, enter the change in investment accounts in the general ledger.
2. If the investment is into stocks, update the Stock Ledger Report (see Exhibit 6.27).
3. If the investment is into bonds, update the Bond Ledger Report (see Exhibit 6.28).

Invest Funds

Stock Ledger Report

Issued by: ___Intergalactic Coal Mining Co.___

Class: ___Common___   Par Value: ___$1.00___

	Bought				Sold			Profit or Loss		Balance	
Date	No. of Shares	Price	Cost*	Date	No. of Shares	Price	Total* Received	Profit or Loss	No. of Shares	Average Price	Cost
1/30/2005	100	$30	$3,020						100	$30.20	$3,020
				9/30/2005	25	$36	$890	$135	75	$30.20	$2,265
10/3/2005	50	$35	$1,770						125	$32.28	$4,035
				11/15/2005	25	$38	$940	$133	100	$32.28	$3,228

* Includes commission.

Exhibit 6.27 Stock Ledger Report

Bond Name: ___Intergalactic Coal Mining Co.___

Purchased
Through ___ABC Bond Sales___

Nominal Rate ___10%___
Actual Rate ___9.3%___

Description:
Numbers: ___B1676, B1677___
Denomination: ___$5,000___
Where Payable: ___Third Trust, Chicago___
Trustee: ___Third Trust, Chicago___

Dated: ___1/1/2008___
When Due: ___12/31/2025___
Interest Payable: ___6/30, 12/31___
Redeemable: ___Yes___

Date	Pieces	Memo	Price	Debit	Credit	Balance	Profit or Loss	Due Date	Interest Amount	Paid Date
4/1/2008	2	ABC Bond	$107.5	$10,750		$10,750		6/30/2008	$500	6/30/2008
6/30/2008		Premium			$50	$10,700		12/31/2008	$500	12/31/2008
12/31/2008		Premium			$100	$10,600		6/30/2009	$500	6/30/2009
6/30/2009		Premium			$100	$10,500	$100			
7/1/2009	1	Denver National	$107.0		$5,200	$5,250	$5,200			

Exhibit 6.28 Bond Ledger Report

Policy/Procedure Statement	Retrieval No.:	FUN-07
Brasto Publishing	Page:	1 of 1
	Issue Date:	10/28/0X
Subject: Transfers Between Investment Portfolios	Supersedes:	N/A

1. **PURPOSE AND SCOPE**
   This procedure is used by the controller to not only specify the correct accounting transactions for a shift between the available-for-sale and trading portfolios, but also to ensure that justification for the change has been documented and approved.

2. **RESPONSIBILITIES**
   CONTROLLER   **Controller**
   GEN LEDGER   **General Ledger Accountant**

3. **PROCEDURES**
   3.1   CONTROLLER   **Document Reason for Transfer**
   1. Document the reason for the shift between portfolios, and summarize the total impact of gains or losses to be recognized in current income as a result of the change, including the tax impact.
   2. If the impact on current earnings is significant, notify the Board of Directors of the prospective change, if required by company policy.

   3.2   GEN LEDGER   **Record Change in Portfolios**
   1. Create a journal entry to shift funds between the available-for-sale and trading portfolios, including the recognition of any gains or losses required to bring the recorded value of the securities to their fair market value as of the transaction date. Log the entry into the accounting system.
   2. Store all documentation of the shift in portfolios, including documentation of Board notification and the related journal entry, in the journal entry binder.

Transfers between Investment Portfolios

Policy/Procedure Statement	Retrieval No.:	FUN-08
	Page:	1 of 1
Brasto Publishing	Issue Date:	10/28/0X
	Supersedes:	N/A
Subject: Create Borrowing Base Certificate		

1. **PURPOSE AND SCOPE**

   This procedure is used by the controller to update the borrowing base certificate at the end of each month, and to send it both to file and all lenders requiring it.

2. **RESPONSIBILITIES**

   CONTROLLER   **Controller**

3. **PROCEDURES**

   3.1   CONTROLLER   **Locate Borrowing Base Certificate File**

   Access the electronic spreadsheet containing the Borrowing Base Certificate (see Exhibit 6.29).

   3.2   CONTROLLER   **Update Borrowing Base Information**

   1. Enter in the "For the month ended" field the month for which financial statements have just been completed.
   2. Enter in the "Accounts receivable balance" field the total amount of accounts receivable listed on the accounts receivable aging report as of the end of the reporting period. Enter in the "Less receivables > 90 days old" field the total in the "90+ days" column in the accounts receivable aging report.
   3. Enter in the "Raw materials inventory balance" field the total amount of raw materials listed in the month-end inventory valuation report.
   4. Enter in the "Finished goods inventory balance" field the total amount of finished goods listed in the month-end inventory valuation report.
   5. Enter in the "Total loan balance" field the amount of loans outstanding pertaining to this borrowing base certificate at the end of the reporting period.
   6. Review the report and sign it.

   3.3   CONTROLLER   **Issue Borrowing Base Certificate**

   Mail the borrowing base certificate to the lender, along with the accounts receivable aging report and inventory valuation report that tie to the amounts listed on the certificate.

Create Borrowing Base Certificate

Company Name
Borrowing Base Certificate

For the month ended: _____

Accounts receivable balance	$1,800,000
Less receivables > 90 days old	−$42,500
Net accounts receivable	$1,757,500

80%	of net accounts receivable balance	$1,406,000

Raw materials inventory balance	$2,020,000

40%	of raw materials inventory balance	$1,010,000

Finished goods inventory balance	$515,000

70%	of finished goods inventory balance	$360,500

Total collateral	$2,776,500
Total loan balance	$2,000,000
Total collateral available for use	$776,500

I assert that the above calculation is correct, and that all bad debts, work-in-process, and obsolete inventory have been removed from the above balances.

CFO Signature: _____   Date: _____

Exhibit 6.29   Borrowing Base Certificate

Policy/Procedure Statement	Retrieval No.:	FUN-09
Brasto Publishing	Page:	1 of 1
	Issue Date:	10/28/0X
	Supersedes:	N/A
Subject: Maintain Stock Subscriptions		

1. **PURPOSE AND SCOPE**

   This procedure is used by the treasurer to calculate periodic cash receipts from stock subscriptions, determine purchase discounts, and allocate shares to participating investors.

2. **RESPONSIBILITIES**

   TREASURER **Treasurer**
   CFO **Chief Financial Officer**

3. **PROCEDURES**

   3.1 TREASURER **Calculate Cash Receipts from Stock Subscriptions**
   1. Access the general ledger account for stock subscriptions and print out the detailed report showing cash receipts by investor for the reporting period.
   2. Compare cash receipts by person to the Stock Subscription Report (see Exhibit 6.30) for the last period to see if there are any anomalies in cash receipts. Investigate any possible cash shortages or overages.

   3.2 TREASURER **Complete Stock Subscription Statement**
   1. Access the Stock Subscription Statement electronic spreadsheet. Add new pages to the report for any new employees for whom stock subscription payroll deductions are now being made.
   2. Transfer the adjusted cash receipt information into the report for each employee, itemizing the date on which cash was deducted from payroll and the amount of the deduction.
   3. Determine the fair market value of company stock at the end of the reporting period and record this amount per share, less the standard subscription discount, in each report.
   4. Record in each report the number of shares purchased by each investor in the reporting period, as well as any remaining unallocated cash.
   5. Print the reports and issue them to all employees enrolled in the stock subscription plan.
   6. Send a copy of the reports to the Chief Financial Officer.

   3.3 CFO **Issue Shares to Investors**
   1. Complete stock certificates in the amount of the shares indicated on the Stock Subscription Statements.
   2. Record the newly issued shares and their identifying certificate numbers, as well as the issuance date, in the stock register.
   3. Issue the certificates to employees by registered mail.

Maintain Stock Subscriptions

Stock Subscription Statement
For [employee name]
as of [date]

| Payroll Dedections | | Stock Purchases | | | | |
Date	Amount	Date	Share Value	10% Discount	Number of Shares	Cash Remainder
1/15/2008	$300.00					
1/31/2008	$300.00	1/31/2008	$ 12.15	$ 10.94	54	$ 9.24
2/15/2008	$300.00					
2/28/2008	$300.00	2/28/2008	$ 13.10	$ 11.79	51	$ 7.95
3/15/2008	$300.00					
3/31/2008	$300.00	3/31/2008	$ 14.05	$ 12.65	48	$ 0.75
4/15/2008	$300.00					
4/30/2008	$300.00	4/30/2008	$ 13.75	$ 12.38	48	$ 6.51
5/15/2008	$300.00					
5/31/2008	$300.00	5/31/2008	$ 13.25	$ 11.93	50	$ 10.01

Exhibit 6.30   Stock Subscription Statement

Policy/Procedure Statement	Retrieval No.:	INV-01
Brasto Publishing	Page:	1 of 1
	Issue Date:	10/28/0X
	Supersedes:	N/A
Subject: Receive Inventory		

1.   **PURPOSE AND SCOPE**
     This procedure is used by the receiving staff to ensure that incoming goods are properly inspected and logged into the accounting database.

2.   **RESPONSIBILITIES**
     RECEIVE   **Receiving Staff**

3.   **PROCEDURES**
3.1 RECEIVE   **Review and Accept Inbound Shipment**
     1. When a shipment arrives, find in the shipping documentation the authorizing purchase order number and locate either a paper-based or electronic copy of the purchase order.
     2. Compare the product quantity and quality to the specifications noted in the purchase order. If there are significant discrepancies, reject the shipment.
     3. Sign a copy of the bill of lading to accept the delivery.
3.2 RECEIVE   **Enter Receipt into Accounting Systems**
     1. Access the authorizing purchase order on the corporate computer system and record both the received quantity and the warehouse location in which they will be stored. If portable bar code scanners are used, then record this transaction at the time the warehouse move is made.
     2. Store a copy of the bill of lading in an indexed file.
     3. Forward a copy of the bill of lading to the accounting department or digitize the image in a scanner and enter the document into the corporate accounting system.

Receive Inventory

Policy/Procedure Statement	Retrieval No.:	INV-02
	Page:	1 of 1
	Issue Date:	10/28/0X
Brasto Publishing	Supersedes:	N/A
Subject: Cycle Count Inventory		

1.   PURPOSE AND SCOPE

This procedure is used by the warehouse staff to ensure that a perpetual inventory's computer records match the physical inventory.

2.   RESPONSIBILITIES

WHSE STAFF   **Warehouse Staff**

3.   PROCEDURES

3.1   WHSE STAFF   Collect Cycle Counting Information

Print a portion of the inventory report, sorted by location (see Exhibit 6.31). Block out a portion of the physical inventory locations shown on the report for cycle counting purposes.

3.2   WHSE STAFF   Compare Physical Inventory to Book Records

1. Go to the first physical inventory location to be cycle counted and compare the quantity, location, and part number of each inventory item to what is described for that location in the inventory report. Mark on the report any discrepancies between the on-hand quantity, location, and description for each item.

2. Use the reverse process to ensure that the same information listed for all items on the report match the items physically appearing in the warehouse location. Note any discrepancies on the report.

3.3   WHSE STAFF   Enter Changes in Accounting Database

1. Verify that the noted discrepancies are not caused by recent inventory transactions that have not yet been logged into the computer system.

2. Correct the inventory database for all remaining errors noted.

3.4   WHSE STAFF   Initiate Corrective Actions

1. Calculate the inventory error rate and post it in the warehouse (see Exhibit 6.32).

2. Call up a history of inventory transactions for each of the items for which errors were noted, and try to determine the cause of the underlying problem. Investigate each issue and recommend corrective action to the warehouse manager, so the problems do not arise again.

Cycle Count Inventory

LOCATION	ITEM NO.	DESCRIPTION	U/M	QUANTITY
A-10-C	Q1458	Switch, 120V, 20A	EA	
A-10-C	U1010	Bolt, zinc, 3 × 1/4	EA	
A-10-C	M1458	Screw, stainless steel, 2 × 3/8	EA	

Exhibit 6.31 Cycle Counting Report

AISLES	RESPONSIBLE PERSON	2 MONTHS AGO	LAST MONTH	WEEK 1	WEEK 2	WEEK 3	WEEK 4
A-B	Fred P.	82%	86%	85%	84%	82%	87%
C-D	Alain Q.	70%	72%	74%	76%	78%	80%
E-F	Davis L.	61%	64%	67%	70%	73%	76%
G-H	Jeff R.	54%	58%	62%	66%	70%	74%
I-J	Alice R.	12%	17%	22%	27%	32%	37%
K-L	George W.	81%	80%	79%	78%	77%	76%
M-N	Robert T.	50%	60%	65%	70%	80%	90%

Exhibit 6.32 Inventory Accuracy Report

Policy/Procedure Statement Brasto Publishing **Subject: Kit Inventory**	Retrieval No.:	INV-03
	Page:	1 of 1
	Issue Date:	10/28/0X
	Supersedes:	N/A

1. **PURPOSE AND SCOPE**
   This procedure is used by the warehouse staff to assemble inventory for production jobs, and to process and returns from the shop floor.

2. **RESPONSIBILITIES**
   WHSE STAFF   **Warehouse Staff**

3. **PROCEDURES**
   3.1   WHSE STAFF   **Collect Parts Kitting Information**
   The materials management department issues a parts request form to the warehouse for each new job to be produced. Upon receipt, set up a pallet on which to store the requested items.

   3.2   WHSE STAFF   **Kit inventory Items**
   1. Collect the requested items from the warehouse, checking off each completed part number on the list and noting the quantity removed and the location from which they were removed.
   2. Access the inventory database record for each removed item and logs out the quantities taken from the appropriate warehouse locations.
   3. Deliver the filled pallet to the production floor.

3.3	WHSE STAFF	**Process Returned Items**

1. If any parts remain after the production job is complete, accept them at the warehouse gate using the Inventory Sign Out and Return form (see Exhibit 6.33), log them back into the computer system, and notify the materials management department of the overage, so they can adjust the bill of material for the products being produced.

2. If any parts are returned in a damaged condition, record them on the Scrap/Rework Transaction Form (see Exhibit 6.34), log them in with a damaged code and stores them in the review area where the Materials Review Board can easily access them. Periodically print out a report listing all items stored in this area, and forward it to the Materials Review Board, so they will be aware that items require their attention.

Kit Inventory

DESCRIPTION	PART NO.	QUANTITY ISSUED	QUANTITY RETURNED	JOB NO.	DATE

Exhibit 6.33   Inventory Sign Out and Return Form

7403

Date: _____

Item Number: _____

Description: _____

Scrapped	Sent to Rework
Quantity Scrapped: _____	Quantity to Rework: _____
Reason: _____	Reason: _____
_____	_____
_____	_____
Signature: _____	Signature: _____

Exhibit 6.34   Scrap/Rework Transaction Form

Policy/Procedure Statement	Retrieval No.:	INV-04
	Page:	1 of 1
Brasto Publishing	Issue Date:	10/28/0X
	Supersedes:	N/A
Subject: Track Inbound Consignment Inventory		

1. **PURPOSE AND SCOPE**

   This procedure is used by the warehouse staff to properly track consignment inventory owned by other parties but stored in the company's warehouse.

2. **RESPONSIBILITIES**

   WHSE STAFF   **Warehouse Staff**

3. **PROCEDURES**

   3.1   WHSE STAFF   **Label Consigned Inventory**

   1. Upon receipt of consigned inventory, prominently label the inventory with a colored tag, clearly denoting its status.
   2. Record the inventory in the computer system using a unique part number to which no valuation is assigned. If a consignment flag is available in the database, flag the part number as being a consignment item.
   3. Store the item in a part of the warehouse set aside for consigned inventory

   3.2   WHSE STAFF   **Review Consigned Inventory**

   Include the consigned inventory in a review by the materials review board (see next procedure, INV-05), which should regularly determine the status of this inventory and arrange for its return if there are no prospects for its use in the near future.

Track Inbound Consignment Inventory

Policy/Procedure Statement	Retrieval No.:	INV-05
	Page:	1 of 1
Brasto Publishing	Issue Date:	10/28/0X
	Supersedes.	N/A
Subject: Review Inventory for Obsolescence		

1. **PURPOSE AND SCOPE**
    This procedure is used by the warehouse staff to periodically review the inventory for obsolete items and account for items considered to be obsolete.

2. **RESPONSIBILITIES**
    WHSE STAFF   **Warehouse Staff**
    GEN LEDGER   **General Ledger Accountant**

3. **PROCEDURES**
    3.1   WHSE STAFF   **Determine Disposition of Inventory**
    1. Schedule a meeting of the materials review board, to meet in the warehouse.
    2. Prior to the meeting, print enough copies of the Inventory Obsolescence Review Report (see Exhibit 6.35) for all members of the committee.
    3. Personally review all items on the report for which there appear to be excessive quantities on hand.
    4. Determine the proper disposal of each item judged to be obsolete, including possible returns to suppliers, donations, inclusion in existing products, or scrap.

    3.2   WHSE STAFF   **Dispose of Inventory**
    1. Have the warehouse staff mark each item as obsolete in the inventory database.
    2. Issue a memo to the materials review board, summarizing the results of its actions.

    3.3   WHSE STAFF   **Dispose of Inventory**
    1. Have the accounting staff write down the value of each obsolete item to its disposal value.

Review Inventory for Obsolescence

DESCRIPTION	ITEM NO.	LOCATION	QUANTITY ON HAND	LAST YEAR USAGE	PLANNED USAGE	EXTENDED COST
Subwoofer case	0421	A-04-C	872	520	180	$9,053
Speaker case	1098	A-06-D	148	240	120	1,020
Subwoofer	3421	D-12-A	293	14	0	24,724
Circuit board	3600	B-01-A	500	5,090	1,580	2,500
Speaker, bass	4280	C-10-C	621	2,480	578	49,200
Speaker bracket	5391	C-10-C	14	0	0	92
Wall bracket	5080	B-03-B	400	0	120	2,800
Gold connection	6233	C-04-A	3,025	8,042	5,900	9,725
Tweeter	7552	C-05-B	725	6,740	2,040	5,630

Exhibit 6.35   Inventory Obsolescence Review Report

Policy/Procedure Statement	Retrieval No.:	INV-06
	Page:	1 of 1
Brasto Publishing	Issue Date:	10/28/0X
	Supersedes:	N/A
Subject: Calculate Period-End Inventory		

1.   **PURPOSE AND SCOPE**
     This procedure is used by the cost accountant to ensure that the inventory valuation created by a computerized accounting system is accurate, as well as to update it with the latest overhead costs.

2.   **RESPONSIBILITIES**
     COST ACCT   **Cost Accountant**

3.   **PROCEDURES**
3.1   COST ACCT   **Verify Inventory Quantities and Costs**
     1.   Following the end of the accounting period, print out and review the computer change log for all bills of material and labor routings. Review them with the materials manager and production engineer to ensure their accuracy. Revise any changes made in error.
     2.   Go to the warehouse and manually compare the period-end counts recorded on the inventory report for the most expensive items in the warehouse to what is in the warehouse racks. If there are any variances, adjust them for any transactions that occurred between the end of the period and the date of the review. If there are still variances, adjust for them in the inventory database.

		3. Print a report that sorts the inventory in declining extended dollar order and review it for reasonableness. Be sure to review not only the most expensive items on the list but also the least expensive, since this where costing errors are most likely to be found. Adjust for any issues found.
3.2	COST ACCT	**Verify Overhead Costs and Allocations** 1. Review all entries in the general ledger during the reporting period for costs added to the cost pool, verifying that only approved costs have been included. Also investigate any unusually large overhead entries. 2. Verify that the overhead allocation calculation conforms to the standard allocation used in previous reporting periods, or that it matches any changes approved by management. 3. Verify that the journal entry for overhead allocation matches the standard journal entry listed in the accounting procedures manual.
3.3	COST ACCT	**Review Variances from Prior Period** Print out the inventory valuation report and compare its results by major category to those of the previous reporting period, both in terms of dollars and proportions. Investigate any major differences.

Calculate Period-End Inventory

Policy/Procedure Statement	Retrieval No.:	INV-07
Brasto Publishing	Page:	1 of 1
	Issue Date:	10/28/0X
	Supersedes:	N/A
Subject: Calculate Lower of Cost or Market Value		

1. **PURPOSE AND SCOPE**

   This procedure is used by the cost accountant to periodically adjust the inventory valuation for those items whose market value has dropped below their recorded cost.

2. **RESPONSIBILITIES**

   COST ACCT **Cost Accountant**

3. **PROCEDURES**

   3.1 COST ACCT **Identify High-Value Inventory Items**

   Export the extended inventory valuation report to an electronic spreadsheet. Sort it by declining extended dollar cost, and delete the 80% of inventory items that do not comprise the top 20% of inventory valuation. Sort the remaining 20% of inventory items by either part number or item description. Print the report.

   3.2 COST ACCT **Conduct Market Price Review**
   1. Send a copy of the report to the materials manager, with instructions to compare unit costs for each item on the list to market prices, and be sure to mutually agree upon a due date for completion of the review.
   2. When the materials management staff has completed its review, meet with the materials manager to go over its results and discuss any major adjustments. Have the materials management staff writes down the valuation of selected items in the inventory database whose cost exceeds their market value.

   3.3 COST ACCT **Document Change in Valuation**
   1. Have the accounting staff expense the value of the write down in the accounting records.
   2. Write a memo detailing the results of the lower of cost or market calculation. Attach one copy to the journal entry used to write down the valuation, and issue another copy to the materials manager.

Calculate Lower of Cost or Market Value

Policy/Procedure Statement	Retrieval No.:	INT-01
	Page:	1 of 1
Brasto Publishing	Issue Date:	10/28/0X
	Supersedes:	N/A
Subject: Construct Audit Methodology		

1.   PURPOSE AND SCOPE

This procedure is used by the internal audit manager to determine the auditing methodology to be used for each audit.

2.   RESPONSIBILITIES

AUDIT MGR   **Internal Audit Manager**

3.   PROCEDURES

3.1   AUDIT MGR   **Compile List of Methodologies**

Consult audit textbooks and the company's external auditors or consultants for copies of audit methodologies.

3.2   AUDIT MGR   **Compare Pros and Cons of Methodologies**

Itemize the differences between the methodologies, not only in terms of investigation techniques and levels, but also reporting formats and control systems.

3.3   AUDIT MGR   **Create Ranking Criteria**

1.   Develop a ranking criteria based on the company's perceived levels of importance when selecting an audit methodology.
2.   Develop a weighting system for each ranking criterion, which reflects the greater importance given to some criteria.

3.4   AUDIT MGR   **Rank Methodologies**

1.   Score each methodology based on the ranking criteria and weighting system.
2.   Select the "winning" methodology based on the ranking system.

3.5   AUDIT MGR   **Train Staff in Methodology**

1.   Develop training materials for using the audit methodology.
2.   Perform "dry runs" of training classes with trainers.
3.   Schedule the internal audit staff for training sessions.
4.   Conduct training.
5.   Incorporate staff comments into revisions of the training materials.

Construct Audit Methodology

Policy/Procedure Statement	Retrieval No.:	INT-02
Brasto Publishing	Page:	1 of 1
	Issue Date:	10/28/0X
	Supersedes:	N/A
Subject: Develop Audit Work Schedule		

1.   **PURPOSE AND SCOPE**
     This procedure is used by the internal audit manager as a guideline in constructing the audit work schedule for all audit teams for the upcoming year.

2.   **RESPONSIBILITIES**
     AUDIT MGR   **Internal Audit Manager**

3.   **PROCEDURES**
3.1   AUDIT MGR   **Compile List of Audit Requests**
     1.   Send an e-mail to all department managers to ask if anyone has requests for specific internal audits.
     2.   Review the recommendations of the external auditors to see if they have spotted weaknesses in the existing control systems.
     3.   Review the results of previous audits to see if there are control problems that may still exist.
     4.   Itemize those areas that have not been audited for a long time.
     5.   Summarize this information into a list of possible audits.

3.2   AUDIT MGR   **Obtain Audit Priorities List from Audit Committee**
     Review this list with the audit committee, and also gain their input regarding additional review areas.

3.3   AUDIT MGR   **Assemble Final Audit List**
     1.   Finalize the list of audits, noting approximations of resources and time requirements.
     2.   Sort the report by priority level.

3.4   AUDIT MGR   **Obtain Audit Committee Approval**
     1.   Present the audit list to the audit committee.
     2.   Make any final adjustments recommended by the audit committee, and obtain their approval.

Develop Audit Work Schedule

Policy/Procedure Statement	Retrieval No.:	INT-03
Brasto Publishing	Page:	1 of 1
	Issue Date:	10/28/0X
	Supersedes:	N/A
Subject: Develop Audit Budget		

1. **PURPOSE AND SCOPE**
   This procedure is used by the internal audit manager to develop a budget for all scheduled audits for the upcoming year.

2. **RESPONSIBILITIES**
   AUDIT MGR   **Internal Audit Manager**

3. **PROCEDURES**

3.1   AUDIT MGR   **Determine Cost of Each Approved Audit**
Determine the cost of each internal audit, which should include the salary cost of audit staff, allocated department overhead costs, travel costs, and the cost of any outsourced audit services.

3.2   AUDIT MGR   **Create Detailed and Summary Budgets**
Summarize the costs of all audits in a summary report, and sort the list in descending dollar order. List the original audit priorities assigned by the audit committee next to each audit so that the audit committee can evaluate the cost of each audit in comparison to its perceived value.

3.3   AUDIT MGR   **Obtain Audit Committee Approval**
1.   Present the audit budget to the audit committee.
2.   Modify the audit budget and list of approved audits in accordance with the wishes of the audit committee.
3.   Gain final approval of the budget.

Develop Audit Budget

Policy/Procedure Statement	Retrieval No.:	INT-04
	Page:	1 of 1
Brasto Publishing	Issue Date:	10/28/0X
	Supersedes:	N/A
Subject: Conduct Internal Audit Review		

1.   **PURPOSE AND SCOPE**
     This procedure is used to determine the reliability of those accounting systems whose failure would have a direct impact on billings to customers or expenses incurred.

2.   **RESPONSIBILITIES**
     ACC PAY   **Accounts Payable Clerk**
     ACC RECV   **Accounts Receivable Clerk**

3.   **PROCEDURES**
3.1 ACC PAY   **Verify Receiving Documentation**
     1.   Take a sample of ___ supplier payments and verify that there is either a signed purchase order attached to the supplier invoice, or the signature of an authorized manager.
     2.   For the same sample, verify that there is a receiving document attached to the supplier invoice.

3.2 ACC RECV   **Verify All Accounts Receivable Credits**
     Take a sample of ___ credits in the accounts receivable journal, and trace the credits back to supporting documentation. Verify that there is an explanation for each credit, as well as an authorized signature on the documentation.

3.3 ACC PAY   **Verify Expense Reports**
     Verify that submitted expenses meet company guidelines for approved travel and entertainment expenses. Take a sample of ___ expense reports and verify that all reported expenses are in accordance with company reimbursement policies.

3.4 ACC PAY   **Review Freight Revenue**
     Verify that customers are charged the correct amount for freight.
     1.   Take a sample of ___ shipments from the shipping log. If the bill of lading states "Prepay" then verify that the customer is one that is not normally charged for freight.
     2.   If the bill of lading states "Prepay and Add" verify that there is a freight amount charged on the corresponding invoice. If not, record this as an error.
     3.   If the invoice does not include a freight charge, trace the amount charged back to the list of standard freight rates by customer. If the rate invoiced does not match the amount on the list of standard rates, record this as an error.

3.5 ACC RECV   **Review Invoicing**
     Verify that all items shipped are invoiced and vice versa. Also, verify that all invoices are printed within one day of shipment. Take a sample of ___ shipments from the shipping log. Trace each shipment back to an invoice, verifying the quantity invoiced. Also, take a sample of invoices and trace them back to the shipping log, verifying that a shipment occurred and that the quantity invoiced is correct.

3.6 ACC RECV   **Review Pricing**
     Verify that customers are being charged the correct prices. Take a sample of ___ invoices and trace the prices for all line items back to the original quote to the customer. Be careful to refer to the sales manager for any subsequent updates to customer quotes.

Conduct Internal Audit Review

Policy/Procedure Statement	Retrieval No.:	INT-05
	Page:	1 of 1
Brasto Publishing	Issue Date:	10/28/0X
	Supersedes.	N/A
Subject: Create and Issue Audit Report		

1. **PURPOSE AND SCOPE**

   This procedure is used by the audit staff to create audits for issuance to management and the audit committee regarding internal control issues discovered by them, along with recommended solutions.

2. **RESPONSIBILITIES**

   AUDIT STAFF   **Internal Audit Staff**

3. **PROCEDURES**

3.1	AUDIT STAFF	**Obtain Audit Report Format**
		Obtain the boilerplate format of the internal audit report, which is located at N: INTERNALX REPORT.DOC.
3.2	AUDIT STAFF	**Create Preliminary Audit Report**

   1. Assemble all findings from the internal audit and enter them into the standard report format.
   2. Add supporting documentation and graphics to the report.
   3. Add recommendations to the report.

| 3.3 | AUDIT STAFF | **Obtain Report Reviews** |

   1. Have the report reviewed by the internal audit manager.
   2. Adjust the report based on any review comments.

| 3.4 | AUDIT STAFF | **Issue Report** |

   1. Review the audit report with the manager of the department whose area was reviewed, with an emphasis on the accuracy of the information presented.
   2. Make final revisions and forward to the internal audit manager.
   3. Send a copy of the report to the manager of the department whose area was reviewed.
   4. Present the report to the internal audit committee.

Create and Issue Audit Report

Policy/Procedure Statement	Retrieval No.:	PAY-01
	Page:	1 of 1
Brasto Publishing	Issue Date:	10/28/0X
	Supersedes:	N/A
Subject: Collect and Reconcile Time Cards		

1.   **PURPOSE AND SCOPE**
     This procedure is used by the payroll clerk to assemble time cards for all hourly employees, as well as to locate and resolve time punching errors.

2.   **RESPONSIBILITIES**
     PR CLERK   **Payroll Clerk**

3.   **PROCEDURES**
3.1 PR CLERK   **Obtain Time Cards**
                       Obtain time cards from all company locations. Check off the receipts against the standard list of company locations, and contact the factory manager of each location from which no cards have been received.

3.2 PR CLERK   **Review Time Cards**
1.   Add up the time on all time cards, circling those time punches that have no clock-ins or clock-outs. Note the total time on all error-free time cards and forward them to the payroll clerk for data entry into the payroll system.
2.   Any time card containing overtime hours must also be initialed by a manager; those cards missing this approval must be returned and signed.

3.3 PR CLERK   **Resolve Time Card Discrepancies**
1.   Review all time cards containing discrepancies with the responsible factory managers. They must initial all time cards for which there is an assumed clock-in or clock-out.
2.   List the total time worked at the top of these time cards.
3.   Forward the cards to the payroll clerk for data entry into the payroll system.

3.4 PR CLERK   **Obtain Commissions Payable**
1.   Obtain the approved commission statements for all sales staff from the commissions clerk.
2.   Compare the commission statements to the list of sales staff to ensure that commission statements have been prepared for all sales staff. Notify the assistant controller of any missing statements.
3.   Verify that each commission statement has an approval signature. If not, send to the assistant controller for review.
4.   Forward the statements to the payroll clerk for data entry into the payroll system.

Collect and Reconcile Time Cards

Policy/Procedure Statement	Procedure No.:	PAY-02
	Page:	1 of 1
	Issue Date:	10/28/0X
	Supersedes.	N/A

Brasto Publishing

Subject: Add or Delete Employees

1. **PURPOSE AND SCOPE**

   This procedure is used by the payroll clerk to add or delete employees from the payroll system.

2. **RESPONSIBILITIES**

   PR CLERK   **Payroll Clerk**

3. **PROCEDURES**

   3.1   PR CLERK   **Obtain Addition or Deletion Documentation**

   1. Receive documentation from the human resources department regarding the addition to or deletion from the payroll database of employees. Review the documentation for correct start or stop dates, extra pay, and (especially) the correct authorization signatures.
   2. Verify if new employees have opted out of the automated 401(k) plan enrollment system by signing the "opt-out" form. If so, ensure that all 401(k) enrollment information has been removed from the new employee packet.

   3.2   PR CLERK   **Update Payroll Database**

   1. Go into the payroll software and access the EMPLOYEE menu. Go to the ADD screen if adding an employee. Enter the employee name and social security number, pay rate, and start date. If deleting an employee go into the DELETE screen from the same menu, enter a "Y" in the "Terminate" field, and enter the final pay date, as well as the amount of any bonus payments.
   2. Print the "Updates" report from the option at the bottom of the screen to verify that the correct entries were made.

   3.3   PR CLERK   **File Documentation**

   Consult the document destruction policy to determine the date at which the filed documents can be destroyed for any terminated employees. Mark this date on the employee's folder and forward it to the document archiving area.

Add or Delete Employees

Policy/Procedure Statement	Retrieval No.:	PAY-03
Brasto Publishing	Page:	1 of 1
	Issue Date:	10/28/0X
	Supersedes:	N/A
Subject: Alter Employee Deductions		

1. **PURPOSE AND SCOPE**

   This procedure is used by the payroll clerk to alter employee deductions in the payroll system.

2. **RESPONSIBILITIES**

   PR CLERK   **Payroll Clerk**

3. **PROCEDURES**

   3.1   PR CLERK   **Obtain Deduction Information**
   1. Obtain employee payroll deduction information from the human resources department.
   2. Verify that all information on the deduction forms are clear, and that each one is authorized by the employee.

   3.2   PR CLERK   **Update Payroll Database**
   1. Go into the payroll software and access the **EMPLOYEE** menu. Go to the DEDUCT screen; enter the deduction code and the amount of the deduction for each documented deduction. Be sure to enter a deduction termination code for deductions that are of limited duration.
   2. Verify that deductions are correctly allocated to each payroll period so that the total amount of each deduction is accurate on a monthly or annual basis.
   3. Print the "Updates" report from the option at the bottom of the screen to verify that the correct entries were made.

   3.3   PR CLERK   **File Documentation**

   Return all employee documentation to the human resources department so that they can file it in employee folders.

Alter Employee Deductions

Policy/Procedure Statement	Procedure No.:	PAY-04
	Page:	1 of 1
	Issue Date:	10/28/0X
Brasto Publishing	Supersedes.	N/A
Subject: Process Payroll Transactions		

1. **PURPOSE AND SCOPE**
   This procedure is used to guide the human resources coordinator or accounting staff through the payroll process.

2. **RESPONSIBILITIES**
   HR COORD   **Human Resources Coordinator**

3. **PROCEDURES**

3.1   HR COORD   **Follow Processing Steps**

1. Review all "Request for Time Off" forms that have been submitted during the most recent pay period.
2. Compare time-off requests to the accrued amounts for each employee, as noted in the pay roll detail report for the last pay period. Notify employees if they do not have enough accrued vacation time available to fulfill their requests. Then process the portion of time they *do* have available into the payroll.
3. Collect all requests for employee transfers to different departments, and enter this information into the payroll software.
4. Enter all manual check payments for the current period into the payroll software, using the MANUAL PAYMENT screen.
5. Collect all requests for pay changes. Verify that there are authorized signatures on the pay change forms. Then enter the changes into the payroll software.
6. Collect all information regarding terminated employees. Calculate final payments due (if they have not already been paid with manual checks), and enter these final amounts into the payroll software.
7. Compare the garnishments file to the detailed payroll records from the last payroll period to see if any changes are needed to current employee deductions. If so, make those changes in the payroll software.
8. On the Friday before the next payroll, clear out all old records from the electronic time clocks that relate back to the previous pay period. Review all electronic time cards for the current period and notify employees if they have incomplete time cards (such as having clocked in but never clocked out).
9. Manually transfer the totals from the electronic time clocks to the payroll processing software. To do this, enter the grand totals of regular and overtime hours into the HOURLY PAY BY EMPLOYEE screen.
10. Verify all data entry by printing the "Payroll Audit" report and comparing all entered data to the source documents. If there are problems, go back and make the changes, and then print this report again to ensure that all payroll data is correct.

11. Print the following error-checking reports to ensure that all payroll data entry has been accurate and complete:
    - *Active employees with no scheduled payments.* Indicates that timekeeping records may be missing.
    - *Time entries for inactive employees.* Indicates that either an inactive employee has returned to work, that an employee has charged time to the wrong employee code, or that some other employee is attempting to falsely record time on behalf of the inactive employee.
    - *Accrued vacation/sick leaves with negative balances.* Indicates that an employee is taking more leave than is authorized.
    - *Negative deductions.* Indicates when a payment is being made to an employee via a negative deduction, requiring review for underlying causes.
    - *Negative taxes.* Indicates either negative pay situations or cases where previous excess tax deductions are being corrected.
    - *Hourly rate less than minimum wage.* Indicates that a payment is being made that is below the legal pay limit.
12. Go to the PROCESS PAYROLL screen and process all employee pay. Be sure to match the check number on the check stock to the check number appearing in the computer.
13. Use a signature stamp to sign the checks. Then stuff them into envelopes, along with any special employee notices, and sort them by department.
14. Back up the payroll database twice. Leave one copy on-site and send the other copy to the off-site storage location.
15. Reset the software to begin processing the payroll for the next pay period.
16. For any off-site locations, send payroll checks by guaranteed overnight delivery.
17. Retrieve the check register from the data center and review it for possible errors. Then file it in the payroll data storage area.

3.2	HR COORD

Process Deductions

1. Move the cafeteria plan amount noted on the payroll summary from the corporate checking account to the cafeteria plan account.
2. Move the 401(k) amount noted on the payroll summary to the 401(k) fund management firm from the corporate checking account.
3. Update the corporate life insurance payment by adjusting it for the total number of employees now on the payroll, as noted in the payroll summary.
4. Issue a check to the United Way based on the amount shown on the payroll summary as having been deducted from employee paychecks.
5. Pay garnishments to the various court authorities. Verify that the amounts paid out match the deductions shown on the payroll summary.

Process Payroll Transactions

Policy/Procedure Statement	Procedure No.:	PAY-05
	Page:	1 of 1
Brasto Publishing	Issue Date:	10/28/0X
	Supersedes:	N/A
Subject: Issue Payments to Employees		

1. **PURPOSE AND SCOPE**
   This procedure is used by the payroll clerk to determine the locations of all employees in the company, and to issue paychecks or deposit advices to them.

2. **RESPONSIBILITIES**
   PR CLERK   **Payroll Clerk**

3. **PROCEDURES**

3.1   PR CLERK   **Print Payroll Checks**
   1. Go to the payroll software and print the payroll test register. Review it to ensure that all paychecks have been correctly calculated.
   2. Insert check stock into the printer.
   3. Use the TEST option to print a sample check and verify that the line spacing is correct. Repeat as necessary.
   4. Print the entire batch of checks.
   5. Reset the printer and print all deposit advices for the employees who use direct deposit.
   6. Print the check register.
   7. Review the file of direct deposits, and export it to tape.

3.2   PR CLERK   **Issue Direct Deposit Data to Bank**
   1. Include the direct deposits tape in a courier package to the bank.
   2. Verify that the bank has received the tape, and that there are no errors in it.

3.3   PR CLERK   **Distribute Payment Notifications**
   1. Have all checks signed by an authorized check signer.
   2. Stuff all pay checks and deposit advices in envelopes.
   3. Batch the envelopes by supervisor and deliver them to supervisors for delivery to employees.

Issue Payments to Employees

Policy/Procedure Statement	Retrieval No.:	PAY-06
Brasto Publishing	Page:	1 of 1
	Issue Date:	10/28/0X
	Supersedes:	N/A
Subject: Delivery Paychecks with IRS Letter Forwarding		

1.   **PURPOSE AND SCOPE**
     This procedure is used by the payroll clerk to deliver paychecks to employees whose current locations are unknown, using the letter forwarding service of the Internal Revenue Service (IRS).

2.   **RESPONSIBILITIES**
     PR CLERK   **Payroll Clerk**

3.   **PROCEDURES**
3.1   PR CLERK   **Send Cover Letter to the IRS**
     1.   Prepare a cover letter directed to the IRS Disclosure Office for the local area where the requester is located. Include the following information in the cover letter:
          • State why the IRS's assistance is being sought.
          • List the names, Social Security numbers, and last known addresses of the individuals who cannot be located.
          • Include the name and address of the person or organization to which the IRS should send an acknowledgment letter.
     2.   Enclosed with the cover letter, include a letter directed to the individuals who cannot be located. Include the following information in the letter:
          • Advise the recipient of the reason for the letter.
          • Include instructions for contacting the company.
          • Note that a response to the letter is entirely voluntary.
          • Include a disclaimer on behalf of the IRS.

Delivery Paychecks with IRS Letter Forwarding

Policy/Procedure Statement	Retrieval No.:	PAY-07
	Page:	1 of 1
Brasto Publishing	Issue Date:	10/28/0X
	Supersedes:	N/A
Subject: Archive Payroll Records		

1. **PURPOSE AND SCOPE**

   This procedure is used by the payroll clerk to properly label and archive all payroll records once they have been processed through the payroll system.

2. **RESPONSIBILITIES**

   PR CLERK   **Payroll Clerk**

3. **PROCEDURES**

   3.1   PR CLERK   **Index Payroll Records**
   1. Extract the personnel folders from the on-site files for all in-active employees.
   2. Batch all the time cards for prior work periods.
   3. Referring to the corporate document destruction policy, mark each item with the legallymandated earliest destruction date.

   3.2   PR CLERK   **Archive Payroll Records**
   1. Box the records by destruction date, mark each box with an index number, and record the index number in the master index, along with the contents of each box.
   2. Send the boxes to the archiving center for storage.

Archive Payroll Records

Policy/Procedure Statement	Retrieval No.:	PAY-08
Brasto Publishing	Page:	1 of 1
	Issue Date:	10/28/0X
	Supersedes:	N/A
Subject: Timekeeping with Automated Systems		

1. **PURPOSE AND SCOPE**
   This procedure is used by a payroll department with automated timekeeping systems to collect and summarize employee hours worked.

2. **RESPONSIBILITIES**
   PAYCLERK1   **Payroll Clerk 1**
   PAYCLERK2   **Payroll Clerk 2**

3. **PROCEDURES**

   3.1   PAYCLERK1   **Review Exception Reports**
   1. Compare the current employee list to the list stored in the automated timekeeping system to verify that all current employees are included, and that terminated employees have been removed.
   2. If this is not the case, add new employees and delete terminated ones from the timekeeping system.
   3. Print exception reports from the timekeeping system that address incomplete time punches or no time punches.
   4. Highlight on the reports all items requiring adjustment prior to the next payroll run.

   3.2   PAYCLERK1   **Correct Errors**
   1. Contact each person on the highlighted report and collect from them all corrections needed.
   2. Review corrections with supervisors to obtain their approval.
   3. Enter the timekeeping system in supervisory mode and make the correcting entries for all employees in one batch.
   4. Reprint the error reports to verify that all adjustments have been correctly made. If not, correct the adjustments and run the reports again.

   3.3   PAYCLERK1   **Send Data to Payroll System**
   1. In the timekeeping system, go to the data transmission interface and press the data transfer button to send the timekeeping data to the timekeeping system.
   2. Contact the clerk in charge of payroll processing and verify that all data was received.

   3.4   PAYCLERK2   **Accumulate and Review Transaction Errors**
   1. Several days after payroll has been processed and paid, go to the pending payroll transactions folder and make copies of all adjusting entries stored there that relate to errors made during the last payroll cycle.
   2. Examine entries made into the payroll system subsequent to the last payroll cycle and note the details of all transactions that are corrections of entries in previous cycles.

		3. Summarize this data into a report, showing a trend line of error types and the detail on each error transaction.
		4. Present the report at the monthly payroll department error review meeting.
3.5	PAY CLERK 2	**Summarize and Review Trends in Hours Worked**
		1. Print from the timekeeping system a listing of hours worked by pay category.
		2. Add this information to an electronic spreadsheet report that stores the data on a trend line.
		3. If there are significant changes in the trend line, investigate the reasons for the change. Note these reasons in an accompanying report.
		4. Issue the summarization and review in a report to the payroll manager as well as the financial analyst in the accounting department.

Timekeeping with Automated Systems

Policy/Procedure Statement	Retrieval No.:	PAY-09
Brasto Publishing	Page:	1 of 1
	Issue Date:	10/28/0X
	Supersedes:	N/A
Subject: Payroll Processing with Automated Systems		

1. PURPOSE AND SCOPE

This procedure is used by a payroll department with fully integrated and computerized timekeeping and payroll processing systems to calculate payments due to employees.

2. RESPONSIBILITIES

PAYCLERK1   **Payroll Clerk 1**
PAYCLERK2   **Payroll Clerk 2**

3. PROCEDURES

3.1   PAYCLERK1   **Review Self-Service Information**

1. Print and review the self-service change reports generated by the manager and employee payroll self-service systems.
2. Contact managers or employees regarding any unusual entries or entries that exceed policy limits.

3.2   PAYCLERK1   **Import Timekeeping Information**

1. Upon notification from the payroll clerk responsible for timekeeping, import the timekeeping data file through the automated interface.
2. Verify that the file has been received without errors.

3.3   PAYCLERK1   **Process Payroll Calculations**

1. Run the payroll calculations for this payroll cycle in the payroll software.
2. Print the transaction register and review it for errors.
3. If there are errors, make corrections and run the payroll calculations again.
4. Once errors are expunged from the payroll cycle, notify the payroll clerk in charge of payroll payments that the payroll information is ready for processing.

3.4   PAYCLERK2   **Calculate Payroll Metrics**

1. Print from the payroll system a summarization of all gross pay, deductions, and net pay by department.
2. Add this information to an electronic spreadsheet report that stores the data on a trend line.
3. If there are significant changes in the trend line, investigate the reasons for the change. Note these reasons in an accompanying report.
4. Issue the summarization and review in a report to the payroll manager as well as the financial analyst in the accounting department.

3.5	PAYCLERK2	**Accumulate and Review Transaction Errors**

1. Several days after payroll has been processed, go to the pending payroll transactions folder and make copies of all adjusting entries stored there that relate to errors made during the last payroll cycle.
2. Examine entries made into the payroll system subsequent to the last payroll cycle and note the details of all transactions that are corrections of entries in previous cycles.
3. Summarize this data into a report, showing a trend line of error types and the detail of each error transaction.
4. Present the report at the monthly payroll department error review meeting.

Payroll Processing with Automated Systems

Policy/Procedure Statement	Retrieval No.:	PAY-10
Brasto Publishing	Page:	1 of 1
	Issue Date:	10/28/0X
	Supersedes:	N/A
Subject: Payment Distribution with Automated Systems		

1. **PURPOSE AND SCOPE**
    This procedure is used by a payroll department with fully integrated and automated payroll systems to issue payments to employees.

2. **RESPONSIBILITIES**
    PAYCLERK1   **Payroll Clerk 1**
    PAYMASTER   **Paymaster**

3. **PROCEDURES**
    3.1   PAYCLERK1   **Investigate Prenotification Failures**
    1. Obtain direct deposit prenotification failure messages from the bank.
    2. Contact all employees for whom these failures occurred, and request a copy of a voided check drawn on their deposit accounts.
    3. Once received, verify the American Bankers Association and account numbers on the checks and resubmit prenotification transactions to the bank.
    4. Enter the employee numbers for all employees having prenotification failures into the payroll system, so they will be issued regular paychecks through the standard paycheck printing process.
    5. Print a report listing the employee numbers and names of these employees.

    3.2   PAYMASTER   **Create Direct Deposit Batch File**
    1. Create the direct deposit batch file using the payroll software.
    2. Print the batch file report and compare it to the prenote failure report to ensure that no employees are listed on both reports.
    3. Electronically transmit the file to the bank handling direct deposit transfers.
    4. Transmit the file to the company's electronic payroll remittance advice system. If this system requires additional information regarding employee tax or other data, then create a separate file from the payroll software and transmit this file instead.

Payment Distribution with Automated Systems

Policy/Procedure Statement	Procedure No.:	PUR-01
	Page:	1 of 1
Brasto Publishing	Issue Date:	10/28/0X
	Supersedes:	N/A
Subject: **Complete Purchase Requisition**		

1.   PURPOSE AND SCOPE
This procedure is used by all employees as the first step in requisitioning purchases through the purchasing department.

2.   RESPONSIBILITIES
ALL   **All Employees**

3.   PROCEDURES

3.1   ALL   **Obtain Requisition Document**
Obtain a multipart purchase requisition form, which is available from all department secretaries.

3.2   ALL   **Compete Purchase Requisition**
1. On the form, fill in the type of item requested, a recommended supplier and part number, and the due date.
2. Obtain the approval signature of the department manager.
3. Remove the pink copy from the form for your records, and forward the remainder of the form to the purchasing department by interoffice mail for further purchasing work.

Complete Purchase Requisition

Policy/Procedure Statement	Retrieval No.:	PUR-02
Brasto Publishing	Page:	1 of 1
	Issue Date:	10/28/0X
	Supersedes:	N/A
Subject: Reorder Supplies with a Visual Review System		

1. **PURPOSE AND SCOPE**
   This procedure is used by the purchasing staff to place orders for supplies not tracked through the inventory system.

2. **RESPONSIBILITIES**
   PUR STAFF   **Purchasing Staff**

3. **PROCEDURES**

3.1 PUR STAFF   **Discuss Visual Review Parameters**
   1. Meet with the production manager and discuss any revisions to the bin sizes and reorder lines used in the current two-bin ordering system.
   2. If necessary, alter the bin sizes used or move the reorder line marked inside the bins.

3.2 PUR STAFF   **Visually Review Stock Supply Levels**
   1. If a two-bin reordering system is in use, note on a reorder form the part number of any item for which its replenishment bin is empty.
   2. If a single-bin reordering system is in use, note on a reorder form the part number of any item for which the inventory level has dropped below the reorder line.
   3. Refer to the standard order quantity summary for each part to be reordered, and note the quantity on the reorder form next to each part number requiring replenishment.

3.3 PUR STAFF   **Reorder Required Supplies**
   1. Obtain a purchase order number for all items shown on the reorder form.
   2. Enter the purchase order number at the top of the form.
   3. Fax the reorder form to the single-source parts supplier.
   4. Call the supplier to confirm receipt of the fax, and obtain an expected delivery date from the supplier.
   5. Enter the delivery date in the purchase order record in the computer system.
   6. File the reorder form.

Reorder Supplies with a Visual Review System

Policy/Procedure Statement	Retrieval No.:	PUR-03
	Page:	1 of 1
Brasto Publishing	Issue Date:	10/28/0X
	Supersedes:	N/A
Subject: Research Purchase		

1. **PURPOSE AND SCOPE**
   This procedure is used by the purchasing staff to determine the best price and delivery terms for requisitioned goods.

2. **RESPONSIBILITIES**
   PURCH STAFF   **Purchasing Staff**

3. **PROCEDURES**

3.1   PURCH STAFF   **Determine Purchase Research Rules**
   Based on the estimated expense of the item to be purchased, consult the company policy on purchasing research rules to determine the minimum required level of pricing research required.

3.2   PURCH STAFF   **Conduct Research**
   1. Based on the rules noted in the last step, obtain the minimum number of supplier bids regarding prices and delivery dates.
   2. Select from this list the best option, with price being the overriding factor for general and administrative purchases, and delivery time being the overriding factor for production purchases. Use other guidelines for purchases in the case of quality-sensitive purchases.

Research Purchase

Policy/Procedure Statement	Retrieval No.:	PUR-04
	Page:	1 of 1
Brasto Publishing	Issue Date:	10/28/0X
	Supersedes:	N/A
Subject: Issue Purchase Order		

1.   **PURPOSE AND SCOPE**
This procedure is used by the purchasing staff to create and issue purchase orders to suppliers.

2.   **RESPONSIBILITIES**
PURCH STAFF   **Purchasing Staff**

3.   **PROCEDURES**

3.1   PURCH STAFF   **Create Purchase Order**
1.   Go to the PO screen with in the PURCHASING menu. Obtain a new purchase order number.
2.   Enter the supplier number.
3.   Enter the account number to which the purchase is to be charged, and then enter either the internal part number or its description.
4.   Enter the unit price and the number of units to be purchased.
5.   Enter the date at which the item is due at the receiving dock.
6.   Press ENTER to store the purchase order, and print it.

3.2   PURCH STAFF   **Create Blanket Purchase Order**
1.   If the purchase order will apply to multiple deliveries, create a blanket purchase order instead of a normal purchase order.
2.   To do so, follow the same steps noted in section 3.1. In addition, check off the "blanket purchase order" flag in the computer. Also, rather than entering the single date at which the item is due at the receiving dock, enter the range of dates over which all receipts will be accepted.

3.3   PURCH STAFF   **Issue Purchase Order to Supplier**
1.   If the supplier is set up for electronic data interchange (EDI), then switch to the EDI screen within the PURCHASING menu and enter the number of the purchase order. A confirming EDI message will arrive through the system once the supplier has accessed the purchase order.
2.   If EDI is not set up, then burst the purchase order, with the white copy going to the supplier, the pink copy staying in the purchasing department files, the blue copy going to accounting, and the goldenrod copy going back to the person who requisitioned the item.

3.4   PURCH STAFF   **Distribute Purchase Order Internally**
1.   Send the goldenrod copy through the interoffice mail to the person who originated the requisition.
2.   File the pink copy in the pending file.
3.   Send the blue copy to the accounts payable staff through the interoffice mail.

Issue Purchase Order

Policy/Procedure Statement	Retrieval No.:	PUR-05
	Page:	1 of 1
Brasto Publishing	Issue Date:	10/28/0X
	Supersedes:	N/A
Subject: Receive Purchased Items		

1. **PURPOSE AND SCOPE**
    This procedure is used by the receiving staff to ensure that all paperwork and computer systems are properly updated as part of a receipt from a supplier.

2. **RESPONSIBILITIES**
    RECV STAFF   **Receiving Staff**

3. **PROCEDURES**

    3.1   RECV STAFF   **Receive Materials**
    1. Verify that there is a company purchase order number on the packing slip attached to a receipt. If not, contact the purchasing staff and inquire about the validity of the item. If it was not ordered through regular channels, then reject the shipment.
    2. If keeping the shipment, verify the condition and quantity of the receipt.

    3.2   RECV STAFF   **Process Computer Entries**
    Go to the RECEIPTS screen in the computer system and call up the purchase order number. Enter the number of items received and the confirm the date on which it was received. Press ENTER to log in the entry.

    3.3   RECV STAFF   **Process Receiving Paperwork**
    Enter the quantity received, the supplier name, and a description of the items received in the receiving log. At the end of the day, attach all bills of lading and packing slips to a copy of the shipping log, and forward it to the accounts payable staff for further processing.

Receive Purchased Items

Policy/Procedure Statement	Retrieval No.:	PUR-06
	Page:	1 of 1
Brasto Publishing	Issue Date:	10/28/0X
	Supersedes:	N/A
Subject: Match Documents		

1. **PURPOSE AND SCOPE**
    This procedure is used by the accounts payable clerk to ensure that all documents related to a payment are properly authorized and matched.

2. **RESPONSIBILITIES**
    AP CLERK   **Accounts Payable Clerk**

3. **PROCEDURES**

3.1   AP CLERK   **Receive and File Documents**
1.   When receiving bills of lading and packing slips from the receiving department, file them in the "Unmatched Receivers" box.
2.   When receiving purchase orders from the purchasing department, file them in the "Unmatched Purchase Orders" box.
3.   When receiving invoices from suppliers, file them in the "Unmatched Invoices" box.

3.2   AP CLERK   **Match Documents**
1.   Alphabetize all the preceding documents by supplier name. Then take a supplier invoice and match it to a supporting company purchase order, verifying that the quantity authorized is the quantity billed. If there is no purchase order, then take it to either the purchasing department or the responsible department manager for authorization.
2.   If the invoice and purchase order match, then match the receiving documentation to them that prove there was a delivery in the correct amount. If the paperwork is missing, review the shipping log to see if it ever arrived, or call the supplier and request a proof of delivery.
3.   Once a set of documents is matched, forward it to the accounts payable clerk for entry into the computer system.

Match Documents

Policy/Procedure Statement	Retrieval No.:	PUR-07
Brasto Publishing	Page:	1 of 1
	Issue Date:	10/28/0X
	Supersedes:	N/A
Subject: Process Expense Reports		

1. **PURPOSE AND SCOPE**

   This procedure helps the accounts payable clerk expedite the payment of expense reports. This is to be used anytime an expense report is being submitted for payment.

2. **RESPONSIBILITIES**

   ACC PAY   **Accounts Payable Clerk**

3. **PROCEDURES**

   3.1   ACC PAY   **Access a Blank Expense Report**
   Access the blank expense report Excel file.

   3.2   ACC PAY   **Fill Out the Form**
   Enter all travel expenses in the top part of the form, which is entitled "Business Travel." Enter all meal information in the middle part of the form, which is entitled "Meals and Entertainment." Enter all remaining expenses in the bottom of the form, which is entitled "Other Expenses." For company policies regarding the allowability of certain expenses, review the policies list at the bottom of the form. Be sure to attach receipts for all expenses exceeding $10.

   3.3   ACC PAY   **Complete the Form**
   Copy the expense form and all receipts, and retain the copy for your records. Sign the form and have your supervisor review and sign it as well.

   3.4   ACC PAY   **Submit the Expense Report**
   Have your supervisor forward the expense report to the accounts payable department for payment.

Process Expense Reports

Policy/Procedure Statement	Retrieval No.:	PUR-08
Brasto Publishing	Page:	1 of 1
	Issue Date:	10/28/0X
	Supersedes:	N/A
Subject: Enter Fixed Asset Payments		

1. **PURPOSE AND SCOPE**
   This procedure is used by the accounts payable clerk to process fixed asset transactions.

2. **RESPONSIBILITIES**
   ACC PAY   **Accounts Payable Clerk**

3. **PROCEDURES**

   3.1   ACC PAY   **Code Account Based on Capitalization Limit**
   Determine if an asset purchase exceeds the corporate capitalization limit. If so, code the purchase into the appropriate asset account. If not, contact the assistant controller to verify which expense account is to be charged for the purchase.

   3.2   ACC PAY   **Enter Transaction in Accounting System**
   1. Open the purchasing module and create a purchase transaction. Include in the asset account all expenses required to bring the asset to the company and install it. In the case of the current invoice in question, this means including the listed sales tax, delivery charges, and shipping insurance in the asset account.
   2. Open the fixed assets register and enter the asset's name, account type, and location within the company. Also enter the fixed asset tag number, if available. The system will automatically assign a depreciation calculation method and period to the asset based on the account type to which it was assigned.

   3.3   ACC PAY   **Verify Entered Data**
   Verify that the amount listed in the fixed asset register matches the amount entered for the purchase transaction.

Enter Fixed Asset Payments

Policy/Procedure Statement	Procedure No.:	PUR-09
	Page:	1 of 1
Brasto Publishing	Issue Date:	10/28/0X
	Supersedes.	N/A
Subject: Adjust and Enter Accounts Payable		

1. **PURPOSE AND SCOPE**

    This procedure guides the accounts payable clerk in paying supplier invoices.

2. **RESPONSIBILITIES**

    ACC PAY   **Accounts Payable Clerk**

3. **PROCEDURES**

    3.1   ACC PAY   **Match Receiving Reports to the Purchase Order**
    1. Receive purchase orders from the receptionist, who is in charge of entering this information.
    2. Collect all receiving documents from the receiving staff, which is located in the warehouse.
    3. Match all receiving reports to purchase orders and supplier invoices. If there is an invoice without an accompanying purchase order, call the supplier and ask who ordered the item being billed. While doing so, also point out to the supplier that all purchases require a purchase order.
    4. If any receiving documents cannot be immediately matched to an invoice or purchase order, file them away for comparison at a later date.

    3.2   ACC PAY   **Set Up Supplier Master File**
    1. If the supplier is a new one, access the supplier master file maintenance screen in the computer system.
    2. Enter the following information into the screen:

        - Supplier name
        - Supplier address
        - Supplier phone number (record 800 number, if available)
        - Supplier fax number
        - Supplier payment terms
        - W-9 form flag
        - Federal tax identification number

    3.3   ACC PAY   **Require Completed W-9 Form**
    1. Access the supplier master file and verify that there is either a Social Security number or federal tax identification number on file. If so, proceed to section 3.4.
    2. If there is no number on file, contact the supplier and tell them that the company will make no payment until a properly completed form W-9 is received.
    3. Shift the payment packet to the "Awaiting W-9 form" bin.
    4. Upon receipt of the completed W-9 form, access the supplier master file and enter the Social Security number or federal tax identification number in the appropriate field. Also, check off the box indicating whether a 1099 form must be issued at the end of the calendar year.

		5. File the completed W-9 form in the W-9 master file.
		6. Remove the payment packet from the "Awaiting W-9 form" bin and enter its billing information into the computer, as noted in section 3.4.
3.4	ACC PAY	**Enter Received Amount into the Computer**
		Go to the payables function in the computer and enter the purchase order number that is displayed on the packing slip. Find the correct line item and then press ENTER. Input the quantity received. Tab forward to the "Transport Via" field and enter the carrier's name. Tab again to the "Packing Slip" field and enter that number, which is listed on the packing slip. Then press ENTER.
3.5	ACC PAY	**Set Up Repetitive Invoicing**
		1. Obtain verification if the invoice appears to be a consistent amount that will be billed again to the company over multiple periods.
		2. If so, access the recurring invoice setup screen in the accounting software.
		3. Enter the supplier code, the recurring amount to be paid, the date on which it should be paid, and the number of months over which it is to be paid.
		4. Call up the "payments due" report to verify that the recurring payment is being correctly processed by the accounting system.
		5. Print the Recurring Payments Report, listing all recurring payments, and give it to the accounts payable clerks, so they do not enter the invoice into the computer system a second time when supplier invoices arrive in the future.
3.6	ACC PAY	**Prepare a Problem List**
		Prepare a list of problems and give them to the purchasing manager to correct. Typical problems include pricing errors, incorrect quantities, or a missing proof of delivery.
3.7	ACC PAY	**Issue Standard Adjustment Letters to Suppliers**
		If there is a problem with a supplier invoice that will result in an adjustment to the payment made to the supplier, prepare Exhibit 6.36 (Supplier Adjustment Letter) and send it to the supplier.
3.8	ACC PAY	**Enter Invoice into the Accounting System**
		Enter the supplier number in the payables screen. Also enter the invoice number, invoice date, and purchase order number. Enter freight charges and taxes, if any. Purchases orders are listed on the left side of the screen. Find the purchase order number that matches the amount, and press ENTER.
3.9	ACC PAY	**Run the Accounts Payable Report**
		Print the accounts payable report. This lists all accounts payable entered into the computer database. Use a highlighter to manually select invoices on the list that must be paid in the current payment period. Add up the amount and verify with the controller that it is acceptable to pay it out, based on current cash levels.

3.10	ACC PAY	**Process Checks**
		1. Access the check printing screen. Check off those items to be paid.
		2. Wait until the "Process Complete" message appears at the bottom of the screen.
		3. Verify the check number to be printed.
		4. Load check stock into the printer. Verify that the check number on the check stock matches the number showing in the computer. If they do not match, change the number in the computer to match the number on the check stock.
		5. Press ENTER to print checks.
		6. Remove the signature stamp from the safe and use it to stamp all checks.
		7. Send the front copy of the check to the supplier.
3.11	ACC PAY	**File Documents**
		File the check copy, invoice, and related information in the supplier file.

Adjust and Enter Accounts Payable

Supplier Contact Name
Supplier Name   Company Logo
Supplier Address
Supplier City, State, ZipCode

Dear Sir:

[Company Name] will short-pay your invoice number _____, dated ___/___/___, by the amount of $_____ due to the following problem(s):

☐ Failed quality test   Notes: _____

☐ Incorrect item shipped   Notes: _____

☐ Incorrect quantity shipped   Notes: _____

☐ Items damaged   Notes: _____

☐ Missing bar code / RFID tag   Notes: _____

☐ Price does not match purchase order   Notes: _____

If you have additional questions about this matter, please contact the [Company Name] accounts payable department at (___) ___-____ or access our Web site at _____.

Exhibit 6.36 Supplier Adjustment Letter

Policy/Procedure Statement	Procedure No.:	PUR-10
Brasto Publishing	Page:	1 of 1
	Issue Date:	10/28/0X
	Supersedes:	N/A
Subject: Create and Issue Payment to Supplier		

1. **PURPOSE AND SCOPE**

   This procedure is used by the accounts payable clerk to print a check or issue an electronic payment authorization, and ensure that either one is sent to the supplier.

2. **RESPONSIBILITIES**

   AP CLERK   **Accounts Payable Clerk**

3. **PROCEDURES**

   3.1 AP CLERK   **Print Checks**
   1. Go to the PAYMENT menu in the accounting software and access the PRINT CHECKS option.
   2. Scan the list of open and approved accounts payable and put a "*" in the "Pay" field to signify that these items will be paid in the upcoming check run.
   3. Print the "Preliminary Check Register" once all line items are selected and verify that the correct items have been selected.
   4. Put check stock in the printer and use the TEST option to correct the line spacing.
   5. Use the PRINT BATCH option to print all checks on the printer.
   6. Switch to regular paper when complete, and print the Check Register.

   3.3 AP CLERK   **Transmit to Supplier**
   1. Burst all check stock and retain the back copy.
   2. Use the check stamp to sign all checks.
   3. Stuff the check into envelopes, affix postage, and mail to suppliers.
   4. Attach check copies to the matched packets of supplier invoices, purchase orders, and receivers.
   5. File the packets by supplier name.
   6. File the check register in the accounting reports cabinet.

Create and Issue Payment to Supplier

Policy/Procedure Statement	Retrieval No.:	PUR-11
Brasto Publishing	Page:	1 of 1
	Issue Date:	10/28/0X
	Supersedes:	N/A
Subject: Close Related Transactions		

1. **PURPOSE AND SCOPE**
   This procedure is used by the accounts payable clerk to close any purchase orders in the computer system related to a paid supplier invoice.

2. **RESPONSIBILITIES**
   AP CLERK   **Accounts Payable Clerk**

3. **PROCEDURES**

   3.1   AP CLERK   **Find Open Transactions after Matching**
   1. Go to the OPEN PO screen in the computer system and select the REPORTS option, which prints out a list of all open purchase orders.
   2. Review the list of open purchase orders to see if there are any orders that have been partially completed as a result of prior supplier deliveries.
   3. Highlight these partial purchase orders.

   3.2   AP CLERK   **Obtain Closing Permissions**
   Forward the updated open purchase orders report to the purchasing manager, with a note to mark all purchase orders that can be closed out.

   3.3   AP CLERK   **Close Related Transactions**
   1. Go to the PURCHASE menu and access the CLOSE PO screen.
   2. Enter the purchase order number to be closed out.
   3. Reduce the quantity ordered so that it matches the quantity already received.
   4. Press ENTER to close the purchase order.

Close Related Transactions

Policy/Procedure Statement	Retrieval No.:	PUR-12
	Page:	1 of 1
Brasto Publishing	Issue Date:	10/28/0X
	Supersedes:	N/A
Subject: File Completed Documents		

1. **PURPOSE AND SCOPE**

   This procedure is used by the accounts payable clerk to ensure that all documentation related to a supplier payment is appropriately grouped together and filed in the correct location.

2. **RESPONSIBILITIES**

   AP CLERK   **Accounts Payable Clerk**

3. **PROCEDURES**

   3.1   AP CLERK   **Assemble and Attach Documentation**

   Combine all paid supplier invoices with a copy of the checks from which they were paid, as well as a copy of the authorizing purchase order and proof of receipt.

   3.2   AP CLERK   **File Documents**

   1. Create storage files for each supplier, and sort them alphabetically.
   2. File the packets of accounts payable documents in the supplier files, sorted by date.

File Completed Documents

Policy/Procedure Statement	Retrieval No.:	PUR-13
	Page:	1 of 1
Brasto Publishing	Issue Date:	10/28/0X
	Supersedes:	N/A
Subject: Void Checks		

1. **PURPOSE AND SCOPE**

   This procedure is used by the accounts payable clerk to void out any checks that have been created but are not to be issued as payments.

2. **RESPONSIBILITIES**

   ACC PAY   **Accounts Payable Clerk**

3. **PROCEDURES**

   3.1   ACC PAY   **Obtain Approval to Void a Check**

   Take the check to be voided to the Controller and request a sign-off on the face of the check, indicating that it is to be voided. Write the reason for the voiding on the back of the check.

   3.2   ACC PAY   **Physically Void the Check**

   Take the check to the stamping machine and stamp the word "void" on the check with sufficient force to punch holes in the check, outlining the word.

   3.3   ACC PAY   **Record Voided Check in the Computer System**

   Go to the Accounts Payable module in the accounting software and access the CHECK PAYMENTS screen. Enter the check number to call up the correct item, and put a "V" in the "Check Status" field.

   3.4   ACC PAY   **Verify That Voided Check Is Removed from Outstanding Check List**

   Go to the Accounts Payable module in the accounting software and access the CLEARED CHECKS screen. Call up the check number for the check that has just been voided, and verify that it has been removed from the list of outstanding checks. If not, go back to the previous step and verify that the check has been listed as void in the accounting database.

   3.5   ACC PAY   **Store Voided Check**

   File the voided check in the voided check folder for the current year, which is kept with the cleared checks that are returned by the bank.

Void Checks

Chapter 7

PURCHASING CARD MANUAL

7.1 INTRODUCTION

This chapter contains the primary procedures and forms required to roll out a successful purchasing card program. A company may find that it eventually purchases 25% or more of its annual acquisitions with purchasing cards, so this is potentially a high-risk area requiring the many controls noted in the following procedures. The procedures enumerate the role of the purchasing card manager, how employees apply for purchasing cards, buy items with the cards, reconcile their monthly statements of items purchased to detailed records, account for missing receipts, reject purchases they claim not to have made, request alterations to their spending limits, report lost cards, and handle card user terminations. Thus, the procedures presented here are intended to address all aspects of the purchasing card process.

Policy/Procedure Statement	Retrieval No.:	PCM-01
Brasto Publishing	Page:	1 of 1
	Issue Date:	10/28/0X
	Supersedes:	N/A
Subject: Purchasing Card Program Overview		

1.	**PURPOSE AND SCOPE**
	This document provides an overview of the purchasing card program, as well as the range of related procedures and forms associated with the program.

2. OVERVIEW

The corporate purchasing card program is intended to simplify the purchasing of low-cost items that would otherwise require a purchase requisition and the involvement of the purchasing department. Purchases under $2,500 generally fall into this category. Card users are nominated by department managers and approved by the purchasing card manager. Expanded purchasing limits require the approval of successively higher levels of company managers, depending on the desired limits.

3. CARD USER RESPONSIBILITIES

Inappropriate purchasing card use can result in significant losses for a company, so the designation of their use is a serious matter. Users are expected to use these cards with the highest sense of ethics. The following rules apply to users of company purchasing cards:

- Do not use purchasing cards for personal transactions.
- Do not use purchasing cards for purchases on Internet auction sites, even if the purchases are intended for company use.
- Do not use purchasing cards to acquire capital items, such as machinery, computer hardware, or vehicles.
- Do not share the card with any other person.
- Use a purchasing card only to purchase items for which your department is responsible for payment.
- Do not receive cash back for purchase card credit transactions; all credits must be processed through the purchasing card.
- Do not split charges into smaller amounts in order to stay within the purchasing restrictions of your purchasing card.
- Promptly forward monthly account statements with attached receipts to the Purchasing Card Manager.
- Promptly report transaction discrepancies or a lost purchasing card to the processing bank.

Improper use of purchasing cards will result in revocation of one's card and possible additional disciplinary action.

4. PURCHASING CARD MANAGER RESPONSIBILITIES

The purchasing card program is managed by the Purchasing Card Manager (PCM). This position is responsible for a payment method that may cover more than 25% of all company expenditures; for that reason, this is a highly responsible position. The following rules apply to the PCM:

- Carefully investigate nominated purchasing card users prior to authorizing card issuances to them.
- Monitor the results of disputed transaction charges to ensure that the company does not pay for items for which it is not responsible.
- Monitor card usage to ensure that cards are being used appropriately.
- Monitor remaining unused department budgets to ensure that managers are aware of approaching budgetary limits.
- Ensure that purchasing cards used by departing or transferring employees are properly canceled and related receipts forwarded to department managers.

5. PROCEDURES

The following procedures apply to the purchasing card program:

Retrieval No.	Procedure Name	Description
PCM-02	Application for Purchasing Card	Used to apply for a corporate purchasing card from the purchasing department.
PCM-03	Purchasing with the Purchasing Card	Used to instruct in the daily use of the purchasing card.
PCM-04	Monthly Statement Reconciliation	Used to reconcile the monthly purchasing card statement to one's payment records.
PCM-05	Purchasing Card Line Item Rejection	Used to reject specific transaction line items on their monthly billing statements.
PCM-06	Request Altered Spending Limits	Used to request changes to the spending limits on their purchasing cards
PCM-07	Report Lost Purchasing Card	Used to provide necessary information to the processing bank regarding a lost or stolen procurement card.
PCM-08	Moved or Terminated Card User	Used to describe the correct procedures for handling purchasing cards if their users either change departments or leave the company.

Purchasing Card Program Overview

Policy/Procedure Statement	Retrieval No.:	PCM-02
Brasto Publishing	Page:	1 of 1
	Issue Date:	10/28/0X
	Supersedes:	N/A
Subject: Application for Purchasing Card		

1. **PURPOSE AND SCOPE**

   This procedure is used by company employees to apply for a corporate purchasing card from the purchasing department.

2. **RESPONSIBILITIES**

   EMPLOYEE   **Employee**

   PCM   **Purchasing Card Manager**

3. **PROCEDURES**

   3.1   EMPLOYEE   **Access the Purchasing Card Application Form**

   Go to the corporate intranet site and access the "Employee Forms" button. Print the "Purchasing Card Application" form. The form is stored in Adobe PDF format, so download the Adobe Acrobat Reader from www.adobe.com if your computer cannot read the PDF document. The form is shown in Exhibit 7.1

3.2	EMPLOYEE	**Complete the Purchasing Card Application Form**

Complete the Purchasing Card Application Form

1. In Section A of the form, complete all fields containing information about your name, title, department, department code, and department mailing address. Also include your contact information: e-mail address, phone number, and fax number. In addition, enter your date of birth and Social Security number. Further, enter the default expense account number to which you would like to have your purchasing card charges debited. Finally, sign and date where indicated at the bottom of the section, and have the department manager do the same.
2. Section B contains the authorized spending limits for your purchasing card, as assigned by the purchasing card manager. These include the maximum single purchase amount, total monthly purchase amount, and the total number of authorization transactions allowed per day.
3. Section C of the form contains approval and processing information, which is for use by the purchasing card manager.
4. Forward the completed form to the purchasing card manager at the address noted at the bottom of the form.

3.3   PCM   **Process Application**

1. Verify that the default expense account number listed on the form is a valid account number for the applying department, with budgeted funding assigned to it.
2. Verify that the manager approval signature is by an authorized department manager.
3. Verify that the applicant is applying for a purchasing card for the first time. If there have been multiple applications, determine why a rejection occurred in the past, or if a credit card was issued and then revoked.
4. Enter the single purchase, monthly purchase total, and number of authorizations allowed per day in Section B of the form, based on company policy regarding purchasing volumes for the position held by the applicant.
5. Sign and date the form in Section C.
6. Enter the date when the form is sent to the purchasing card provider, and fax the form to the provider. File the form in the pending file.

3.3   PCM   **Issue Purchasing Card**

1. Upon receipt of the purchasing card, withdraw the associated form from the pending file and note on it in Section C the date when the card was received.
2. Notify the applicant of the next purchasing card orientation meeting.
3. Make a copy of the purchasing card application and retain it. File the original in the permanent purchasing card file.
4. Issue the purchasing card to the applicant at the orientation meeting, as well as the copy of the purchasing card application.

Application for Purchasing Card

Purchasing Card Application
[Company Name]

<u>Applicant Information:</u>   (A)

   Applicant Name/Title: _____ / _____

   Department Name/Number: _____ / _____

   Department Mailing Address: _____

                                         _____

   Applicant Contact Information:

        E-Mail: _____

        Phone: _____

        Fax: _____

   Applicant Identification Information:

        Date of Birth: _____

        S/S Number: _____

   Default Expense Account Number: ☐☐☐☐☐☐

   Applicant Signature: _____ Date: _____

   Manager Signature: _____ Date: _____

Do Not Write Below This Line

	Single Purchase	Monthly Purchase Total	Authorizations Allowed/Day
(B)			
<u>Spending Limits:</u>	$ _____	$ _____	# _____

<u>Processing and Approval Information:</u>   (C)

   Purchasing Card Manager Approval/Date: _____ / _____

   Date Sent to Card Provider/Received From: _____ / _____

Mail To:
      Purchasing Card Manager
      Company Name
      Street
      City, State, Zip Code   Form No. PUR-193

Exhibit 7.1 Purchasing Card Application Form

Policy/Procedure Statement	Retrieval No.:	PCM-03
	Page:	1 of 1
Brasto Publishing	Issue Date:	10/28/0X
	Supersedes:	N/A
Subject: Purchasing with the Purchasing Card		

1. PURPOSE AND SCOPE

This procedure is used by company employees to determine the correct processing of daily purchases with a purchasing card.

2. RESPONSIBILITIES

EMPLOYEE   **Employee**

3. PROCEDURES

3.1 EMPLOYEE   **Pay with Purchasing Card**

1. When first making a purchase with a purchasing card, inquire if the supplier accepts credit card payments. If so, pay with the card if the purchase is less than the per-transaction purchasing maximum for the card. When making the transaction, give the supplier the address listed on the purchasing card billing statement.

2. If a purchase is declined by the supplier, refer the matter to the Purchasing Card Manager. This may call for an increase in the authorized spend limit on the card (see the "Request Altered Spending Limits" procedure).

3. Always obtain an itemized receipt for all purchases made with the purchasing card. Receipts will be used at month-end to verify purchases listed on the purchasing card statement.

4. Log all receipts into the Purchasing Card Transaction Log, which is shown in Exhibit 7.2. The "Trans. No." is a sequential numbering of the transactions on the page. The "Date" field is for the date of the purchase transaction as noted on the supplier's receipt. Also fill in the remaining descriptive information as noted in the form. This form is available on the company intranet site.

5. Verify that items ordered are actually received. It is easiest to do this by requiring that all purchases be delivered directly to you. If there is evidence of nonreceipt, dispute supplier billings as noted later in the "Purchasing Card Line Item Rejection" procedure.

Purchasing with the Purchasing Card

TRANS. NO.	DATE	SUPPLIER NAME	PURCHASED ITEM DESCRIPTION	TOTAL PRICE	COMMENTS
1	5/1/08	Acme Electric Supply	200w floodlights	$829.00	
2	5/2/08	Wiley Wire Supply	Breaker panels	741.32	
3	5/5/08	Coyote Electrical	12 gauge cable	58.81	Returned for credit
4	5/7/08	Roadrunner Electric	Foot light trim	940.14	

Exhibit 7.2 Purchasing Card Transaction Log

Policy/Procedure Statement	Retrieval No.:	PCM-04
	Page:	1 of 1
Brasto Publishing	Issue Date:	10/28/0X
	Supersedes:	N/A
Subject: Monthly Statement Reconciliation		

1. **PURPOSE AND SCOPE**

   This procedure is used by company employees to reconcile the monthly purchasing card statement to their payment records.

2. **RESPONSIBILITIES**

   | EMPLOYEE | **Employee** |
   | PCM | **Purchasing Card Manager** |

3. **PROCEDURES**

   3.1 EMPLOYEE **Review Monthly Billing Statement**

   1. You will receive a purchasing card account statement at the end of each month (a sample statement is shown in Exhibit 7.3). When it arrives, compare the line items on the statement to your manual purchasing card transaction log (as shown earlier in Exhibit 7.2). Verify all matching items and attach receipts to the statement for those items.

   2. If any receipts are missing, contact the supplier and attempt to obtain a replacement receipt.

   3. If any receipts are still missing, list them on the Purchasing Card Missing Receipt form (as shown in Exhibit 7.4), which is located on the company intranet site. In Section A of this form, list your contact information, including your name, address, phone number, and fax number. In Section B, list the month and year of the purchasing card account statement and reference number in which the item is listed for which you have no receipt. Then list in the expense matrix the statement line item number for each missing receipt, as well as the date and dollar amount of the expense as listed on the statement. Also fill in the supplier name and the description of the expense. Sign in Section C to certify that the expenditures with missing receipts were legitimate business expenses, and also obtain the signature of the department manager.

   4. Once all line items have been reviewed, go back to Section C of the statement and write the expense account number in the "Account Number" column next to any line items that are different from the default expense account used for the card.

   5. If you are disputing any line items, circle them in Section C of the statement and write "in dispute" next to them.

   6. Sign and date the billing statement.

   7. Make a copy of the entire expense packet and store it in a safe place. Company policy requires that you retain this document for three years. This is also useful for researching possible double billings that may appear on multiple account statements.

| | | 8. Review and check off the reconciliation checklist in Section D of the statement to ensure that you have completed all reconciliation tasks.
9. Forward the statement, with attached receipts and Purchasing Card Missing Receipt form, to the Purchasing Card Manager for review.

Note: If you do not forward the completed packet to the accounts payable department by the required date, all charges made during the month will be charged to a default departmental expense account and the department will be charged a $ 100 processing fee by the accounting department. |
| 3.2 | PCM | **Review Forwarded Expense Packet**
1. Upon receipt of each employee's expense packet, scan the list of purchased items to determine if any inappropriate purchases were made, or if there is any evidence of split purchases being made. If so, discuss the issue with the employee's manager to see if further action should be taken.
2. Promptly forward the expense packet to the accounts payable department for payment. |

Monthly Statement Reconciliation

Purchasing Card Statement of Account
[Company Name]

A   **Statement Date:**   <u>May 2006</u>   **Statement Reference Number:** <u>12345678</u>

Cardholder: Mary Follett
123 Sunny Lane
Anywhere, USA 01234

B

	Single Purchase	Monthly Purchase Total	Authorizations Allowed per Day
Spending Limits:	$2,500	$25,000	10

C   **Transaction Detail:**

Transaction Date	Reference Number	Supplier	SIC Code	Account Number	Amount
5/1/06	1234567AB043	Acme Electric Supply	7312	-	$829.00
5/2/06	2345678CD054	Wiley Wire Supply	7312	-	741.32
5/5/06	3456789DL065	Coyote Electrical	7312	040-1720	58.81
5/7/06	4567890EF076	Roadrunner Electric	7312	-	940.14
				Total	$2,569.27

D   **Reconciliation Checklist:**

☐   I have reconciled this statement of account

☐   I have attached all receipts to this statement of account

☐   I have completed and attached the Purchasing Card Missing Receipt form for all line items for which I have no receipts

☐   I have entered account numbers in the "Account Number" column for those line items that vary from the default expense account number

☐   I have circled any items currently under dispute with suppliers

☐   I have signed and dated this statement of account

☐   I have retained a copy and understand that it must be retained for three years

Cardholder Signature: _____   Date: _____

Exhibit 7.3   Sample Monthly Purchasing Card Account

Purchasing Card Missing Receipt Form
[Company Name]

A

Your Contact Information:

Name: _____   Address Line 1: _____

Phone Number: _____   Address Line 2: _____

Fax Number: _____

B

Account Statement Information:

Statement Month/Year: _____/_____

Statement Reference Number: _____

Line Item Number	Line Item Date	Line Item Amount	Supplier Name	Description

C

I certify that the above expenditures were legitimate business expenditures on behalf of the company.

Card Holder
Signature: _____   Date: _____

Department Manager
Signature: _____   Date: _____

Form PUR-196

Exhibit 7.4   Purchasing Card Missing Receipt Form

Policy/Procedure Statement	Retrieval No.:	PCM-05
Brasto Publishing	Page:	1 of 1
	Issue Date:	10/28/0X
	Supersedes:	N/A
Subject: Purchasing Card Line Item Rejection		

1.   **PURPOSE AND SCOPE**

This procedure is used by company employees to reject specific transaction line items on their monthly billing statements.

2.   **RESPONSIBILITIES**

EMPLOYEE   **Employee**

3.   **PROCEDURES**

3.1   EMPLOYEE   **Review Monthly Billing Statement**

When you receive the monthly billing statement from the purchasing card provider, carefully review all line items and verify that all charges match your purchasing records. If there are any discrepancies calling for rejection of specific line items, go to the following step.

3.2   EMPLOYEE   **Complete the Line Item Rejection Form**

1.   Go to the corporate intranet site and access the "Purchasing Card Line Item Rejection" form. The form is shown in Exhibit 7.5.

2.   In Section A of the form, fill in your contact information under the "Your Contact Information" heading. Also specify your card number under the "Dispute Information" heading, as well as the number, date, dollar amount, and supplier name for the line item you are disputing. Note that a separate form must be used for each line item.

3.   In Section B of the form, check off the box next to the dispute description most closely matching the problem you have encountered. Follow the instructions next to the checked box, either to attach a receipt or to include additional detail regarding the nature of the problem.

4.   In Section C of the form, sign and date the form. Make a copy of the form. Send the original to the purchasing card provider in accordance with the mailing or fax instructions noted at the bottom of the section, and send the copy to the purchasing card manager.

Purchasing Card Line Item Rejection

Purchasing Card Line Item Rejection

A

Your Contact Information:	**Dispute Information:**
Name: _____	Card Number: _____
Phone Number: _____	Line Item Number: _____
Fax Number: _____	Line Item Date: _____
Address Line 1: _____	Line Item Amount: _____
Address Line 2: _____	Supplier Name: _____

B

Check the box next to the reason for your line item rejection, and add explanations as requested. Sign and mail **or** fax the completed form to the location indicated at the bottom of this form.

☐   I did not authorize the purchasing transaction represented by this line item.

☐   I have a receipt indicating a different amount than was charged in this line item. (attach a copy of the receipt)

☐   I have already been billed for this amount in a previous account statement. Date of the previous charge: _____

☐   I have a credit voucher offsetting this line item, but which does not appear on the account statement. (attach a copy of the credit voucher)

☐   I have not received the goods ordered or have returned them. Details of the dispute: _____ _____

☐   I am disputing this line item for other reasons. Details of the dispute: _____ _____

C

Signature: _____   Date: _____

Mail To: **Fax To: (111) 111-1111**

     Bank Name
     Bank Address
     City, State, Zip

Form No. PUR-194

Exhibit 7.5   Purchasing Card Line Item Rejection Form

Policy/Procedure Statement	Retrieval No.:	PCM-06
	Page:	1 of 1
Brasto Publishing	Issue Date:	10/28/0X
	Supersedes:	N/A
Subject: Request Altered Spending Limits		

1. **PURPOSE AND SCOPE**

    This procedure is used by company employees to request changes to the spending limits on their purchasing cards.

2. **RESPONSIBILITIES**

    EMPLOYEE   **Employee**
    PCM   **Purchasing Card Manager**

3. **PROCEDURES**

    3.1   EMPLOYEE   **Review Monthly Billing Statement**

    1. Each purchasing card is limited in terms of the total monthly allowable spending, as well as smaller daily limits and in terms of the number of authorized purchases per day. If your regular purchasing patterns are being impacted by these limits, fill out the Purchasing Card Spending Limit Change Request Form (shown in Exhibit 7.6).
    2. In Section A of the form, enter your name, phone number, fax number, and address.
    3. In Section B of the form, enter the purchasing card number in the squares provided.
    4. In Section C of the form, enter the requested spending limit changes. If you are not requesting a change in all three of the limitation areas, enter "N/A" in the unused fields.
    5. In Section D of the form, obtain approval signatures in accordance with the approval policy in the signature table.
    6. Retain a copy of the form and forward the original to the purchasing card manager.

    3.2   PCM   **Complete the Line Item Rejection Form**

    1. Verify that the signed approval level on the form matches the requested spending limit, as per the company policy on purchasing card monthly spending limits, which follows:

        - $10,000 limit—department manager approval
        - $10,001–$25,000 limit—Operations VP approval
        - $25,000+ limit—COO approval

    2. If the required signatures are missing, return the form to the relevant department manager with an explanatory note. Otherwise, sign and date the form and make a copy. Forward the original to the purchasing card bank to have the revised purchasing levels updated for the purchasing card.
    3. At month-end, request from the bank a summary statement of authorization levels for all purchasing cards. Verify that the requesting employee's card spending limits have been changed. If not, follow up with the bank.

Request Altered Spending Limits

Purchasing Card Spending Limit Change Request Form
[Company Name]

A   **Your Contact Information:**

Name: _____   Address Line 1: _____

Phone Number: _____   Address Line 2: _____

Fax Number: _____

B   **Purchasing Card Number:**

☐☐☐☐ - ☐☐☐☐ - ☐☐☐☐ - ☐☐☐☐

C   **Requested Spending Limits:**

Single Purchase	Monthly Purchase Total	Authorizations Allowed per Day
$ _____	$ _____	$ _____

D   **Authorization Signatures:**

Monthly Spending Limit	Authorized Approver	Signature	Print Name	Date
$10,000	Dept. Manager	_____	_____	_____
$10,001–$25,000	Operations Vice President	_____	_____	_____
$25,000+	Chief Operating Officer	_____	_____	_____

E   **Purchasing Card Manager Approval:**

_____   _____   _____
Signature   Print Name   Date

Form PUR-195

Exhibit 7.6   Purchasing Card Spending Limit Change Request Form

Policy/Procedure Statement	Retrieval No.:	PCM-07
Brasto Publishing	Page:	1 of 1
	Issue Date:	10/28/0X
	Supersedes:	N/A
Subject: Report Lost Purchasing Card		

1.   PURPOSE AND SCOPE
This procedure is used by company employees to provide necessary information to the processing bank regarding a lost or stolen procurement card.

2.   RESPONSIBILITIES
EMPLOYEE	**Employee**
PCM	**Purchasing Card Manager**

3.   PROCEDURES

3.1   EMPLOYEE   **Notify Bank Regarding Lost Card**
Notify the card issuing bank as soon as you realize that your purchasing card is missing. Write down the name of the person you contact, as well as the date and time when the contact was made.

3.2   EMPLOYEE   **Complete Missing Purchase Card Form**
1.   Download the Missing Purchasing Card form from the company intranet site (as shown in Exhibit 7.7).
2.   Complete the contact information shown in Section A of the form.
3.   In Section B, check off the appropriate box to indicate what happened to the card.
4.   In Section C, enter the card number in the boxes provided. If you do not have this information, check the box immediately below the spaces provided for the card number.
5.   Based on your notification call to the bank, enter in Section D the name of the person contacted, as well as the date and time when the call occurred.
6.   In Section E, check the box indicating how you would like to have a replacement card delivered to you. If the shipment is by overnight delivery, include your department's account number to which the delivery cost will be charged.
7.   Sign and date the form.
8.   Forward the completed form to the Purchasing Card Manager.
9.   If you locate your original purchasing card at a later date, cut it in half and send it to the Purchasing Card Manager.

3.3   PCM   **Report and Record Missing Purchasing Card Information**
1.   Upon receipt of the completed Missing Purchasing Card form from the employee, review it for accuracy and forward it to the bank.
2.   File the form in the lost cards file. On a monthly basis, transfer the information from all newly received Missing Purchasing Card forms to a lost cards tracking spreadsheet.
3.   Review the spreadsheet to determine if some employees are losing a disproportionate number of purchasing cards. If so, discuss the situation with the employee's manager to determine if purchasing card privileges should be revoked.

Report Lost Purchasing Card

Missing Purchasing Card Form
[Company Name]

A   **Your Contact Information:**

Name: _____   Address Line 1: _____

Phone Number: _____   Address Line 2: _____

Fax Number: _____

B   **Loss Information:**

☐   Card was stolen

☐   Card was lost

☐   Other (describe): _____

C   **Purchasing Card Number:**

☐☐☐☐ - ☐☐☐☐ - ☐☐☐☐ - ☐☐☐☐

☐   I do not have a record of the purchasing card number.

D   **Bank Notification Information:**

Name of person contacted at bank: _____

Date of contact: _____   Time of contact: _____

E   **Card Replacement Information:**

☐   Send me a replacement card by regular mail.

☐   Send me a replacement card by overnight delivery.

My FedEx account number is: _____

F   Card Holder
Signature: _____   Date: _____

Form PUR-197

Exhibit 7.7   Missing Purchasing Card Form

Policy/Procedure Statement	Retrieval No.:	PCM-08
![Brasto Publishing logo]	Page:	1 of 1
	Issue Date:	10/28/0X
Brasto Publishing	Supersedes:	N/A
Subject: Moved or Terminated Card User		

1.   PURPOSE AND SCOPE

This procedure is used by company employees to determine the correct procedures for handling purchasing cards if their users either change departments or leave the company.

2.   RESPONSIBILITIES

EMPLOYEE	**Employee**
DEPT MANAGER	**Department Manager**

3.   PROCEDURES

3.1   EMPLOYEE   **Handling of Purchasing Card for Departing Employee**

1. If the card user moves to a different location or leaves the company, notify the Purchasing Card Manager and the department manager of the effective date of this event.
2. Collect all receipts related to purchases made since the last account statement, sorted by date of purchase, and turn them over to the department manager.
3. Cut up the card and properly dispose of it.

3.2   DEPT MANAGER   **Processing of Final Account Statement**

1. The department manager is responsible for the reconciliation of the final account statement for the departed employee's purchasing card. The department manager should reconcile the statement as per the "Monthly Statement Reconciliation" procedure.
2. The department manager initials the reconciled expense packet before forwarding it to the Purchasing Card Manager, and should also prominently note on the form the departure date of the employee.

Moved or Terminated Card User

Chapter 8

ACCOUNTING CONTROLS MANUAL

8.1 INTRODUCTION

The controls in this controls manual can be used as a checklist to ensure that a complete control system is in place for all major accounting transactions. The following list itemizes the groups of controls to be found within this accounting controls manual:

Basic order entry	Obsolete inventory
Computerized order entry	Manufacturing resources planning
Electronic order entry	Just-in-time manufacturing
Basic credit granting	Basic shipping
Computerized credit granting	Drop shipping
Basic purchasing	Shipping—evaluated receipts
Basic inventory procurement	Basic billing
Computerized purchasing	Computerized billing
Procurement cards	Advanced billing systems
Goods in transit	Credit memos
Manual receiving	Basic cash receipts
Computerized receiving	Basic check handling
Receiving—evaluated receipts	Computerized check handling
Manual accounts payable	Credit card receipts
Computerized accounts payable	Lockbox receipts
Manual cash disbursements	Petty cash
Computerized cash disbursements	Investments
Electronic payments	Basic payroll

Basic inventory storage/movement	Computerized timekeeping
Basic perpetual inventory tracking	Computerized payroll
Computerized perpetual inventory tracking	Payroll self-service
Inventory bar code scanning	Cash payroll payments
Inventory zone putaway and picking	Electronic payroll payments
Inventory pick-to-light	Electronic payroll remittances
Inventory cross-docking	Outsourced payroll
Inventory valuation	Fixed assets

The sequence of controls in the list follows the standard transaction flow of a business enterprise—receipt of a customer order, credit management, inventory procurement and receipt, shipping, billing, cash receipts, and funds investment. Controls for payroll and fixed assets, which do not fall within this transaction flow, are listed at the end of the manual.

8.2 BASIC ORDER ENTRY CONTROLS

The controls for a basic order entry system are centered on data accuracy verification, and are as follows:

- *Verify approved buyer for customer.* The order entry staff will contact the customer and verify that the buyer who signed a received purchase order exceeding $_____ is approved to do so by the customer.

- *Verify price against price book.* The order entry staff will compare the prices listed on each customer purchase order to the official prices listed in the latest version of the company price book and contact the customer for resolution if any discrepancies are found.

- *Contact customers regarding significant freight charges.* The order entry staff will notify customers if anticipated freight charges are expected to exceed $_____ .

- *Prenumber sales orders.* The order entry staff will order all new sales order forms with sequential numbers that are in sequence from the last set of sales orders purchased.

- *Review the sales order for accuracy.* The order entry staff will compare the sales order to the originating customer purchase order to ensure that all information has been accurately transferred to the sales order.

8.3 COMPUTERIZED ORDER ENTRY CONTROLS

The controls for a computerized order entry system mostly involve data accuracy verification, and are as follows:

- *Control access to the order entry system.* Access to the order entry software will be password protected.

- *Maintain a transaction log.* The computer system automatically creates a keystroke log for every order entry transaction.

- *Data entry validation checks.* The computer system automatically performs data entry validation checks, including addresses, delivery dates, and part or product numbers that do not exist.

- *Check on-hand Inventory status.* The computer system automatically compares the amount of unallocated on-hand inventory to the customer order, and notifies the customer if there is insufficient inventory to fulfill their order.

- *Automatic price matching.* The computer system automatically sets up product prices from the standard corporate price book.

- *Supervisory override of special pricing.* The computer system routes all nonstandard pricing to the order entry supervisor for manual override authorization.

- *Set up complex billing terms.* The order entry staff enters complex billing terms into the order entry database on the order placement date and routes the billing terms to the controller for review.

8.4 ELECTRONIC ORDER ENTRY CONTROLS

The controls for electronic order entry involve having the computer conduct all aspects of the order entry process, and are as follows:

- *Automated payment processing.* The computer system will automatically process payments using the customer's credit card, or notify the customer that there is insufficient credit remaining on the card.

- *Automated credit review.* The computer system will automatically match customer orders against a table listing available credit, and notify the credit staff if the credit level has been exceeded.

- *Flag order as approved for shipment.* The computer system will automatically flag customer orders as approved for shipment, once either a credit card payment has been processed or an automated credit review has been conducted.

- *Communicate order status to customer.* The computer system will automatically issue a confirmation message to the customer, stating that the order has been processed.

8.5 BASIC CREDIT GRANTING CONTROLS

The controls for a basic credit granting operation are primarily targeted at the timely review of customer credit and ensuring that all orders within certain parameters are subject to credit reviews. The controls are as follows:

- *Create credit policy.* The credit manager will create and enforce the use of a credit policy that defines how to calculate a credit limit, information required of customers in order to determine a credit limit, standard terms of sale, and collection techniques to be employed.

- *Conduct staff training.* The credit manager will conduct periodic training of the credit staff in credit procedures.

- *Require credit approval prior to shipment.* The shipping manager will not ship a customer order unless the sales order contains a credit approval stamp.

- *Investigate unanswered questions on the credit application.* The credit staff will follow up with prospective customers on all unanswered questions on the standard credit application form.

- *Verify the existence of a new customer.* The credit staff will verify the existence of a new customer, through either a credit report or online inquiry to the state secretary of state's office.

- *Verify credit limit at time of order placement.* The credit staff will log new orders into a manually maintained customer credit log, and determine if there is sufficient available credit for a new customer order.

- *Determine credit level using credit decision table.* The credit staff will use a standardized credit decision table to determine credit levels based on fixed criteria.

- *Require supervisory approval of credit changes.* The credit manager will approve all changes in the level of credit granted each customer.

- *Stamp approval on sales order.* The credit manager will stamp "Approved" on each sales order that has successfully completed a credit review, as well as sign and date the sales order.

- *Securely store credit approval stamp.* The credit manager will securely store the credit approval stamp when it is not in use.

- *Review credit if check is returned.* The credit manager will require customers to complete a new credit application if any of their payments are returned due to not-sufficient funds.

- *Require periodic credit reviews.* The credit manager will require customers to complete a new credit application once every _____ years if their annualized order quantity exceeds $_____ .

- *Require credit review for reduced payment scenarios.* The credit manager will review the credit status of all customers who skip payments or stop taking early payment discounts.

- *Review credit for large orders.* The credit manager will review the credit of all customer orders for which the order amount exceeds $_____ .

8.6 COMPUTERIZED CREDIT GRANTING CONTROLS

The controls for a computerized credit granting system are primarily targeted at the replacement of manual credit controls with automated ones, as noted below:

- *Link customers to an online credit application form.* The computer system will automatically route new customers to an online credit application form with built-in validation checks.

- *Automatically review credit for smaller orders.* The computer system will automatically use a rules based credit engine to review and grant credit for smaller orders.

- *Automatically assign approval flag for customers with sufficient credit.* The computer system will compare the dollar amount of each incoming customer order to its predetermined credit limit and set a flag in the accounting database to indicate credit approval if the remaining credit limit exceeds the amount of the order.

- *Flag order as approved for shipment.* The credit staff will set a flag in the accounting database for each approved order, indicating that it is approved for shipment.

- *Investigate credit levels exceeded.* The credit staff will print a listing of credit levels exceeded from the computer system, and investigate which credit management system breakdowns caused the excessive levels of credit.

- *Audit orders below the credit review threshold.* The internal audit staff will conduct a periodic review of selected customer orders falling below the minimum credit review threshold, and notify the CFO if it finds a pattern of orders being placed by low-credit entities just below the credit threshold.

- *Receive electronic credit rating change notifications.* The credit manager will automatically receive electronic credit rating change notifications for a designated list of customers from a reputable credit rating organization.

8.7 BASIC PURCHASING CONTROLS

The key controls for general purchasing address the proper use and tracking of purchase orders, as noted below. Additional purchasing controls are noted in sections 8.8, "Basic Inventory Procurement Controls," and 8.9, "Computerized Purchasing Controls."

- *Require purchase order beyond a threshold amount.* The purchasing manager will require all acquisitions exceeding a purchase price of $____ to be authorized in advance with a signed purchase order.

- *Prenumber purchase orders.* The purchasing clerk will order all new purchase order forms with sequential numbers that are in sequence from the last set of purchase orders purchased.

- *Secure blank purchase orders.* The purchasing clerk will store all purchase order stock in a locked storage cabinet. The clerk will not post the combination to the storage cabinet's lock in a public location.

- *Track purchase order numbers.* The purchasing clerk will retain in a secure location a list of all purchase order numbers used that is separate from the purchase order storage area, and update this list promptly whenever blank purchase order forms are used. The clerk will promptly notify the purchasing manager when purchase order numbers are missing.

- *Countersign large purchase orders*. The purchasing manager will sign all purchase orders having dollar amounts exceeding $____.

- *Notify suppliers regarding authorized buyers*. The purchasing manager will periodically notify suppliers of the names of buyers who are authorized to issue purchase orders for specific commodity groups.

8.8 BASIC INVENTORY PROCUREMENT CONTROLS

There are a multitude of controls related to the purchase of inventory, with particular attention to the proper requisitioning of inventory from within the warehouse. Controls are as follows:

- *Assign requisitions to one person*. The warehouse manager will assign requisition responsibility for each inventory item to one person to avoid duplicate requisitions.

- *Conduct daily inventory review*. The warehouse manager or designated requisitioning staff will conduct a daily review of the inventory to determine if additional inventory should be requisitioned.

- *Use prenumbered purchase requisition forms*. The warehouse staff will use prenumbered purchase requisition forms to request inventory purchases from the purchasing department.

- *Investigate purchase requisition forms*. The warehouse staff will review its open requisitions to determine if any do not have an attached purchase order, and follow up with the purchasing department to verify if they have issued a purchase order for the missing requisitions.

- *Purchase using minimum order quantities*. The purchasing staff will place orders for inventory items based on minimum economic order quantities.

- *Verify that purchase order matches requisition*. The warehouse staff will compare its copy of the purchase order to the initiating purchase requisition to ensure that the correct items were ordered.

- *Complete receiving report*. The warehouse staff will enter the quantity and product description for all items received in a receiving report and send this report to the accounts payable department.

- *Three-way matching required for payment*. The accounts payable staff will match the receiving report to the authorizing purchase order and supplier invoice to ensure that all deliveries are properly authorized, in the correct amount, and for the correct price before issuing payment.

- *Put away items immediately after receipt*. The warehouse staff will put away inventory items immediately after receipt in order to reduce the risk of issuing requisitions for items that have already arrived.

- *Verify projected shipping dates for overdue deliveries.* The purchasing staff will regularly investigate with suppliers the reasons for overdue deliveries and notify the purchasing manager of significant projected delivery delays.

- *Regularly update visual reorder points.* The materials manager will regularly schedule a review of all visual reorder points based on changes in demand, reordering costs, and holding costs, and modify the reorder points as necessary.

8.9 COMPUTERIZED PURCHASING CONTROLS

Using a computer system to process purchases allows for a number of controls that take advantage of the automation characteristics of the computer, including running reports for control reviews, securing file access, and tracking changes to records. The controls are as follows:

- *Segregate vendor master file duties.* The person responsible for updating the vendor master file will not be allowed to approve payments to suppliers.

- *Restrict access to vendor master file.* The computer system will allow access to the vendor master file only if a correct user identification and password are provided.

- *Restrict access to purchasing system.* The computer system will allow access to the purchasing system only if a correct user identification and password are provided.

- *Run a credit report on new suppliers.* The purchasing clerk will run a credit report on each new supplier for whom purchases exceed a cumulative year-to-date total of $____. If the credit report reveals that the supplier is a company employee or related to such a person, the purchasing clerk will notify the purchasing manager and controller.

- *Compare ordered to received quantities.* The purchasing manager will match the purchasing, receiving, and payables databases to determine if any suppliers are shipping lower quantities than ordered and then billing the company for the full amount ordered. The purchasing manager will bring these issues to the attention of the purchasing clerks responsible for those suppliers.

- *Review old open purchase orders.* The purchasing staff will periodically run a report listing all open purchase orders, sorted by purchase order date, and determine if the open items shown in older purchase orders are still needed. If not, the purchasing staff will cancel these purchase orders.

- *Review customer complaints database.* The purchasing manager will review the customer complaints database to determine if any suppliers have reduced their product quality on items resold by the company to its customers, and bring any possible issues to the attention of the purchasing clerks responsible for those suppliers.

- *Eliminate duplicate suppliers.* The purchasing manager will periodically review the vendor master file for duplicate supplier records and purge excess records.

- *Audit acquisitions made within authorized purchase levels.* The internal audit staff will run a report listing multiple small payments to suppliers within a short time period to see if the payments are related to a single acquisition, and determine if this payment pattern is caused by a circumvention of maximum purchasing authorization rules.

- *Audit the vendor master file change log.* The internal audit staff will periodically review the change log for the vendor master file to determine if changes are being inappropriately made to the file.

- *Match quantities ordered to MRP requirements.* The internal audit staff will match quantities ordered by the purchasing department to actual material requirements indicated by the material requirements planning (MRP) system to determine if excessive quantities are being purchased and possibly diverted.

- *Track short-term price changes by suppliers.* The internal audit staff will compare a history of price changes by supplier to market rates for the commodities being purchased to determine if there is evidence of excessive pricing. The internal audit staff will then sort suppliers for whom pricing appears excessive by the purchasing clerk assigned to each supplier to reveal possible kickback trends.

8.10 PROCUREMENT CARD CONTROLS

The bulk of procurement card controls involve the proper tracking, reconciliation, and investigation of purchases reported on the procurement card statement, with additional controls governing card usage and credit limit changes. Controls are as follows:

- *Sign usage agreement.* Procurement card users will sign an agreement with the company, detailing their responsibilities in using procurement cards, and stating the consequences of misuse.

- *Maintain transaction log.* Procurement card users will maintain a written log of all purchases made, as well as retain receipts matching the logged items.

- *Reconcile log to statement.* Procurement card users will use a standard checklist to reconcile their written log of all purchases made to the monthly card statement.

- *Report missing receipts.* Procurement card users will promptly report missing receipts on a standard form, itemizing each line item on the monthly card statement for which there is no receipt.

- *Reject items on monthly statement.* Procurement card users will promptly report line items on the monthly card statement that they are rejecting on the grounds of lack of receipt, incorrect pricing, incorrect product delivery, or items having been returned.

- *Approve charged expenses.* Department managers to whose departments procurement card expenses are charged will review and approve all such expenses.

- *Track card expenditures on a trend line.* The internal audit staff will periodically track purchasing totals by expense type for each procurement card user to locate trends or spikes indicating inappropriate purchases.

- *Verify that purchases are made through an approved supplier.* The internal audit staff will verify that procurement card purchases are being made through approved suppliers, and notify the purchasing manager of incorrect purchases.

- *Report lost cards.* Procurement card users will report lost cards promptly, both by calling a hotline number and by filling out a form that provides evidence of when notification was given to the card provider.

- *Approve credit limit changes.* Department managers will approve all requests for changes in procurement card credit limits.

- *Avoid inventory purchases.* Procurement card users will not purchase inventory that is normally ordered automatically through a manufacturing resources planning (MRP II) system.

8.11   GOODS IN TRANSIT CONTROLS

The primary controls concern for in-transit goods is to ensure that the purchasing staff has addressed the risks associated with any special shipping terms. Controls are as follows:

- *Review shipping terms on customer orders.* The order entry staff will review shipping terms listed on customer orders and notify the corporate risk management staff of any special insurance requirements.

- *Audit shipping terms.* The internal audit staff will periodically review shipment terms mandated by customers to verify if the corporate risk management staff was notified of special insurance requirements.

- *Audit the receiving dock.* The internal audit staff will periodically conduct a review of the receiving area to verify that all received items are promptly entered in the inventory database.

8.12   MANUAL RECEIVING CONTROLS

Controls in a noncomputerized environment center on the proper authorization for received items and the communication of receiving information to the rest of the company. Controls are as follows:

- *Reject deliveries not having purchase order support.* The receiving manager will reject all supplier deliveries for which there is no authorizing purchase order, or for which there is not a sufficient authorized quantity to cover the unit quantity of the delivery.

- *Prenumber receiving reports.* The receiving clerk will order all receiving forms with sequential numbers that are in sequence from the last set of receiving forms purchased.

- *Track receiving report numbers.* The disbursements clerk will track the sequence of receiving report numbers to ascertain if any reports are missing, and notify the receiving manager of the form numbers of missing reports.

- *Secure blank receiving reports.* The receiving clerk will store all receiving report stock in a locked storage cabinet. The clerk will not post the combination to the storage cabinet's lock in a public location.

8.13   COMPUTERIZED RECEIVING SYSTEM CONTROLS

When a computer system is used to enhance the receiving process, additional controls can be used to match information in the receiving and purchasing databases to uncover shipping and product return anomalies. Controls are as follows:

- *Review flagged duplicate packing slip numbers.* The computer system will automatically flag duplicate packing slip numbers and not allow receipt until the transaction is approved by the receiving manager.

- *Investigate product returns.* The receiving staff will compare items returned by customers to the originating customer purchase order and internal sales order, and forward error information to the controller.

8.14   RECEIVING–EVALUATED RECEIPTS CONTROLS

An in-house evaluated receipts system requires suppliers to attach purchase order information to all deliveries, which is the principle information used to pay the supplier. Controls center on the accurate and consistent use of the purchase order number, as well as the identification of suppliers who are paid under this system. Controls are as follows:

- *Add evaluated receipts flag.* The purchasing clerk will enter an evaluated receipts flag in the vendor master file for all suppliers using the evaluated receipts system. This flag prevents the accounts payable staff from paying invoices sent by suppliers for the payments already processed through the evaluated receipts system.

- *Communication of system changes.* The purchasing clerk will promptly notify suppliers in the evaluated receipts system of all changes to their reporting requirements.

- *Reject invoices referencing a purchase order number.* The accounts payable staff will reject all supplier invoices referencing a purchase order number, since these invoices are paid through the evaluated receipts system.

- *Notify supplier of incorrect units of measure.* The purchasing clerk will notify suppliers of any incorrect units of measure shown on supplier packing slips.

- *Notify suppliers of packing slips not sent in bar-coded format.* The purchasing clerk will notify suppliers if bar coding is not used on packing slip information.

- *Audit manually issued purchase orders.* The internal audit staff will periodically review a selection of purchase orders issued outside the automated material requirements planning system, with particular attention to unusual quantities and items not normally purchased.

- *Audit automated purchase orders.* The internal audit staff will periodically review a selection of purchase orders automatically issued by the material requirements planning system, focusing on orders resulting in either excessive on-hand inventory or production shortages.

8.15 MANUAL ACCOUNTS PAYABLE CONTROLS

Controls for the manual handling of accounts payable address proper authorization of payment, avoidance of duplicate payments, and timely payment. Controls are as follows:

- *Compare supplier invoices to authorizing purchase orders.* The payables staff will match supplier invoices to purchase orders, and forward all supplier invoices with no supporting purchase order authorization to the controller for approval.

- *Track all unapproved supplier invoices.* The payables staff will maintain a register of all supplier invoices issued to managers for approval, and which have not been returned by the approvers. This register will be updated on a daily basis.

- *Duplicate number review.* The payables staff will manually compare the numbers on new supplier invoices to open and paid supplier invoices to ensure that supplier invoices are not paid twice.

- *Conduct a three-way match.* The payables staff will compare the pricing and quantities listed on each supplier invoice to the quantities actually received, as listed on receiving documents, and to the price originally agreed to, as noted in the company's purchase order.

- *Require additional approval for payment from copies.* The controller must approve any supplier invoice for which payment is being made from a duplicate copy.

- *Track all unmatched supplier invoices.* The payables staff will maintain a record of all unpaid supplier invoices for which related purchasing or receiving documentation has not yet been received, and investigate missing documents on a daily basis.

- *File by due date.* The payables staff will file unpaid supplier invoices by due date to ensure that each invoice is paid on the designated date.

- *Reconcile supplier credits to returned goods documentation.* The disbursements clerk will maintain a register of returned goods and match it against supplier credits. If no credits arrive, then the clerk will use the register to continually remind suppliers to issue credit memos.

- *Create a payment escalation schedule.* The disbursements clerk will create a schedule showing the dates on which recurring payments are scheduled to change at various times in the future, and use it to revise recurring payments on an ongoing basis.

- *Create a recurring payment termination schedule.* The disbursements clerk will create a schedule showing the dates on which recurring payments are terminated, and use it to stop recurring payments.

8.16 COMPUTERIZED ACCOUNTS PAYABLE CONTROLS

When a computer system is used to process accounts payable, controls can take advantage of the additional features of the computer system, so that supplier invoices, payment dates, and potential fraud situations can be more easily investigated. Controls are as follows:

- *Use standard naming convention in vendor master file.* The payables staff will use a standard naming convention to create supplier names in the vendor master file.

- *Use duplicate invoice search feature.* The payables staff will turn on the duplicate invoice tracking feature in the accounting software, and investigate all invoices flagged by the system as being duplicates of invoices already entered into the system.

- *Access the vendor history file when paying from a copy.* When entering a copy of a supplier invoice in the computer system, the payables staff will review the vendor history file to see if the same invoice has already been paid.

- *Identify and investigate invoices with no authorizing purchase order.* The payables staff runs a computer report listing all supplier invoices received for which there is no authorizing purchase order, and investigates why no purchase order was issued.

- *Search for duplicate remit-to addresses.* The payables staff will sort the vendor master file by address to determine if there are multiple supplier records having the same remit-to address. If so, each set of duplicate records shall be merged into a single supplier record, following consultation with the purchasing manager.

- *Match supplier addresses to employee addresses.* The payables staff will compare the employee and supplier address files to determine if any employees are posing as suppliers. Any matching incidents will be brought to the attention of the controller.

- *Track payment due dates with computer report.* The payables staff will print the open payables report, sorted by due date, and use it to ensure that all supplier invoices are paid on time, including invoices for which early payment discounts are available.

- *Terminate recurring payments on escalation dates.* The payables staff will set up recurring payments in the accounting software to terminate as of their escalation dates, which forces the staff to review the new payment amounts and reset this information in the accounting software.

8.17   MANUAL CASH DISBURSEMENT CONTROLS

In a manual cash disbursement environment, there is extremely tight control over the check stock, supporting documents, and check signers. Controls are as follows:

- *Secure the check stock.* The disbursements clerk will store all check stock in a locked storage cabinet. The clerk will not post the combination to the storage cabinet's lock in a public location.

- *Track check stock numbers.* The disbursements clerk will retain in a secure location a list of all check numbers used that is separate from the check stock storage area, and update this list promptly whenever new check stock is used. The clerk will also promptly notify the controller when check stock numbers are missing.

- *Verify that all check stock ordered has been received.* The disbursements clerk will compare the number of checks ordered to the number that arrive, and notify the bank to cancel all checks having the missing check numbers.

- *Segregate check-signing duties.* The check signer will not be responsible for or have access to any other accounting activities.

- *Avoid signing blank checks.* The check signer will not sign a blank check under any circumstances.

- *Compare check to voucher package.* The check signer will review the backup information in the voucher package attached to each check, compare the dollar amount of the voucher package to the amount being paid on the face of the check, and bring instances of unauthorized payment to the attention of the controller.

- *Perforate voucher package.* The disbursements clerk will perforate the voucher package with the "Paid" stamp once the associated payment has been sent to the supplier to ensure that the voucher package is not used again as backup material for another payment.

- *Destroy or perforate and lock up canceled checks.* The disbursements clerk will perforate all canceled checks with the word "canceled" and store them in a locked cabinet, or shred them with a cross-cut shredder.

- *Fund bank account to match issued checks.* The treasurer will only fund the checking account in an amount sufficient to cover checks identified in the check register.

- *Segregate bank reconciliation duties.* The person reconciling the checking account will have no responsibility for or access to any disbursement functions.

- *Reconcile supplier statements to payment detail.* The internal audit staff will investigate overdue payment notices on supplier statements to determine if an employee is diverting supplier payments for their own use.

8.18 COMPUTERIZED CASH DISBURSEMENT CONTROLS

Many of the controls already noted for a manual cash disbursements system also apply to a computerized system. In addition, the following controls should be added that provide additional control over check payments:

- *Secure signature plates.* The disbursement staff will store signature plates and signature stamps in a locked safe at all times other than when check printing is being conducted.

- *Require manual signature on large checks.* A senior manager must review and manually sign all checks exceeding $____.

- *Use positive pay.* The disbursements clerk will send a list of issued checks to the company's bank, which the bank shall use as the basis for accepting checks.

- *Conduct a daily bank reconciliation.* The person assigned to the reconciliation task will conduct a bank reconciliation every business day for every checking account, using online access to the bank's account records. This person will notify the controller at once of any anomalies discovered as part of these reconciliations.

8.19 ELECTRONIC PAYMENT CONTROLS

Electronic payments present the possibility of large cash outflows, and so require a number of controls to ensure that those payments are fully authorized. The controls are as follows:

- *Control access to payment software.* The electronic payment system will allow access only to authorized users.

- *Require payment approval document.* The disbursement clerk will not process an electronic payment without a signed approval document.

- *Set up debit blocks.* The treasurer will require the company's bank to install automated clearinghouse (ACH) debit filters on all company accounts, with debits allowed only on an individual approval basis.

- *Set up daily cumulative debit limits.* The treasurer will require the company's bank to install daily cumulative debit limits for all suppliers who are allowed to charge ACH debits against company bank accounts.

- *Issue electronic payments from a single account.* The treasurer will process electronic payments only from a single bank account, which will be funded only to cover specific electronic payments.

- *Request notification of duplicate debits.* The treasurer will periodically verify that the bank is notifying the company whenever a duplicate debit is being presented for posting.

- *Examination of duplicate debits.* Upon notification by the bank of a duplicate debit, the treasurer will notify the purchasing manager and internal audit manager of the details of the transaction.

- *Verify approved ACH debits.* The treasurer will verify with the bank that specific suppliers are allowed to initiate an ACH debit from the company's account.

- *Conduct an end-of-day payments review.* The controller will verify all electronic payments made at the end of each business day, which should encompass a comparison of authorizing documents to the actual amounts paid, as well as verification that payments are made to the correct supplier accounts. This review should not be conducted by someone within the treasury department.

8.20 BASIC INVENTORY STORAGE/MOVEMENT CONTROLS

Controls over inventory involve restricted access, proper review of incoming materials, and timely identification and recordation of all receipts. The controls are as follows:

- *Restrict warehouse access.* The warehouse manager will restrict access to the warehouse solely to the warehouse staff.

- *Reject unauthorized deliveries.* The receiving staff will reject all supplier deliveries for which there is no authorizing purchase order.

- *Conduct receiving inspections with a receiving checklist.* The receiving staff will use a formal receiving checklist for all receipts, which includes specific inspection points such as timeliness of the delivery, quality, quantity, and the presence of an authorizing purchase order number.

- *Complete inspection prior to recordation.* The warehouse staff will complete its receiving inspection prior to recording incoming inventory in the inventory database.

- *Identify and tag all received inventory.* The receiving staff will identify and tag each received item with the correct part number and description.

- *Record all receipts in a receiving log.* The receiving staff will record item descriptions and numbers for all items received, as well as quantities received and the dates of receipt.

- *Segregate customer-owned inventory.* The warehouse staff will store customer-owned inventory in a physically separate location.

- *Preassign inventory to specific locations.* The warehouse manager will assign specific storage locations to inventory items, and will direct the warehouse staff to congregate inventory in these locations.

- *Pick from the source document.* The picking staff will pick from a copy of the customer sales order or purchase order.

- *Restrict publicity about warehouse locations.* The webmaster will not list the locations of company warehouses on the corporate web site.

8.21 BASIC PERPETUAL INVENTORY TRACKING CONTROLS

The principal controls over a manual perpetual inventory system are the use of move tickets, centralized record keeping, and ongoing cycle counts. The controls are as follows:

- *Record transactions on move tickets.* The warehouse staff will record inventory move transactions on move tickets.

- *Use prenumbered move tickets.* The warehouse clerk will issue prenumbered move tickets to the warehouse staff and investigate all missing move tickets at the end of each shift.

- *Assign blocks of move tickets to specific personnel.* The warehouse clerk will issue blocks of consecutively numbered move tickets to the warehouse staff in order to more easily track responsibility for missing move tickets.

- *Require centralized record updating.* The warehouse clerk will be the only person allowed to record information in the central perpetual inventory card file.

- *Conduct a physical inventory count.* The warehouse manager will conduct a physical inventory count to correct inaccuracies in the perpetual inventory records.

- *Conduct ongoing cycle counts.* The warehouse staff will conduct ongoing cycle counts and investigate the reasons for inventory record inaccuracies.

- *Investigate negative-balance perpetual records.* The warehouse staff will promptly investigate the reasons for negative quantities in the perpetual inventory records and adjust the records as necessary.

8.22 COMPUTERIZED PERPETUAL INVENTORY TRACKING CONTROLS

The key controls for a computerized perpetual inventory system are rapid database updates to keep the records accurate in real time, and ongoing cycle counts. All of the other controls noted below are used to deal with a small number of situations involving specialty transactions:

- *Restrict access to database.* The perpetual inventory system will restrict access to authorized personnel.

- *Require rapid data updates.* The warehouse staff will use radio frequency scanners to update inventory records in real time.

- *Flag customer-owned inventory.* The warehouse clerk will turn on the customer-owned inventory flag in the item master record when in-stock inventory is owned by customers.

- *Require centralized record updating.* The warehouse clerk will be the only person allowed to record information about specialty inventory transactions in the perpetual inventory database.

- *Use prenumbered forms for specialty transactions.* The warehouse staff shall use prenumbered forms to record scrap and rework transactions.

- *Investigate missing forms.* The warehouse clerk will investigate all missing specialty inventory transaction forms at the end of each shift.

- *Conduct a physical inventory count.* The warehouse manager will conduct a physical inventory count to correct inaccuracies in the perpetual inventory records.

- *Conduct ongoing cycle counts.* The warehouse staff will conduct ongoing cycle counts and investigate the reasons for inventory record inaccuracies.

- *Investigate negative-balance perpetual records.* The warehouse staff will promptly investigate the reasons for negative quantities in the perpetual inventory records and adjust the records as necessary.

8.23 INVENTORY BAR CODE SCANNING CONTROLS

The use of bar code scanners requires controls for timely uploads, scanning error avoidance, and the proper use and maintenance of bar code labels. The controls are as follows:

- *Require timely data uploads.* The warehouse staff will upload data from their portable scanners at every scheduled work break.

- *Require specific character lengths.* The computer system will require the entry of specific character lengths for bar code scanner data entry fields to avoid having scans entered into the wrong database fields.

- *Print part descriptions on labels.* The receiving staff will print bar-coded identification labels for all incoming materials that include the part number and description on each label.

- *Review and replace location tags.* The warehouse staff regularly reviews the condition of all warehouse location tags and replaces them with laminated tags as needed.

- *Assign picking and putaway responsibilities.* The warehouse manager will assign responsibility for inventory record accuracy within warehouse areas to specific employees.

8.24 INVENTORY ZONE PUTAWAY AND PICKING CONTROLS

The principal controls for putaway and picking are the assignment of responsibility for record accuracy. Those and other controls are as follows:

- *Identify putaway locations.* The computer will automatically identify putaway locations and communicate this information to the stock putaway staff.

- *Assign putaway responsibilities.* The warehouse manager will assign responsibility for putaway tasks by location to specific employees.

- *Assign picking responsibilities.* The warehouse manager will assign picking responsibility by warehouse area to specific warehouse employees.

- *Record picks at the central packing area.* The warehouse clerk will record all picked items as they arrive in the packing area from stock pickers.

8.25 INVENTORY PICK-TO-LIGHT CONTROLS

Controls over a pick-to-light situation require the assignment of picking and putaway responsibilities, as outlined in the following controls:

- *Assign putaway responsibilities by location.* The warehouse manager will assign responsibility for putaway tasks by pick-to-light location to specific employees.

- *Assign picking responsibilities by location.* The warehouse manager will assign responsibility for picking tasks by pick-to-light location to specific employees.

8.26 INVENTORY CROSS-DOCKING CONTROLS

When inventory is being cross-docked, it is too inefficient to conduct standard receiving inspections. Instead, the primary control (as noted below) is to use advance shipping notices from shippers as the receiving document, thereby allowing goods to be more rapidly transshipped from the warehouse.

- *Use advance shipping notices.* The warehouse clerk will use advance shipping notices as receiving documents.

8.27 INVENTORY VALUATION CONTROLS

Controls for inventory valuation cover a broad range of issues, since valuation can be affected by such items as cost pool calculations, standard cost updates, and layering calculations. The controls are as follows:

- *Restrict file access.* The computer system will restrict access to the bill of materials and labor routing files to authorized users.

- *Review the bill of materials and labor routing change log.* The cost accountant will review the keystroke log for changes to bills of materials and labor routings, and investigate unusual changes.

- *Compare unextended product costs to those for prior periods.* The cost accountant will review a report comparing the unextended cost of each product to its cost in a prior period, and investigate significant changes.

- *Review sorted list of extended product costs in declining dollar order.* The cost accountant will review a report listing the extended cost of all inventory on hand in declining order of cost, and review items having unusually high or low valuations.

- *Review variances from standard cost.* The cost accountant will review a report listing the standard cost and most recent price paid for inventory items, and investigate significant variances from the standard cost.

- *Investigate entries to the inventory or cost of goods sold accounts.* The cost accountant will review the inventory and cost of goods sold general ledger accounts, and investigate unusual or unauthorized journal entries.

- *Review inventory layering calculations.* The cost accountant will review the underlying calculations for manually calculated inventory layering systems and correct any errors found. This review will include tracing layered costs back to invoices, tracing invoices forward to layered costs, and verifying the consistency of sales tax and freight cost allocations to layers.

- *Verify the calculation and allocation of overhead cost pools.* The cost accountant will review the costs included in allocation pools and how those costs are allocated to other general ledger accounts, and adjust entries as necessary.

- *Review assigned standard costs.* The cost accountant will periodically compare standard costs to actual costs, and recommend to the controller that standard costs be altered to more closely match actual costs.

- *Determine the lower of cost or market.* The cost accountant will regularly compare market prices to actual costs for larger inventory items, and write down actual costs to market costs if market costs are lower.

- *Remove scrap promptly.* The production manager will actively seek out and eliminate scrapped inventory from the company premises as well as from the inventory database.

- *Review production setup cost calculations.* The cost accountant will review the calculations for the per-unit cost of equipment setup, with particular attention to the assumed number of units in each production run, and change the assigned cost as necessary.

8.28 OBSOLETE INVENTORY CONTROLS

The primary control over obsolete inventory is to conduct regular inventory reviews, and then to follow through on the decisions made during those reviews. The controls are as follows:

- *Conduct periodic reviews.* The Materials Review Board will conduct obsolescence reviews on at least a quarterly basis.

- *Turn off automatic reordering.* The materials management staff will deactivate the inventory reorder flag in the item master file when it eliminates inventory from stock, thereby avoiding automated reordering.

- *Reduce impacted inventory prior to change order implementation.* The materials manager will implement engineering change orders after impacted inventory levels have been reduced to the greatest extent possible.

- *Move obsolete inventory to a segregated area.* The Materials Review Board will move all items designated as obsolete to a segregated area for easier review and disposition.

- *Track cash receipts against disposition estimates.* The cash receipts clerk will record all cash receipts from obsolete inventory dispositions in a separate account, and the cost accountant will match these cash receipts against estimated disposition values and report significant variances to the Materials Review Board.

- *Match obsolete inventory to disposal authorizations.* The internal audit staff will periodically compare inventory tagged for disposition to obsolescence authorizations in the minutes of the Materials Review Board, and investigate any tagged items for which no authorization exists.

8.29 MANUFACTURING RESOURCES PLANNING CONTROLS

Controls for MRP II systems center on the accuracy of information being used by the system, as well as prompt investigation of variances reported by it. The controls are as follows:

- *Maintain high levels of record accuracy.* The materials manager will maintain inventory record accuracy of at least 95%, labor routing record accuracy of at least 95%, and bill of materials record accuracy of at least 98%.

- *Restrict record access.* The MRP II system will restrict access to the inventory item master file to authorized personnel.

- *Restrict purchase order issuances.* The purchasing staff will restrict its inventory purchases to recommendations made by the MRP II system.

- *Enter under/over receipt notifications.* The receiving staff will enter into the MRP system the presence of any under/over quantity receipts from the ordered amounts.

- *Enter scrap/rework quantities.* The warehouse staff will enter into the MRP II system the amounts of any scrapped or reworked inventory.

- *Investigate returned inventory.* The warehouse staff will investigate the reasons why items picked for production are returned to the warehouse, and correct the underlying problems.

- *Investigate additional issuances.* The warehouse staff will investigate the reasons why additional items are requested from the warehouse in addition to the quantities already picked for a job.

- *Review action/exception messages.* The production planning staff will immediately review all action/exception messages reported by the MRP II system and correct the underlying problems as necessary.

- *Review the production area for excess inventory.* The materials management staff will regularly review the production area for excess inventory not returned to the warehouse, and transport it back to the warehouse.

8.30   JUST-IN-TIME MANUFACTURING CONTROLS

Just-in-time controls are unique to that process, and include supplier precertification, *kanban* usage, and downstream inspection. Related controls are as follows:

- *Certify suppliers.* The industrial engineering manager will investigate and certify suppliers for their product quality and delivery reliability.

- *Maintain a supplier performance scoring system.* The materials manager will regularly update a supplier performance scoring system and communicate its results to suppliers.

- *Work only with* kanban *authorizations.* Workstation operators will process work only when there is a *kanban* authorization to create a specific quantity of inventory.

- *Use standard container sizes.* The materials manager will enforce the use of standard container sizes to move, store, and count inventory.

- *Inspect parts at downstream locations.* Workstation operators will inspect the work-in-process inventory provided to it by the immediately preceding workstation and issue a notification of quality problems.

8.31   BASIC SHIPPING CONTROLS

The key shipping control is to not ship without a credit authorization, while other controls address the identification of backorders and consignment inventory. The controls are as follows:

- *Require credit authorization prior to shipment.* The warehouse staff will not ship an order unless a credit approval stamp is located on the sales order.

- *Compare quantity ordered to amount shipped.* The warehouse staff will compare the sales order to the quantity picked, note shortages on the sales order, and forward the revised sales order to the warehouse manager for backorder notifications.

- *Identify consignment inventory.* The warehouse staff will clearly identify company-owned consignment inventory that is being shipped to a reseller in both the shipping log and inventory tracking system.

8.32 DROP SHIPPING CONTROLS

When a supplier ships goods directly to a company's customers, the main control emphasis is on monitoring the shipment status of the order. Controls are as follows:

- *Verify receipt of customer order by supplier*. The order entry staff will verify that the supplier has received a copy of the customer order.

- *Match supplier's bill of lading to customer order*. The order entry staff will match the supplier's bill of lading to the customer to the customer order, and either forward this documentation to the billing department (if the order is complete) or correspond with the supplier regarding additional shipping (if the order is incomplete).

- *Investigate old open orders*. The order entry staff will regularly investigate the status of all open customer orders with suppliers.

- *Reconcile backlogged remainder items*. The order entry staff will investigate remainder items on shipped customer orders and either cancel the items, communicate with customers regarding replacement items, or obtain shipping information from the supplier.

8.33 SHIPPING—EVALUATED RECEIPTS CONTROLS

When shipping goods to a company that operates an evaluated receipts system, key controls are to ensure that a purchase order number is attached to each shipment, and that no invoice is sent. The controls are as follows:

- *Attach purchase order number*. The warehouse manager will attach an identifying purchase order number and other customer-required information to every delivery sent to a customer using an evaluated receipts system.

- *Set evaluated receipts flag*. The order entry staff will set the evaluated receipts flag in the customer master file to indicate that no invoices are to be sent to any customer using an evaluated receipts system and that an evaluated receipts shipping tag must be attached to all deliveries to those customers.

- *Audit billings to ensure that invoices are not issued*. The internal audit staff will extract from the master customer file all customer records with an activated evaluated receipts flag, and compare this list to the sales journal to see if invoices are being printed, and notify the controller of any issues found.

- *Review customer complaints for issues related to evaluated receipts*. The order entry staff will periodically review the customer complaints log for issues with evaluated receipts tags not being in the proper format or invoices incorrectly being sent to customers who do not want them, and forward any issues found to the controller.

8.34 BASIC BILLING SYSTEM CONTROLS

Many billing controls have the objective of ensuring billing accuracy, thereby reducing collection problems and accelerating cash flow. These and other controls are as follows:

- *Segregate billing and collection functions.* The controller will ensure that the billing staff does not perform collection functions.

- *Review sales order for credit approval stamp.* The billing clerk will examine the sales order for a signed credit approval stamp and notify the credit manager if this approval information is not shown on the sales order.

- *Prenumber sales invoices.* The billing clerk will order prenumbered sales invoices that are in sequence from the last numeric series of invoices ordered.

- *Verify contract terms.* The billing clerk will verify the terms of any contracts upon which billings are based.

- *Issue invoices promptly.* The billing clerk will issue all invoices within one day of shipment or service delivery.

- *Proofread invoices.* A second billing clerk will compare completed invoices to the source documentation to verify the accuracy of all billing information. Invoices will be adjusted based on this review.

- *Mark envelopes as "address correction requested."* The billing clerk will stamp envelopes containing invoices to suppliers with "address correction requested" to obtain updated address information from the Postal Service.

- *Route address changes to the billing department.* The mailroom staff will route all returned billing envelopes to the billing department for address correction.

- *Reconcile goods shipped to billed.* The billing clerk will compare the shipping log to the sales journal to identify items billed but not shipped, and investigate as necessary.

- *Monitor billing complaints.* The billing manager will monitor all complaints from customers regarding billing issues and resolve them as necessary.

- *Simplify invoices.* The billing manager will periodically revise the layout of the invoice form to eliminate unneeded information and clarify payment terms, amounts, and due dates.

- *Review performance metrics.* The controller will periodically review performance metrics for billings and follow up on any issues with the billing manager.

- *Audit billings.* The internal audit staff will periodically review billings to ensure that invoices correctly carry forward billing information in the supporting documents and that all items shipped are billed. The audit will also include a review of unusual entries in the accounts receivable account in the general ledger.

8.35 COMPUTERIZED BILLING SYSTEM CONTROLS

Billing controls in a computerized billing environment should make use of automated links to the shipping database, as well as use all available data entry error checking facilities. The controls are as follows:

- *Restrict system access*. The billing software will restrict access to authorized users, especially in regard to the issuance of credit memos.

- *Compare shipping log to sales journal*. The billing clerk will review a computer report comparing shipped to billed goods, and investigate any unbilled items.

- *Preview invoices*. The billing clerk will print an invoice preview report from the computer system and review it for errors prior to printing final invoices.

- *Data entry error checking*. The computer system will automatically flag incorrect pricing, product descriptions, and customer addresses as part of an invoicing data entry system.

- *Block invoices.* The computer system will automatically block invoices from being generated until the related products have been flagged by the warehouse staff as having been shipped.

- *Issue month-end statements*. A person not in the billing department will issue month-end statements to customers, and will follow up on irregularities reported by customers.

- *Review billing terms*. The billing manager will print a monthly report showing all credit terms listed on invoices during the past month, and review unusual terms with the collections manager and controller.

8.36 ADVANCED BILLING SYSTEM CONTROLS

Web Invoice Entry

Some customers have created web sites on which they require suppliers to manually enter invoices. Related controls are as follows:

- *Match confirmation sheet to invoice*. The billing clerk will compare the web site's confirmation page to the invoice for errors, and attach it to the invoice.

- *Create activity checklist for customer*. The billing clerk will use a customized checklist for entering web site invoices for each customer, specifying how invoices are to be entered.

- *Confirm entry*. The billing clerk will contact the customer to confirm correct entry of an invoice if the customer's web site does not create a confirmation page.

Invoicing at the Delivery Point

In situations where the amount delivered is not finalized until the point of delivery, the person delivering the goods must create an invoice and hand it directly to the supplier. Related controls are as follows:

- *Use a prenumbered invoice in duplicate.* The delivery person will create a manual invoice using a prenumbered duplicate invoice, and return one copy to the accounting department for recording of the sale.

- *Track invoice numbers issued to the delivery staff.* The billing clerk will issue blocks of prenumbered invoice forms to the delivery staff, and follow up on invoice numbers that are not returned.

- *Match delivery schedule to invoices.* The billing clerk will match the list of customers on the daily delivery schedule to the completed invoice copies returned by the delivery staff, and follow up on any customers on the schedule for which there are no invoices.

Electronic Data Interchange

When electronic data interchange (EDI) is used, the company sends an electronic message to the customer in which is embedded an invoice in a strictly defined format. An EDI invoice can be manually entered in EDI software before being sent, or can be automatically created and issued by the computer system. Related controls are as follows:

- *Match EDI transmission receipt to invoice.* If an EDI transmission is manually keypunched, the billing clerk will match the EDI transmission receipt to the original invoice to ensure the accuracy of transmitted information.

- *Verify that an acknowledgment has been received.* The billings clerk will verify that an acknowledgment EDI message has been sent back from the customer following an EDI billing, and follow up on any missing acknowledgments.

- *Send EDI statement of account.* A person not in the billing department will issue EDI month-end statements to customers, and will follow up on irregularities reported by customers.

8.37   CREDIT MEMO CONTROLS

Credit memos can be used to hide the theft of customer payments, so the level of required control is relatively high, and involves physical and supervisory control, as well as the segregation of duties. The controls are as follows:

- *Segregate the collections and credit memo recordation functions.* The controller will ensure that the collections staff does not also have responsibility for or access to the credit memo system.

- *Prenumber credit memos.* The billing clerk will order prenumbered credit memos that are in sequence from the last numeric series of credit memos ordered.

- *Match credit memos to receiving documents.* A person not in the billing or collection departments will match the list of returned goods on the receiving log to issued credit memos, and investigate all credit memos for which there is no matching receipt.

- *Approve credit memos.* The credit manager will approve all credit memo requests exceeding $____.

- *Audit credit memos.* The internal audit staff will periodically review a sample of credit memos and their supporting documentation and approvals, as well as the handling of any subsequent cash receipts for which credit memos had previously been issued.

8.38 BASIC CASH RECEIPT CONTROLS

There are a multitude of controls needed for cash receipts, extending from the point of cash receipt to depositing at the bank. Key controls are as follows:

- *Enter cash in cash register.* The sales clerk enters each sale into a cash register or fills out a prenumbered receipt.

- *Give receipt copy to customer.* The sales clerk gives a copy of each sale receipt from the cash register or a copy of a prenumbered receipt to the customer.

- *Give gift to customers if no receipt given.* The sales clerk will give customers a gift if no sales receipt is given to the customer.

- *Authorize cash refunds.* The sales clerk supervisor will authorize all cash refunds to customers.

- *Reconcile cash to cash register.* A supervisor will reconcile the cash in each cash register to the total sale recorded on the sale register, and investigate any differences.

- *Deposit cash daily.* A bonded clerk will deposit cash daily.

- *Transport cash in secure container.* A bonded clerk will transport cash to the bank in a locked cash pouch.

- *Reconcile validated deposit slip to deposit ticket.* The accounting supervisor will compare the bank-validated deposit slip to the original deposit slip filled out by the cashier, and investigate any differences.

- *Review unapplied cash.* The assistant controller will review unapplied cash on a daily basis and investigate items that have been unapplied for more than one day.

- *Monitor metrics.* The internal audit staff will monitor those metrics indicating cash fraud, including increased levels of inventory shrinkage and the proportion of refunds to sales over time.

8.39 BASIC CHECK HANDLING CONTROLS

Checks are tightly monitored with a number of controls that begin in the mailroom and continue through the cashier, cash application, depositing, and bank reconciliation functions. The controls are as follows:

- *Several staff open the mail.* Two mailroom employees will open the mail together, and mutually verify the contents of the check pre-list report.

- *Endorse checks "for deposit only."* The mailroom staff will stamp incoming checks with a "for deposit only" stamp.

- *Prepare check pre-list.* The mailroom staff will prepare a list of checks received through the mail prior to forwarding checks for cashing.

- *Review restrictive endorsements.* The cashier will review checks for restrictive endorsements and forward any such checks to the legal staff prior to cashing them.

- *Match check pre-list to cash receipts journal.* The cashier will compare checks listed in the cash receipts journal to the check pre-list prepared by the mailroom staff, and investigate any differences.

- *Reconcile check pre-list to remittance advices.* The receivables clerk will compare the check pre-list to the remittance advices forwarded by the cashier, and investigate any differences.

- *Apply cash within one day.* The receivables clerk will apply cash to open accounts receivable within one day of receipt of the associated check.

- *Review unapplied cash.* The collections staff will promptly contact customers regarding the proper disposition of cash receipts for which there is no information regarding the invoice number to which they are to be assigned.

- *Review NSF checks.* The cashier will route not-sufficient funds (NSF) checks to the collections manager for further action.

- *Reconcile bank statement.* The accounting manager will reconcile the monthly bank statement to the corporate accounting records and investigate any differences.

- *Review metrics.* The controller will review metrics for the presence of decreasing cash to total current assets, decreasing ratio of cash to credit card sales, and flat or declining sales with an increasing cost of sales, and investigate possible skimming issues if these conditions are present.

- *Require cash application staff to take vacations.* The controller will require the cash application staff to take the full amount of their earned vacations each year.

8.40 COMPUTERIZED CHECK HANDLING CONTROLS

Controls for computerized check handling are similar to those used for a manual system, but improve the speed with which the check pre-list is made accessible to downstream users of this information. The controls are as follows:

- *Restrict software access.* The computer system will restrict access to the cash receipts system to authorized users.

- *Prepare check pre-list.* The mailroom staff will prepare a list of checks received through the mail, and enter this information into the computer system.

- *Match check pre-list to cash receipts journal.* The cashier will run a report comparing checks listed in the cash receipts journal to the mailroom's check pre-list, and investigate any differences.

- *Match check pre-list to remittance advices and cash receipts journal.* The receivables clerk will run a report comparing checks listed in the cash receipts journal to the mailroom's check pre-list, as well as to remittances advices, and investigate any differences.

- *Reconcile bank statement.* The accounting manager will conduct a daily reconciliation of bank records to the corporate accounting records using online access to the bank database, and investigate any differences.

- *Convert customers to electronic payments.* The controller will periodically contact customers regarding conversion to electronic payments.

8.41 CREDIT CARD RECEIPT CONTROLS

Though the key transactional control for credit card receipts is to ensure that all such receipts are applied to receivables, it is also very important to ensure that access to credit card information is tightly controlled. The controls are as follows:

- *Restrict access to credit card information.* The computer system will restrict access to customer credit card information to authorized users.

- *Match credit receipts and cash receipt transactions.* The receivables clerk will match credit card receipts on a daily basis with the cash receipts journal to ensure that all credit card receipts have been entered in the accounting system, and will investigate any variances.

- *Shred credit card information.* The receivables clerk will shred all customer information containing credit card numbers and expiration dates once payment transactions have been completed.

8.42 LOCKBOX RECEIPT CONTROLS

Controls are much less rigorous for lockbox receipts, since cash is no longer on the premises. The controls are as follows:

- *Checks are routed to the lockbox.* The mailroom staff redirects all checks received by the company to the corporate lockbox.

- *Reconcile remittance advices to cash receipts journal.* The receivables clerk will print the cash receipts journal for the date associated with remittance advices and check copies forwarded by the bank, match the report to the received items, and investigate any differences.

- *Reconcile lockbox truncation report to checks.* If the company uses lockbox truncation, then the cashier will reconcile the lockbox truncation report printed by the truncation software to the checks entered into the system, and investigate any differences.

- *Reconcile bank statement.* The accounting manager will conduct a daily reconciliation of bank records to the corporate accounting records using online access to the bank database, and investigate any differences.

8.43   PETTY CASH CONTROLS

Controls over petty cash ensure the validity of reimbursements and the security of on-hand cash balances. The controls are as follows:

- *Issue payment based on a valid receipt.* The petty cash clerk will issue petty cash payments only upon presentation of a valid expense receipt or affidavit thereof.

- *Require a signature on petty cash receipts.* The petty cash clerk will require the signature of every petty cash recipient on a "received of petty cash" form, which is then stapled to the receipt.

- *Restrict petty cash reimbursements.* The petty cash clerk will restrict petty cash reimbursements to amounts not exceeding $____. Reimbursements will also not include advances, or the reimbursement of gifts, personal loans, traffic citations, personal expenses, or interest charges.

- *Minimize on-hand petty cash balance.* The controller will restrict the amount of on-hand petty cash to an amount requiring replenishment about twice per month.

- *Lock petty cash.* The petty cash clerk will store petty cash in a locked storage container when it is not in use.

- *Audit petty cash.* The internal audit staff will periodically audit petty cash for the presence of IOU vouchers, incomplete or suspicious receipts, missing "received of petty cash" vouchers, and missing cash.

8.44   INVESTMENT CONTROLS

The primary controls for funds investment involve the proper authorization of specific types of investment, while other controls address investment quotes, record storage, and notifications regarding investment balances. The controls are as follows:

- *Create a cash forecast*. The financial analyst will create a cash forecast, which shall include recommended levels and durations of investment needed, and which will be reviewed and approved by the chief financial officer.

- *Obtain approval of investment recommendation*. The chief financial officer will review and approve the amount, duration, and type of any recommended investment.

- *Obtain investment quotes*. The investment manager will obtain multiple quotes for investments and document these quotes on a quotation sheet.

- *Issue investment authorization*. The investment manager will issue a signed investment authorization form to the bank with which it elects to invest its funds.

- *Match authorization form to transaction report*. The investment manager will match the signed authorization form to any investment transaction report issued by the bank, and investigate any variances.

- *Store records*. The investment manager will forward all investment-related documents to a separate department for storage in a secure location.

- *Notify Board of changes in investment designations*. The treasurer will notify the Board of Directors of the reasons for any significant shift in the designation of securities among the held-to-maturity, available-for-sale, and trading portfolios, and the approximate impact of such changes on different categories of income.

- *Notify Board of unrecognized gains or losses*. The treasurer will periodically notify the Board of Directors of the amount of unrecognized gains or losses on held-to-maturity securities.

- *Audit investment records*. The internal audit staff will periodically compare a selection of the approved cash forecast, quote sheets, investment authorization, and accounting entries to verify that investments have occurred as authorized.

8.45 BASIC PAYROLL SYSTEM CONTROLS

Controls are required for nearly every aspect of the basic payroll system, covering hours to be paid, deductions, pay rates, tax remittances, and pay distributions. The controls are as follows:

- *Verify time card receipt*. The payroll staff will match received time cards against the current employer list and investigate all missing time cards.

- *Obtain approval for hours worked*. The payroll staff will obtain the written approval of supervisors for hours worked by their direct reports, including overtime hours.

- *Obtain approval of pay rate changes.* The payroll staff will obtain the written approval of a high-level manager on the standard pay change form for all changes in pay rates.

- *Obtain approval of negative deductions.* The payroll manager will approve all negative payroll deductions

- *Obtain approval of payroll advances.* An employee's immediate supervisor and the controller will approve any request for a payroll advance.

- *Review wage and tax calculations.* A second payroll clerk will review the payroll wage and tax calculations for errors, and adjust any errors found.

- *Match payroll register to authorizing documents.* A second payroll clerk will compare the payroll register to authorizing deduction forms, pay requests, change forms, and so on to ensure that all components of the payroll were properly authorized.

- *Issue checks directly to recipients.* The paymaster will require a photo identification before issuing paychecks to employees, and require recipients to sign for checks received.

- *Retain unclaimed paychecks.* The paymaster will retain an employee's check in a secure location until the employee is personally available to receive it.

- *Segregate the paymaster function.* The paymaster will not have responsibility for any other payroll activities.

- *Review uncashed payroll checks.* The paymaster will follow up with employees regarding uncashed paychecks.

- *Review tax remittances.* A second payroll clerk will review the amount of tax remittances and the completeness of accompanying remittance documents prior to the remittances being delivered to the government.

- *Remit taxes on a timely basis.* The payroll manager will ensure that all payroll taxes are remitted to the appropriate government entities on a timely basis.

- *Review outstanding advances.* The payroll staff will regularly review the repayment status of all outstanding pay advances.

- *Limit access to completed change authorization forms.* The payroll clerk will store signed payroll change authorization forms in a secure location to reduce the risk of subsequent document modification.

- *Issue paycheck list to department managers.* The paymaster will issue a list of paychecks distributed to the department managers, with instructions to search the list for ghost employees.

- *Reconcile the payroll bank account.* The controller will reconcile the payroll bank account and investigate any variances.

- *Audit pay deductions.* The internal audit staff will periodically compare deduction authorizations to the actual deductions being taken from employee pay, and investigate any variances.

- *Audit no-deduction paychecks.* The internal audit staff will periodically search for paychecks having no deductions, and determine if these are being written for ghost employees.

- *Audit employee addresses.* The internal audit staff will periodically search for matching employee addresses on multiple paychecks, and determine if multiple instances of the same address are caused by employees fraudulently paying themselves through ghost employees.

- *Compare W-2 forms to pay documentation.* The internal audit staff will periodically match year-end employee W-2 forms to employee pay change authorizations and termination documentation, and investigate any variances.

- *Compare payroll payments to human resources files.* The internal audit staff will periodically verify that human resources files exist for all employees being paid, and investigate any missing files.

- *Review paychecks for double endorsements.* The internal audit staff will periodically review a selection of paychecks for double endorsements, indicating the possible use of ghost employees.

- *Compare the payroll salary budget to actual expenditures.* The internal audit staff will match the expected payroll as outlined in the budget to actual payments, and investigate any differences.

8.46 COMPUTERIZED TIMEKEEPING CONTROLS

Controls for computerized timeclocks are used to ensure that the correct numbers of hours are recorded by the employees who actually worked the recorded hours. The controls are as follows:

- *Timeclock controls employee hours.* The computerized timeclock will block out hours when employees are allowed to clock in or out.

- *Timeclock requires overtime approval.* The computerized timeclock will require a supervisory approval code before an employee can record overtime hours.

- *Review timeclock reports.* The payroll clerk will review timeclock exception reports for such items as missed punches, late punches, and overtime hours worked, and investigate problems as necessary.

- *Use biometric clocks.* Biometric clocks will not allow time recording by anyone but people specifically identified as being current employees.

- *Link photo images of employees to badge scanner.* An electronic camera will record the image of each employee as they enter time in the timeclock, which the payroll clerk will monitor to detect buddy punching.

- *Review hours worked.* Supervisors will regularly review timeclock reports itemizing hours worked by employee, and investigate any unusual amounts.

8.47   COMPUTERIZED PAYROLL SYSTEM CONTROLS

Controls in a computerized payroll system should incorporate many of the controls already noted for a manual system, but can be streamlined in the area of timekeeping controls. The controls are as follows:

- *Restrict access to the employee master file.* The computer system will restrict access to the employee master file to authorized employees.

- *Automatic reporting of missing time cards.* The computer will automatically compare the employee master file to submitted time cards, and report on employees for whom no timecard has been received.

- *Compare time card totals to data entry totals.* A non-data entry person will compare keypunched employee time records to time cards for data entry errors, and correct any errors found.

- *Review payroll register for errors.* The payroll staff will compare source documents to the payroll register report, and correct any errors found.

- *Independent review of payroll register.* The payroll manager will independently print the payroll register and review it for evidence of improper payments.

- *Review exception reports.* The payroll manager will print and review computer-generated exception reports, addressing such areas as negative deductions, as well as unusually large base pay, overtime, or hours being paid, and investigate as necessary.

- *Send a manual check copy to the general ledger clerk.* The payroll staff will copy each manual check created and forward it to the general ledger clerk for recording in the general ledger.

- *Audit employee master file.* The internal audit staff will periodically determine if all employees listed in the employee master file are actual employees who are currently employed, and investigate any differences.

8.48   PAYROLL SELF-SERVICE CONTROLS

When payroll self-service systems are used, all related controls are automated, and center on data entry issues and user notifications. The controls are as follows:

- *Limit the preallowed amount of pay rate changes.* The self-service system will impose restrictions on the amount of pay raises that managers can grant employees, above which supervisory approval is required.

- *Send change verification e-mails.* The self-service system will automatically send an e-mail message to the person initiating a payroll change, verifying the change made.

- *Issue notification of bank account changes.* The self-service system will notify the controller by e-mail if the bank account information for any employee is changed.

- *Reject entry of unauthorized residency states.* The self-service system will reject the entry of a state of residence for which the company is not set up to record state income or unemployment tax remittances, and notify the payroll staff.

- *Link termination information to self-service system.* The human resources system will be linked to the payroll self-service system, so that entry of termination information by the human resources staff will automatically shut down access to the payroll self-service system.

8.49   CASH PAYROLL PAYMENT CONTROLS

When employees are paid their wages in cash, strong controls are required to ensure that the correct amount of cash is received by the intended recipient. The controls are as follows:

- *Complete pay envelope information in ink.* The payroll clerk will write employee pay information on the pay envelope in ink to avoid subsequent modification of pay amounts.

- *Match payroll register to pay envelopes.* A second clerk will compare the payroll register to the pay amount listed on each pay envelope, investigate any differences, and initial each correct envelope.

- *Complete cash requirements form in ink.* The payroll clerk will complete a cash requirements form (on which specific bill and coin amounts are requested) in ink to avoid subsequent modification.

- *Require approval of the cash requirements form.* The payroll manager will review and approve each completed cash requirements form before cash is issued.

- *Casher retains copy of cash requirements form.* The cashier will retain a copy of the cash requirements form once cash has been issued.

- *Count and sign for received cash.* The paymaster will count cash received from the cashier and match the amount received to the cash requirements form prior to signing for receipt of the cash.

- *Employee signs pay receipt.* Each employee being paid will count the cash received from the paymaster and match it to the pay amount listed on the pay envelope prior to signing for receipt of the cash.

8.50   ELECTRONIC PAYROLL PAYMENT CONTROLS

The primary controls over electronic payments are the proper authorization and verification of electronic payment information. The controls are as follows:

- *Require electronic payments.* The human resources manager will enforce the use of direct deposit or payroll card payments to all employees.

- *Match routing and account numbers on employee check to submitted information.* The payroll clerk will verify that the routing and account numbers on the check accompanying any employee request for direct deposit payment match the corresponding numbers entered in the payroll software.

- *Require direct deposit verification.* The payroll clerk will not process a change to an employee's direct deposit information without the employee's signature and formal identification.

- *Securely store direct deposit authorization forms.* The payroll clerk will store all completed direct deposit authorization forms in a locked cabinet.

- *Investigate multiple payments to the same bank account.* The payroll manager will periodically print a computer report itemizing all bank accounts referenced multiple times in the payroll database, and investigate any payments from multiple employees to such accounts.

8.51 ELECTRONIC PAYROLL REMITTANCE CONTROLS

When payroll remittance information is provided online, there is no risk of asset loss, but there is a risk of inappropriate access to personal information, which is mitigated by the following control:

- *Require user verification.* Employees will create user identification and password information for access to their online payroll remittance and W-2 accounts.

8.52 OUTSOURCED PAYROLL CONTROLS

When the payroll function is outsourced, the key additional controls are to verify that the supplier is indeed remitting taxes, and that paychecks are still routed through the company paymaster. These controls are shown below:

- *Obtain verification of tax remittances.* The payroll manager will obtain receipts for all tax remittances made by the payroll supplier and match them to required remittance information.

- *Route incoming paychecks through a paymaster.* The payroll supplier will send all employee paychecks to a paymaster rather than directly to employees; the paymaster will verify the existence of each employee prior to issuing the paychecks.

8.53 FIXED ASSET CONTROLS

The primary fixed asset controls over fixed assets cover their proper acquisition and disposal. The controls are as follows:

- *Segregate fixed asset duties.* The controller will ensure that responsibility for fixed asset acquisitions, transaction recording, custody, disposal, and reconciliation are assigned to different employees.

- *Use prenumbered acquisition and disposal forms.* The financial analyst will purchase prenumbered asset acquisition and disposal forms, and track the status of each form.

- *Require a signed capital investment approval form.* Company managers must complete an asset acquisition form and have it reviewed and signed prior to acquiring capital assets.

- *Include funding approval in the annual budget.* The financial analyst will include capital expenditure requests in the capital expenditures portion of the annual budget, which shall require the standard approval process prior to inclusion.

- *Create return on investment calculation.* The financial analyst will work with applicants to derive the net present value and payback period of each capital investment for which an application is being made.

- *Record purchases as fixed assets.* The payables clerk will code invoices for purchases greater than $____ as fixed assets.

- *Create fixed asset record.* The assistant controller will create and maintain a detailed record of each fixed asset in the fixed asset master file.

- *Reconcile fixed asset additions to authorizations.* The internal audit staff will periodically reconcile all fixed asset additions to the file of approved capital expenditure authorizations, and investigate any differences.

- *Conduct a postcompletion project analysis.* The financial analyst will conduct regular reviews of the results of asset acquisitions in comparison to initial predictions, and report the results to senior management.

- *Affix identification plate to fixed assets.* The financial analyst will affix an identification plate to each asset that contains a unique identification number.

- *Compare fixed asset serial numbers.* The internal audit staff will periodically compare the serial numbers of all acquired assets for duplicate numbers to see if employees are stealing assets from the company and selling them back to the company.

- *Restrict access to the fixed asset master file.* The computer system will restrict access to the fixed asset master file to authorized personnel.

- *Review fixed asset master file additions.* The internal audit staff will periodically review the accuracy of fixed asset master file additions for asset classification, location code, and pricing, and investigate variances.

- *Verify depreciation calculations.* The internal audit staff will periodically review the asset categories in which assets are recorded, as well as the depreciation periods and salvage values assigned to those assets.

- *Conduct a periodic fixed asset audit.* The internal audit staff will periodically conduct a comparison of the physical presence of fixed assets to book records, and investigate any differences.

- *Assign responsibility for assets.* The controller will formally assign responsibility for each acquired asset to the department manager whose staff uses the asset, and send all managers a quarterly notification of what assets are under their control.

- *Verify fair value assumptions on asset exchanges.* An independent appraisal firm will periodically verify the fair value assumptions used in the recording of gains or losses on the exchange of dissimilar assets.

- *Test for asset impairment.* The controller will periodically review the potential impairment of the value of significant assets and reduce their recorded cost to fair value, if necessary.

- *Authorize changes in asset retirement obligation assumptions.* The controller will review and approve all assumption changes related to the amount of future cash flows associated with asset retirement obligations.

- *Use a transfer document to shift asset locations.* Company managers will fill out a formal transfer document to shift an asset to a new location, which must be signed by the managers of the sending and receiving locations.

- *Conduct asset disposition reviews.* The financial analyst will coordinate a periodic review of fixed assets to determine if any assets should be disposed of before they lose their resale value.

- *Obtain formal approval prior to disposition.* The chief operating officer will sign a capital asset disposition form before any assets with original costs exceeding $____ are disposed of.

- *Investigate handling of cash receipts from asset sales.* The internal audit staff will periodically verify that a bill of sale or receipt from a buyer accompanies the file for every asset that has been disposed of, and investigate any differences.

- *Warn of asset removal.* The computer system will automatically issue a warning if RFID-tagged assets are removed from the premises.

Chapter 9

PERIOD-END MANUAL

9.1 INTRODUCTION

The users of a company's financial statements—investors, lenders, and management—wish to see accurate results from the latest reporting period as soon as possible. In past years, these have been conflicting goals, under the premise that a rapid financial closing required the use of so many estimates that the results would be less accurate than those achieved after a prolonged wait. However, by using a carefully designed period-end closing manual, the accounting department can create accurate financial statements in short order. The author regularly issues 20-page financial statements within two days of the period-end, primarily by closely following a tight production schedule that is itemized in a closing procedure.

9.2 PERIOD-END MANUAL

The keys to the success of this manual include its constant review and updating to achieve continual improvements in the closing process; careful delineation of the tasks required of each person; and shifting of closing tasks forward into the accounting period to be closed. By paying constant attention to these mechanics, it is possible to close the accounting records and achieve a high degree of accuracy within just a few days of the end of an accounting period.

An example of the period-end closing manual is shown in Exhibit 9.1. This manual is the master copy that is maintained by the controller, showing the work tasks of every person who is involved in the closing process. The left column of the exhibit shows the number of days either before or after the date of the month-end; for example, the first

Policy/Procedure Statement			Retrieval No.:	10-250
			Page:	1 of 3
Brasto Publishing			Issue Date:	4/30/0X
			Supersedes:	N/A
Subject: Period-End Closing Activities				

Days from Month-End	Responsibility	Task Description
−4	Controller	1. Review closing schedule and distribute to staff.
−4	General Ledger Accountant	1. Verify that recurring journal entries are still correct for the current reporting period. 2. Review financial statements with the most recent information and investigate unusual variances. 3. Set up journal entry forms for the coming close.
−4	Cost Accountant	1. Audit bills of material and adjust for any inaccuracies found.
−2	Payables and Receivables Clerks	1. Review the contract schedule and verify that all contractual agreements have been either paid to suppliers or billed to customers.
−2	Cost Accountant	1. Complete all allocation bases.
−1	Cost Accountant	1. Conduct an inventory audit to determine the inventory accuracy level.
−1	Controller	1. Complete footnotes.
−1	General Ledger Clerk	1. Go online and complete a preliminary bank reconciliation. 2. Accrue estimated bank charges and the interest income and interest expense.
−1	General Ledger Accountant	1. Review financial statements with the most recent information and investigate unusual variances.
−1	Accounts Receivable Clerk	1. Conduct a preliminary review of the shipping log to ensure that all deliveries have been billed.
0	General Ledger Accountant	1. Process the period-end closing program in the computer. 2. Print and distribute all period-end reports.
0	Cost Accountant	1. Verify the quantities and descriptions of all offsite inventories that are on consignment. 2. Complete a physical inventory count if the inventory record accuracy is below 95%. 3. Collect Acknowledgment of bill and hold transaction forms from customers.
+1	General Ledger Accountant	1. Compare all period-end reports to general ledger balances and reconcile differences. 2. Complete the preliminary bank reconciliation. 3. Cancel all outstanding checks more than 90 days old. 4. Complete a petty cash reconciliation.

Exhibit 9.1   Period-End Closing Procedure

task listed is −4 days from the month-end, which is four days prior to that date. The next column lists the job title of the person responsible for each task, and the third and final column describes the task that must be completed on that date.

The procedure shown in Exhibit 9.1 is based on several underlying assumptions, which may call for a change in the contents of the procedure if the assumptions are incorrect.

Policy/Procedure Statement			Retrieval No.:	10-250
			Page:	2 of 3
Brasto Publishing			Issue Date:	4/30/0X
			Supersedes:	N/A
Subject: Period-End Closing Activities				

Days from Month-End	Responsibility	Task Description
+1	Payroll Clerk	1. Accrue for unpaid wages. 2. Accrue for unused vacation and sick time. 3. Prepare a detailed list of withheld taxes and pension deductions, tying back to individual payrolls, identified by date. 4. Prepare accrual for the amount of any company-paid matching funds to be deposited in pension account. 5. Prepare commission statement following completion of customer billings.
+1	Accounts Receivable Clerk	1. Complete billings to all customers. 2. Close the accounts receivable module. 3. Review accounts receivable aging with the controller and determine the amount of a bad debt accrual. 4. Review old accounts receivable and write off selected balances with controller approval. 5. Prepare a detailed schedule of other accounts receivable.
+1	Financial Analyst	1. Prepare a detailed list of short-term investments, showing the name of the investment, the date purchased, the face amount, interest rate, and total accrued interest.
+2	Controller	1. Review the bank reconciliation.
+2	Accounts Payable Clerk	1. Review cut-off information and accrue for any missing supplier invoices based on purchase order costs. 2. Accrue for any unpaid medical or dental insurance, or other employee benefits. 3. Review the repairs and maintenance account to see if any items charged here should be shifted to a fixed asset account. 4. Close the accounts payable module.
+2	Cost Accountant	1. Review inventory balances and conduct a reasonableness test of quantities on hand and costs in comparison to previous periods. 2. Conduct sample test counts for all inventory classes exceeding 10% of total inventory value. 3. Print inventory reports and issue to distribution list. 4. Close the inventory module.
+2	Fixed Assets Clerk	1. Review asset sales and disposals, and update fixed asset records accordingly. 2. Record gains and losses on the sale of assets. 3. Update the fixed assets schedule and calculate depreciation. 4. Verify that depreciation totals do not exceed the totals of asset valuations less salvage values. 5. Reconcile the general ledger fixed asset and accumulated depreciation balances to the detail ledger balances, and correct any variances. 6. Close the fixed asset module.

Exhibit 9.1   Continued

They are:

- *That bills of material are used to cost the inventory.* The procedure requires the cost accountant to verify the accuracy of a selection of bills of material in advance of the period-end. By doing so, one can gain some confidence that the costs assigned to work-in-process and finished goods inventories are reasonably accurate, and will require minimal further review or adjustment subsequent to

Policy/Procedure Statement		Retrieval No.:	10-250
		Page:	3 of 3
Brasto Publishing		Issue Date:	4/30/0X
		Supersedes:	N/A
Subject: Period-End Closing Activities			

Days from Month-End	*Responsibility*	*Task Description*
+2	General Ledger Clerk	1. Complete all remaining accruals. 2. Summarize prepaid assets and compare to balances from the previous period. Review balances with the controller and determine the extent of prepaid write-downs for the period. 3. Review the construction in progress account to see if any projects can be finalized; if so, shift to a fixed assets account and initiate depreciation. 4. Prepare royalty statements.
+3	General Ledger Clerk	1. Update detailed schedules for all balance sheet accounts. 2. Trace all journal entries to the summary-level general ledger, and investigate all variances.
+3	Financial Analyst	1. Complete all operating data for inclusion in the financial statements.
+3	Controller	1. Consolidate incoming entries from subsidiaries. 2. Complete a preliminary set of financial statements.
+3	Tax Manager	1. Accrue for income taxes expense.

+4	Controller	1. Finalize the financial statements and issue to the distribution list. The following reports should be included in the statements:
		  a. Balance sheet
		  b. Income statement
		  c. Statement of cash flows
		  d. Income statements by department
		  e. Key operating statistics

+4	Financial Analyst	1. Calculate the borrowing base certificate and send it to the lender, along with a set of financial statements.
+5	General Ledger Clerk	1. Review variances too small to be checked during the closing process.
+6	Controller	1. Review the size of the cutoff level used to eliminate variance investigations. 2. Review the closing schedule for the next month. 3. Review job assignments for the next month's closing schedule. 4. Review the closing schedules for subsidiaries for the next month. 5. Review the contents and layout of the financial statements, and plan for changes in advance of the next close.
+7	All Staff	1. Review problems with the last close and agree on necessary changes to be made for the next close.

Source: *Accounting Best Practices*, 2nd Edition, Steven Bragg, copyright ©2001 John Wiley & Sons. This material is used by permission of John Wiley & Sons, Inc.

Exhibit 9.1   Continued

the period-end. If there are no bills of material, or if they are not used to assign costs to inventory, or if they contain significant inaccuracies, then the procedure must include additional (and time-consuming) steps to review costed inventory valuations subsequent to the end of the period.

- *That there are standardized overhead allocations.* The procedure requires the cost accountant to complete the calculation of overhead allocation bases two days before the period-end date. This is possible if one uses a one-month delay in the allocation period so that allocations can be completed in advance. If such a system

Vacation Accrual

Name	Annualized Salary	Maximum Hours	Maximum Accrual	Division	Maximum Accrual	Current Accrued Balance	Required Entry
Adams, Latrone	$45,000	40.00	$865	Subsidiary A			
Benning, Brian	$103,500	40.00	$1,990	Subsidiary A			
Blotten, Charles	$75,250	40.00	$1,447	Subsidiary A	$7,253	$5,250	$2,003
Clarion, Alice	$97,000	40.00	$1,865	Subsidiary A			
Corey, David	$56,400	40.00	$1,085	Subsidiary A			
Brower, Franklin	$85,000	80.00	$3,269	Subsidiary B			
Hustle, James	$48,000	80.00	$1,846	Subsidiary B			
Innes, Mandy	$99,000	80.00	$3,808	Subsidiary B	$13,346	$12,000	$1,346
Mandrel, Steven	$65,000	80.00	$2,500	Subsidiary B			
Van den Plee, Joe	$100,000	40.00	$1,923	Subsidiary B			
Chao, Brian	$60,000	40.00	$1,154	Subsidiary C			
Dunwiddy, John	$51,039	40.00	$982	Subsidiary C			
Ephraim, Joe	$48,900	40.00	$940	Subsidiary C	$5,225	$5,000	$225
Horvath, Mark	$37,752	40.00	$726	Subsidiary C			
McKenna, Jason	$74,000	40.00	$1,423	Subsidiary C			

Journal Entry:

Account Description	Account No.	Debit	Credit
Salary expense—Subsidiary A	6000-01	$2,003	
Salary expense—Subsidiary B	6000-02	$1,346	
Salary expense—Subsidiary C	6000 02	$225	
Vacation Accrual	22300		$3,574

Exhibit 9.4   Vacation Accrual Spreadsheet

June 2008 Commissions

Salesperson Name: Smith

Date	Invoice Number	Amount	Less: Supplier Cost	Net Sale	Customer	Product	Commission Type	Rate	Commission Dollars
6/1/2008	5527	$1,117.00	$0.00	$1,117.00	Oregon Land Title	LandTitle Database update	Repeat	4%	$44.68
6/4/2008	5570	−$883.75	$0.00	−$883.75	Arizona Title Search	Credit on customer return	Split	4%	($35.35)
6/30/2008	5638	$14,898.40	$8,332.00	$6,566.40	Iowa Land Equity	LandTitle Database update	Split	4%	$ 262.66
6/30/2008	5643	$9,191.00	$0.00	$9,191.00	Oregon Land Title	GPS Trak2000 software	Split	4%	$367.64
6/5/2008	5577	$700.60	$0.00	$700.60	Oregon Land Title	LandParcel Database update	New	7%	$49.04
6/5/2008	5578	$9,009.00	$0.00	$9,009.00	Iowa Land Equity	LandParcel Database update	New	8%	$720.72
6/5/2008	5579	$7,850.00	$5,000.00	$2,850.00	Missouri Flood Insurance	GPS Trak2000 software	New	8%	$228.00
6/6/2008	5582	$400.00	$0.00	$400.00	Missouri Flood Insurance	LandTitle Database update	New	7%	$28.00
6/9/2008	5583	$4,229.25	$0.00	$4,229.25	Arizona Title Search	LandParcel Database update	New	8%	$338.34
6/30/2008	5641	$686.80	$0.00	$686.80	Arizona Title Search	GPS Trak2000 software	New	7%	$48.08
		$47,198.30	$13,332.00	$33,866.30					$ 2,051.80

Manager Override Commissions				
Sales trainee #1	$ 2,500	Override	2%	$50.00
Sales trainee #2	$ 1,750	Override	2%	$35.00
			Total Commission	$2,136.80

Exhibit 9.5   Commission Calculation Report

paid. The report also itemizes any override commissions paid to managers based on the sales volume of their trainees.

The general ledger clerk is required to calculate royalties due as of day +2 in the period-end closing procedure. To accomplish this, one can use the royalty statement shown in Exhibit 9.6. It notes the royalty rate paid on each incremental block of sales, as well as royalties already paid and the amount still due for payment.

---

is not used, the allocation calculation must be delayed until after the accounts payable module is closed subsequent to period-end.

- *That there is an accurate perpetual inventory system.* The procedure requires the cost accountant to review the accuracy of the inventory with an audit prior to the period-end. If the accuracy level is high, then the controller does not need to conduct a physical inventory count (which can seriously delay the completion of the financial statements). There may not even be a need for a formal accuracy review by the cost accountant as long as cycle counts are regularly performed and yield high accuracy levels. If there is no perpetual inventory system or cycle counting procedure in place, then this procedure step must be replaced by a physical inventory count after the period-end.

- *That the bank reconciliation can be completed online.* Many larger banks now make daily account balance and detailed transaction information available online. This allows one to complete a running bank reconciliation so that there are no surprises at the end of the accounting period. The author completes bank reconciliations on all accounts by 8 A.M. every morning, so the period-end bank reconciliation is a nonevent. If a company does not have such account access, it must wait up to a week after period-end to obtain a mailed statement from the bank; this places the controller in the uncomfortable position of either delaying the close until the statement is received, or of issuing financial results before that date and hoping that there will be no significant changes contained within the statement.

- *That a receiving log is used.* The procedure requires the accounts payable clerk to accrue for any supplier invoices not yet received by reviewing the receiving log to see what deliveries have been received for which there is no accompanying invoice. This is a particularly easy step in an integrated computerized accounting system that links purchase order numbers to specific receipts, allowing the computer to present an accrual list to the clerk. If this capability is not present, then the controller must authorize a lengthy manual analysis of receipts, or wait a number of days for supplier invoices to be received, or accrue based on a guess of the amount received (which can be incorrect to a significant degree).

The procedure assumes that the accounting staff will issue financial statements on the fourth day after the period-end. However, this is merely a sample target, which will not be reached at once, and which can be surpassed after a number of months of attention to the underlying processes. One can easily use the basic text of Exhibit 9.1 for a tailored procedure, changing the due dates to match the reality of one's current closing process.

Of particular note in this procedure are the steps listed on days six and seven. They require the controller and his or her staff to review the just-completed closing process to see what steps can be made more efficient, thereby contributing to the ongoing reduction of time required to complete the closing process.

As noted under the day 0 task in the preceding period-end closing procedure for the cost accountant, it is necessary to collect acknowledgment forms for all bill and hold transactions from any customers who have agreed to such inventory holding situations. A sample form that can be used for this acknowledgment is shown in Exhibit 9.2. The form

Acknowledgment of
Bill and Hold Transaction

Customer Name: _____

This document indicates your acknowledgment that a bill and hold transaction exists in regard to purchase order number_____, which you ordered from [company name]. Please indicate your acknowledgment of this transaction by initialing next to each of the following statements and signing at the bottom of the page. If you disagree with any of the statements, please indicate your concerns at the bottom of the page. Thank you!

_____ I agree that I ordered the items noted in the purchase order.
(initial)

_____ I agree that [company name] is storing the items noted in the purchase order on my behalf.
(initial)

_____ I acknowledge that I have taken on all risks of ownership related to this purchase order.
(initial)

_____ I agree that I requested the bill and hold transaction, and my reason for doing so is as
(initial) follows:

_____

_____

_____ I agree that all performance issues related to this purchase order were completed no
(initial) later than _____.

_____ I agree that the held goods will be delivered to me no later than _____.
(initial)

I disagree with some or all of the statements on this page. My concerns are as follows:

_____

_____

_____

_____   _____
Signature   Date

_____   _____
Name (Please Print)   Title

Exhibit 9.2   Acknowledgment of Bill and Hold Transaction

Wage Accrual Spreadsheet   For the month of: Jul-08

Department	Hourly Personnel	Pay Rate per Hour	Unpaid Hours in Month	Pay Accrual
Marketing	Belowe, Melissa	$ 40.00	14.00	$ 560.00
Production	Brandon, Andrew	$ 18.15	72.00	$ 1,306.80
Production	Gutierrez, Pablo	$ 17.25	72.00	$ 1,242.00
Production	Holloway, Tim	$ 16.43	72.00	$ 1,182.96
Production	Innes, Sean	$ 15.00	72.00	$ 1,080.00
Production	Smith, Michael	$ 15.00	72.00	$ 1,080.00
Consulting	Verity, Thomas	$ 50.00	72.00	$ 3,600.00

Journal Entry:	Account Number	Debit	Credit
Production Wages	62150-02	$ 5,891.76	
Production Payroll Taxes	62250-02	$ 365.29	
Marketing Wages	62150-01	$ 560.00	
Marketing Payroll Taxes	62250-01	$ 34.72	
Consulting Wages	50050-03	$ 3,600.00	
Consulting Payroll Taxes	62250-03	$ 223.20	
Wage Accrual	22800		$ 10,674.97

NOTE: Hourly personnel are paid through the Sunday prior to the payroll date.

Exhibit 9.3   Wage Accrual Spreadsheet

requires a customer to sign off on each aspect of the accounting transaction required by generally accepted accounting principles. The form is then kept on file and is used as proof of customer agreement with each transaction.

The payroll clerk's wage accrual noted on day +1 in the preceding period-end closing procedure typically requires the use of a wage accrual spreadsheet such as the one noted in Exhibit 9.3. The spreadsheet itemizes the names of all hourly staff persons for whom unpaid wages must be accrued, as well as each one's pay rate per hour and the number of unpaid hours. This is automatically translated by the spreadsheet into a journal entry that is listed at the bottom of the spreadsheet.

The payroll clerk also accrues vacation time on day +1 in the period-end closing procedure. This requires the use of a vacation accrual spreadsheet such as the one shown in Exhibit 9.4. The spreadsheet clusters employees by operating division, noting the maximum number of vacation hours allowed under the current company policy, comparing this to the current accrual level, and automatically creating a journal entry to fully recognize any shortfall in vacation hours accrued.

The payroll clerk is also required to calculate commissions for the sales staff once all billings have been completed by the accounts receivable clerk. This can be done with a sample spreadsheet such as the one shown in Exhibit 9.5. The spreadsheet allows one to itemize all invoices created during the reporting period, as well as the type of commission to be paid (e.g., repeat, split, or new), and the commission percentage and dollar amount

```
                    [Supplier Name] Royalty Statement
                       for the Third Fiscal Quarter Ended
                                   [Date]

Product Name                                              $  128,000
Product Name                                              $   34,500
Product Name                                              $   98,250
Total Product Revenue                                    $  260,750


Royalty Calculation:
           4% × First $50,000                             $    2,000
           7% × Excess over $50,000, up to $200,000       $   10,500
           11% × Excess over $200,000                     $    6,683
Total Royalty for the Fiscal Year                         $   19,183


Less: Previous Payments Made                              $   14,750
Total Payment                                            $    4,433



[Company Name],



By: _____          Date: _____
        Signature of Authorized Officer
```

Exhibit 9.6   Royalty Statement

9.3 CLOSING PROCEDURE BY POSITION

Each member of the accounting staff is interested only in those tasks requiring his or her involvement. The other activities listed in the Exhibit 9.1 procedure only contribute to one's knowledge of how other employees' activities may interact with one's tasks. Accordingly, it is common to see the closing procedure broken down into smaller procedures, with each accounting position receiving a procedure only dealing with those tasks for which it is responsible. The procedures listed in the following exhibits show the same tasks in Exhibit 9.1, but itemized by position:

- Closing procedure for the general ledger clerk (Exhibit 9.7)

- Closing procedure for the accounts receivable clerk (Exhibit 9.8)

- Closing procedure for the controller (Exhibit 9.9)

- Closing procedure for the cost accountant (Exhibit 9.10)

- Closing procedure for the fixed assets clerk (Exhibit 9.11)

- Closing procedure for the accounts payable clerk (Exhibit 9.12)

Policy/Procedure Statement **Brasto Publishing** **Subject: Accounts Payable Closing Activities**		Retrieval No.:	10-251
		Page:	1 of 1
		Issue Date:	4/30/0X
		Supersedes:	N/A

Days from Month-End	Responsibility	Task Description
−2	Accounts Payable Clerk	1. Review the contract schedule and verify that all contractual agreements have been either paid to suppliers or billed to customers.
+2	Accounts Payable Clerk	1. Review cutoff information and accrue for any missing supplier invoices based on purchase order costs. 2. Accrue for any unpaid medical or dental insurance, or other employee benefits. 3. Review the repairs and maintenance account to see if any items charged here should be shifted to a fixed asset account. 4. Close the accounts payable module.
+7	Accounts Payable Clerk	1. Review problems with the last close and agree on necessary changes to be made for the next close.

Exhibit 9.7   Closing Procedure for the Accounts Payable Clerk

Policy/Procedure Statement **Brasto Publishing** **Subject: Accounts Receivable Closing Activities**		Retrieval No.:	10-252
		Page:	1 of 1
		Issue Date:	4/30/0X
		Supersedes:	N/A

Days from Month-End	Responsibility	Task Description
−2	Accounts Receivable Clerk	1. Review the contract schedule and verify that all contractual agreements have been either paid to suppliers or billed to customers.
−1	Accounts Receivable Clerk	1. Conduct a preliminary review of the shipping log to ensure that all deliveries have been billed.
+1	Accounts Receivable Clerk	1. Complete billings to all customers. 2. Close the accounts receivable module. 3. Review accounts receivable aging with the controller and determine the amount of a bad debt accrual. 4. Review old accounts receivable and write off selected balances with controller approval. 5. Prepare a detailed schedule of other accounts receivable.
+7	Accounts Receivable Clerk	1. Review problems with the last close and agree on necessary changes to be made for the next close.

Exhibit 9.8   Closing Procedure for the Accounts Receivable Clerk

9.4 SOFT CLOSE

Some organizations avoid the hassle of closing the books every month, instead focusing on a quarterly close. This is most common for entities that are publicly held, and which are therefore required by law to provide complete quarterly financial statements. Even in these cases, it is useful to complete a "soft close" at the end of those months that are

	Policy/Procedure Statement		Retrieval No.:	10-253
	Brasto Publishing		Page:	1 of 1
			Issue Date:	4/30/0X
	Subject: Controller Closing Activities		Supersedes:	N/A

Days from Month-End	Responsibility	Task Description
−4	Controller	1. Review closing schedule and distribute to staff.
−1	Controller	1. Complete footnotes.
+2	Controller	1. Review the bank reconciliation.
+3	Controller	1. Consolidate incoming entries from subsidiaries. 2. Complete a preliminary set of financial statements.

+4	Controller	1. Finalize the financial statements and issue to the distribution list. The following reports should be included in the statements:
		  a. Balance sheet
		  b. Income statement
		  c. Statement of cash flows
		  d. Income statements by department
		  e. Key operating statistics

+6	Controller	1. Review the size of the cutoff level used to eliminate variance investigations. 2. Review the closing schedule for the next month. 3. Review job assignments for the next month's closing schedule. 4. Review the closing schedules for subsidiaries for the next month. 5. Review the contents and layout of the financial statements, and plan for changes in advance of the next close.
+7	Controller	1. Review problems with the last close and agree on necessary changes to be made for the next close.

Exhibit 9.9 Closing Procedure for the Controller

not at the end of a quarter so that management has some idea of the company's financial results as it approaches its quarterly reporting period. It is especially useful if a company is closely tracked by outside analysts who may ask the company for information about expected results as the end of each quarter approaches.

A soft close requires somewhat less work than the normal period-end close, because inventory counts are usually avoided and accruals are more roughly estimated. An example of the procedure for a period-end soft close is noted in Exhibit 9.13.

A comparison of the soft close procedure to the earlier period-end procedure reveals that the soft close contains less than half the number of closing steps. Here are some of the items that one can avoid through the soft close:

- *Petty cash reconciliation.* Though there can be a control problem if petty cash is not reconciled regularly, any adjustments to the account (even if the entire balance is missing) will still be too small to impact the income statement; thus, one can avoid it.

- *Cancel old checks.* Canceling checks that have exceeded a set amount will merely increase the amount of cash and accounts payable, and will have no impact on the income statement at all. Also the dollar amount of cancelled checks tends to be a

Policy/Procedure Statement		Retrieval No.:	10-254
		Page:	1 of 1
Brasto Publishing		Issue Date:	4/30/0X
		Supersedes:	N/A
Subject: Cost Accountant Closing Activities			

Days from Month-End	Responsibility	Task Description
−4	Cost Accountant	1. Audit bills of materials and adjust for any inaccuracies found.
−2	Cost Accountant	1. Complete all allocation bases.
−1	Cost Accountant	1. Conduct an inventory audit to determine the inventory accuracy level.
0	Cost Accountant	1. Verify the quantities and descriptions of all off-site inventories that are on consignment. 2. Complete a physical inventory count if the inventory record accuracy is below 95%.
+2	Cost Accountant	1. Review inventory balances and conduct a reasonableness test of quantities on hand and costs in comparison to previous periods. 2. Conduct sample test counts for all inventory classes exceeding 10% of total inventory value. 3. Print inventory reports and issue to distribution list. 4. Close the inventory module.
+7	Cost Accountant	1. Review problems with the last close and agree on necessary changes to be made for the next close.

Exhibit 9.10   Closing Procedure for the Cost Accountant

Policy/Procedure Statement		Retrieval No.:	10-255
		Page:	1 of 1
Brasto Publishing		Issue Date:	4/30/0X
		Supersedes:	N/A
Subject: Fixed Assets Closing Activities			

Days from Month-End	Responsibility	Task Description
+2	Fixed Assets Clerk	1. Review asset sales and disposals, and update fixed asset records accordingly. 2. Record gains and losses on the sale of assets. 3. Update the fixed assets schedule and calculate depreciation. 4. Verify that depreciation totals do not exceed the totals of asset valuations less salvage values. 5. Reconcile the general ledger fixed asset and accumulated depreciation balances to the detail ledger balances, and correct any variances. 6. Close the fixed asset module.
+7	Fixed Assets Clerk	1. Review problems with the last close and agree on necessary changes to be made for the next close.

Exhibit 9.11   Closing Procedure for the Fixed Assets Clerk

is not used, the allocation calculation must be delayed until after the accounts payable module is closed subsequent to period-end.

- *That there is an accurate perpetual inventory system.* The procedure requires the cost accountant to review the accuracy of the inventory with an audit prior to the period-end. If the accuracy level is high, then the controller does not need to conduct a physical inventory count (which can seriously delay the completion of the financial statements). There may not even be a need for a formal accuracy review by the cost accountant as long as cycle counts are regularly performed and yield high accuracy levels. If there is no perpetual inventory system or cycle counting procedure in place, then this procedure step must be replaced by a physical inventory count after the period-end.

- *That the bank reconciliation can be completed online.* Many larger banks now make daily account balance and detailed transaction information available online. This allows one to complete a running bank reconciliation so that there are no surprises at the end of the accounting period. The author completes bank reconciliations on all accounts by 8 A.M. every morning, so the period-end bank reconciliation is a nonevent. If a company does not have such account access, it must wait up to a week after period-end to obtain a mailed statement from the bank; this places the controller in the uncomfortable position of either delaying the close until the statement is received, or of issuing financial results before that date and hoping that there will be no significant changes contained within the statement.

- *That a receiving log is used.* The procedure requires the accounts payable clerk to accrue for any supplier invoices not yet received by reviewing the receiving log to see what deliveries have been received for which there is no accompanying invoice. This is a particularly easy step in an integrated computerized accounting system that links purchase order numbers to specific receipts, allowing the computer to present an accrual list to the clerk. If this capability is not present, then the controller must authorize a lengthy manual analysis of receipts, or wait a number of days for supplier invoices to be received, or accrue based on a guess of the amount received (which can be incorrect to a significant degree).

The procedure assumes that the accounting staff will issue financial statements on the fourth day after the period-end. However, this is merely a sample target, which will not be reached at once, and which can be surpassed after a number of months of attention to the underlying processes. One can easily use the basic text of Exhibit 9.1 for a tailored procedure, changing the due dates to match the reality of one's current closing process.

Of particular note in this procedure are the steps listed on days six and seven. They require the controller and his or her staff to review the just-completed closing process to see what steps can be made more efficient, thereby contributing to the ongoing reduction of time required to complete the closing process.

As noted under the day 0 task in the preceding period-end closing procedure for the cost accountant, it is necessary to collect acknowledgment forms for all bill and hold transactions from any customers who have agreed to such inventory holding situations. A sample form that can be used for this acknowledgment is shown in Exhibit 9.2. The form

Acknowledgment of
Bill and Hold Transaction

Customer Name: _____

This document indicates your acknowledgment that a bill and hold transaction exists in regard to purchase order number_____, which you ordered from [company name]. Please indicate your acknowledgment of this transaction by initialing next to each of the following statements and signing at the bottom of the page. If you disagree with any of the statements, please indicate your concerns at the bottom of the page. Thank you!

_____ I agree that I ordered the items noted in the purchase order.
(initial)

_____ I agree that [company name] is storing the items noted in the purchase order on my behalf.
(initial)

_____ I acknowledge that I have taken on all risks of ownership related to this purchase order.
(initial)

_____ I agree that I requested the bill and hold transaction, and my reason for doing so is as
(initial) follows:

_____

_____

_____ I agree that all performance issues related to this purchase order were completed no
(initial) later than _____.

_____ I agree that the held goods will be delivered to me no later than _____.
(initial)

I disagree with some or all of the statements on this page. My concerns are as follows:

_____

_____

_____

_____   _____
            Signature   Date

_____   _____
        Name (Please Print)   Title

Exhibit 9.2   Acknowledgment of Bill and Hold Transaction

Wage Accrual Spreadsheet   For the month of: Jul-08

Department	Hourly Personnel	Pay Rate per Hour	Unpaid Hours in Month	Pay Accrual
Marketing	Belowe, Melissa	$ 40.00	14.00	$ 560.00
Production	Brandon, Andrew	$ 18.15	72.00	$ 1,306.80
Production	Gutierrez, Pablo	$ 17.25	72.00	$ 1,242.00
Production	Holloway, Tim	$ 16.43	72.00	$ 1,182.96
Production	Innes, Sean	$ 15.00	72.00	$ 1,080.00
Production	Smith, Michael	$ 15.00	72.00	$ 1,080.00
Consulting	Verity, Thomas	$ 50.00	72.00	$ 3,600.00

Journal Entry:

	Account Number	Debit	Credit
Production Wages	62150-02	$ 5,891.76	
Production Payroll Taxes	62250-02	$ 365.29	
Marketing Wages	62150-01	$ 560.00	
Marketing Payroll Taxes	62250-01	$ 34.72	
Consulting Wages	50050-03	$ 3,600.00	
Consulting Payroll Taxes	62250-03	$ 223.20	
Wage Accrual	22800		$ 10,674.97

NOTE: Hourly personnel are paid through the Sunday prior to the payroll date.

Exhibit 9.3 Wage Accrual Spreadsheet

requires a customer to sign off on each aspect of the accounting transaction required by generally accepted accounting principles. The form is then kept on file and is used as proof of customer agreement with each transaction.

The payroll clerk's wage accrual noted on day +1 in the preceding period-end closing procedure typically requires the use of a wage accrual spreadsheet such as the one noted in Exhibit 9.3. The spreadsheet itemizes the names of all hourly staff persons for whom unpaid wages must be accrued, as well as each one's pay rate per hour and the number of unpaid hours. This is automatically translated by the spreadsheet into a journal entry that is listed at the bottom of the spreadsheet.

The payroll clerk also accrues vacation time on day +1 in the period-end closing procedure. This requires the use of a vacation accrual spreadsheet such as the one shown in Exhibit 9.4. The spreadsheet clusters employees by operating division, noting the maximum number of vacation hours allowed under the current company policy, comparing this to the current accrual level, and automatically creating a journal entry to fully recognize any shortfall in vacation hours accrued.

The payroll clerk is also required to calculate commissions for the sales staff once all billings have been completed by the accounts receivable clerk. This can be done with a sample spreadsheet such as the one shown in Exhibit 9.5. The spreadsheet allows one to itemize all invoices created during the reporting period, as well as the type of commission to be paid (e.g., repeat, split, or new), and the commission percentage and dollar amount

Vacation Accrual

Name	Annualized Salary	Maximum Hours	Maximum Accrual	Division	Maximum Accrual	Current Accrued Balance	Required Entry
Adams, LaTrone	$45,000	40.00	$865	Subsidiary A			
Benning, Brian	$103,500	40.00	$1,990	Subsidiary A			
Blotten, Charles	$75,250	40.00	$1,447	Subsidiary A	$7,253	$5,250	$2,003
Clarion, Alice	$97,000	40.00	$1,865	Subsidiary A			
Corey, David	$56,400	40.00	$1,085	Subsidiary A			
Brower, Franklin	$85,000	80.00	$3,269	Subsidiary B			
Hustle, James	$48,000	80.00	$1,846	Subsidiary B			
Innes, Mandy	$99,000	80.00	$3,808	Subsidiary B	$13,346	$12,000	$1,346
Mandrel, Steven	$65,000	80.00	$2,500	Subsidiary B			
Van den Plee, Joe	$100,000	40.00	$1,923	Subsidiary B			
Chao, Brian	$60,000	40.00	$1,154	Subsidiary C			
Dunwiddy, John	$51,039	40.00	$982	Subsidiary C			
Ephraim, Joe	$48,900	40.00	$940	Subsidiary C	$5,225	$5,000	$225
Horvath, Mark	$37,752	40.00	$726	Subsidiary C			
McKenna, Jason	$74,000	40.00	$1,423	Subsidiary C			

Journal Entry:	Account Description	Account No.	Debit	Credit
	Salary expense — Subsidiary A	6000-01	$2,003	
	Salary expense — Subsidiary B	6000-02	$1,346	
	Salary expense — Subsidiary C	6000-02	$225	
	Vacation Accrual	22300		$3,574

Exhibit 9.4 Vacation Accrual Spreadsheet

June 2008 Commissions

Salesperson Name: Smith

Date	Invoice Number	Amount	Less: Supplier Cost	Net Sale	Customer	Product	Commission Type	Rate	Commission Dollars
6/1/2008	5527	$1,117.00	$0.00	$1,117.00	Oregon Land Title	LandTitle Database update	Repeat	4%	$44.68
6/4/2008	5570	-$883.75	$0.00	-$883.75	Arizona Title Search	Credit on customer return	Split	4%	($35.35)
6/30/2008	5638	$14,898.40	$8,332.00	$6,566.40	Iowa Land Equity	LandTitle Database update	Split	4%	$ 262.66
6/30/2008	5643	$9,191.00	$0.00	$9,191.00	Oregon Land Title	GPS Trak2000 software	Split	4%	$367.64
6/5/2008	5577	$700.60	$0.00	$700.60	Oregon Land Title	LandParcel Database update	New	7%	$49.04
6/5/2008	5578	$9,009.00	$0.00	$9,009.00	Iowa Land Equity	LandParcel Database update	New	8%	$720.72
6/5/2008	5579	$7,850.00	$5,000.00	$2,850.00	Missouri Flood Insurance	GPS Trak2000 software	New	8%	$228.00
6/6/2008	5582	$400.00	$0.00	$400.00	Missouri Flood Insurance	LandTitle Database update	New	7%	$28.00
6/9/2008	5583	$4,229.25	$0.00	$4,229.25	Arizona Title Search	LandParcel Database update	New	8%	$338.34
6/30/2008	5641	$686.80	$0.00	$686.80	Arizona Title Search	GPS Trak2000 software	New	7%	$48.08
		$47,198.30	$13,332.00	$33,866.30					$ 2,051.80

Manager Override Commissions							
	Sales trainee #1	$		2,500	Override	2%	$50.00
	Sales trainee #2	$		1,750	Override	2%	$35.00
					Total Commission		$2,136.80

Exhibit 9.5 Commission Calculation Report

paid. The report also itemizes any override commissions paid to managers based on the sales volume of their trainees.

The general ledger clerk is required to calculate royalties due as of day +2 in the period-end closing procedure. To accomplish this, one can use the royalty statement shown in Exhibit 9.6. It notes the royalty rate paid on each incremental block of sales, as well as royalties already paid and the amount still due for payment.

[Supplier Name] Royalty Statement
for the Third Fiscal Quarter Ended
[Date]

Product Name	$ 128,000
Product Name	$ 34,500
Product Name	$ 98,250
Total Product Revenue	$ 260,750
Royalty Calculation:	
4% × First $50,000	$ 2,000
7% × Excess over $50,000, up to $200,000	$ 10,500
11% × Excess over $200,000	$ 6,683
Total Royalty for the Fiscal Year	$ 19,183
Less: Previous Payments Made	$ 14,750
Total Payment	$ 4,433

[Company Name],

By: _____   Date: _____
          Signature of Authorized Officer

Exhibit 9.6 Royalty Statement

9.3 CLOSING PROCEDURE BY POSITION

Each member of the accounting staff is interested only in those tasks requiring his or her involvement. The other activities listed in the Exhibit 9.1 procedure only contribute to one's knowledge of how other employees' activities may interact with one's tasks. Accordingly, it is common to see the closing procedure broken down into smaller procedures, with each accounting position receiving a procedure only dealing with those tasks for which it is responsible. The procedures listed in the following exhibits show the same tasks in Exhibit 9.1, but itemized by position:

- Closing procedure for the general ledger clerk (Exhibit 9.7)

- Closing procedure for the accounts receivable clerk (Exhibit 9.8)

- Closing procedure for the controller (Exhibit 9.9)

- Closing procedure for the cost accountant (Exhibit 9.10)

- Closing procedure for the fixed assets clerk (Exhibit 9.11)

- Closing procedure for the accounts payable clerk (Exhibit 9.12)

Policy/Procedure Statement **Brasto Publishing** Subject: Accounts Payable Closing Activities		Retrieval No.:	10-251
		Page:	1 of 1
		Issue Date:	4/30/0X
		Supersedes:	N/A

Days from Month-End	Responsibility	Task Description
−2	Accounts Payable Clerk	1. Review the contract schedule and verify that all contractual agreements have been either paid to suppliers or billed to customers.
+2	Accounts Payable Clerk	1. Review cutoff information and accrue for any missing supplier invoices based on purchase order costs. 2. Accrue for any unpaid medical or dental insurance, or other employee benefits. 3. Review the repairs and maintenance account to see if any items charged here should be shifted to a fixed asset account. 4. Close the accounts payable module.
+7	Accounts Payable Clerk	1. Review problems with the last close and agree on necessary changes to be made for the next close.

Exhibit 9.7 Closing Procedure for the Accounts Payable Clerk

Policy/Procedure Statement **Brasto Publishing** Subject: Accounts Receivable Closing Activities		Retrieval No.:	10-252
		Page:	1 of 1
		Issue Date:	4/30/0X
		Supersedes:	N/A

Days from Month-End	Responsibility	Task Description
−2	Accounts Receivable Clerk	1. Review the contract schedule and verify that all contractual agreements have been either paid to suppliers or billed to customers.
−1	Accounts Receivable Clerk	1. Conduct a preliminary review of the shipping log to ensure that all deliveries have been billed.
+1	Accounts Receivable Clerk	1. Complete billings to all customers. 2. Close the accounts receivable module. 3. Review accounts receivable aging with the controller and determine the amount of a bad debt accrual. 4. Review old accounts receivable and write off selected balances with controller approval. 5. Prepare a detailed schedule of other accounts receivable.
+7	Accounts Receivable Clerk	1. Review problems with the last close and agree on necessary changes to be made for the next close.

Exhibit 9.8 Closing Procedure for the Accounts Receivable Clerk

9.4 SOFT CLOSE

Some organizations avoid the hassle of closing the books every month, instead focusing on a quarterly close. This is most common for entities that are publicly held, and which are therefore required by law to provide complete quarterly financial statements. Even in these cases, it is useful to complete a "soft close" at the end of those months that are

Policy/Procedure Statement			Retrieval No.:	10-253
			Page:	1 of 1
Brasto Publishing			Issue Date:	4/30/0X
			Supersedes:	N/A
Subject: Controller Closing Activities				

Days from Month-End	Responsibility	Task Description
−4	Controller	1. Review closing schedule and distribute to staff.
−1	Controller	1. Complete footnotes.
+2	Controller	1. Review the bank reconciliation.
+3	Controller	1. Consolidate incoming entries from subsidiaries. 2. Complete a preliminary set of financial statements.
+4	Controller	1. Finalize the financial statements and issue to the distribution list. The following reports should be included in the statements: a. Balance sheet b. Income statement c. Statement of cash flows d. Income statements by department e. Key operating statistics
+6	Controller	1. Review the size of the cutoff level used to eliminate variance investigations. 2. Review the closing schedule for the next month. 3. Review job assignments for the next month's closing schedule. 4. Review the closing schedules for subsidiaries for the next month. 5. Review the contents and layout of the financial statements, and plan for changes in advance of the next close.
+7	Controller	1. Review problems with the last close and agree on necessary changes to be made for the next close.

Exhibit 9.9 Closing Procedure for the Controller

not at the end of a quarter so that management has some idea of the company's financial results as it approaches its quarterly reporting period. It is especially useful if a company is closely tracked by outside analysts who may ask the company for information about expected results as the end of each quarter approaches.

A soft close requires somewhat less work than the normal period-end close, because inventory counts are usually avoided and accruals are more roughly estimated. An example of the procedure for a period-end soft close is noted in Exhibit 9.13.

A comparison of the soft close procedure to the earlier period-end procedure reveals that the soft close contains less than half the number of closing steps. Here are some of the items that one can avoid through the soft close:

- *Petty cash reconciliation.* Though there can be a control problem if petty cash is not reconciled regularly, any adjustments to the account (even if the entire balance is missing) will still be too small to impact the income statement; thus, one can avoid it.

- *Cancel old checks.* Canceling checks that have exceeded a set amount will merely increase the amount of cash and accounts payable, and will have no impact on the income statement at all. Also the dollar amount of cancelled checks tends to be a

Policy/Procedure Statement		Retrieval No.:	10-254
Brasto Publishing		Page:	1 of 1
		Issue Date:	4/30/0X
		Supersedes:	N/A
Subject: Cost Accountant Closing Activities			

Days from Month-End	Responsibility	Task Description
−4	Cost Accountant	1. Audit bills of materials and adjust for any inaccuracies found.
−2	Cost Accountant	1. Complete all allocation bases.
−1	Cost Accountant	1. Conduct an inventory audit to determine the inventory accuracy level.
0	Cost Accountant	1. Verify the quantities and descriptions of all off-site inventories that are on consignment. 2. Complete a physical inventory count if the inventory record accuracy is below 95%.
+2	Cost Accountant	1. Review inventory balances and conduct a reasonableness test of quantities on hand and costs in comparison to previous periods. 2. Conduct sample test counts for all inventory classes exceeding 10% of total inventory value. 3. Print inventory reports and issue to distribution list. 4. Close the inventory module.
+7	Cost Accountant	1. Review problems with the last close and agree on necessary changes to be made for the next close.

Exhibit 9.10   Closing Procedure for the Cost Accountant

Policy/Procedure Statement		Retrieval No.:	10-255
Brasto Publishing		Page:	1 of 1
		Issue Date:	4/30/0X
		Supersedes:	N/A
Subject: Fixed Assets Closing Activities			

Days from Month-End	Responsibility	Task Description
+2	Fixed Assets Clerk	1. Review asset sales and disposals, and update fixed asset records accordingly. 2. Record gains and losses on the sale of assets. 3. Update the fixed assets schedule and calculate depreciation. 4. Verify that depreciation totals do not exceed the totals of asset valuations less salvage values. 5. Reconcile the general ledger fixed asset and accumulated depreciation balances to the detail ledger balances, and correct any variances. 6. Close the fixed asset module.
+7	Fixed Assets Clerk	1. Review problems with the last close and agree on necessary changes to be made for the next close.

Exhibit 9.11   Closing Procedure for the Fixed Assets Clerk

Policy/Procedure Statement **Brasto Publishing** **Subject: General Ledger Closing Activities**	Retrieval No.: Page: Issue Date: Supersedes:	10-256 1 of 1 4/30/0X N/A

Days from Month-End	Responsibility	Task Description

−4	General
	Ledger Clerk
		1. Verify that recurring journal entries are still correct for the current
		    reporting period.
		2. Review financial statements with the most recent information and
		    investigate unusual variances.
		3. Set up journal entry forms for the coming close.

−1	General
	Ledger Clerk
		1. Go online and complete a preliminary bank reconciliation.
		2. Accrue estimated bank charges and the interest income and
		    interest expense.
		3. Review financial statements with the most recent information and
		    investigate unusual variances.

0	General Ledger Clerk	1. Process the period-end closing program in the computer. 2. Print and distribute all period-end reports.
+1	General Ledger Clerk	1. Compare all period-end reports to general ledger balances and reconcile differences. 2. Complete the preliminary bank reconciliation. 3. Cancel all outstanding checks more than 90 days old. 4. Complete a petty cash reconciliation.

+2	General
	Ledger Clerk
		1. Complete all remaining accruals.
		2. Summarize prepaid assets and compare to balances from
		    the previous period. Review balances with the controller and determine
		    the extent of prepaid write-downs for the period.
		3. Review the construction in progress account to see if any projects can be
		    finalized; if so, shift to a fixed assets account and initiate depreciation.

+3	General Ledger Clerk	1. Update detailed schedules for all balance sheet accounts. 2. Trace all journal entries to the summary-level general ledger, and investigate all variances.
+5	General Ledger Clerk	1. Review variances too small to be checked during the closing process.
+7	General Ledger Clerk	1. Review problems with the last close and agree on necessary changes to be made for the next close.

Exhibit 9.12   Closing Procedure for the Accounts Payable Clerk

small number. Consequently, avoiding this step has little impact on the financial
statements.

- *Bad debt write-off.* There is no point in writing off uncollectible accounts receivable during the closing period, as the amount is offset by the bad debt allowance. Thus, there is no impact on the income statement at all, and the accounts receivable balance net of the reserve for bad debts will be unchanged. This does not mean that write-offs will only occur at the end of a quarter, but that the write-off process can occur at other times besides the closing period.

- *Detailed balance sheet schedules.* Though it is good practice to maintain a detailed schedule of the contents of every balance sheet account, one can review these both before and after the closing period to ascertain their accuracy, thereby

Policy/Procedure Statement			Retrieval No.:	10-257
Brasto Publishing			Page:	1 of 1
			Issue Date:	4/30/0X
Subject: Soft Close Activities			Supersedes:	N/A

Days from Month-End	Responsibility	Task Description
−1	Controller	1. Review closing schedule and distribute to staff.
−1	General Ledger Accountant	1. Verify that recurring journal entries are still correct for the current reporting period. 2. Review financial statements with the most recent information and investigate unusual variances. 3. Set up journal entry forms for the coming close.
+1	General Ledger Accountant	1. Complete the online bank reconciliation. 2. Accrue estimated bank charges and the interest income and interest expense.
+1	Payroll Clerk	1. Accrue for unpaid wages. 2. Accrue for unused vacation and sick time.
+1	Accounts Receivable Clerk	1. Complete billings to all customers. 2. Review accounts receivable aging with the controller and determine the amount of a bad debt accrual.
+2	Controller	1. Review the bank reconciliation.
+2	Accounts Payable Clerk	1. Review cutoff information and accrue for any missing supplier invoices based on purchase order costs. 2. If no purchase order system in use, accrue based on history of recurring supplier invoices. 3. Accrue for any unpaid medical or dental insurance, or other employee benefits. 4. Review the repairs and maintenance account to see if any items charged here should be shifted to a fixed asset account.
+2	Cost Accountant	1. Allocate overhead costs at the historical rate. 2. Charge cost of goods sold at the historical percentage, comparing to the mix of products sold at their standard costs for verification.
+2	Fixed Assets Clerk	1. Review asset sales and disposals, and update fixed asset records accordingly. 2. Record gains and losses on the sale of assets. 3. Update the fixed assets schedule and calculate depreciation.
+2	General Ledger Clerk	1. Complete all remaining accruals. 2. Review the construction in progress account to see if any projects can be finalized; if so, shift to a fixed assets account and initiate depreciation.
+3	Financial Analyst	1. Complete all operating data for inclusion in the financial statements.
+3	Controller	1. Consolidate incoming entries from subsidiaries. 2. Complete a preliminary set of financial statements.
+3	Tax Manager	1. Accrue for income tax expense.

+4	Controller	1. Finalize the financial statements and issue to the distribution list. The following reports should be included in the statements:
		  a. Balance sheet
		  b. Income statement
		  c. Statement of cash flows
		  d. Income statements by department
		  e. Key operating statistics

Exhibit 9.13   Period-End Soft Close Procedure

avoiding this time-consuming task during the soft close. However, if the accounting department has a history of having incorrect schedules, this may have to be reviewed during the close for accounts with larger balances.

- *Bill of materials (BOM) accuracy review.* The soft close substitutes a review of BOM accuracy with a cost of goods sold calculation that is based on the historical cost of goods sold percentage. This figure is the most likely to be inaccurate, because the mix of products sold may vary in the current month from that of the periods from which the historical average was taken. If this appears to be the case, one may still have to use bills of materials to derive a standard cost of goods sold, which can be used as a cross-check of the historical cost of goods sold percentage.

- *Physical inventory count.* As long as historically derived cost of goods sold percentage is used to calculate the cost of goods sold for the soft close, there is no need to determine the actual amount of the ending inventory. This can be a very time-consuming step, so it is one of the most common tasks that is dropped from the soft close. If there is an ongoing problem with the accuracy of the inventory, then the controller can always conduct an inventory review at any other time besides the soft close to determine the extent of any variances from the inventory book balance and incorporate this variance into the results for the following accounting period.

- *Elimination of prepaid expenses.* Unless there is a large quantity of prepaid expenses on the balance sheet, the incremental shifting of these items to expenses will rarely have a significant impact on the income statement, so it can be avoided for a soft close. Even if the decision is made to reduce the amount of prepaid expenses amount, this task can easily be completed during some other time than the closing process.

- *Pension and payroll tax accruals.* Though the expense associated with a company's contribution to the employee pension plan and all payroll taxes must certainly be recorded as part of the soft close, there is no need to spend time verifying the exact amount of the liability that has not yet been sent to the pension plan or government entity. This later calculation only impacts the balance sheet, so it can be avoided for the soft close.

- *Software module closing.* Though some accounting software packages will require users to close out the current month before shifting to the next one, others will allow several periods to be kept open at the same time. This can save a small amount of time during the soft close, as some time for processing and report printing is usually associated with a module closing.

The number of tasks just described that can be skipped in a soft close is considerable. However, these deductions from the standard closing procedure must only be made in light of the accuracy of records within the accounting department. In particular, using a historical cost of goods sold percentage can yield surprising results when the quarterly "hard" close must be completed, because the historical percentage may have no bearing on the different mix of sales, production operating costs, and changes in overhead costs that have occurred since the last hard close. If this appears to be the case, be sure to cross-check the figure with a compilation of product standard costs from a company's bills of materials.

9.5 YEAR-END CLOSE

The year-end close results in information that may be subject to an audit, if a company has outside lenders who require audited results or if the owners or management insist upon this extra step. In any case, the year-end audit will require the accounting department to integrate a number of extra steps into its standard closing procedure. An example of this more comprehensive procedure is shown in Exhibit 9.14, with the additional closing steps noted in bold print.

Policy/Procedure Statement		Retrieval No.:	10-258
Brasto Publishing		Page:	1 of 4
		Issue Date:	4/30/0X
		Supersedes:	N/A
Subject: Year-End Closing Activities			

Days from Month-End	Responsibility	Task Description
−4	Controller	1. Review closing schedule and distribute to staff. **2. Assist the auditors in conducting a controls review.** **3. Assist the auditors in planning their overview of the physical inventory.**
−4	General Ledger Clerk	1. Verify that recurring journal entries are still correct for the current reporting period. 2. Review financial statements with the most recent information and investigate unusual variances. 3. Set up journal entry forms for the coming close.
−4	Cost Accountant	1. Audit bills of material and adjust for any quantity inaccuracies found. **2. Conduct annual update of standard costs in bills of materials to reflect actual costs.** **3. Audit the scrap rates in bills of materials and adjust to match actual scrap rates.**
−2	Payables and Receivables Clerks	1. Review the contract schedule and verify that all contractual agreements have been either paid to suppliers or billed to customers.
−1	General Ledger Clerk	1. Go online and complete the bank reconciliation. 2. Accrue actual bank charges and the interest income and interest expense.
−1	Payroll Clerk	**1. Prepare payroll checks that include as recognized income to employees the amount of company-paid life insurance that exceeds the federally mandated maximum value.**
−1	General Ledger Clerk	1. Review financial statements with the most recent information and investigate unusual variances.
−1	Accounts Receivable Clerk	1. Conduct a review of the shipping log to ensure that all deliveries have been billed.
0	General Ledger Clerk	1. Process the period-end closing program in the computer. 2. Print and distribute all period-end reports.
0	Cost Accountant	1. Verify the quantities and descriptions of all off-site inventories that are on consignment.
+1	General Ledger Clerk	1. Compare all period-end reports to general ledger balances and reconcile differences. 2. Complete the preliminary bank reconciliation. 3. Cancel all outstanding checks more than 90 days old. 4. Complete a petty cash reconciliation.

Exhibit 9.14 Year-End Closing Procedures

Policy/Procedure Statement			Retrieval No.:	10-258
			Page:	2 of 4
Brasto Publishing			Issue Date:	4/30/0X
			Supersedes:	N/A
Subject: Year-End Closing Activities				

Days from Month-End	Responsibility	Task Description
+1	Payroll Clerk	1. Accrue for unpaid wages. 2. Accrue for commissions earned but not paid. 3. Accrue for unused vacation and sick time. 4. Prepare a detailed list of withheld taxes and pension deductions, tying back to individual payrolls, identified by date. 5. Prepare accrual for the amount of any company-paid matching funds to be deposited in pension account. **6. Prepare a listing of employees and their annual pay, and set aside for the auditors.**
+1	Accounts Receivable Clerk	1. Complete billings to all customers. 2. Close the accounts receivable module. 3. Review accounts receivable aging with the controller and determine the amount of a bad debt accrual. 4. Review old accounts receivable and write off selected balances with controller approval. 5. Prepare a detailed schedule of other accounts receivable. **6. Print the year-end aged accounts receivable listing and set aside for the auditors.** **7. Print the bad debt accrual calculation and set aside for the auditors.** **8. Assist auditors in sending receivable confirmations to customers.**
+1	Financial Analyst	1. Prepare a detailed list of short-term investments, showing the name of the investment, the date purchased, the face amount, interest rate, and total accrued interest. Set aside a copy for the auditors.
+1	Cost Accountant	**1. Conduct a physical inventory count.**
+2	Controller	1. Review the bank reconciliation. **2. Compile a list of all current contracts, with attached contracts, and set aside for auditors.** **3. Assist auditors in sending legal opinion letters to company lawyers.**
+2	Accounts Payable Clerk	1. Review cutoff information and accrue for any missing supplier invoices based on purchase order costs. 2. Accrue for any unpaid medical or dental insurance, or other employee benefits. 3. Review the repairs and maintenance account to see if any items charged here should be shifted to a fixed asset account. **4. Print the accounts payable listing for year-end and set aside for the auditors.**

Exhibit 9.14 Continued

As shown in the procedure, the accounting staff must allocate additional time prior to the close to work with the auditors in reviewing control systems and planning the year-end physical inventory count.

The payroll staff must record on the final employee paychecks of the calendar year the amount of any company-paid life insurance that exceeds (at the time of this writing) $50,000, discounted by a factor that is based on each employee's age. If the year-end close does not fall on the calendar year-end, this step can be avoided. The auditors will also want to see a list of all employees and their annual pay, which is used for control testing. The payroll staff should have this information on hand for them.

Policy/Procedure Statement		Retrieval No.:	10-258
		Page:	3 of 4
Brasto Publishing		Issue Date:	4/30/0X
		Supersedes:	N/A
Subject: Year-End Closing Activities			

Days from Month-End	Responsibility	Task Description
+2	Cost Accountant	1. Print inventory reports and issue to distribution list. 2. Close the inventory module.
+2	Fixed Assets Clerk	1. Review asset sales and disposals, and update fixed asset records accordingly. 2. Record gains and losses on the sale of assets. 3. Update the fixed assets schedule and calculate depreciation. 4. Verify that depreciation totals do not exceed the totals of asset valuations less salvage values. 5. Reconcile the general ledger fixed asset and accumulated depreciation balances to the detail ledger balances, and correct any variances. **6. Calculate depreciation as per tax regulations, and set aside for the auditors.** 7. Close the fixed asset module.
+2	General Ledger Clerk	1. Complete all remaining accruals. 2. Summarize prepaid assets and compare to balances from the previous period. Review balances with the controller and determine the extent of prepaid write-downs for the period. 3. Review the construction in progress account to see if any projects can be finalized; if so, shift to a fixed assets account and initiate depreciation.
+3	General Ledger Clerk	**1. Update detailed schedules for all balance sheet accounts and set aside for the auditors.** 2. Trace all journal entries to the summary-level general ledger, and investigate all variances.
+3	Accounts Payable Clerk	**1. Record any late supplier invoices.** **2. Compile all legal invoices for the year and set aside for the auditors.** **3. Close the accounts payable module.**
+3	Cost Accountant	1. Compile allocation bases through the final month and allocate overhead. **2. Document allocation methodology and set aside for auditors.**
+3	Tax Manager	1. Accrue for income taxes expense.
+3	Financial Analyst	1. Complete all operating data for inclusion in the financial statements.
+3	Controller	1. Consolidate incoming entries from subsidiaries. 2. Complete a preliminary set of financial statements. **3. Complete financial footnotes.**
+4	Controller	1. Finalize the financial statements and issue to the distribution list. The following reports should be included in the statements: a. Balance sheet b. Income statement

Exhibit 9.14 Continued

The accounts receivable clerk is much busier than usual at this time, having to set aside a final accounts receivable aging for the auditors, write down the reasoning for the final bad debt accrual of the year, and assist the auditors in issuing to customers a selection of confirmations of year-end balances owed.

The cost accountant will have to conduct a physical inventory count for all company locations, and allow for extra time for the auditors to conduct test counts. This must be done as soon after the year-end as possible. This person must also fully document the allocation methodology used for the allocation of overhead costs, and have this information available

Policy/Procedure Statement		Retrieval No.:	10-258
(Brasto Publishing logo)		Page:	4 of 4
		Issue Date:	4/30/0X
Subject: Year-End Closing Activities		Supersedes:	N/A

Days from Month-End	*Responsibility*	*Task Description*
+4	Controller (Continued)	c. Statement of cash flows **d. Stockholders' equity statement** e. Income statements by department f. Key operating statistics
+4	Financial Analyst	1. Calculate the borrowing base certificate and send it to the lender, along with a set of financial statements.
+5	General Ledger Clerk	1. Review variances too small to be checked during the closing process.
+6	Controller	**1. Review all documents required by the auditors, comparing them to the check-off list supplied by the auditors.**
+7	Controller	1. Review the size of the cutoff level used to eliminate variance investigations. 2. Review the closing schedule for the next month. 3. Review job assignments for the next month's closing schedule. 4. Review the closing schedules for subsidiaries for the next month. 5. Review the contents and layout of the financial statements, and plan for changes in advance of the next close.
+8	All Staff	1. Review problems with the last close and agree on necessary changes to be made for the next close.

Exhibit 9.14 Continued

for the auditors. In addition, the cost accountant usually updates the bills of materials with a comprehensive review of costs; this is not necessary for the audit, but the year-end close is frequently used as the time to update bills.

The accounts payable clerk must run a final accounts receivable detail report for the auditors. This position may be required to hold the books open for at least a week subsequent to the date of the year-end to wait for extra supplier invoices to reach the company through the mail. Though Exhibit 9.14 shows that only a three-day wait is used, the books may be held open much longer. If this is not done, then the auditors will probably review supplier invoices that are received subsequent to the closing and require the company to include them in the results for the prior year. This position must also compile all the legal invoices that were received in the past year, which the auditors will review to see if there are any legal disclosures that they must make in the footnotes to the financial statements.

If the company is also hiring the auditors to complete its annual tax return, the fixed assets clerk or the tax manager can calculate the tax depreciation on all depreciable assets and forward this information to the auditors.

The controller must compile a list of current contracts as well as the underlying contract detail, and have this information available for the auditors' review. This person must also create a preliminary set of footnotes, which the auditors will amplify upon if their work reveals extra information that must be included. The controller should also conduct the final review of documents that have been set aside for the auditors and ensure that they are complete.

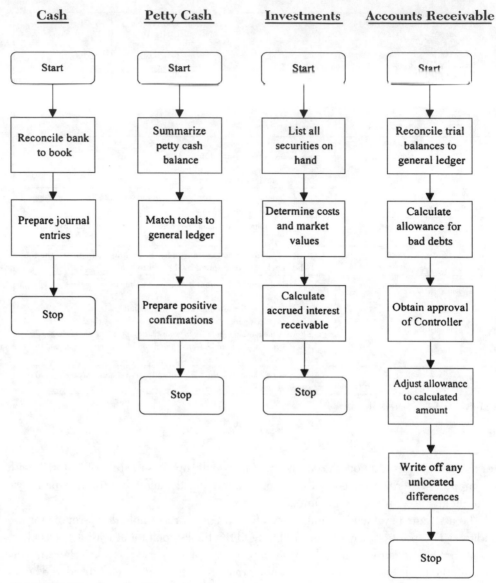

Exhibit 9.15 Closing Tasks by Position, in a Flowchart Format

The volume of extra tasks required for the year-end close can make this a much longer closing process than usual. The procedure in Exhibit 9.14 shows the financial statements being produced one day later than usual, but it is quite common for this process to take one or more weeks of extra time to complete.

An alternative format to the year-end procedure is to break down the various tasks by job position and then convert them into flow charts. An example of this approach is shown in Exhibit 9.15. Though this method will make the tasks of each person quite easy to view, it does not show the due dates for each task, nor does it show the interrelationships between the tasks performed by each person. Consequently, it should only be used if the controller continues to use the master year-end closing procedure so that he or she has access to information about the entire process.

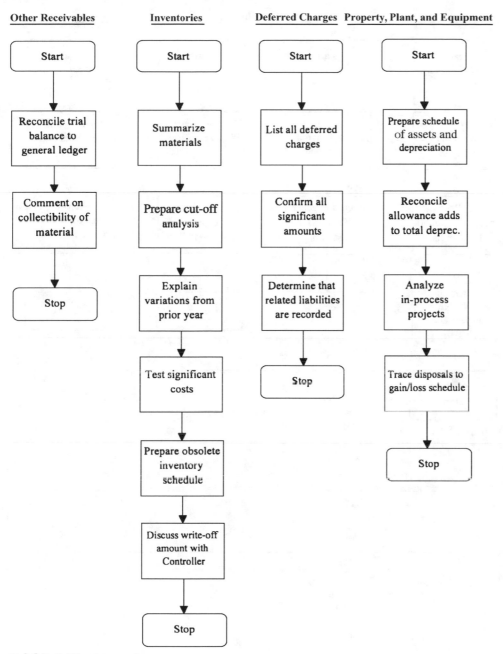

Exhibit 9.15 Continued

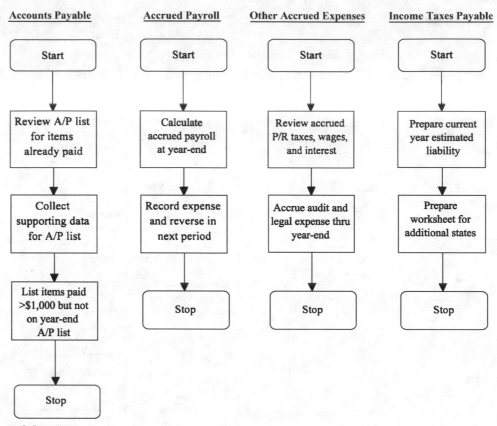

Exhibit 9.15 Continued

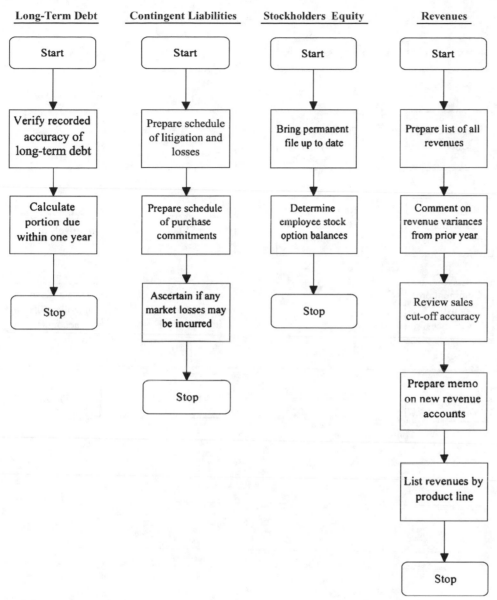

Exhibit 9.15   Continued

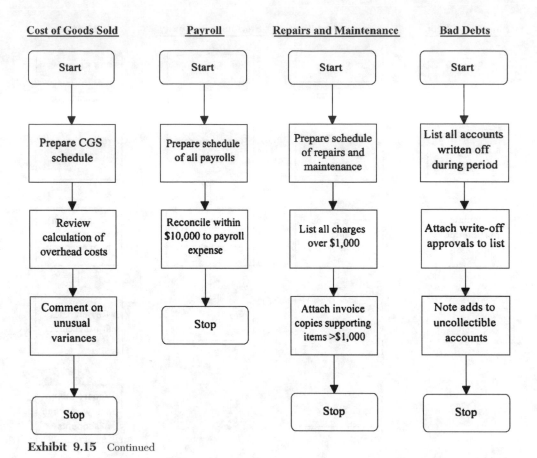

Exhibit 9.15 Continued

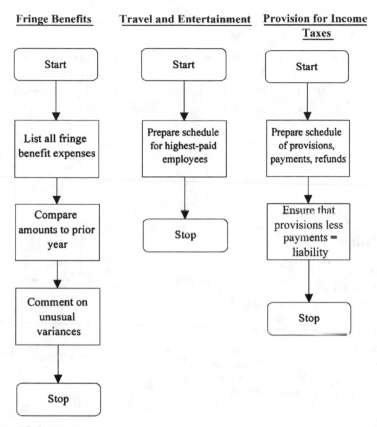

Exhibit 9.15 Continued

9.6 NEW YEAR STARTUP

Though the accounting staff tends to be most concerned with the completion of the year-end financial statements and the associated audit, it is equally important to ensure that ongoing accounting operations are set up to run for the next fiscal year. The following procedure details the typical startup tasks required of the accounting department.

Policy/Procedure Statement		Retrieval No.:	10-259
		Page:	1 of 1
Brasto Publishing		Issue Date:	10/28/0X
		Supersedes:	N/A
Subject: New Year Startup			

1.   **PURPOSE AND SCOPE**
     This procedure is used by the accounting staff to set up systems for a new accounting year.

2.   **RESPONSIBILITIES**
     GL ACCT   **General Ledger Accountant**
     ACCT RECV   **Accounts Receivable Clerk**
     ACCT PAY   **Accounts Payable Clerk**
     PAY CLERK   **Payroll Clerk**

3.   **PROCEDURES**

3.1   GL ACCT   **Roll Forward Accounting Balances to New Year**
1.   Obtain approval from the controller to roll forward balances to the new year and archive records from the oldest year listed in the accounting database.
2.   Lock all users out of the accounting system.
3.   Backup all accounting database records.
4.   Print the following year-end reports for the preceding accounting year:
     • Accounts Payable Detail
     • Accounts Receivable Aging
     • Cash Receipts Journal
     • Financial Statements
     • Fixed Assets Register
     • General Ledger
     • Sales Journal
5.   Initiate the automated system roll-forward routine.
6.   Allow user access back into the system.

3.2   GL ACCT   **Eliminate Small-Balance Accounts**
1.   Select all general ledger accounts for which there was less than $____ of activity in the preceding year.
2.   Compile a recommended list of larger-balance alternative accounts into which these smaller accounts can be rolled.
3.   Obtain controller approval to eliminate the small-balance accounts from the general ledger.

		4. Access the Supplier Master File and adjust all supplier accounts for which accounts to be eliminated are used as the default account.
		5. Access all transactions listed in the small-balance accounts, and shift the transaction charges to the new replacement accounts.
		6. Verify that all small-balance accounts to be eliminated have zero balances.
		7. Access the chart of accounts file and switch all designated small-balance accounts to inactive status.
		8. Issue a memo to the accounts payable data entry staff, detailing these changes.
3.3	GL ACCT	**Adjust Chart of Accounts to Match Business Structure**
		1. Discuss with the controller any planned structural changes to the business that will mandate changes in the chart of accounts.
		2. Discuss with the controller any planned changes in the homogenization of charts of accounts among subsidiaries.
		3. Discuss with the controller any planned cost accounting changes, such as activity-based costing, that will require new accounts in which to store data.
		4. Modify the chart of accounts as required.
3.4	GL ACCT	**Organize Bank Statements**
		1. Box all binders containing bank statements from the preceding year, index them, and forward to the archives staff for storage.
		2. Create a new binder with tabbed pages for each bank account.
3.5	ACCT PAY	**Roll Forward Supplier Files**
		1. Box all supplier files from the preceding year, index them, and forward to the archives staff for storage.
		2. Print the Supplier Ledger for the preceding year. If there were more than ____ transactions for a supplier in the previous year, highlight the supplier name on the report.
		3. Forward the highlighted report to the payables manager, who eliminates all highlighted suppliers from the report with whom the company no longer does business.
		4. Access the supplier master file and switch all designated suppliers with whom the company no longer does business to inactive status.
		5. Create folder labels for all remaining highlighted suppliers, affix the labels to folders, and store them in alphabetical order in the accounts payable filing cabinets.
3.6	ACCT RECV	**Roll Forward Supplier Files**
		1. Box all customer files from the preceding year, index them, and forward to the archives staff for storage.
		2. Print the Customer Ledger for the preceding year. If there were more than ____ transactions for a customer in the previous year, highlight the customer name on the report.
		3. Forward the highlighted report to the sales manager, who eliminates all highlighted customers from the report with whom the company no longer does business.
		4. Access the customer master file and switch all designated customers with whom the company no longer does business to inactive status.
		5. Create folder labels for all remaining highlighted customers, affix the labels to folders, and store them in alphabetical order in the accounts receivable filing cabinets.

3.7	PAY CLERK	**Update Unemployment Information**
		1. Verify the amount of unemployment tax rates and associated wage limits to be used for the new calendar year.
		2. Determine if a voluntary unemployment contribution should be made to reduce the upcoming unemployment tax rate for the new year.
3.8	PAY CLERK	**Update Payroll Withholdings and Deductions**
		1. Notify employees to review their W-4 forms, and update employee withholdings based on any revised W-4 forms that are submitted.
		2. Notify employees of unused flexible spending account deductions.
		3. Verify the amount of standard employee deductions for the new year.
		4. Reset pension plan deductions for the new year.
3.9	PAY CLERK	**Create and Distribute Payroll Processing Schedule**
		1. Verify that upcoming payroll processing dates do not conflict with weekends or planned holidays.
		2. Issue a schedule of payroll processing and pay distribution dates for the new year to employees.
3.10	PAY CLERK	**Organize Payroll Files**
		1. Box all binders containing payroll registers and the company copy of W-2 forms from the preceding year, index them, and forward to the archives staff for storage.
		2. Create a new binder for payroll registers.
		3. Purge terminated employees from the payroll database.

New Year Startup

Chapter 10

BUDGETING MANUAL[1]

10.1 INTRODUCTION

Budgeting is one of the most important activities that an accountant can engage in, for it provides the basis for the orderly management of activities within a company. A properly created budget will funnel funding into those activities that a company has determined to be most essential, as defined in its strategic plan. Furthermore, it provides a bridge between strategy and tactics by itemizing the precise tactical events that will be funded, such as the hiring of personnel or acquisition of equipment in a key department. Once the budget has been approved, it also acts as the primary control point over expenditures, because it should be compared to purchase requisitions before purchases are so the level of allowed funding can be ascertained. In addition, the results of specific departments can be compared to their budgets, which is an excellent tool for determining the performance of department managers. For all of these reasons, a comprehensive knowledge of the budgeting process is crucial for the accountant.

In this chapter, we look at the system of budgets and how they are linked together, review a sample budget, cover the key elements of flex budgeting, address the processes required to construct a budget, and finish with coverage of the control systems that can be used if a budget is available.

10.2 SYSTEM OF INTERLOCKING BUDGETS

A properly designed budget is a complex web of spreadsheets that account for the activities of virtually all areas within a company. As noted in Exhibit 10.1, the budget begins in two

---

[1] Adapted with permission from Bragg, *Accounting Reference Desktop* (John Wiley & Sons), pp. 258–91.

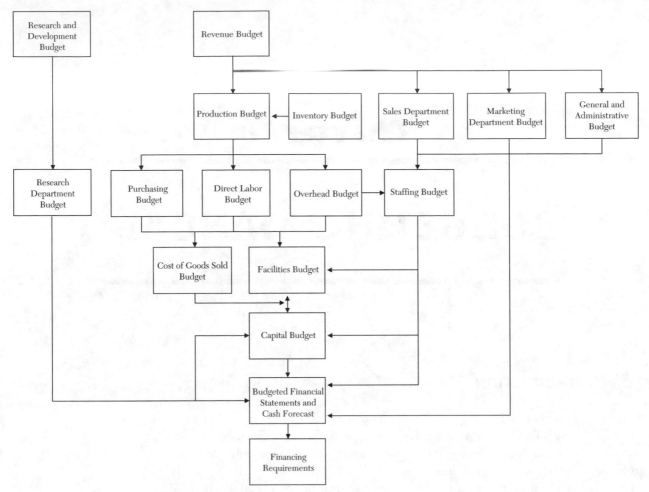

Exhibit 10.1   System of Budgets

places, with both the revenue budget and research and development budget. The revenue budget contains the revenue figures that the company believes it can achieve for each upcoming reporting period. These estimates come partially from the sales staff, which is responsible for estimates of sales levels for existing products within their current territories. Estimates for the sales of new products that have not yet been released, and for existing products in new markets will come from a combination of the sales and marketing staffs, who will use their experience with related product sales to derive estimates. The greatest fallacy in any budget is to impose a revenue budget from the top management level without any input from the sales staff, as this can result in a company-wide budget that is geared toward a sales level that is most unlikely to be reached.

A revenue budget requires prior consideration of a number of issues. For example, a general market share target will drive several other items within the budget, as greater market share may come at the cost of lower unit prices or higher credit costs. Another issue is the compensation strategy for the sales staff; a shift to higher or lower commissions for specific products or regions will be a strong incentive for the sales staff to alter their selling behavior, resulting in some changes in estimated sales levels. Yet another consideration is which sales territories are to be entered during the budget period—those with high target populations may yield very high sales per hour of sales effort, while the reverse will be true if the remaining untapped regions have smaller target populations. It is also necessary to review the price points that will be offered during the budget period, especially in relation to the pricing strategies that are anticipated from competitors. If there is a strategy to increase market share as well as to raise unit prices, the budget may fail due to conflicting activities. Another major factor is the terms of sale, which can be extended, along with easy credit, to attract more marginal customers; conversely, they can be retracted to reduce credit costs and focus company resources on a few key customers. A final point is that the budget should address any changes in the type of customer to whom sales will be made. If an entirely new type of customer will be added to the range of sales targets during the budget period, then the revenue budget should reflect a gradual ramp-up that will be required for the sales staff to work through the sales cycle of the new customers.

Once all of these factors have been ruminated upon and combined to create a preliminary budget, the sales staff should also compare the budgeted sales level per person to the actual sales level that has been experienced in the recent past to see if the company has the existing capability to make the budgeted sales. If not, the revenue budget should be ramped up to reflect the time it will take to hire and train additional sales staff. The same cross-check can be conducted for the amount of sales budgeted per customer to see if historical experience validates the sales levels noted in the new budget.

Another budget that initiates other activities within the system of budgets is the research and development budget. This is not related to the sales level at all (as opposed to most other budgets), but instead is a discretionary budget that is based on the company's strategy to derive new or improved products. The decision to fund a certain amount of project-related activity in this area will drive a departmental staffing and capital budget that is, for the most part, completely unrelated to the activity conducted by the rest of the company. However, there can be a feedback loop between this budget and the cash budget, because financing limitations may require management to prune some projects from this area. If so, the management team must work with the research and development manager to determine the correct mix of projects with both short-range and long-range payoffs that will still be funded. This is as much an art as a science, though the process can be helped along by a capital budgeting evaluation.

The production budget is largely driven by the sales estimates contained within the revenue budget. However, it is also driven by the inventory-level assumptions in the inventory budget. The inventory budget contains estimates by the materials management supervisor regarding the inventory levels that will be required for the upcoming budget period. For example, a new goal may be to reduce the level of finished goods inventory from 10 turns per year to 15. If so, some of the products required by the revenue budget can be bled off from the existing finished goods inventory stock, requiring smaller production requirements during the budget period. Alternatively, if there is a strong focus on improving the level of customer service, then it may be necessary to keep more finished goods in stock, which will require more production than is strictly called for by the revenue budget. This concept can also be extended to work-in-process (WIP) inventory, where the installation of advanced production planning systems, such as manufacturing resources planning or just-in-time, can be used to reduce the level of required inventory. Also, just-in-time purchasing techniques can be used to reduce the amount of raw materials inventory that is kept on hand. All of these assumptions should be clearly delineated in the inventory budget so that the management team is clear about what systemic changes will be required to effect altered inventory turnover levels. Also, one should be aware that any advanced production planning system takes a considerable amount of time to install and tune, so it is best if the inventory budget contains a gradual ramp-up to different planned levels of inventory.

Given this input from the inventory budget, the production budget is used to derive the unit quantity of required products that must be manufactured to meet revenue targets for each budget period. This involves a number of interrelated factors, such as the availability of sufficient capacity for production needs. Of particular concern should be the amount of capacity at the bottleneck operation. This tends to be the most expensive capital item, so it is important to budget a sufficient quantity of funding to ensure that this operation includes enough equipment to meet the targeted production goals. If the bottleneck operation involves skilled labor rather than equipment, the human resources staff should be consulted regarding its ability to bring in the necessary personnel in time to improve the bottleneck capacity in a timely manner.

Another factor that drives the budgeted costs contained within the production budget is the anticipated size of production batches. If the batch size is expected to decrease, then more overhead costs should be budgeted in the production scheduling, materials handling, and machine setup staffing areas. If longer batch sizes are planned then there may be a possibility of proportionally reducing overhead costs in these areas. This is a key consideration that is frequently overlooked but can have an outsized impact on overhead costs. If management attempts to contain overhead costs in this area while still using smaller batch sizes, then it will likely run into larger scrap quantities and quality issues that are caused by rushed batch setups and the allocation of incorrect materials to production jobs.

Step costing is also an important consideration when creating the production budget. Costs will increase in large increments when certain capacity levels are reached. The management team should be fully aware of when these capacity levels will be reached so that it can plan appropriately for the incurrence of added costs. For example, the addition of a second shift to the production area will call for added costs in the areas of supervisory staff as well as an increased pay rate and higher maintenance costs. The inverse of this condition can also occur, where step costs can decline suddenly if capacity levels fall below a specific point.

Production levels may also be impacted by any lengthy tooling setups or changeovers to replacement equipment. These changes may halt all production for extended periods and so must be carefully planned for. This is the responsibility of the industrial engineering staff. The accountant would do well to review the company's history of actual equipment setup times to see if the current engineering estimates are sufficiently lengthy, based on past history.

The expense items included in the production budget should be driven by a set of subsidiary budgets, which are the purchasing, direct labor, and overhead budgets. These budgets can simply be included in the production budget, but they typically involve such a large proportion of company costs that it is best to lay them out separately in greater detail in separate budgets. Comments on these budgets are as follows:

Purchasing Budget

The purchasing budget is driven by several factors, first of which is the bill of materials that comprises the products that are planned for production during the budget period.

These bills must be accurate, or else the purchasing budget can include seriously incorrect information. In addition, there should be a plan for controlling material costs, perhaps through the use of concentrated buying through few suppliers, or perhaps through the use of long-term contracts. If materials are highly subject to market pressures, are a large proportion of total product costs, and have a history of sharp price swings, then a best-case and worst-case costing scenario should be added to the budget so that managers can review the impact of costing issues in this area. If a just-in-time delivery system from suppliers is contemplated, then the purchasing budget should reflect a possible increase in material costs caused by the increased number of deliveries from suppliers. It is also worthwhile to budget for a raw material scrap and obsolescence expense; there should be a history of costs in these areas that can be extrapolated based on projected purchasing volumes.

Direct Labor Budget

One should not make the mistake of budgeting for direct labor as a fully variable cost. The production volume from day to day tends to be relatively fixed, and requires a set number of direct labor personnel on a continuing basis to operate production equipment and manually assemble products. Further, the production manager will realize much greater production efficiencies by holding on to an experienced production staff rather than letting them go as soon as production volumes make small incremental drops. Accordingly, it is better to budget based on reality, which is that direct labor personnel are usually retained, even if there are ongoing fluctuations in the level of production. Thus, direct labor should be shown in the budget as a fixed cost of production, within certain production volume parameters.

Also, this budget should describe staffing levels by type of direct labor position; this is driven by labor routings, which are documents that describe the exact type and quantity of staffing needed to produce a product. When multiplied by the unit volumes located in the production budget, this results in an expected level of staffing by direct labor position. This information is most useful for the human resources staff, which is responsible for staffing the positions.

The direct labor budget should also account for any contractually mandated changes in hourly rates that may be itemized in a union agreement. Such an agreement may also have restrictions on layoffs, which should be accounted for in the budget if this will keep labor levels from dropping in proportion with budgeted reductions in production levels. Such an agreement may also require that layoffs be conducted in order of seniority, which may force higher-paid employees into positions that would normally be budgeted for less expensive laborers. Thus, the presence of a union contract can result in a much more complex direct labor budget than would normally be the case.

The direct labor budget may also contain features related to changes in the efficiency of employees, and any resulting changes in pay. For example, one possible pay arrangement is to pay employees based on a piece rate, which directly ties their performance to the level of production achieved. If so, this will probably only apply to portions of the work force, so the direct labor budget may involve pay rates based on both piece rates and hourly pay. Another issue is that any drastic increases in the budgeted level of direct labor personnel will likely result in some initial declines in labor efficiency, as it takes time for new employees to learn their tasks. If this is the case, the budget should reflect a low level of initial efficiency, with a ramp-up over time to higher levels that will result in greater initial direct labor costs. Finally, efficiency improvements may be rewarded with staff bonuses from time to time; if so, these bonuses should be included in the budget.

Overhead Budget

The overhead budget can be a simple one to create if there are no significant changes in production volume from the preceding year, because this involves a large quantity of static costs that will not vary much over time. Included in this category are machine maintenance; utilities; supervisory salaries, wages for the materials management, production scheduling, and quality assurance personnel; and facilities maintenance and depreciation expenses. Under the no-change scenario, the most likely budgetary alterations will be to machinery or facilities maintenance, which depend on the condition and level of usage of company property.

If there is a significant change in the expected level of production volume, or if new production lines are to be added, then one should examine this budget in great detail, for the underlying production volumes may cause a ripple effect that results in wholesale changes to many areas of the overhead budget. Of particular concern is the number of overhead-related personnel who must be either laid off or added when capacity levels reach certain critical points, such as the addition or subtraction of extra work shifts. Costs also tend to rise substantially when a facility is operating at very close to 100% capacity, as this tends to call for an inordinate amount of effort to maintain on an ongoing basis.

The purchasing, direct labor, and overhead budgets can then be summarized into a cost of goods sold budget. This budget should incorporate, as a single line item, the total amount of revenue so that all manufacturing costs can be deducted from it to yield a gross profit margin on the same document. This budget is referred to constantly during the budget creation process, because it tells management if its budgeting assumptions are yielding an acceptable gross margin result. As it is a summary-level budget for the production side of the budgeting process, this is also a good place to itemize any production-related statistics, such as the average hourly cost of direct labor, inventory turnover rates, and the amount of revenue dollars per production person.

Thus far, we have reviewed the series of budgets that descend in turn from the revenue budget and then through the production budget. However, there are other expenses that are unrelated to production. These are categories in a separate set of budgets. The first is the sales department budget. This includes the expenses that the sales staff must incur to achieve the revenue budget, such as travel and entertainment, as well as sales training. Of particular concern in this budget is the amount of budgeted headcount that is required to meet the sales target. It is essential that the actual sales per salesperson from the most recent completed year of operations be compared to the same calculation in the budget to ensure that there is a sufficiently large budget available for an adequate number of sales personnel. This is a common problem, for companies will make the false assumption that the existing sales staff can make heroic efforts to wildly exceed its previous-year sales efforts. Furthermore, the budget must account for a sufficient time period in which new sales personnel can be trained and form an adequate base of customer contacts to create a meaningful stream of revenue for the company. In some industries, this learning curve may be only a few days, but it can be the better part of a year if considerable technical knowledge is required to make a sale. If the latter situation is the case, it is likely that the procurement and retention of qualified sales staff is the key element of success for a company, which makes the sales department budget one of the most important elements of the entire budget.

The marketing budget is also closely tied to the revenue budget, for it contains all of the funding required to roll out new products, merchandise them properly, advertise for them, test new products, and so on. A key issue here is to ensure that the marketing budget is fully funded to support any increases in sales noted in the revenue budget. It may be necessary to increase this budget by a disproportionate amount if one is trying to create a new brand, issue a new product, or distribute an existing product in a new market. These costs can easily exceed any associated revenues for some time. A common budgeting problem is not to provide sufficient funding in these instances, leading to a significant drop in expected revenues.

Another nonproduction budget that is integral to the success of the corporation is the general and administrative budget. This contains the cost of the corporate management staff, plus all accounting, finance, and human resources personnel. Because this is a cost center, the general inclination is to reduce these costs to the bare minimum. However, to do so there must be a significant investment in technology to achieve reductions in the manual labor usually required to process transactions; thus, there must be some provision in the capital budget for this area.

There is a feedback loop between the staffing and direct labor budgets and the general and administrative budget, because the human resources department must staff itself based on the amount of hiring or layoffs that are anticipated elsewhere in the company. Similarly, a major change in the revenue volume will alter the budget for the accounting department, as many of the activities in this area are driven by the volume of sales transactions. Furthermore, a major increase in the capital budget, especially for items requiring prolonged construction activities, will require an investment in additional cost accounting personnel who will track these expenditures. Thus, the general and administrative budget generally requires a number of iterations in response to changes in many other parts of the budget.

Though salaries and wages should be listed in each of the departmental budgets, it is useful to list the total headcount for each position through all budget periods in a separate staffing budget. By doing so, the human resources staff can tell when specific positions must be filled so that they can time their recruiting efforts most appropriately. This budget also provides good information for the person responsible for the facilities budget; he or she can use it to determine the timing and amount of square footage requirements for office space. Rather than being a standalone budget, the staffing budget tends to be one whose formulas are closely intertwined with those of all other departmental budgets, so a change in headcount information on this budget will automatically translate into a change in the salaries expense on other budgets. It is also a good place to store the average pay rates, overtime percentages, and average benefit costs for all positions. By centralizing this cost information, the human resources staff can more easily update budget information. Salary-related costs tend to be the highest proportion of costs in a company (excluding materials costs), making this a heavily used budget.

The facilities budget is based on the level of activity that is estimated in many of the budgets just described. For this reason, it is one of the last budgets to be completed. This budget is closely linked to the capital budget, because expenditures for additional facilities will require more maintenance expenses in the facilities budget. This budget typically contains expense line items for building insurance, maintenance, repairs, janitorial services, utilities, and the salaries of the maintenance personnel employed in this function. It is crucial to estimate the need for any upcoming major repairs to facilities when constructing this budget, as these can greatly amplify the total budgeted expense.

Another budget that includes input from virtually all areas of a company is the capital budget. This should comprise either a summary listing of all main fixed asset categories for which purchases are anticipated, or else a detailed listing of the same information; the latter case is only recommended if there are comparatively few items to be purchased. The capital budget is of great importance to the calculation of corporate financing requirements because it can involve the expenditure of sums far beyond those that are normally encountered through daily cash flows. The contents of the capital budget should be carefully examined to determine whether it has an impact on a company's bottleneck operation. All too often expenditures are made that make other operations more efficient but do not increase the ability to produce more product by increasing the capacity of the bottleneck operation.[2] It is also necessary to ensure that capital items are scheduled for procurement far enough in advance of related projects that they will be fully installed and operational before the scheduled first activity date of the project. For example, a budget should not itemize revenue from a printing press for the same month in which the press is scheduled to be purchased, for it may take months to set up the press. A final item is that capital purchases may be tied to the pet projects of senior managers, rather than to the strategic or tactical goals of the company. Consequently, it may be useful to review all capital items in the budget to ensure that they are all needed to meet these goals.

The end result of all budgets just described is a set of financial statements that reflect the impact on the company of the upcoming budget. At a minimum, these statements should include the income statement and cash flow statement, which are the best evidence of fiscal health during the budget period. The balance sheet is less necessary because the key factors on which it reports are related to cash, and that information is already contained within the cash flow statement. These reports should be directly linked to all the other budgets so that any changes to the budgets will immediately appear in the financial statements. The management team will closely examine these statements and make numerous adjustments to the budgets to arrive at a satisfactory financial result.

The budget-linked financial statements are also a good place to store related operational and financial ratios so that the management team can review this information and revise the budgets to alter the ratios to match benchmarking or industry standards that may have been set as goals. Typical measurements in this area can include revenue and income per person, inventory turnover ratios, and gross margin percentages. This type of information is also useful for lenders, who may have required minimum financial performance results as part of loan agreements, such as a minimum current ratio or debt-to-equity ratio.

The cash forecast is of exceptional importance, for it tells company managers if the proposed budget model will be feasible. If cash projects result in major cash needs that cannot be met by any possible financing, then the model must be changed. The assumptions that go into the cash forecast should be based strictly on historical fact rather than on the wishes of managers. This stricture is particularly important in the case of cash receipts from accounts receivable. If the assumptions are changed in the model to reflect an advanced

---

[2] For more information about this topic, See Chapter 14, "Throughput Accounting," in Bragg, *Cost Accounting* (John Wiley & Sons, 2001).

rate of cash receipts that exceeds anything the company has heretofore experienced, then it is very unlikely that it will be achieved during the budget period. Instead, it is better to use proven collection periods as assumptions and alter other parts of the budget to ensure that cash flows remain positive.

The cash forecast is a particularly good area in which to spot the impact of changes in credit policy. For example, if a company wishes to expand its share of the market by allowing easy credit to marginal customers, then it should lengthen the assumed collection period in the cash forecast to see if there is a significant downgrading of the resulting cash flows.

The other key factor in the cash forecast is the use of delays in budgeted accounts payable payments. It is common for managers to budget for extended payment terms to fund other cash flow needs, but there are several problems that can result from this policy. One is the possible loss of key suppliers who will not tolerate late payments. Another is the risk of being charged interest on late payments to suppliers. A third problem is that suppliers may relegate a company to a lower level on their lists of shipment priorities because they are being paid late. Finally, suppliers may simply raise their prices to absorb the cost of the late payments. Consequently, the late payment strategy must be followed with great care, only using it on those suppliers who do not appear to notice, and otherwise only doing it after prior negotiation with targeted suppliers to make the changed terms part of the standard buying agreement.

The last document in the system of budgets is the discussion of financing alternatives. This is not strictly a budget, though it will contain a single line item, derived from the cash forecast, which itemizes funding needs during each period itemized in the budget. In all other respects, it is simply a discussion of financing alternatives, which can be quite varied. This may involve a mix of debt, supplier financing, preferred stock, common stock, or some other, more innovative approach. The document should contain a discussion of the cost of each form of financing, the ability of the company to obtain it, and when it can be obtained. Managers may find that there are so few financing alternatives available, or that the cost of financing is so high, that the entire budget must be restructured to avoid the negative cash flow that calls for the financing. There may also be a need for feedback from this document back into the budgeted financial statements in order to account for the cost of obtaining the funding, as well as any related interest costs.

In the next section, we will review an example of the budgets that have just been described to see how they are formatted and link together in a cohesive set of budgets that can be used to conduct the future operations of a business.

10.3 SAMPLE BUDGET

In this section, we will review several variations on how a budget can be constructed, using a number of examples. The first budget covered is the revenue budget, which is shown in Exhibit 10.2. To conserve space, the exhibit uses quarterly revenue figures for a budget year rather than monthly. It contains revenue estimates for three different product lines that are designated as Alpha, Beta, and Charlie.

The Alpha product line uses a budgeting format that identifies the specific quantities that are expected to be sold in each quarter, as well as the average price per unit sold. This format is most useful when there are not so many products that such a detailed delineation

REVENUE BUDGET FOR THE FISCAL YEAR ENDED XX/XX/08

	Quarter 1	Quarter 2	Quarter 3	Quarter 4	Totals
Product Line Alpha					
Unit price	$15.00	$14.85	$14.80	$14.75	—
Unit volume	14,000	21,000	25,000	31,000	91,000
Revenue subtotal	$210,000	$311,850	$370,000	$457,250	$1,349,100
Product Line Beta					
Revenue subtotal	$1,048,000	$1,057,000	$1,061,000	$1,053,000	$4,219,000
Product Line Charlie					
Region 1	$123,000	$95,000	$82,000	$70,000	$370,000
Region 2	80,000	89,000	95,000	101,000	365,000
Region 3	95,000	95,000	65,000	16,000	271,000
Region 4	265,000	265,000	320,000	375,000	1,225,000
Revenue subtotal	$563,000	$544,000	$562,000	$562,000	$2,231,000
Revenue grand total	$1,821,000	$1,912,850	$1,993,000	$2,072,250	$7,799,100
Quarterly revenue proportion	23.3%	24.5%	25.6%	26.6%	100.0%
Statistics					
Product line proportion:					
Alpha	11.5%	16.3%	18.6%	22.1%	17.3%
Beta	57.6%	55.3%	53.2%	50.8%	54.1%
Charlie	30.9%	28.4%	28.2%	27.1%	28.6%
Product line total	100.0%	100.0%	100.0%	100.0%	100.0%

Exhibit 10.2 Revenue Budget

would create an excessively lengthy budget. It is a very useful format, for the sales staff can go into the budget model and alter unit volumes and prices quite easily. An alternative format is only to reveal this level of detail for the most important products, and to lump the revenue from other products into a single line item, as is the case for the Beta product line.

The most common budgeting format is used for the Beta product line, where we avoid the use of detailed unit volumes and prices in favor of a single lump-sum revenue total for each reporting period. This format is used when there are multiple products within each product line, making it cumbersome to create a detailed list of individual products. However, this format is the least informative and gives no easy way to update the supporting information.

Yet another budgeting format is shown for the Charlie product line, where projected sales are grouped by region. This format is most useful when there are many sales personnel, each of whom has been assigned a specific territory in which to operate. This budget can then be used to judge the ongoing performance of each salesperson.

These revenue reporting formats can also be combined so that the product line detail for the Alpha product can be used as underlying detail for the sales regions used for the Charlie product line—though this will result in a very lengthy budget document.

PRODUCTION AND INVENTORY BUDGET FOR THE FISCAL YEAR ENDED XX/XX/08

	Quarter 1	Quarter 2	Quarter 3	Quarter 4	Totals
Inventory Turnover Goals					
Raw materials turnover	4.0	4.5	5.0	5.5	4.8
W-I-P turnover	12.0	15.0	18.0	21.0	16.5
Finished goods turnover	6.0	6.0	9.0	9.0	7.5
Product Line Alpha Production					
Beginning inventory units	15,000	21,000	20,000	15,000	—
Unit sales budget	14,000	21,000	25,000	31,000	91,000
Planned production	20,000	20,000	20,000	27,375	87,375
Ending inventory units	21,000	20,000	15,000	11,375	
Bottleneck unit capacity	20,000	20,000	20,000	40,000	
Bottleneck utilization	100%	100%	100%	68%	
Planned finished goods turnover	15,167	15,167	11,375	11,375	

Exhibit 10.3 Production and Inventory Budgets

There is also a statistics section at the bottom of the revenue budget that itemizes the proportion of total sales that occurs in each quarter, plus the proportion of product line sales within each quarter. Though it is not necessary to use these exact measurements, it is useful to include some type of measure that informs the reader of any variations in sales from period to period.

Both the production and inventory budgets are shown in Exhibit 10.3. The inventory budget is itemized at the top of the exhibit, where we itemize the amount of planned inventory turnover in all three inventory categories. There is a considerable ramp-up in work-in-process inventory turnover, indicating the planned installation of a manufacturing planning system of some kind that will control the flow of materials through the facility.

The production budget for just the Alpha product line is shown directly below the inventory goals. This budget is not concerned with the cost of production, but rather with the number of units that will be produced. In this instance, we begin with an on-hand inventory of 15,000 units, and try to keep enough units on hand through the remainder of the budget year to meet both the finished goods inventory goal at the top of the exhibit and the number of required units to be sold, which is referenced from the revenue budget. The main problem is that the maximum capacity of the bottleneck operation is 20,000 units per quarter. To meet the revenue target, we must run that operation at full bore through the first three quarters, irrespective of the inventory turnover target. This is especially important because the budget indicates a jump in bottleneck capacity in the fourth quarter from 20,000 to 40,000 units—this will occur when the bottleneck operation is stopped for a short time while additional equipment is added to it. During this stoppage, there must be enough excess inventory on hand to cover any sales that will arise. Consequently, production is planned for 20,000 units per quarter for the first three quarters, followed by a more precisely derived figure in the fourth quarter that will result in inventory turns of 9.0 at the end of the year, exactly as planned.

The production budget can be enhanced with the incorporation of planned machine downtime for maintenance, as well as for the planned loss of production units to scrap. It is also useful to plan for the capacity needs of nonbottleneck work centers, as these areas will require varying levels of staffing depending on the number of production shifts needed.

The purchasing budget is shown in Exhibit 10.4. This contains several different formats for planning budgeted purchases for the Alpha product line. The first option summarizes the planned production for each quarter; this information is brought forward from the production budget. We then multiply this by the standard unit cost of materials to arrive at the total amount of purchases that must be made to adequately support sales. The second option identifies the specific cost of each component of the product so that management can see where cost increases are expected to occur. Though this version provides more information, it occupies a great deal of space on the budget if there are many components in each product or many products. A third option is shown at the bottom of the exhibit that summarizes all purchases by commodity type. This format is most useful for the company's buyers, who usually specialize in certain commodity types.

The purchasing budget can be enhanced by adding a scrap factor for budgeted production, which will result in slightly higher quantities to buy, thereby leaving less chance of running out of raw materials. Another upgrade to the exhibit would be to schedule purchases for planned production some time in advance of the actual manufacturing date so that the purchasing staff will be assured of having the parts on hand when manufacturing begins. A third enhancement is to round off the purchasing volumes for each item into the actual buying volumes that can be obtained on the open market. For example, it may only be possible to buy the required labels in volumes of 100,000 at a time, which would result in a planned purchase at the beginning of the year that would be large enough to cover all production needs through the end of the year.

The direct labor budget is shown in Exhibit 10.5. This budget assumes that only one labor category will vary directly with revenue volume. That category is the final assembly department, where a percentage in the far right column indicates that the cost in this area will be budgeted at a fixed 3.5% of total revenues. In all other cases, there are assumptions for a fixed number of personnel in each position within each production department. All of the wage figures for each department (except for final assembly) are derived from the planned hourly rates and headcount figures noted at the bottom of the page. This budget can be enhanced with the addition of separate line items for payroll tax percentages, benefits, shift differential payments, and overtime expenses. The cost of the final assembly department can also be adjusted to account for worker efficiency, which will be lower during production ramp-up periods when new, untrained employees are added to the work force.

A sample of the overhead budget is shown in Exhibit 10.6. In this exhibit, we see that the overhead budget is really made up of a number of subsidiary departments, such as maintenance, materials management, and quality assurance. If the budgets of any of these departments are large enough, it makes a great deal of sense to split them off into a separate budget so that the managers of those departments can see their budgeted expectations more clearly. Of particular interest in this exhibit is the valid capacity range noted on the far right side of the exhibit. This signifies the production activity level within which the budgeted overhead costs are accurate. If the actual capacity utilization were to fall outside of this range, either high or low, a separate overhead budget should be constructed with costs that are expected to be incurred within those ranges.

PURCHASING BUDGET FOR THE FISCAL YEAR ENDED XX/XX/08					
	Quarter 1	Quarter 2	Quarter 3	Quarter 4	Totals
Inventory Turnover Goals					
Raw materials turnover	4.0	4.5	5.0	5.5	4.8
Product Line Alpha Purchasing (Option 1)					
Planned production	20,000	20,000	20,000	27,375	
Standard material cost/Unit	$5.42	$5.42	$5.67	$5.67	
Total material cost	$108,400	$108,400	$113,400	$155,216	$485,416
Product Line Alpha Purchasing (Option 2)					
Planned production	20,000	20,000	20,000	27,375	
Molded part	$4.62	$4.62	$4.85	$4.85	
Labels	$0.42	$0.42	$0.42	$0.42	
Fittings and fasteners	$0.38	$0.38	$0.40	$0.40	
Total cost of components	$5.42	$5.42	$5.67	$5.67	
Product Line Alpha Purchasing (Option 2)					
Plastic Commodities					
Molded Part Units	20,000	20,000	20,000	27,375	
Molded Part Cost	$4.62	$4.62	$4.85	$4.85	
Adhesives Commodity					
Labels Units	20,000	20,000	20,000	27,375	
Labels Cost	$0.42	$0.42	$0.42	$0.42	
Fasteners Commodity					
Fasteners Units	20,000	20,000	20,000	27,375	
Fasteners Cost	$0.38	$0.38	$0.40	$0.40	
Statistics					
Materials as percent of revenue	36%	36%	38%	38%	

Exhibit 10.4 Purchasing Budget

A sample cost of goods sold budget is shown in Exhibit 10.7. This format splits out each of the product lines noted in the revenue budget for reporting purposes, and subtracts from each one the materials costs that are noted in the purchases budget. This results in a contribution margin for each product line that is the clearest representation of the impact of direct costs (i.e., material costs) on each one. We then summarize these individual contribution margins into a summary-level contribution margin, and then subtract the total direct labor and overhead costs (as referenced from the direct labor and overhead budgets) to arrive at a total gross margin. The statistics section also notes the number of production personnel budgeted for each quarterly reporting period, plus the average annual revenue per production employee—these statistics can be replaced with any operational information that management wants to see at a summary level for the production function, such as efficiency levels, capacity utilization, or inventory turnover.

DIRECT LABOR BUDGET FOR THE FISCAL YEAR ENDED XX/XX/08

	Quarter 1	Quarter 2	Quarter 3	Quarter 4	Totals	Notes
Machining Department						
Senior Machine Operator	$15,120	$15,372	$23,058	$23,058	$76,608	
Machining Apprentice	4,914	4,964	9,929	9,929	29,736	
Expense subtotal	$20,034	$20,336	$32,987	$32,987	$106,344	
Paint Department						
Senior Paint Shop Staff	$15,876	$16,128	$16,128	$16,128	$64,260	
Painter Apprentice	$5,065	$5,216	$5,216	$5,216	$20,714	
Expense subtotal	$20,941	$21,344	$21,344	$21,344	$84,974	
Polishing Department						
Senior Polishing Staff	$16,632	$11,844	$11,844	$11,844	$52,164	
Polishing Apprentice	4,360	4,511	4,511	4,511	17,892	
Expense subtotal	$20,992	$16,355	$16,355	$16,355	$70,056	
Final Assembly Department						
General Laborer	$63,735	$66,950	$69,755	$72,529	$272,969	3.5%
Expense subtotal	$63,735	$66,950	$69,755	$72,529	$272,969	
Expense grand total	$125,702	$124,985	$140,441	$143,215	$534,343	
Statistics						
Union Hourly Rates						
Senior Machine Operator	$15.00	$15.25	$15.25	$15.25		
Machining Apprentice	9.75	9.85	9.85	9.85		
Senior Paint Shop Staff	15.75	16.00	16.00	16.00		
Painter Apprentice	10.05	10.35	10.35	10.35		
Senior Polishing Staff	11.00	11.75	11.75	11.75		
Polishing Apprentice	8.65	8.95	8.95	8.95		
Headcount by Position						
Senior Machine Operator	2	2	3	3		
Machining Apprentice	1	1	2	2		
Senior Paint Shop Staff	2	2	2	2		
Painter Apprentice	1	1	1	1		
Senior Polishing Staff	3	2	2	2		
Polishing Apprentice	1	1	1	1		

Exhibit 10.5   Direct Labor Budget

The sales department budget is shown in Exhibit 10.8. This budget shows several different ways in which to organize the budget information. At the top of the budget is a block of line items that lists the expenses for those overhead costs within the department that cannot be specifically linked to a salesperson or region. In cases where the number of sales staff is quite small, *all* of the department's costs may be listed in this area.

Another alternative is shown in the second block of expense line items in the middle of the sales department budget, where all of the sales costs for an entire product line are lumped together into a single line item. If each person on the sales staff is exclusively

						Valid Capacity
OVERHEAD BUDGET FOR THE FISCAL YEAR ENDED XX/XX/08						
	Quarter 1	Quarter 2	Quarter 3	Quarter 4	Totals	Range
Supervision						
Production Manager Salary	$16,250	$16,250	$16,250	$16,250	$65,000	—
Shift Manager Salaries	22,000	22,000	23,500	23,500	91,000	40%-70%
Expense subtotal	$38,250	$38,250	$39,750	$39,750	$156,000	
Maintenance Department						
Equipment Maintenance Staff	$54,000	$56,500	$58,000	$60,250	$228,750	40%-70%
Facilities Maintenance Staff	8,250	8,250	8,500	8,500	33,500	40%-70%
Equipment Repairs	225,000	225,000	275,000	225,000	950,000	40%-70%
Facility Repairs	78,000	29,000	12,000	54,000	173,000	40%-70%
Expense subtotal	$365,250	$318,750	$353,500	$347,750	$1,385,250	
Materials Management Department						
Manager Salary	$18,750	$18,750	$18,750	$18,750	$75,000	—
Purchasing Staff	28,125	18,750	18,750	18,750	84,375	40%-70%
Materials Management Staff	28,000	35,000	35,000	35,000	133,000	40%-70%
Production Control Staff	11,250	11,250	11,250	11,250	45,000	40%-70%
Expense subtotal	$86,125	$83,750	$83,750	$83,750	$337,375	
Quality Department						
Manager Salary	$13,750	$13,750	$13,750	$13,750	$55,000	—
Quality Staff	16,250	16,250	16,250	24,375	73,125	40%-70%
Lab Testing Supplies	5000	4,500	4,500	4,500	18,500	40%-70%
Expense subtotal	$35,000	$34,500	$34,500	$42,625	$146,625	
Other Expenses						
Depreciation	$14,000	$15,750	$15,750	$15,750	$61,250	—
Utilities	60,000	55,000	55,000	60,000	230,000	40%-70%
Boiler Insurance	3,200	3,200	3,200	3,200	12,800	—
Expense subtotal	$77,200	$73,950	$73,950	$78,950	$304,050	
Expense grand total	$601,825	$549,200	$585,450	$592,825	$2,329,300	

Exhibit 10.6   Overhead Budget

assigned to a single product line, then it may make sense to break down the budget into separate budget pages for each product line, and list all of the expenses associated with each product line on a separate page.

A third alternative is shown next in Exhibit 10.8, where we list a summary of expenses for each salesperson. This format works well when combined with the departmental overhead

COST OF GOODS SOLD BUDGET FOR THE FISCAL YEAR ENDED XX/XX/08

	Quarter 1	Quarter 2	Quarter 3	Quarter 4	Totals
Product Line Alpha					
Revenue	$210,000	$311,850	$370,000	$457,250	$1,349,100
Materials expense	108,400	108,400	113,400	155,216	485,416
Contribution Margin $$	$101,600	$203,450	$256,600	$302,034	$863,684
Contribution Margin %	48%	65%	69%	66%	64%
Product Line Beta					
Revenue	$1,048,000	$1,057,000	$1,061,000	$1,053,000	$4,219,000
Materials expense	12,000	14,000	15,000	13,250	54,250
Contribution Margin $$	$1,036,000	$1,043,000	$1,046,000	$1,039,750	$4,164,750
Contribution Margin %	99%	99%	99%	99%	99%
Revenue—Product Line Charlie					
Revenue	$563,000	$544,000	$562,000	$562,000	$2,231,000
Materials expense	$268,000	$200,000	$220,000	$230,000	$918,000
Contribution Margin $$	$295,000	$344,000	$342,000	$332,000	$1,313,000
Contribution Margin %	52%	63%	61%	59%	59%
Total Contribution Margin $$	$1,432,600	$1,590,450	$1,644,600	$1,673,784	$6,341,434
Total Contribution Margin %	79%	83%	83%	81%	81%
Direct Labor Expense	$125,702	$124,985	$140,441	$143,215	$534,343
Overhead Expense	$601,825	$549,200	$585,450	$592,825	$2,329,300
Total Gross Margin $$	$705,073	$916,265	$918,709	$937,744	$3,477,791
Total Gross Margin %	39%	48%	46%	45%	44%
Statistics:					
Number of Production Staff*	23	22	22	23	
Average Annual Revenue per Production Employee	$316,696	$347,791	$362,364	$360,391	

*Not including general assembly staff.

Exhibit 10.7   Cost of Goods Sold Budget

expenses at the top of the budget, because this accounts for all of the departmental costs. However, this format brings up a confidentiality issue, because the compensation of each salesperson can be inferred from the report. Also, this format would include the commission expense paid to each salesperson; commissions are a variable cost that is directly associated with each incremental dollar of sales, so they should be itemized as a separate line item within the cost of goods sold.

A final option listed at the bottom of the example is to itemize expenses by sales region. This format works best when there are a number of sales personnel within the department who are clustered into a number of clearly identifiable regions. If there were no obvious regions or if there were only one salesperson per region, then the better format would be to list expenses by salesperson.

```
SALES DEPARTMENT BUDGET FOR THE FISCAL YEAR ENDED XX/XX/08
```

	Quarter 1	Quarter 2	Quarter 3	Quarter 4	Totals
Departmental Overhead					
Depreciation	$500	$500	$500	$500	$2,000
Office supplies	$750	$600	$650	$600	$2,600
Payroll taxes	$2,945	$5,240	$5,240	$8,186	$21,611
Salaries	$38,500	$68,500	$68,500	$107,000	$282,500
Travel and entertainment	$1,500	$1,500	$1,500	$2,000	$6,500
Expense subtotal	$44,195	$76,340	$76,390	$118,286	$315,211
Product Line Alpha	$32,000	$18,000	$0	$21,000	$71,000
Expenses by Salesperson					
Jones, Milbert	$14,000	$16,500	$17,000	$12,000	$59,500
Smidley, Jefferson	$1,000	$9,000	$8,000	$12,000	$30,000
Verity, Jonas	$7,000	$9,000	$14,000	$12,000	$42,000
Expense subtotal	$22,000	$34,500	$39,000	$36,000	$131,500
Expenses by Region					
East Coast	$52,000	$71,000	$15,000	$0	$138,000
Midwest	$8,000	$14,000	$6,000	$12,000	$40,000
West Coast	$11,000	$10,000	$12,000	$24,000	$57,000
Expense subtotal	$71,000	$95,000	$33,000	$36,000	$235,000
Expense grand total	$137,195	$205,840	$148,390	$190,286	$681,711
Statistics					
Revenue per salesperson	$607,000	$637,617	$664,333	$690,750	$2,599,700
T&E per salesperson	$500	$500	$500	$667	$2,167

Exhibit 10.8 Sales Department Budget

At the bottom of the budget is the usual statistics section. The sales department budget is only concerned with making sales, so it should be no surprise that revenue per salesperson is the first item listed. Also, as the primary sales cost associated with this department is usually travel costs, the other statistical item is the travel and entertainment cost per person.

Exhibit 10.9 shows a sample marketing budget. As was the case for the sales department, this one also itemizes departmental overhead costs at the top, which leaves space in the middle for the itemization of campaign-specific costs in the middle. The campaign-specific costs can be lumped together for individual product lines, as is the case for product lines Alpha and Beta in the exhibit, or with subsidiary line items, as is shown for product line Charlie. A third possible format, which is to itemize marketing costs by marketing tool (e.g., advertising, promotional tour, or coupon redemption) is generally not recommended if there is more than one product line, because there is no way for an analyst to determine the impact of individual marketing costs on specific product lines. The statistics at the bottom of the page attempt to compare marketing costs to sales; however, this should only be treated as an approximation; marketing efforts will usually not result in immediate sales,

```
            MARKETING BUDGET FOR THE FISCAL YEAR ENDED XX/XX/08

                         Quarter 1   Quarter 2   Quarter 3   Quarter 4    Totals

Departmental Overhead
  Depreciation               650         750         850       1,000       3,250
  Office supplies            200         200         200         200         800
  Payroll taxes            4,265       4,265       4,265       4,265      17,060
  Salaries               $55,750     $55,750     $55,750     $55,750     223,000
  Travel and entertainment 5,000       6,500       7,250       7,250      26,000
    Expense subtotal      65,865      67,465      68,315      68,465     270,110

Campaign-Specific Expenses
  Product Line Alpha      14,000      26,000      30,000           0      70,000
  Product Line Beta       18,000           0           0      24,000      42,000
  Product Line Charlie                                                         0
   Advertising            10,000           0      20,000           0      30,000
   Promotional tour        5,000      25,000       2,000           0      32,000
   Coupon redemption       2,000       4,000       4,500       1,200      11,700
   Product samples         2,750       5,250       1,250           0       9,250
    Expense subtotal      51,750      60,250      57,750      25,200     194,950


  Expense grand total    117,615     127,715     126,065      93,665     465,060

Statistics
  Expense as percent of total sales  6.5%    6.7%      6.3%       4.5%       6.0%
  Expense proportion by quarter     25.3%   27.5%     27.1%      20.1%     100.0%
```

Exhibit 10.9   Marketing Budget

but rather will result in sales that build over time. Thus, there is a time lag after incurring a marketing cost that makes it difficult to determine the efficacy of marketing activities.

A sample general and administrative budget is shown in Exhibit 10.10. This budget can be quite lengthy, including such additional line items as postage, copier leases, and office repair. Many of these extra expenses have been pruned from the exhibit to provide a compressed view of the general format to be used. The exhibit does not lump together the costs of the various departments that are typically included in this budget, but rather identifies each one in separate blocks; this format is most useful when there are separate managers for the accounting and human resources functions so that they will have a better understanding of their budgets. The statistics section at the bottom of the page itemizes a benchmark target of the total general and administrative cost as a proportion of revenue. This is a particularly useful statistic to track, because the general and administrative function is a cost center and requires such a comparison to inform management that these costs are being held in check.

A staffing budget is shown in Exhibit 10.11. This itemizes the expected headcount in every department by major job category. It does not attempt to identify individual positions, which could lead to an excessively lengthy list. Also, because there may be multiple positions identified within each job category, the *average* salary for each cluster of jobs is identified. If a position is subject to overtime pay, its expected overtime percentage

GENERAL AND ADMINISTRATIVE BUDGET FOR THE FISCAL YEAR ENDED XX/XX/08						
	Quarter 1	Quarter 2	Quarter 3	Quarter 4	Totals	Notes
Accounting Department						
Depreciation	4,000	4,000	4,250	4,250	16,500	
Office supplies	650	650	750	750	2,800	
Payroll taxes	4,973	4,973	4,973	4,973	19,890	
Salaries	$65,000	$65,000	$65,000	$65,000	260,000	
Training	500	2,500	7,500	0	10,500	
Travel and entertainment	0	750	4,500	500	5,750	
Expense subtotal	75,123	77,873	86,973	75,473	315,440	
Corporate Expenses						
Depreciation	450	500	550	600	2,100	
Office supplies	1,000	850	750	1,250	3,850	
Payroll taxes	6,598	6,598	6,598	6,598	26,393	
Salaries	$86,250	$86,250	$86,250	$86,250	345,000	
Insurance, business	4,500	4,500	4,500	4,500	18,000	
Training	5,000	0	0	0	5,000	
Travel and entertainment	2,000	500	500	0	3,000	
Expense subtotal	105,798	99,198	99,148	99,198	403,343	
Human Resources Department						
Benefits programs	7,284	7,651	7,972	8,289	31,196	**0.4%**
Depreciation	500	500	500	500	2,000	
Office supplies	450	8,000	450	450	9,350	
Payroll taxes	2,869	2,869	2,869	2,869	11,475	
Salaries	$37,500	$37,500	$37,500	$37,500	150,000	
Training	5,000	0	7,500	0	12,500	
Travel and entertainment	2,000	1,000	3,500	1,000	7,500	
Expense subtotal	55,603	57,520	60,291	50,608	224,021	
Expense grand total	236,523	234,591	246,411	225,278	942,804	
Statistics						
Expense as proportion of revenue	13.0%	12.3%	12.4%	10.9%	12.1%	
Benchmark comparison	11.5%	11.5%	11.5%	11.5%	11.5%	

Exhibit 10.10   General and Administrative Budget

is identified on the right side of the budget. Many sections of the budget should have linkages to this page so that any changes in headcount here will be automatically reflected in the other sections. This budget may have to be restricted from general access, for it contains salary information that may be considered confidential.

The facilities budget tends to have the largest number of expense line items. A sample of this format is shown in Exhibit 10.12. These expenses may be offset by some rental or sublease revenues if a portion of the company facilities is rented out to other organizations. However, this revenue is only shown in this budget if the revenue amount is small; otherwise, it is more commonly found as an "other revenue" line item on the revenue

```
          STAFFING BUDGET FOR THE FISCAL YEAR ENDED XX/XX/08
```

	Quarter 1	Quarter 2	Quarter 3	Quarter 4	Average Salary	Overtime Percent
Sales Department						
Regional Sales Manager	1	2	2	3	$120,000	0%
Salesperson	2	4	4	6	$65,000	0%
Sales Support Staff	1	1	1	2	$34,000	6%
Marketing Department						
Marketing Manager	1	1	1	1	$85,000	0%
Marketing Researcher	2	2	2	2	$52,000	0%
Secretary	1	1	1	1	$34,000	6%
General and Administrative						
President	1	1	1	1	$175,000	0%
Chief Operating Officer	1	1	1	1	$125,000	0%
Chief Financial Officer	1	1	1	1	$100,000	0%
Human Resources manager	1	1	1	1	$80,000	0%
Accounting Staff	4	4	4	4	$40,000	10%
Human Resources Staff	2	2	2	2	$35,000	8%
Executive Secretary	1	1	1	1	$45,000	6%
Research Department						
Chief Scientist	1	1	1	1	$100,000	0%
Senior Engineer Staff	3	3	3	4	$80,000	0%
Junior Engineer Staff	3	3	3	3	$60,000	0%
Overhead Budget						
Production Manager	1	1	1	1	$65,000	0%
Quality Manager	1	1	1	1	$55,000	0%
Materials Manager	1	1	1	1	$75,000	0%
Production Scheduler	1	1	1	1	$45,000	0%
Quality Assurance Staff	2	2	2	3	$32,500	8%
Purchasing Staff	3	2	2	2	$37,500	8%
Materials Management Staff	4	5	5	5	$28,000	8%
Total headcount	39	42	42	48		

Exhibit 10.11   Staffing Budget

budget. A statistics section is found at the bottom of this budget, which refers to the total amount of square feet occupied by the facility. A very effective statistic is the amount of unused square footage, which can be used to conduct an ongoing program of selling off, renting, or consolidating company facilities.

The research department's budget is shown in Exhibit 10.13. It is most common to segregate the department-specific overhead that cannot be attributed to a specific project at the top of the budget, and then cluster costs by project below that. By doing so, the management team can see precisely how much money is being allocated to each project. This may be of use in determining which projects must be cancelled or delayed as part of the budget review process. The statistics section at the bottom of the budget notes

FACILITIES BUDGET FOR THE FISCAL YEAR ENDED XX/XX/08

	Quarter 1	Quarter 2	Quarter 3	Quarter 4	Totals
Facilty Expenses					
Contracted services	$ 5,500	$ 5,400	$ 5,000	$ 4,500	$ 20,400
Depreciation	29,000	29,000	28,000	28,000	114,000
Electricity charges	4,500	3,500	3,500	4,500	16,000
Inspection fees	500	0	0	500	1,000
Insurance	8,000	0	0	0	8,000
Maintenance supplies	3,000	3,000	3,000	3,000	12,000
Payroll taxes	1,148	1,148	1,148	1,186	4,628
Property taxes	0	5,000	0	0	5,000
Repairs	15,000	0	29,000	0	44,000
Sewage charges	250	250	250	250	1,000
Trash disposal	3,000	3,000	3,000	3,000	12,000
Wages—Janitorial	5,000	5,000	5,000	5,500	20,500
Wages—Maintenance	10,000	10,000	10,000	10,000	40,000
Water charges	1,000	1,000	1,000	1,000	4,000
Expense grand total	$85,898	$66,298	$88,898	$61,436	$302,528
Statistics					
Total square feet	52,000	52,000	78,000	78,000	
Square feet/Employee	839	813	1,219	1,099	
Unused square footage	1,200	1,200	12,500	12,500	

Exhibit 10.12 Facilities Budget

the proportion of planned expenses between the categories of overhead, research, and development. These proportions can be examined to see if the company is allocating funds to the right balance of projects that most effectively meets it product development goals.

The capital budget is shown in Exhibit 10.14. This format clusters capital expenditures by a number of categories. For example, the first category, entitled "budget-related expenditures," clearly focuses attention on those outgoing payments that will increase the company's key productive capacity. The payments in the third quarter under this heading are directly related to the increase in bottleneck capacity that was shown the production budget (Exhibit 10.3) for the fourth quarter. The budget also contains an automatic assumption of $7,000 in capital expenditures for any net increase in nondirect labor headcount, which encompasses the cost of computer equipment and office furniture for each person. If the company's capitalization limit is set too high to list these expenditures on the capital budget, then a similar line item should be inserted into the general and administrative budget so that the expense can be recognized under the office supplies or some similar account.

The capital budget also includes a category for profit-related expenditures. Any projects listed in this category should be subject to an intensive expenditure review, using cash flow discounting techniques to ensure that they return a sufficient cash flow to make their acquisition profitable to the company. Other categories in the budget cover expenditures for safety or required items, which tend to be purchased with no cash flow discounting review. An alternative to this grouping system is to only list the sum total of all capital expenditures in each category, which is most frequently used when there are far too

RESEARCH DEPARTMENT FOR THE FISCAL YEAR ENDED XX/XX/08

	Quarter 1	Quarter 2	Quarter 3	Quarter 4	Totals
Departmental Overhead					
Depreciation	$ 500	$ 500	$ 400	$ 400	1,800
Office supplies	750	2,000	1,500	1,250	5,500
Payroll taxes	9,945	9,945	9,945	11,475	41,310
Salaries	130,000	130,000	130,000	150,000	540,000
Travel and entertainment	0	0	0	0	0
Expense subtotal	$141,195	$142,445	$141,845	$163,125	$588,610
Research—Specific Expenses					
Gamma Project	$20,000	$43,500	$35,000	$12,500	$111,000
Omega Project	5,000	6,000	7,500	9,000	27,500
Pi Project	14,000	7,000	7,500	4,500	33,000
Upsilon Project	500	2,500	5,000	0	8,000
Expense subtotal	$39,500	$59,000	$55,000	$26,000	$179,500
Development—Specific Expenses					
Latin Project	$ 28,000	$ 29,000	$ 30,000	$ 15,000	$ 102,000
Greek Project	14,000	14,500	15,000	7,500	51,000
Mabinogian Project	20,000	25,000	15,000	10,000	70,000
Old English Project	6,250	12,500	25,000	50,000	93,750
Expense subtotal	$ 68,250	$ 81,000	$ 85,000	$ 82,500	$ 316,750
Expense grand total	$248,945	$282,445	$281,845	$271,625	$1,084,860
Statistics					
Budgeted number of patent applications filed	2	0	1	1	4
Proportion of expenses:					
Overhead	56.7%	50.4%	50.3%	60.1%	217.5%
Research	15.9%	20.9%	19.5%	9.6%	65.8%
Development	27.4%	28.7%	30.2%	30.4%	116.6%
Total Expenses	100.0%	100.0%	100.0%	100.0%	400.0%

Exhibit 10.13 Research Department Budget

many separate purchases to list on the budget. Another variation is to only list the largest expenditures on separate budget lines, and cluster together all smaller ones. The level of capital purchasing activity will determine the type of format used.

All of the preceding budgets roll up into the budgeted income and cash flow statement, which is noted in Exhibit 10.15. This format lists the grand totals from each preceding pages of the budget to arrive at a profit or loss for each budget quarter. In the example, we see that a large initial loss in the first quarter is gradually offset by smaller gains in later quarters to arrive at a small profit for the year. However, the presentation continues with a cash flow statement that has less positive results. It begins with the net profit figure for each quarter, adds back the depreciation expense for all departments, and subtracts out all planned capital expenditures from the capital budget to arrive at cash flow needs for

CAPITAL BUDGET FOR THE FISCAL YEAR ENDED XX/XX/08

	Quarter 1	Quarter 2	Quarter 3	Quarter 4	Totals
Bottleneck-Related Expeditures					
Stamping machine			$150,000		$150,000
Facility for Machine			$72,000		$72,000
Headcount-Related Expenditures					
Headcount change × $7,000					
added staff	$0	$21,000	$0	$42,000	$63,000
Profit-Related Expenditures					
Blending machine		$50,000			$50,000
Polishing machine		$27,000			$27,000
Safety-Related Expenditures					
Machine shielding		$3,000	$3,000		$6,000
Handicapped walkways	$8,000	$5,000			$13,000
Required Expenditures					
Clean air scrubber			$42,000		$42,000
Other Expenditures					
Tool crib expansion				$18,500	$18,500
Total expenditures	$8,000	$106,000	$267,000	$60,500	$441,500

Exhibit 10.14 Capital Budget

the year. This tells us that the company will experience a maximum cash shortfall in the third quarter. This format can be made more precise by adding in time lag factors for the payment of accounts payable and the collection of accounts receivable.

The final document in the budget is an itemization of the finances needed to ensure that the rest of the budget can be achieved. An example is shown in Exhibit 10.16, which carries forward the final cash position at the end of each quarter that was the product of the preceding cash flow statement. This line shows that there will be a maximum shortfall of $223,727 by the end of the third quarter. The next section of the budget outlines several possible options for obtaining the required funds (which are rounded up to $225,000)—debt, preferred stock, or common stock. The financing cost of each one is noted in the far right column, where we see that the interest cost on debt is 9.5%, the dividend on preferred stock is 8%, and the expected return by common stockholders is 18%.

The third section on the page lists the existing capital structure, its cost, and the net cost of capital. This is quite important, for anyone reviewing this document can see what impact the financing options will have on the capital structure if any of them are selected. For example, the management team may prefer the low cost of debt, but can also use the existing capital structure presentation to see that this will result in a very high proportion of debt to equity, which increases the risk that the company cannot afford to repay the debt to the lender.

The fourth and final part of the budget calculates any changes in the cost of capital that will arise if any of the three financing options are selected. A footnote points out the incremental corporate tax rate—this is of importance to the calculation of the cost of

INCOME AND CASH FLOW STATEMENT FOR THE FISCAL YEAR ENDED XX/XX/08

	Quarter 1	Quarter 2	Quarter 3	Quarter 4	Totals
Revenue	$1,821,000	$1,912,050	$1,993,000	$2,072,250	$7,799,100
Cost of Goods Sold					
Materials	$388,400	$322,400	$348,400	$398,466	$1,457,666
Direct Labor	125,702	124,985	140,441	143,215	534,343
Overhead					
Supervision	38,250	38,250	39,750	39,750	156,000
Maintenance Department	365,250	318,750	353,500	347,750	1,385,250
Materials Management	86,125	83,750	83,750	83,750	337,375
Quality Department	35,000	34,500	34,500	42,625	146,625
Other Expenses	77,200	73,950	73,950	78,950	304,050
Total Cost of Goods Sold	$1,115,927	$996,585	$1,074,291	$1,134,506	$4,321,309
Gross Margin	$705,073	$916,265	$918,709	$937,744	$3,477,791
Operating Expenses					
Sales Department	$137,195	$205,840	$148,390	$190,286	$681,711
General and Administrative					
Department					
Accounting	75,123	77,873	86,973	75,473	315,440
Corporate	105,798	99,198	99,148	99,198	403,343
Human Resources	55,603	57,520	60,291	50,608	224,021
Marketing Department	117,615	127,715	126,065	93,665	465,060
Facilities Department	85,898	66,298	88,898	61,436	302,528
Research Department	248,945	282,445	281,845	271,625	1,084,860
Total Operating Expenses	$826,176	$916,888	$891,609	$842,290	$3,476,963
Net Profit (Loss)	−$121,103	−$624	$27,100	$95,455	$828

	Quarter 1	Quarter 2	Quarter 3	Quarter 4	Totals
Cash Flow					
Beginning Cash	$100,000	$20,497	−$34,627	−$223,727	
Net Profit (Loss)	−$121,103	−$624	$27,100	$95,455	$828
Add Depreciation	$49,600	$51,500	$50,800	$51,000	$202,900
Minus Capital Purchases	−$8,000	−$106,000	−$267,000	−$60,500	−$441,500
Ending Cash	$20,497	−$34,627	−$223,727	−$137,772	

Exhibit 10.15   Budgeted Income and Cash Flow Statement

capital, because the interest cost of debt can be deducted as an expense, thereby reducing its net cost. In the exhibit, selecting additional debt as the preferred form of financing will result in a reduction in the cost of capital to 10.7%, whereas a selection of high-cost common stock will result in an increase in the cost of capital to 12.9%. These changes can have an impact on what types of capital projects are accepted in the future, for the cash flows associated with them must be discounted by the cost of capital in order to see if they result in positive cash flows. Accordingly, a reduction in the cost of capital will mean that projects with marginal cash flows will become more acceptable, while the reverse will be true for a higher cost of capital.

```
                 FINANCING BUDGET FOR THE FISCAL YEAR ENDED XX/XX/08

                                                                      Financing
                      Quarter 1   Quarter 2   Quarter 3   Quarter 4     Cost

Cash Position          $20,497    -$34,627   -$223,727   -$137,772

Financing Option One
  Additional Debt                  $225,000                              9.5%

Financing Option Two
  Additional Preferred Stock  $225,000                                   8.0%

Financing Option Three
  Additional Common Stock   $225,000                                    18.0%

Existing Capital Structure
  Debt                      $400,000                                     9.0%
  Preferred Stock           $150,000                                     7.5%
  Common Stock              $500,000                                    18.0%
    Existing Cost of Capital    11.8%

Revised Cost of Capital
  Financing Option One         10.7%
  Financing Option Two         11.2%
  Financing Option Three       12.9%

Note: Tax rate equals 38%.
```

Exhibit 10.16   Financing Requirements

The budgeting examples shown here can be used as the format for a real-life corporate budget. However, it must be adjusted to include a company's chart of accounts and departmental structure so that it more accurately reflects actual operations. Also, it should include a detailed benefits and payroll tax calculation page, which will itemize the cost of social security taxes, Medicare, unemployment insurance, worker's compensation insurance, medical insurance, and so on. These costs are a substantial part of a company's budget, and yet are commonly lumped together into a simplistic budget model that does not accurately reflect their true cost.

Though the budget model presented here may seem excessively large, it is necessary to provide detailed coverage of all aspects of the corporation so that prospective changes to it can be accurately modeled through the budget. Thus, a detailed format is strongly recommended over a simple, summarized model.

10.4 FLEX BUDGET

One problem with the budget model shown in the last section is that many of the expenses listed in it are directly tied to the revenue level. If the actual revenue incurred is significantly different from the budgeted figure, then so many expenses will also shift in association with the revenue that the comparison of budgeted to actual expenses will not be valid. For example, if budgeted revenues are $1 million and budgeted material costs are $450,000, one would expect a corresponding drop in the actual cost of materials incurred if actual revenues drop to $800,000. A budget-to-actual comparison would then show a significant difference in the cost of materials, which would in turn cause a difference in the gross margin and net profit. This issue also arises for a number of other variable or semivariable expenses, such as salesperson commissions, production supplies, and maintenance costs. Also, if there are really large differences between actual and budgeted revenue levels, other costs that are more fixed in nature will also change, such as the salaries, office supplies, and even facilities maintenance (facilities may be sold off or added to, depending on which direction actual revenues have gone). These represent large step cost changes that will skew actual expenses so far away from the budget that it is difficult to conduct any meaningful comparison between the two.

A good way to resolve this problem is to create a flexible budget, or "flex" budget, that itemizes different expense levels depending on changes in the amount of actual revenue. In its simplest form, the flex budget will use percentages of revenue for certain expenses rather than the usual fixed numbers. This allows for an infinite series of changes in budgeted expenses that are directly tied to revenue volume. However, this approach ignores changes to other costs that do not change in accordance with small revenue variations. Consequently, a more sophisticated format will also incorporate changes to many additional expenses when certain larger revenue changes occur, thereby accounting for step costs. By making these changes to the budget, a company will have a tool for comparing actual to budgeted performance at many levels of activity.

Though the flex budget is a good tool, it can be difficult to formulate and administer. One problem with its formulation is that many costs are not fully variable, instead having a fixed cost component that must be included in the flex budget formula. Another issue is that a great deal of time can be spent developing step costs, which is more time than the typical accounting staff has available, especially when in the midst of creating the standard budget. Consequently, the flex budget tends to include only a small number of step costs, as well as variable costs whose fixed cost components are not fully recognized.

Implementation of the flex budget is also a problem, for very few accounting software packages incorporate any features that allow one to load in multiple versions of a budget that can be used at different revenue levels. Instead, some include the option to store a few additional budgets, which the user can then incorporate into the standard budget-to-actual comparison reports. This option does not yield the full benefits of a flex budget; it only allows for a few changes in expenses based on a small number of revenue changes, rather than a set of expenses that will automatically change in proportion to actual revenue levels incurred. Furthermore, the option to enter several different budgets means that someone must enter this additional information into the accounting software, which can be a considerable chore if the number of budget line items is large. For these reasons, it is more common to see a flex budget incorporated into an electronic spreadsheet, with actual results being manually posted to it from other accounting reports.

10.5 BUDGETING PROCESS

The budgeting process is usually rife with delays, which are caused by several factors. One is that information must be input to the budget model from all parts of the company—some of which may not put a high priority on the submission of budgeting information. Another reason is that the budgeting process is highly iterative, sometimes requiring dozens of budget recalculations and changes in assumptions before the desired results are achieved. The typical budgeting process is represented in Exhibit 10.17, where we see that there is a sequential process that requires the completion of the revenue plan before the production plan can be completed, which in turn must be finished before the departmental expense budgets can be finished, which then yields a financing plan. If the results do not meet expectations, then the process starts over again at the top of the exhibit. This process is so time consuming that the budget may not be completed before the budget period has already begun.

A number of best practices can be used to create a more streamlined budgeting process:

- *Reduce the number of accounts.* The number of accounts included in the budget should be reduced, thereby greatly reducing the amount of time needed to enter and update data in the budget model.

- *Reduce the number of reporting periods.* One can consolidate the 12 months shown in the typical budget into quarterly information, thereby eliminating two-thirds of the information in the budget. If the budget must later be reentered into the accounting system to provide budget-to-actual comparisons, then a simple formula can be used to divide the quarterly budget back into its monthly components—which is still much less work than maintaining 12 full months of budget information.

- *Use percentages for variable cost updates.* When key activities, such as revenues, are changed in the budget model, one must peruse the entire budget to determine what related expenses must change in concert with the key activities. A much easier approach is to use percentage-based calculations for variable costs in the budget model so that these expenses will be updated automatically. They should also be color-coded in the budget model so that they will not be mistaken for items that are manually changed.

- *Report on variables in one place.* A number of key variables will impact the typical budget model, such as the assumed rate of inflation in wages or purchased parts, tax rates for income, payroll, and worker's compensation, and medical insurance rates. These variables are much easier to find if they are set up in a cluster within the budget so that one can easily reference and alter them. Under this arrangement, it is also useful to show key results (such as net profits) on the same page with the variables so that one can make alterations to the variables and immediately see their impact without having to search through the budget model to find the information.

- *Use a budget procedure and timetable.* The budget process is plagued by many iterations; the first results will nearly always yield profits or losses that do not meet a company's expectations. Furthermore, it requires input from all parts of a company, some of which may lag in sending in information in a timely manner. Accordingly, it is best to construct a budgeting procedure that specifically identifies what job positions must send budgeting information to the budget coordinator, what information is required of each person, and when that information is due. Furthermore, there should be a clear timetable of events that is carefully

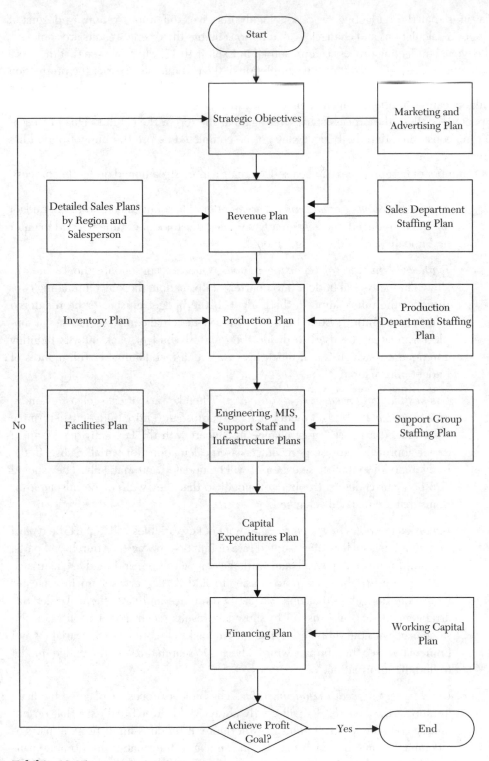

Exhibit 10.17   Traditional Budgeting Process

adhered to so that plenty of time is left at the end of the budgeting process for the calculation of multiple iterations of the budget.

In addition to these efficiency-improvement issues, the budgeting process can be modified in other ways so that it can be completed much more quickly:

- *Itemize the corporate strategy.* The strategy and related tactical goals that the company is trying to achieve should be listed at the beginning of the budget model. All too frequently, management loses sight of its predetermined strategy when going through the many iterations that are needed to develop a realistic budget. By itemizing the corporate strategy in the budget document, it is much less likely that the final budget model will deviate significantly from the company's strategic direction.

- *Identify step-costing change points.* The budget model should have notations incorporated into it that specify the capacity levels at which expenses are valid. For example, if the production level for Product A exceeds 100,000 per year, then a warning flag should be generated by the budget model that informs the budget manager of the need to add an extra shift to accommodate the increased production requirements. Another example is to have the model generate a warning flag when the average revenue per salesperson exceeds $1 million, because this may be the maximum expectation for sales productivity and will require the addition of more sales personnel to the budget. These flags can be clustered at the front of the budget model so that problems will be readily apparent to the reader.

- *Specify maximum amounts of available funding.* One of the warning flags just noted should include the maximum level of funding that the company can obtain. If an iteration of the budget model results in excessively high cash requirements, then the flag will immediately point out the problem. It may be useful to note next to the warning flag the amount by which the maximum funding has been exceeded so that this information is readily available for the next budget iteration.

- *Base expense changes on cost drivers.* Many expenses in the budget will vary in accordance with changes in various activities within the firm. As noted earlier in this section, expenses can be listed in the budget model as formulas so that they vary in direct proportion to changes in budgeted revenue. This same concept can be taken a step farther by listing other types of activities that drive cost behavior, and linking still other expenses to them with formulas. For example, the amount of telephone expense is directly related to the number of employees, so it can be linked to the total number of employees on the staffing budget. Another example is the number of machine setup personnel, which will change based on the planned number of production batches to be run during the year. This level of automation requires a significant degree of knowledge of how selected expenses interact with various activities within the company.

- *Budget by groups of staff positions.* A budget can rapidly become unwieldy if every position in the company is individually identified, especially if the names of all employees are listed. This format requires constant updating as the budget progresses through multiple iterations. A better approach is to itemize by job title, which allows one to vastly reduce the number of job positions listed in the budget.

- *Rank projects.* A more complex budget model can incorporate a ranking of all capital projects so that any projects with a low ranking will be automatically eliminated by the model if the available amount of cash drops below the point where they could be funded. However, this variation requires that great attention be paid to the ranking of projects, because there may be some interrelationship between projects—if one is dropped but others are retained, the ones retained may not be functional without the missing project.

- *Issue a summary-level model for use by senior management.* The senior management team is primarily concerned with the summary results of each department, product line, or operating division, and does not have time to wade through the details of individual revenue and expense accounts. Further, they may require an increased level of explanation from the budgeting staff if they *do* choose to examine these details. Accordingly, the speed of the iteration process can be enhanced by producing a summary-level budget that is directly linked to the main budget so that all fields in it are updated automatically. The senior management team can more easily review this document, yielding faster updates to the model.

- *Link budget results to employee goal and reward system.* The budgeting process does not end with the final approval of the budget model. Instead, it then passes to the human resources department, which uses it as the foundation for an employee goal and reward system. The trouble is that, if budget approval is delayed, the human resources department will have very little time in which to create its goal and reward system. Accordingly, this add-on project should be incorporated directly into the budget model so that it is approved alongside the rest of the budget. For example, a goals and rewards statement added to the budget can specify a bonus payment to the manager of the production department if he or she can create the number of units of product specified in the production budget. Similarly, the sales manager can receive a bonus based on reaching the sales goals noted in the revenue budget. By inserting the bonus amounts in this page of the budget, the model can automatically link them to the final targets itemized in the plan, requiring minimal further adjustments by the human resources staff.

As a result of these improvements, the budgeting process will change to the format shown in Exhibit 10.18, where the emphasis changes away from many modeling iterations toward the incorporation of a considerable level of automation and streamlining into the structure of the budget model. By following this approach, the budget will require much less manual updating, allowing it to sail through the smaller number of required iterations with much greater speed.

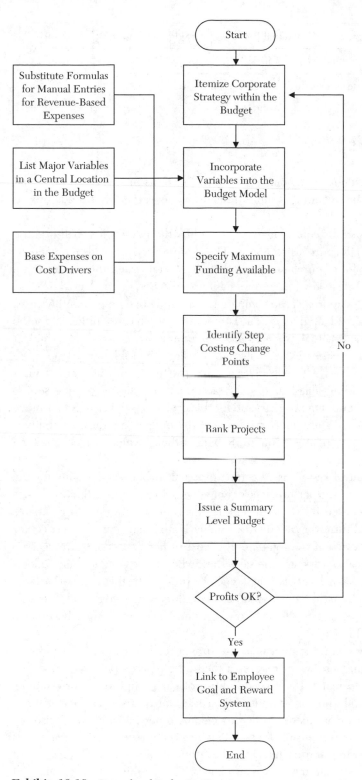

Exhibit 10.18   Streamlined Budgeting Process

Account No.	Description	Actual Results	Budgeted Results	Variance
4500-010	Arizona Revenue	$43,529	$51,000	−$7,471

Exhibit 10.19   Line Item Budget Reporting for Specific Employees

10.6 BUDGETARY CONTROL SYSTEMS

A budget can be used to enhance a company's control systems in several ways so that objectives are met more easily and it is more difficult for costs to stray from approved levels.

One of the best methods for controlling costs is to link the budget for each expense within each department to the purchasing system. The computer system will automatically accumulate the total amount of purchase orders that have been issued thus far against a specific account, and will refuse any further purchase orders when the budgeted expense total has been reached. This approach can compare the monthly budget to monthly costs, or compare costs to annual budgeted totals. The later approach can cause difficulty for the inattentive manager, because actual expenses may be running well ahead of the budget for most of the year, but the system will not automatically flag the problem until the entire year's budget has been depleted. Alternatively, a comparison to monthly budgeted figures may result in so many warning flags on so many accounts that the purchasing staff is unable to purchase many items. One workaround for this problem is to use a fixed overage percentage by which purchases are allowed to exceed the budget; another possibility is to only compare cumulative expenses to quarterly budget totals, which reduces the total number of system warning flags.

Another budgetary control system is to compare actual to budgeted results for the specific purpose of evaluating the performance of employees. For example, the warehouse manager may be judged based on actual inventory turnover of 12×, which compares unfavorably to a budgeted turnover rate of 15×. Similarly, the manager of a cost center may receive a favorable review if the total monthly cost of her cost center averages no more than $152,000. This also works for the sales staff, who can be assigned sales quotas that match the budgeted sales levels for their sales territories. In this manner, a large number of employees can have their compensation levels directly tied to the achievement of budgeted goals. This is a highly effective way to ensure that the budget becomes a fixture in the lives of employees.

Yet another budgetary control system is to use it as a feedback loop to employees. This can be done by issuing a series of reports at the end of each reporting period that are specifically designed to match the responsibilities of each employee. For example, Exhibit 10.19 shows a single revenue line item that is reported to a salesperson for a single territory. The salesperson does not need to see any other detailed comparison to the budget, because he is not responsible for anything besides the specific line item that is reported to him. This reporting approach focuses the attention of many employees on just those segments of the budget that they have control over. Though this approach can result in the creation of dozens or even hundreds of reports by the accounting department, they can be automated on most packaged accounting software systems so that only the initial report creation will take up much accounting time.

An additional control use for the budget is to detect fraud. The budget is usually based upon several years of actual operating results, so unless there are major changes in activity levels, actual expense results should be fairly close to budgeted expectations. If not, variance analysis is frequently used to find out what happened. This process is an excellent means for discovering fraud, as the resulting variance analysis will detect a sudden surge in expense levels. The two instances in which this control will not work is when the fraud has been in existence for a long time (and so is incorporated into the budgeted expense numbers already) or the amount of fraud is so low that it will not create a variance large enough to warrant investigation.

Chapter 11

PROPERTY ACCOUNTING MANUAL

11.1 INTRODUCTION

The weakest documentation area in many organizations is the description of various types of property. Though this may not be considered a significant issue in some service organizations that are oriented toward human capital, many other types of entities have invested a large amount of capital in land, buildings, equipment, vehicles, and leasehold improvements. In the later case, it is extremely important to maintain a high level of record accuracy so that company management maintains proper control over its investment. Good record keeping in this area is also necessary for audit reviews, cost accounting allocations, insurance claims, and warranty tracking.

This chapter is oriented toward a large number of examples of property tracking forms, which include project cost sheets, land records, land improvement records, building records, equipment records, vehicle records, leasehold improvement records, and lease records. The formats shown can be expanded to included additional information required by individual organizations.

Property accounting should be assigned to a senior accountant who will be responsible for updating and maintaining the records. This person should have a descriptive title, such as Physical Property Manager, Fixed Asset Accounting Manager, or (as used herein) Property Accounting Manager.

The amount of record keeping recommended in this chapter may appear voluminous, but it is necessary to maintain sufficient information about the warranties, maintenance, vendor contact information, and other items about each asset. However, one can reduce the amount of record keeping by using a relatively high capitalization limit, below which assets are immediately charged to expense rather than being recorded as an asset.

Depreciation records used to be manually calculated for each of the records noted in this chapter, and stored with them. However, the advent of inexpensive computerized depreciation software has rendered this approach inefficient. Instead, one should record all depreciable asset information in a central database, from which depreciation calculations can be easily made.

11.2 PROJECT COST REPORT

If any capital assets are acquired or constructed that need additional work, one should use the Project Cost Sheet, noted later under retrieval number 2-520, to accumulate the changes. To complete the form for each asset, enter the descriptive heading information such as the name of the project or asset, assigned project number with a prefix letter to indicate the asset category (e.g., **L**and, **B**uilding, **F**actory, **E**quipment), the balance sheet account where the item will be recorded, and a brief description of the project. Additional information recorded on the form should include:

- Date project initiated
- Budget approval amount
- Asset serial number
- Materials used, including description, supplier, and cost
- Labor used, including date incurred and cost
- Contractors, including date incurred and cost
- Date of project completion
- Account number to which accumulated costs were transferred
- Summary totals for all cost categories

11.3 RECORD KEEPING FOR LAND PROJECTS

Maintain a record of the purchase price of land, including tax stamps, recording fees, surveys, title insurance, and any state fees. However, this should not include property taxes or the cost of land improvements (see the next section). Information about each land purchase should be maintained on a separate property accounting record, noted later under retrieval number 2-530, which should contain:

- General description of the land site
- Purchase cost
- Postal address of the location

- Township (if in a Western state) and county location

- Approximate size

- Legal description

- Zoning classification, such as residential single or multiple unit, commercial retail, or light or heavy industry

- Easements for electricity, water, sewers, or gas lines

- Use restrictions

- Year of valuation and assessed value

11.4   RECORD KEEPING FOR LAND IMPROVEMENT PROJECTS

Land improvements are depreciable. Examples of land improvements are fences and gates, parking lots, roads, sewage ponds, and signs. Information about each land improvement should be maintained on a separate property accounting record, noted later under retrieval number 2-540, which should contain:

- General description

- Purchase cost

- Date put into use

- Approximate size

- Construction materials used

- Useful life

- Assessed valuation

In the category of "Construction materials used," the description for fences and gates should note whether they are constructed of wood, brick, or chain link. For roads or parking lots, the description should note the use of gravel, asphalt, or concrete.

11.5   RECORD KEEPING FOR BUILDING PROJECTS

A record of each company-owned building should be maintained. Use a sufficiently high capitalization limit to ensure that small additions, such as a small wall or shed attachment, do not become part of the building asset. Each building should have a name or number for reference purposes.

Information about each building should be maintained on a separate property accounting record, noted later under retrieval number 2-550, which should contain:

- Building name or number

- General description

- Type of construction

- Intended use

- Cost, date put into use, and useful life

- Approximate size

- Assessed valuation

11.6 RECORD KEEPING FOR FACTORY EQUIPMENT PROJECTS

In a manufacturing environment, the factory equipment is the largest-dollar asset category and therefore requires special attention, especially in regard to asset warranty information that may be used.

Information about each piece of factory equipment should be maintained on a separate property accounting record, noted later under retrieval number 2-560, which should contain:

- General description

- Purpose of the equipment

- Fixed or portable equipment designation

- Location by building and room number

- Cost, date put into use, and useful life

- Model and serial number

- Vendor name and address

- Warranty provisions and the period covered

- Property tag number

11.7 RECORD KEEPING FOR OFFICE EQUIPMENT PROJECTS

The increasing uses of technology in the modern office mean that the volume of office equipment can make this the largest asset category, especially in service industries where the entire staff is equipped with computers. Examples of office equipment are personal computers, video presentation equipment, fax machines, and copiers.

Information about each piece of office equipment should be maintained on a separate property accounting record, noted later under retrieval number 2-570, which should contain:

- General description

- Purpose of the equipment

- Fixed or portable equipment designation

- Location by building and room number

- Cost, date put into use, and useful life

- Model and serial number

- Vendor name and address

- Warranty provisions and the period covered

- Property tag number

11.8   RECORD KEEPING FOR VEHICLES

Anything that is portable and can be ridden upon by a person is a vehicle. Cars, trucks, trailers, motorcycles, boats, airplanes, lift trucks, snowmobiles, riding lawnmowers, and construction equipment are all vehicles.

Information about each vehicle should be maintained on a separate property accounting record, noted later under retrieval number 2-580, which should contain:

- General description

- Serial or vehicle identification number

- Purpose of equipment

- Location where stored

- Cost

- Vendor name and address

- Warranty provisions and period covered

- Property tag number

- Person assigned to

11.9   RECORD KEEPING FOR LEASEHOLD IMPROVEMENTS

Leasehold improvements are additions to leased land and buildings. Examples are storage cabinets, shelves, counters, refrigeration units, drapes, air conditioning, parking lots, roads, signs, fences and gates, or anything else that will be abandoned when the lease contract expires. The amortization of these improvements is recorded over the time period of the lease agreement. If the lease term exceeds the useful life, only calculate depreciation through the useful life of the asset.

Information about each leasehold improvement should be maintained on a separate property accounting record, noted later under retrieval number 2-590, which should contain:

- General description
- Serial number (if available)
- Purpose of improvement
- Location where stored
- Cost, date put into use, and useful life
- Vendor name and address
- Warranty provisions and period covered
- Property tag number
- Lease record number

11.10 RECORD KEEPING FOR LEASES

Maintain a separate record for each lease entered into by the organization. All leasehold improvements recorded elsewhere are tied to these lease records by the item number of the lease. If the company is required to have annual financial statements prepared by a certified public accountant, the lease information is needed for a footnote disclosure in the financial statements, itemizing the future lease payments for each of the following five years.

Information about each lease should be maintained on a separate property accounting record, noted later under retrieval number 2 600, which should contain:

- Description of the leased property
- Serial number (if available)
- Location of property
- Name and address of lessor
- Beginning and ending dates of the lease
- Lease amount
- Required maintenance by the lessee
- Lease renewal provisions
- Termination provisions

11.11 SAMPLE PROPERTY ACCOUNTING MANUAL

The remaining pages of this chapter contain a sample property accounting policy and procedure manual.

PROPERTY ACCOUNTING
POLICY/PROCEDURE MANUAL
COMPANY NAME

Distribution: Chief Financial Officer
                                 Controller
                                 Facilities Manager
                                 Tax Manager
                                 Property Accounting Manager

Property Accounting Policy/Procedure	Retrieval No.:	Index
	Page:	1 of 1
	Issue Date:	7/1/0X
Company Name		

Subject: Index

Retrieval Number	Subject
1-010	General Policy and Procedures

Property Accounting Policy/Procedure	Retrieval No.:	1-010
	Page:	1 of 1
	Issue Date:	7/1/0X
Company Name	Supersedes:	

Subject: General Policy and Procedures Policy

The Company will maintain a detailed record of each fixed asset acquired. Current property categories are:

- Land
- Land Improvements
- Buildings
- Factory Equipment
- Office Equipment
- Vehicles
- Leasehold Improvements
- Leased Land, Buildings, and Equipment

The purpose of these records is to:

- Support the recorded cost of fixed assets on the balance sheet.
- Calculate annual depreciation and amortization on these assets.
- Assist the internal and external auditors in their audits.
- Determine if casualty insurance coverage is adequate in case of a catastrophe.
- Determine compliance with lease provisions.
- Compile information for the personal property tax return.
- Take equipment inventories at least annually.

Procedures

Data on all purchases recorded as physical asset properties will be reported to the Property Accounting Manager who will then prepare a record for each item costing over $500, the minimum capitalization amount. The Manager will prepare correcting journal entries if any items under $500 were misclassified. The Manager will review all entries to repair and maintenance accounts to determine that no assets over $500 were misclassified to expense.

The Manager will maintain the Project Cost Sheets for items under construction, modification, or installation.

The Manager will maintain copies of the active records in an off-premise location for insurance purposes in case of a catastrophe such as a fire, explosion, or acts of God.

FORMS MANUAL
PROPERTY ACCOUNTING
COMPANY NAME

Departmental Copy

Normal Distribution
Chief Financial Officer
Controller
Property Accounting Manager
Internal Auditor
External Auditor

Forms Manual		Retrieval No.:	Index
Property Accounting		Page:	1 of 1
		Date:	7/1/0X
Company Name			

Subject: Index

Retrieval Number			Form
2-520	PA—1		Project Cost Sheet
2-530	PA—2		Land Record
2-540	PA—3		Land Improvement Record
2-550	PA—4		Building Record
2-560	PA—5		Factory Equipment Record
2-570	PA—6		Office Equipment Record
2-580	PA—7		Vehicle Record
2-590	PA—8		Leasehold Improvement Record
2-600	PA—9		Lease Record

Forms Manual Property Accounting	Retrieval No.:	2-520
	Page:	1 of 4
	Date:	7/1/0X
Company Name	Supersedes:	
Name of Form: Project Cost Sheet Form Number: PA-1	Date of Last Revision:	

Purpose: To maintain details of costs of land, land improvements, buildings, equipment, and leasehold improvements which require alterations, additions, or installation before being put into use.

Copy	Color	Destination or Distribution of Copies
1.	White	Prepared and maintained by Property Accounting Manager
2.		
3.		
4.		

IS THE FORM PRENUMBERED? _ YES <u>X</u> NO

DEPARTMENT SUPPLYING FORM: Property Accounting

PRINTING SOURCE: C:\WPDATA\PROPERTY\PROJECT.1

DISTRIBUTION OF THIS RELEASE: Normal

INSTRUCTIONS FOR COMPLETING THE "PROJECT COST SHEET"

Front of Form PA-1, enter:

1. Project no.: Enter consecutive project number.
2. Name of project: Describe project such as Building x, Factory Equipment milling machine, and so on.
3. B/S a/c: Enter balance sheet account where this project will be entered.
4. Description of project: Describe what is to be done to complete project.
5. Date initiated: Enter date project began.
6. Budget approval amount: Enter amount budgeted for project, if required.
7. Serial no.: Enter, if available for this item.
8. Materials: For purchased items, enter date received, vendor invoice number, vendor name, description of item, and amount paid, including freight and sales tax, if any.
9. Direct labor: If company labor is used, enter date of payroll, payroll ending date or number, type of work done such as electrical, installation, and so forth, and gross amount of labor on that payroll for this project.
10. Contractors: If any outside contractors are used, for example to install or modify machine, enter date of service, contractor invoice number, description of service, and amount paid.
11. Date project completed: Enter date completed and put into use.
12. Transferred to balance sheet a/c: Enter account number.
13. Summary: Enter the listed totals for materials, direct labor, and contractor services.

Back of Form PA-1:

Same as 8, 9, and 10 above.

When completed, the form is held by Property Accounting.

Retrieval No.:   2-520

Page: 3 of 4

Front of Form PA-1

PROJECT COST SHEET   Project No._____

Name of Project _____   _____ B/S a/c _____

Description of Project _____

Date Initiated _____   Budget approval amount _____   Serial No. _____

Item	Date	Inv. #	Vendor or Payroll	Item or Service	Amount	
Materials						
Direct Labor						
Contractors						

Date Project completed _____

Transferred to Balance Sheet a/c _____

Total Materials

Total Direct Labor

Total Contractors

Total Project

Retrieval No.:   2-520

Page: 4 of 4

Back of Form PA-1

PROJECT COST SHEET				Project No.___		
Item	Date	Inv. #	Vendor or Payroll	Item or Service	Amount	
Materials						
Direct Labor						
Contractors						

Forms Manual			Retrieval No.:	2-530
Property Accounting			Page:	1 of 4
			Date:	7/1/0X
Company Name			Supersedes:	

Name of Form: Land Record
Form Number: PA-2   Date of Last Revision:

Purpose: To record details of land acquisitions.

Copy	Color	Destination or Distribution of Copies
1.	White	Prepared and held by Property Accounting Manager
2.		
3.		
4.		

IS THE FORM PRENUMBERED? _ YES X NO
DEPARTMENT SUPPLYING FORM: Property Accounting
PRINTING SOURCE: C:\WPDATA\PROPERTY\PA2LAND.1
DISTRIBUTION OF THIS RELEASE: Normal

Retrieval No.:   2-530

Page: 2 of 4

INSTRUCTIONS FOR COMPLETING THE "LAND RECORD"

Front of Form PA-2, enter:

Consecutive property number.

1. General description such as factory site, retail stores, and so on
2. Purchase cost which may be allocated portion of purchase price, and date purchased
3. Postal address of this location
4. City, state, and zip code of this address
5. Township and county where this property is located
6. Approximate size of land area
7. Legal description of property as shown by deed or tax bills
8. Zoning classification which may be single residence, multiple residence, commercial retail, light industry, and so on
9. List any easements such as "south 6 feet for utility lines."
10. List any restriction on use such as height of buildings permitted, protected wetlands, type of fence permitted, and so forth.

Back of Form PA-2:

1. Enter year of valuation and assessed valuation for property tax purposes.
2. Enter brief descriptions of land improvements on this property.
3. Enter brief description of buildings on this property.

When completed, the form is held by Property Accounting.

Retrieval No.:   2-530

Page: 3 of 4

Front of Form PA-2

PROPERTY ACCOUNTING – LAND RECORD

                                              Property No: L _____

1. **General Description:**
2. **Cost:**   **Date Purchased:**
3. **Address:**
4. **City, State, Zip Code:**
5. **Township:**   **County:**
6. **Approximate Size:**
7. **Legal Description:**
8. **Zoning Classification:**
9. **Easements:**
10. **Restrictions on use:**
11. **Assessed valuation for property taxes:**
    Form PA-2

Back of Form PA-2

PROPERTY ACCOUNTING – LAND RECORD

                                                    Property No: L _____

1. **Assessed Valuation:**   Year _____   Amount _____
                              Year _____   Amount _____
                              Year _____   Amount _____

2. **Land Improvements:**

3. **Buildings:**

Form PA-2

Forms Manual	Retrieval No.:	2-540
Property Accounting	Page:	1 of 3
	Date:	7/1/0X
Company Name	Supersedes:	
Name of Form: Land Improvement Record		
Form Number: PA-3	Date of Last Revision:	

Purpose: To maintain a detailed record of each land improvement such as fences
  and gates, parking lots, roadways, signs, and other such improvements to the
  land. Buildings are not recorded as land improvements

Copy	Color	Destination or Distribution of Copies
1.	White	Prepared and maintained by Property Accounting Manager
2.		
3.		
4.		

IS THE FORM PRENUMBERED? YES X NO

DEPARTMENT SUPPLYING FORM: Property Accounting

PRINTING SOURCE: C:\WPDATA\PROPERTY\LANDIMF.1

DISTRIBUTION OF THIS RELEASE: Normal

Retrieval No.:	2-540
Page:	2 of 3

COMPLETING THE "LAND IMPROVEMENT RECORD"

Front of Form PA-3, enter:

Consecutive property number.

1. General description such as factory site, retail stores, and so on
2. Purchase cost which may be allocated portion of purchase price or completed project cost
3. Date put in use is date purchased or project completed date
4. Approximate size:
   Fences, height and length
   Roadways, width and length or square feet
   Parking lot, width and length or square feet
   Sign, width and height
5. Construction materials: Describe general materials such as chain link, concrete, wood, asphalt, steel, and so on

When completed, the form is held by Property Accounting.

Retrieval No.:   2-540

Page: 3 of 3

Form PA-3

PROPERTY ACCOUNTING – LAND IMPROVEMENT RECORD

Property No: LI_____

1. **General Description:**
2. **Cost:**
3. **Date Put in Use:**
4. **Approximate Size:**
5. **Construction Materials:**
6. **Useful Life:**
7. **Assessed valuation increase, if applicable (See Land):**

Form PA-3

Forms Manual Property Accounting	Retrieval No.:	2-550
	Page:	1 of 3
	Date.	7/1/0X
Company Name	Supersedes:	
Name of Form: Building Record Form Number: PA-4	Date of Last Revision:	

Purpose: To maintain a detailed record of each building.

Copy	Color	Destination or Distribution of Copies
1.	White	Prepared and maintained by Property Accounting Manager
2.		
3.		
4.		

IS THE FORM PRENUMBERED? _ YES X NO

DEPARTMENT SUPPLYING FORM: Property Accounting

PRINTING SOURCE: C:\WPDATA\PROPERTY\BUILDING.1

DISTRIBUTION OF THIS RELEASE: Normal

Retrieval No.:   2-550

Page: 2 of 3

COMPLETING THE "BUILDING RECORD"

Front of Form PA-4, enter:

Consecutive property number.

1. Building name and/or number as appropriate
2. General description: Purpose, general style of architecture
3. Type of construction: Brick, concrete block, wood, steel, and so on
4. General use of building: Retail stores, factory, office, storage, and so forth
5. Cost: Total cost, excluding land
   Date put in use: Date first occupied or used
   Useful life: Estimated useful life for depreciation purposes
6. Approximate size
   Length and width of main floor
   No. of floors
   Approximate square feet of useable floor space
7. Assessed valuation: Enter date and property taxing authority valuation
   each time it changes

When completed, the form is held by Property Accounting.

Form PA-4

PROPERTY ACCOUNTING – BUILDING RECORD

Property No: B _____

1. **Building Name and/or Number:**
2. **General Description:**
3. **Type of Construction:**
4. **General Use of Building:**
5. **Cost:**   **Date Put in Use:**   **Useful Life:**
6. **Approximate Size: Length:**   **Width:**
               No. of Floors:
               Approximate Square Feet of Floor Space:
7. **Assessed Valuation:**   <u>Year</u>   <u>Valuation</u>
               _____   _____
               _____   _____
               _____   _____

Form PA-4

Forms Manual	Retrieval No.:	2-560
Property Accounting	Page:	1 of 3
	Date:	7/1/0X
Company Name	Supersedes:	
Name of Form: Factory Equipment Record		
Form Number: PA-5	Date of Last Revision:	

Purpose: To maintain a detailed record of each unit of factory equipment,
  whether permanently installed or portable.

Copy	Color	Destination or Distribution of Copies
1.	White	Prepared and maintained by Property Accounting Manager
2.		
3.		
4.		

IS THE FORM PRENUMBERED?. YES <u>X</u> NO
DEPARTMENT SUPPLYING FORM: Property Accounting
PRINTING SOURCE: C:\WPDATA\PROPERTY\FACTORY.1
DISTRIBUTION OF THIS RELEASE: Normal

Retrieval No.:   2-560

Page: 2 of 3

COMPLETING THE "FACTORY EQUIPMENT RECORD"

Front of Form PA-5, enter:

Consecutive property number.

1. General description: Size of machine or equipment
2. Purpose of equipment: Describe general use of equipment
3. Fixed or portable: enter as appropriate
4. Location, building and room: Enter building name or number, and room number or use
5. Cost: Total cost, including installation
   Date put in use: Date first installed or put into use
   Useful life: Estimated useful life for depreciation purposes
6. Model and serial number, if any: Enter appropriate data
7. Vendor name and address: Enter name of company from whom purchased
8. Warranty provisions and period covered: Period of guaranty and any
   exclusions and inclusions
9. Property tag no.: Enter metal or plastic tag placed on equipment
   by Property Accounting.

When completed, the form is held by Property Accounting.

Retrieval No.:   2-560

Page: 3 of 3

Form PA-5

PROPERTY ACCOUNTING – FACTORY EQUIPMENT RECORD

Property No: FE _____

1. **General Description:**
2. **Purpose of Equipment:**
3. **Fixed or Portable:**
4. **Location, Building and Room:**
5. **Cost:**   **Date Put in Use:**   **Useful Life:**
6. **Model and Serial Number:**
7. **Vendor Name and Address:**
8. **Warranty provisions and period covered:**
9. **Property Tag No.**

Form PA-5

Forms Manual	Retrieval No.:	2-570
Property Accounting	Page:	1 of 3
	Date:	7/1/0X
Company Name	Supersedes.	
Name of Form: Office Equipment Record		
Form Number: PA-6	Date of Last Revision:	

Purpose: To maintain a detailed record of each piece of office equipment, whether permanently installed or portable.

Copy	Color	Destination or Distribution of Copies
1.	White	Prepared and maintained by Property Accounting Manager
2.		
3.		
4.		

IS THE FORM PRENUMBERED? _ YES X NO

DEPARTMENT SUPPLYING FORM: Property Accounting

PRINTING SOURCE: C:\WPDATA\PROPERTY\OFFICE.1

DISTRIBUTION OF THIS RELEASE: Normal

Retrieval No.:   2-570

Page: 2 of 3

COMPLETING THE "OFFICE EQUIPMENT RECORD"

Front of Form PA-6, enter:
Consecutive property number.

1. General description: Size of machine or equipment
2. Purpose of equipment: Describe general use of equipment
3. Fixed or Portable: Enter as appropriate.
4. Location, building and room. Enter building name or number, and room number or use
5. Cost: Total cost, including installation
   Date put in use: Date first installed or put into use
   Useful life: Estimated useful life for depreciation purposes
6. Model and serial number, if any: Enter appropriate data
7. Vendor name and address: Enter name of company from whom purchased
8. Warranty provisions and period covered: Period of guaranty and any
   exclusions and inclusions
9. Property tag no.: Enter metal or plastic tag placed on equipment
   by Property Accounting.

When completed, the form is held by Property Accounting.

Form PA-6

PROPERTY ACCOUNTING – OFFICE EQUIPMENT RECORD

                                                     Property No: OE _____

1. General Description:
2. Purpose of Equipment:
3. Fixed or Portable:
4. Location, Building and Room:
5. Cost: Date Put in Use: Useful Life:
6. Model and Serial Number:
7. Vendor Name and Address:
8. Warranty provisions and period covered:
9. Property Tag No.

Form PA-6

Forms Manual			Retrieval No.:	2-580
Property Accounting			Page:	1 of 3
			Date:	7/1/0X
Company Name			Supersedes:	
Name of Form: Vehicle Record				
Form Number: PA-7			Date of Last Revision:	

Purpose: To maintain a detailed record of each Vehicle, including anything that a
    person rides upon except permanent installations such as hoists.

Copy	Color	Destination or Distribution of Copies
1.	White	Prepared and maintained by Property Accounting Manager
2.		
3.		
4.		

IS THE FORM PRENUMBERED? _ YES <u>X</u> NO

DEPARTMENT SUPPLYING FORM: Property Accounting

PRINTING SOURCE: C:\WPDATA\PROPERTY\VEHICLE.1

DISTRIBUTION OF THIS RELEASE: Normal

Retrieval No.:   2-580

Page: 2 of 3

COMPLETING THE "VEHICLE RECORD"

Front of Form PA-7, enter:
Consecutive property number.

1. General description: Make: Enter make such as Ford, Toro, and so on.
   Model: Enter 4-dr or other model description.
   Color: Enter predominant color.
2. Serial or vehicle identification no.: Enter as appropriate.
3. Purpose of equipment: Describe general use of equipment such as
   delivery or snow removal, and so forth.
4. Location where stored: Building name or number and room number, if applicable.
5. Cost: Total cost, including special equipment added
   Date put in use: Date purchased or put into use
   Useful life: Estimated useful life for depreciation purposes
6. Vendor name and address: Enter name of company from whom purchased
7. Warranty provisions and period covered: Period of guaranty and any
   exclusions and inclusions
8. Property tag no.: Enter metal or plastic tag placed on equipment
   by Property Accounting.
9. Person assigned to: Enter name.

When completed, the form is held by Property Accounting.

Retrieval No.:   2-580

Page: 3 of 3

Form PA-7

PROPERTY ACCOUNTING – VEHICLE RECORD

Property No: V _____

1. **General Description:**
   Make:
   Model:
   Color:
2. **Serial or Vehicle Identification No. (VIN):**
3. **Purpose of Equipment:**
4. **Location, where stored or parked:**
5. **Cost:**   **Date Put in Use:**   **Useful Life:**
6. **Vendor Name and Address:**
7. **Warranty provisions and period covered:**
8. **Property Tag No.**
9. **Person assigned to, if appropriate**

Form PA-7

Forms Manual		Retrieval No.:	2-590
Property Accounting		Page:	1 of 3
		Date.	7/1/0X
Company Name		Supersedes.	
Name of Form: Leasehold Improvement Record		Date of Last Revision:	
Form Number: PA-8			

Purpose: To maintain a detailed record of each Leasehold Improvement
   which has a shorter lease life than the useful life.

Copy	Color	Destination or Distribution of Copies
1.	White	Prepared and maintained by Property Accounting Manager
2.		
3.		
4.		

IS THE FORM PRENUMBERED? _ YES X NO

DEPARTMENT SUPPLYING FORM: Property Accounting

PRINTING SOURCE: C:\WPDATA\PROPERTY\LEASEIMP.1

DISTRIBUTION OF THIS RELEASE: Normal

Retrieval No.:   2-590

Page: 2 of 3

COMPLETING THE "LEASEHOLD IMPROVEMENT RECORD"

Front of Form PA-8, enter:

Consecutive property number.

1. General description: Brief description of improvement
2. Serial no.: Enter if appropriate.
3. Purpose of improvement: Describe general use of improvement such as air conditioning, drapes, and so forth.
4. Location where stored: Building name or number and room number, if applicable.
5. Cost: Including special equipment added
   Date put in use: Date purchased or put into use
   Useful life: Estimated useful life for depreciation purposes
6. Vendor name and address: Enter name of company from whom purchased
7. Warranty provisions and period covered: Period of guaranty and any exclusions and inclusions
8. Property tag no.: Enter metal or plastic tag placed on equipment by Property Accounting.
9. Lease record no.: Enter lease number to which this improvement is attached.

When completed, the form is held by Property Accounting.

Form PA 8

PROPERTY ACCOUNTING – LEASEHOLD IMPROVEMENT RECORD

Property No: LSI _____

1. General Description:
     Make:
     Model:
2. Serial No, if applicable:
3. Purpose of Improvement:
4. Location, where installed, Building and Room:
5. Cost: Date Put in Use: Leasehold Life:
6. Vendor Name and Address:
7. Warranty provisions and period covered:
8. Property Tag No.
9. Lease Record No.:

Form PA-8

Forms Manual	Retrieval No.:	2-600
Property Accounting	Page:	1 of 4
	Date:	7/1/0X
Company Name	Supersedes:	
Name of Form: Lease Record		
Form Number: PA-9	Date of Last Revision:	

Purpose: To maintain a record of all leased land and buildings, equipment, and
   vehicles. This information is used to audit rent payments and the
   future lease calculations for the footnote to the financial statements.
   Leasehold Improvements are related to these records by the LE
   number shown on the Lease Record.

Copy	Color	Destination or Distribution of Copies
1.	White	Held by Property Accounting Manager
2.		
3.		
4.		

IS THE FORM PRENUMBERED? _ YES <u>X</u> NO

DEPARTMENT SUPPLYING FORM: Property Accounting

PRINTING SOURCE: C:\WPDATA\PROPERTY\LEASE.1

DISTRIBUTION OF THIS RELEASE: Normal

Retrieval No.:	2-600
Page:	2 of 4

COMPLETING THE "LEASE RECORD"

Front of Form PA-9, enter:

Consecutive property number.

1. Description of property rented: Brief description of land and building, equipment, or vehicle
2. Serial no.: Enter if appropriate.
3. Location of property: Address if land and building, building and room number or area if equipment
4. Name and address of lessor: Enter for communication purposes.
5. Date of lease: Beginning and ending date of lease period
6. Rental amount: Monthly rent and annual rental if different
7. Maintenance by lessee, type and frequency: Any periodic maintenance required by our company should be described
8. Lease renewal or extension provisions: Enter as appropriate.
9. Provision for termination by lessor or lessee: Enter all pertinent provisions.

Back of Form PA-9, enter:

1. Year paid
2. Amount of rent paid for that year

Retrieval No.: 2-600

Page: 3 of 4

Front of Form PA-9

PROPERTY ACCOUNTING – LEASE RECORD

                                              No: LE

1. Description of property rented:
2. Serial Number, if any:
3. Location of Property:
4. Name and Address of Lessor:
5. Dates of Lease: Begin Date   **End Date**
6. Rental Amount: Monthly Rental   **Annual Rental**
7. Maintenance by Lessee, type and frequency:
8. Lease Renewal or Extension provisions:
9. Provision for termination by lessor or lessee:

PA-9

Back of Form PA-9

ANNUAL RENTAL					
Year	Total Rent	Comments	year	Total Rent	Comment

Chapter 12

FORMS MANUAL

12.1 INTRODUCTION

The forms manual is the easiest documentation module to prepare. However, given the absence of a forms specialist, this documentation is rarely completed, and it typically includes forms that reduce the efficiency with which accounting transactions are completed. In this chapter, we will cover the identification of needed forms, review the rules for constructing forms, and describe how to create the forms manual. There is also a brief discussion of ways to eradicate the use of superseded forms from an organization.

12.2 IDENTIFY NEEDED FORMS

The first step in the creation of a forms manual is to complete a forms survey. In a small accounting operation, the controller could probably describe adequately all the forms used in the operation without a forms survey, but a larger organization will contain so many forms that the survey method is mandatory. The survey can be handled by various employees who are familiar with specific forms, or may be done on a consulting basis by one or two experienced people discussing the form with the person most familiar with its use. If a large number of forms are to be surveyed, the consultant method is more efficient.

Exhibit 12.1 shows a form survey worksheet that simplifies the information-gathering process. The survey is generally limited to forms initiated or processed by the accounting department, such as purchase orders, remittance vouchers, and forms for time reporting, payroll deduction authorizations, travel expense reimbursements, inventory moves, sales, and petty cash transactions.

FORM SURVEY   Survey No. _____

Name of Form   _____

Form No. _____ _____ Date of Last Revision _____

Copies and destination or use. Number of parts _____
Copy No.   Color   Destination or Use

   1   _____   _____

   2   _____   _____

   3   _____   _____

   4   _____   _____

   5   _____   _____

Is the form prenumbered?   ____ Yes   ____ No

Source of supply:

   ____ Purchased. Name of printer, if known _____

   ____ Own Print Shop

   ____ From another department? Which? _____

   ____ Other. Describe _____

If retained in Accounting, how is form filed? _____

Estimated quantity used per month _____

Originating Department _____

How is Form completed: ____ Handwritten
                         ____ Typewriter
                         ____ Computer output (Invoice, check, etc.)
                         ____ Terminal device or Personal Computer
                         ____ Other _____

Remarks: _____

_____

_____

                                          Information
Prepared by _____ Date _____ Provided by _____

Attach original or copy of Form

Exhibit 12.1 Form Survey Worksheet

In either case, the requested information is entered on the form survey and an actual form or a copy of it is attached. If possible, a copy of a completed form should be attached to show what information is entered by users. The survey forms should be numbered so they can be located later when writing the forms manual. The survey form is completed as follows:

1. If making a general survey of existing forms, enter a generated survey number, such as "Payroll 1" or "Accounts Payable 3."
2. Enter the form's name, identifying number, and last revision date.
3. Enter the number of copies, their identifying colors, and the use of each one.
4. Indicate if the form is prenumbered.
5. Indicate the supplying vendor.
6. If a copy is retained in the accounting department, note the method of filing, such as alphabetically, numerically, or by date.
7. Estimate the quantity of forms used per year.
8. Note the department that first enters information on the form.
9. Indicate the normal method of preparation, such as handwriting, typing, stamping, or bar coding.
10. Enter the name of the person preparing the survey form and the date on which it is prepared.

12.3 RULES FOR FORM CREATION

As a result of the forms survey, the controller may find that several forms must be rewritten or new forms created. If so, several rules for creating forms can contribute to lower costs, more efficient use, and easier user comprehension:

- *Purpose of the form.* Determine which function within the accounting department will be the primary user, because the data needed by that function will generally determine the form's minimum content. Next, determine whether the form relates to the updating of a master file—such as an employee payroll file, price file, or supplier master file—or whether it is a dollar or quantity accounting transaction form. If the form updates a master file, its layout can be somewhat informal, because the preparer is probably an accountant familiar with the information and how it is used. A transaction form initiated by an outside department typically needs to be more explicit in its content and preparation, due to the user's reduced level of accounting training.

- *Usage of the form.* Determine which department initiates the form and how the data are developed and entered. The answer determines where the working supply of forms will be stored. Follow the form through its various processing steps and indicate by number or letter which person or function enters information in each space. For example, assign a letter to each person or function entering data on the form. The foreman could be "A," the production supervisor "B," the cost accountant "C," and so on. An "A" would then be placed in each space on the form completed by the foreman. Continue this process until every blank space requiring information has been filled.

- *Number of copies and distribution*. Forms are expensive, especially if multipart forms are printed. Retention of a copy implies permanent storage and future reference, both expensive operations. Thus, there must be a strong reason given when a department wants to retain a copy. If information is to be entered manually on a form, the maximum number of copies that may be used is usually four, including the original. Any form of more than four copies must be typewritten or computer printed in order to obtain readable copies.

- *Permanent or interim document*. If the form is to be retained permanently, how will it be filed and how will it be accessed after filing? The answers determine the type and quantity of future storage and the quality of paper and printing used. For example, some photocopies do not retain images well, and will not be legible after a few years.

- *Forms numbering*. Prenumbering a form with consecutive numbers is only done to establish control over them. Printing forms with consecutive numbers is very expensive and should be avoided unless required for reference and control purposes. Be certain of the need for numbering before adding this feature to a form.

- *Form size*. Unless required by the volume of data needed, an accounting form should match the standard paper size of 8 $\frac{1}{2}$ by 11 inches. To avoid extra printing charges, forms smaller than a full-size page should be designed to be cut from regular paper stock sizes. Oversize pages are difficult to file and require more expensive storage cabinets. Very small forms, if retained, may also require special storage trays. Small forms that are attached to other documents tend to become separated in the filing process.

- *Manual or typewritten entry*. If entries are to be typed on the form, all spacing from top to bottom should be in multiples of one-sixth of an inch, which is standard vertical typewriter spacing. If entries are to be handwritten, vertical spacing should be one-quarter to one-third of an inch or multiples thereof. Because most typing is done with elite print of 12 characters to the inch, a grid chart with both horizontal and vertical lines spaced at intervals of one-sixth of an inch is very useful in designing a rough draft of a form for subsequent printing.

- *Data entry form layout*. Entering data from a form to other media is usually done manually via a data entry terminal, though some fields may include a preprinted bar code that can be scanned directly into the terminal. In all cases, the forms should be designed so the needed items are selected in a logical sequence. If the reader's eyes have to jump all over the form to pick up the information for transcription or data entry operations, the form itself is causing significant inefficiency in the transcription of data. This problem leads to fatigue, transcription errors, and even the loss of data. Exhibit 12.2 shows an accounting input document that is difficult to use due to the location of required data fields. If a document is relatively simple, one can add a section that summarizes the information in the proper sequence for the data entry operation. For instance, Exhibit 12.3 shows

PERMISSION TO TRAVEL

Submit at least two weeks prior to date of proposed trip.

①_____, 20_____

TO: President

FROM: _____ Title _____ S. S. No. _____

Request is made for authorization to attend the following convention, association, or meeting:

_____

Complete Name of Convention, Association or Meeting (Do Not Abbreviate)   Place of Meeting

_____

Dates of Meeting   Departmental Name   Departmental Code

Purpose of convention, association, or meeting

Estimated Cost $ _____

I acknowledge that I have read and that I understand the summary of travel policies on the back of this form.

Signature of Applicant _____

Southern Station Box No. _____

1. Chairman _____

2. Vice President _____

3. Funds Available—Accounting _____

4. President _____

FOR ACCOUNTING AND BUSINESS OFFICE USE ONLY

S. S. No.	Encumbered Control No.	P. O. Date
F/GL ②	OBJ ③	DEPT./S. S. No.	AMOUNT ⑤

④

Amount of advance $ _____

I hereby certify that the above trip has been properly approved. The amount advanced will be repaid from reimbursement check for travel expenses, and it is expressly understood and agreed that unless this amount is repaid by me before the next full pay period after the date of my return, it may be deducted from my next salary check.

Signature _____

Date _____

White Copy—Accounting   •   Canary Copy—Employee (For Advance)   •   Pink Copy—File with Voucher   •   Goldenrod Copy—Dept. File Copy

ACC. 1 (Revised 7/81)

Exhibit 12.2   Poorly Designed Input Document

PERMISSION TO TRAVEL

Submit at least two weeks prior to date of proposed trip (90 days prior to foreign travel).

_____ , 20

Name: _____ Title _____ S.S. No. _____

Request is made for authorization to attend the following convention, association, or meeting:

_____   _____

Complete Name of Convention, Association or Meeting (Do Not Abbreviate)   Place of Meeting

_____   _____   _____

Dates of Meeting   Department Name   Department Code

Purpose of convention, association, or meeting (If an advance is needed, but cost of trip will be reimbursed by an outside organization, please explain).

Domestic Travel

Estimated Cost $ _____   1. Chairman _____

I acknowledge that I have read and that I understand the sum-   2. Funds Available—Accounting (5143) _____
mary of travel policies on the back of this form.

Foreign, Hawaii, Alaska Travel

3. Vice President _____

_____   4. President _____

Signature of Applicant

Southern Station Box No. _____

_____

FOR ACCOUNTING AND BUSINESS OFFICE USE ONLY _____

ADVANCE (Cannot exceed estimated cost above)

Amount of advance $ _____ Signature _____ Date _____

I hereby certify that the above trip has been properly approved. The amount advanced will be repaid from reimbursement check for travel expenses, and it is ex-pressly understood and agreed that unless this amount is repaid by me before the next full pay period after the date of my return, it may be deducted from my next salary check.

ACCOUNT RECEIVABLE

Date MMDDYY	F/GL	OBJ	SOCIAL SEC. NO.	AMOUNT	DR
①	② 1014	③ 1169	④	⑤	4

ENCUMBRANCE

P.O. CONTROL	F/GL	OBJ.	DEPARTMENT	SOCIAL SEC. NO.	AMOUNT	DATE MMDDY

White Copy—Accounting • Canary Copy—Employee (For Advance) • Pink Copy—File with Voucher • Goldenrod Copy—Dept. File Copy

ACC 1 (Revised 7/84)

Exhibit 12.3 Input Document Designed for Efficient Data Entry

the same information as Exhibit 12.2, but with the addition of a data entry block. In this real data entry situation, the data entry error rate dropped from 5% to almost zero.

12.4 CREATING THE FORMS MANUAL

Having learned how to collect information about available forms and how to create them, we can now assemble the forms manual. It contains sections that describe the physical characteristics of each form, examples of the forms, and exactly what information should be entered in each field. Also shown are the position titles or department names that are responsible for completing each part of the form. Most forms require three pages in the manual to impart this information. An example of the contents of a three page description is as follows:

Page 1. *Physical description of the form* (Exhibit 12.4). This contains the following information:

- Name of the form being described.

- The identifying number of the form.

- Its last revision date.

- The number of parts, the color of each one, and its destination or use.

- A prenumbering identifier.

- The name of the department that stores blank copies of the form (which is the chief internal source of this document).

- The name of the supplier that prints the form.

- The form's purpose, such as to "request payment of items not requiring a supplier invoice, such as payments for dues, subscriptions, and periodic tax payments."

- The names of the employees, departments, or outside entities to whom the copies are sent. This can include notes on how the forms are delivered, such as by certified mail or an overnight delivery service.

An example of a completed form description is shown in Exhibit 12.5.

Page 2. *Copy of the form with sequential numbers/letters added.* The reference numbers or letters should be in bold print so they are not confused with the form itself. A simple approach is to draw quarter-inch circles in the center of each form field, and then type the identifying numbers or letters within these circles. An example is shown in Exhibit 12.6. It is useful to have the form completion and form pages on facing pages of the manual so that the reader can more readily reference back and forth between a picture of the form and a description of how the form is filled out.

Page 3. *Completing the form.* To complete the description, one must enter sequential numbers or letters in each area of the form requiring data, in the order in which

FORM DESCRIPTION

NAME OF FORM _____

FORM NO. _____ DATE OF LAST REVISION _____

COPY NO.   COLOR   DESTINATION OR USE

   1   _____   _____

   2   _____   _____

   3   _____   _____

   4   _____   _____

   5   _____   _____

IS THE FORM PRENUMBERED? ____ YES ____ NO

DEPARTMENT SUPPLYING FORM:

PRINTING SOURCE:

PURPOSE:

DISTRIBUTION OF THE COPIES:

Exhibit 12.4   Form Description Page in the Forms Manual

```
                            FORM DESCRIPTION

        NAME OF FORM     Multiple-Invoice Voucher

        FORM NO.    ACC 11          DATE OF LAST REVISION     1-01

        COPY NO.          COLOR                  DESTINATION OR USE

           1           White             Accounting

           2           Canary            Vendor

           3           Pink              Department

           4           _____           _____

           5           _____           _____

        IS THE FORM PRENUMBERED?  ____  YES    X   NO

        DEPARTMENT SUPPLYING FORM:  Accounting

        PRINTING SOURCE:  Printing Center

        PURPOSE:

        Used by those departments who handle their own large-volume purchasing such
        as the Bookstore, Library and Food Services.  It is also used by the
        Athletic Department for required medical examination fees and by Accounting
        Services to process partial payments or payments on standing purchase
        orders for the Physical Plant operations.

        The form is identical to the Remittance Voucher form ACC 14 except for the
        description area.

        Supporting documents are to be attached to the accounting copy of the form.




        DISTRIBUTION OF THE COPIES:

        Accounting - Permanent accounts payable file.

        Vendor - Mailed with check.

        Department - Retains and compares to next monthly Budget Report.
```

Exhibit 12.5 Completed Form Description Page in the Forms Manual

MULTIPLE-INVOICE VOUCHER

DEPT NAME	A
ACCT NU	B
TEL NO	C

VENDOR **D**

VENDOR CODE **L**

PURCHASE ORDER NUMBER	INVOICE NUMBER	INVOICE DATE	RECEIVING REPORT NUMBER	INVOICE PRICE	LESS DISCOUNT	NET PRICE
E1	E2	E3	E4	E5	E6	F

REQUESTED BY	DATE	APPROVED BY	DATE	TOTAL	
H		I			G

ACCOUNTING USE		GL	OBJECT	DEPARTMENT	LIQUIDATION	EXPENDITURE
VOUCHER NUMBER	M		J		T	K
VOUCHER DATE	N					
PURCHASE ORDER NUMBER	O					
PROCESSED BY DATE	P					
VERIFIED BY:	Q	SPECIAL CHECK NO. R	ACCOUNTING USE S			

ACC. 11 (REV. 1-83)   WHITE—ACCOUNTING   CANARY—VENDOR   PINK—DEPARTMENT

Exhibit 12.6   Form with Sequential Numbering Added

COMPLETING THE MULTIPLE-INVOICE VOUCHER

Department enters:

A. Department name.
B. Account number.
C. Telephone number of preparer.
D. Name and address of vendor.
E. Description of each invoice to be paid.

    1. Purchase order number assigned to the purchase.
    2. Vendor invoice number.
    3. Invoice date.
    4. Receiving report number.
    5. Total dollar amount of the invoice.
    6. Dollar amount of cash discount permitted by vendor.

F. Amount to be paid. Attach supporting document, if any.
G. Total to be paid on this voucher.
H. Signature of person requesting payment and date signed.
I. Approval signature and date. Payments to individuals require two approval signatures if an invoice is not available.
J. General Ledger Code, Object Code and Department to be charged. If Department is not entered, the charge will be made to the account shown at the top of the form.
K. Amount to be charged to this account. Form provides distribution for up to eight accounts.

Financial Affairs enters:

L. Vendor code number.
M. Voucher number.
N. Voucher date.
O. Purchase Order Number, if any.
P. Name of person processing the voucher and date processed.
Q. Name of person reviewing or verifying information.
R. Preprinted number of special check used to pay voucher.
S. Special handling required or enclosure to be mailed with check.
T. Amount of encumbrance to be liquidated, if any.

Exhibit 12.7 Form Completion Page

the data is entered. This sequence is vital as it permits separating the entries into groups of sequential users. With this numbering in place, once can then create a sequential description of how to fill out the form. An example is shown in Exhibit 12.7, where there is a complete description of the fields previously shown in Exhibit 12.6.

If a form is two-sided, use the same approach, except that two pages are added to show the back page and instructions on how to complete it. The form documentation would consist of the following five pages:

1. Physical description of the form
2. Front of the actual form
3. Instructions for completing the front of the form
4. Back of the actual form
5. Instructions for completing the back of the form

12.5 ELECTRONIC FORMS

A common difficulty for companies of any size is that too many versions of the same form are being used. This can be a major problem if people are using an old form that does not require certain information that is now necessary to complete a transaction. As a result, the recipient of the form must track down the person who completed the old form and have him or her add the extra information. Not only is this a waste of time for the form recipient, but it also increases the time before the transaction represented by the form is completed. Further, the new form may exclude information that was required on the old form, resulting in extra labor by anyone using the old form, because they are adding unnecessary information. In the days before computer systems, it was nearly impossible to eradicate old forms from a company, because each employee kept a "stash" of forms for use whenever needed, which might last for months or years after the forms were superseded.

However, one can use electronic forms to completely eliminate old form versions. This can be done in two ways. One is to program forms right into the computer system so one can enter information directly into the computer database, with no need for any paperwork at all. This is the best approach from the standpoint of avoiding old form versions, but requires the most programming time to accomplish. A simpler, though less effective approach is to store the files for all forms in the computer system, in a location where the majority of employees can access them. Employees then print out the forms, complete them, and submit them in the usual manner. This approach allows any company with a computer network to eliminate any paper files of forms. However, once a form file is printed, an employee may be tempted to retain a paper-based copy rather than go back to the computer network for a new version each time the form is needed; this can still result in caches of old forms scattered throughout an organization. Thus, though it is a simple and easily implemented approach, it is not as effective as the complete elimination of paper forms that can be achieved through the first approach.

No matter which variation is used, a company can achieve a significant improvement in its ability to store and disseminate forms to its employees by using electronic forms.

Chapter 13

DOCUMENT MANAGEMENT MANUAL

13.1 INTRODUCTION

The world has become an increasingly litigious place, so companies require highly organized document management systems that they can rely on to find exactly the right documents when needed to respond to legal and other queries. This document management module walks the user through the document indexing and box labeling process for both regular and permanent file documents, as well as how to identify and store confidential documents, and document the transfer of these documents to and from storage. There is also a procedure for formally documenting the destruction of records, which can be an important issue if the company is accused of eliminating records in an irregular manner. Finally, there is a procedure for documenting the proper layout of the storage area in order to combine the maximization of storage space with the accessibility of records for rapid retrieval.

Policy/Procedure Statement	Retrieval No.:	DOC-01
Brasto Publishing	Page:	1 of 1
	Issue Date:	10/28/0X
	Supersedes:	N/A
Subject: Document Management Overview		

1. **PURPOSE AND SCOPE**

    This document provides an overview of the document management program, as well as the range of related procedures and forms associated with the program.

2. **OVERVIEW**

    The document management program is designed to extract from the current operations staff all documents that it no longer needs to conduct day-to-day business, and transfer these documents into a long-term storage facility that balances cost-effective storage with the need to occasionally transfer documents to requestors for a variety of purposes.

3. **DOCUMENT MANAGER RESPONSIBILITIES**

    The document management program is managed by the Document Manager. This position is responsible for the proper indexing, storage, security, and retrieval of all company documents. Because of the company's need to have proper documentation available in case of a lawsuit, worker claim, product design issue, and so on, this is a key position. The following rules apply to the Document Manager:

    - Ensure that all storage box indexes are correctly applied and that the contents of all storage boxes are verified and documented.
    - Ensure that all permanent file and confidential documents are segregated.
    - Manage all aspects of the document storage area, including proper warehouse layout, risk mitigation, and efficient storage.
    - Ensure that requested documents are promptly retrieved from storage and delivered to requestors, and that these documents are returned to storage within a reasonable time period.
    - Determine restrictions on access to stored documents, as well as the level of approval required to authorize retrieval.
    - Update the document retention policy to match government-mandated storage requirements.
    - Periodically conduct a records inventory throughout the company to ensure that all documents are being properly managed.

4. **DOCUMENT MANAGEMENT POLICIES**

    - *Document Retention*. The document manager shall destroy documents in accordance with the standard retention periods listed in the following table:[1]

TYPE OF RECORD	RETENTION PERIOD
Articles of incorporation	Permanent
Audit report, external	Permanent
Audit report, internal	10 years
Audit work papers, internal	4 years
Bank reconciliation	6 years
Bank statement	6 years
Bond, fidelity	10 years
Budget	5 years
Check, canceled	6 years
Collection notes	While customer is active

[1] Adapted with permission from Bragg Roehl-Anderson, *Controllership* 7 *E*, John Wiley & Sons, New York, 2004, p. 1081.

Contract document	5 years after termination
Cost estimates	5 years
Credit application, customer	While customer is active
Debit/credit memo	5 years
Deposit slip	6 years
E-mail	5 years
Expense reports	5 years
Financial statements	Permanent
Guarantees	5 years after termination
Inventory, count sheet	3 years
Invoice, company	5 years
Invoice, supplier	5 years
Journal entry	7 years
Lease document	5 years after termination
Ledger, general	Permanent
License, business	10 years
Minute book	Permanent
Note payable/receivable	5 years after termination
Overhead allocation calculations	5 years
Proxy statement	5 years
Purchase order	5 years
Receiving record	5 years
Report, to shareholders	Permanent
Royalty calculations	5 years

- *Local Storage.* The document manager shall balance the need for low-cost long-term document storage with employees' need to obtain rapid access to selected documents. This may result in a smaller, high cost storage area adjacent to operating areas that is used to retain frequently accessed items.
- *E-Mail Storage.* The company shall retain e-mail records in a central repository that is directly linked to the e-mail server, with automated daily backups.
- *Electronic Data Migration.* Records stored electronically shall be periodically migrated to new storage media to avoid the obsolescence of media currently used as a repository for the records.

5. PROCEDURES
- The following procedures apply to the document management program:

RETRIEVAL NO.	PROCEDURE NAME	DESCRIPTION
DOC-02	Storage Box Indexing	Used to create index labels and update the index database for boxes of temporary and permanent documents being sent into long-term storage.
DOC-03	Confidential Document Storage	Used to determine which documents are considered confidential and how they are to be stored.
DOC-04	Document Transfer to Storage	Used to verify the contents of storage boxes and organize the boxes for storage.

DOC-05	Document Retrieval from Storage	Used to request the transfer of selected files from long-term storage, log them out of storage, move them to the requesting employee, and verify the status of withdrawn documents.
DOC-06	Document Destruction	Used to ensure that documents are destroyed in accordance with the company document retention policy.
DOC-07	Storage Area Layout	Used to properly plan all aspects of the records storage area, including layout, maximization of storage space, record segregation, security, control systems, and insurance.

Document Management Overview

Policy/Procedure Statement	**Retrieval No.:**	**DOC-02**
	Page:	1 of 1
Brasto Publishing	Issue Date:	10/28/0X
	Supersedes:	N/A
Subject: Storage Box Indexing		

1.   PURPOSE AND SCOPE

This procedure is used by company employees to create index labels and update the index database for boxes of both temporary and permanent documents being sent into long-term storage.

2.   RESPONSIBILITIES

DOC MGR   **Document Manager**

3.   PROCEDURES

3.1   DOC MGR   **Labeling of Indexes on Storage Boxes**

1. When loading documents into each storage box, set aside permanent files that cannot be destroyed; these documents are to be stored separately.
2. Sort all remaining documents in alphabetical order and load them into the storage box. Remove all hanging Pendaflex folders at this time, so no metal hangers project over the edge of the box.
3. On the label end of the box, list the document year and the year in which the documents are to be destroyed. For example, for 2005 documents with an intended destruction interval of seven years, the label would read:

| Year: | 2005 |
| Destroy: | 2012 |

4. Just below the year designation, write the document year followed by the sequential box number for that year. For example, if this is the twelfth storage box to be used during the year 2005, its index number should be 2005–12.

5. On the label end of the box, list the general types of documents being stored. The following table lists some of the more common summary labels that can be used:

DOCUMENT TYPE	LABEL
Accounts Payable, supplier names ranging from A to Q	A/P—A to Q
Accounts Receivable, customer names ranging from M-Z	A/R—M to Z
Payroll, third-quarter records	P/R—3rd Qtr
Bank statements	Cash

The following label is an example of a completed box index for documents being stored in 2005 with a planned destruction interval of five years, being the 20th box of stored items for that year, containing accounts receivable records for customer names from H to N:

Year: 2008
Destroy: 2015
Index: 2005-20
Description: A/R—H to N

6. List in an index database the contents of the documents contained within the storage box, using the box index number as the record key. The following table shows an example of a proper entry in the database:

INDEX NO.	DOCUMENT YEAR	DESCRIPTION
2005-15	2008	Payroll register, 3rd quarter
2005-15	2008	Canceled checks
2005-15	2008	Budget files

3.2 DOC MGR

Labeling of Indexes on Permanent File Boxes

1. The following documents must be stored in the permanent file boxes:

Bylaws	Directors minutes
Capital stock records	Patents
Certificate of incorporation	Powers of attorney
Constitution	Product designs
Copyrights	Stockholder lists
Deeds and leases	Stockholder proxies

2. Load all permanent files into a separate box. On the label end of the box, list the general types of permanent documents being stored, such as "Board Minutes" or "Articles of Incorporation."

3. Label the box with "PERM" to indicate a permanent file, and add the sequential box number in the permanent file series. For example, if this is the seventh box of permanent files, its index number should be PERM-07. Finally, include in the index file a complete listing of all documents stored in the permanent file.

4. List in an index database the contents of the documents contained within the permanent file storage box, using the box index number as the record key. The following table shows an example of a proper entry in the database for box number PERM-07.

INDEX NO.	DESCRIPTION
PERM-07	Board minutes, 2008 full year
PERM-07	Vehicle titles
PERM-07	Insurance binders, 2008

Confidential Document Storage

Policy/Procedure Statement		Retrieval No.:	DOC-03
Brasto Publishing		Page:	1 of 1
		Issue Date:	10/28/0X
		Supersedes:	N/A
Subject: Confidential Document Storage			

1. PURPOSE AND SCOPE

This procedure is used by company employees to determine which documents are considered confidential and how they are to be stored.

2. RESPONSIBILITIES

DOC MGR   **Document Manager**

3. PROCEDURES

3.1   DOC MGR   **Identification of Confidential Documents**

1. Some general categories of documents are considered to be confidential, requiring all documents of these types to be stored in areas designated for confidential documents. The following general categories are considered confidential:
   - All Human Resources Department files
   - All Legal Department files
   - All Payroll Department documents

2. In addition to these general categories, specific documents are considered to be confidential, and must be stored in areas designated for confidential documents. The following documents are considered confidential:
   - Commission agreements
   - Corporate minutes book
   - Customer credit card files
   - Fidelity bond documentation
   - Job performance reviews retained at the department level
   - Notes payable documentation
   - Patent filings
   - Personal guarantee documents
   - Shareholder lists
   - Titles to property

3.2	DOC MGR	**Storage of Confidential Documents**

1. Once identified, all confidential documents are to be set aside for separate document storage, using the standard labeling procedure noted earlier in the Storage Box Indexing procedure. To ensure that these documents are not stored in the main document storage area, mark the index information on a colored label.
2. Store the confidential documents in a storage area with the following minimum security and document safety features:
   - Biometric lock access, with the only approved person having access being the Document Manager.
   - No window access to the storage area.
   - Walls extend to the roof, with no potential access through overhead crawl spaces.
   - Concrete floor, with no access possible from subfloor compartments.
   - Requests for document retrieval require approval by the Chief Administrative Officer.
   - All documents are stored in containers that are proof against fire and water damage up to a minimum temperature of 600 degrees.
   - Non-water fire-suppression system.
   - Fire alarm system automatically contacts emergency services in the event of a fire.

Confidential Document Storage

Policy/Procedure Statement **Brasto Publishing** **Subject: Document Transfer to Storage**	**Retrieval No.:**	**DOC-04**
	Page:	1 of 1
	Issue Date:	10/28/0X
	Supersedes:	N/A

1. PURPOSE AND SCOPE

This procedure is used by company employees to verify the contents of storage boxes and organize the boxes for storage.

2. RESPONSIBILITIES

DOC MGR   **Document Manager**

3. PROCEDURES

3.1	DOC MGR	**Review Storage Box Contents**

1. Verify that the summary-level description noted on the storage box label coincides with the contents of each box. In particular, look for any permanent file or confidential documents that may have been mixed into the box.
2. Compare the destruction date listed on the label to the standard company policy for document destruction dates to ensure that the correct destruction date has been assigned to the box.

		3. If there is any uncertainty about the destruction date for a specific document, complete a Records Retention/Disposition Analysis form (see Exhibit 13.1). It can be downloaded from the company intranet site. In Section A of the form, enter today's date as well as the company division and department from which the document originates. In Section B, enter the document name, form number, the name of the person from whom it comes, and the purpose of the document. Then send the document to the department manager, controller, tax counsel, and legal counsel. This group enters their remarks concerning the document in the Remarks field, and also checks off its retention status to the right of the Remarks field. This group then signs and dates the document in Section D. Once the completed form is returned, dispose of the document as indicated in Section C of the form and store the form.
3.2	DOC MGR	**Document Putaway**
		1. Once the storage box arrives at the warehouse facility, allocate it to a storage area based on its status as permanent file, confidential, or regular storage, as well as by destruction year (if any). Transport the box to the assigned storage area and write down the aisle, rack, and bin number where it was stored, as well as the information on the box label.
		2. Enter all information on the box index label, as well as the storage location, into the warehouse location database.

Document Transfer to Storage

Records Retention/Disposition Analysis
and Authorization
[Company Name]

A

Date: _____

Division: _____

Department: _____

B

Record or Document Title: _____

Form No. (if applicable): _____ Originator: _____

Description and Purpose: _____

C

Retention Period: _____

Remarks:

☐ Confidential   ☐ Regular Storage

☐ Permanent   ☐ No Storage

D **Approval Signatures:**

Department Manager   _____ Date _____

Controller   _____ Date _____

Tax Counsel   _____ Date _____

Legal Counsel   _____ Date _____

DOC-101

Exhibit 13.1   Records Retention/Disposition Analysis Form

Policy/Procedure Statement	Retrieval No.:	DOC-05
	Page:	1 of 1
Brasto Publishing	Issue Date:	10/28/0X
	Supersedes:	N/A
Subject: Document Retrieval from Storage		

1.   PURPOSE AND SCOPE

This procedure is used by company employees to request the transfer of selected files from long-term storage, log them out of storage, move them to the requesting employee, and verify the status of withdrawn documents.

2.   RESPONSIBILITIES

DOC MGR   **Document Manager**
EMPLOYEE   **Employee**

3.   PROCEDURES

3.1   EMPLOYEE   **Determine Index Number of Desired Documents**

Go to the archive indexing database and type in the document year and type of record to be retrieved from storage. If the exact storage box cannot be determined, then determine the range of boxes in which the document is most likely to be stored.

3.2   EMPLOYEE   **Complete Document Request Form**

1. Download the Document Request form (see Exhibit 13.2), which is available on the company intranet site.
2. In Section A of the form, enter your name, division, department, and contact phone number. In Section B, check off the box indicating a request for either a full-box retrieval or just a specific document, followed by the index number of the storage box. If you checked the specific document box, then provide a description of the document. Complete a separate line on the form for each document retrieval request. Have the department manager sign the request at the bottom of Section B.

3.3   DOC MGR   **Retrieve and Log Out Documents**

1. Upon receipt of the approved Document Request form, use the warehouse location database to determine the location of the requested storage boxes.
2. Print a pick list for the requested items.
3. Using the pick list, retrieve the requested storage boxes.
4. If the request is for only a portion of a storage box, then extract the requested items, mark the location of the missing items in the storage box with a colored divider, and return the remaining portion of the box to storage.
5. Log the withdrawn documents out of the warehouse location database.
6. Upon delivery of the documents, have the recipient sign in Section C of the Document Request form. Then file the form.

3.4   DOC MGR   **Verify Status of Withdrawn Documents**

1. On a weekly basis, run the Withdrawn Documents Report (see Exhibit 13.3) and issue it to the managers of all departments whose employees still retain documents withdrawn from the archives warehouse.

2. If documents are still outstanding after one month, contact each document recipient and verify with them the dates by which they expect to return documents to the warehouse.
3. Contact the document recipients on the day before their promised document return dates, and arrange to have a warehouse person arrive at a specific time on the designated day to retrieve the documents.
4. On the designated retrieval date, remove the Document Request form from the file and take it to the recipient. Verify the receipt of all items on the list, and initial in the Return Initials section of Section B of the form to signify that each box or document has been returned.
5. Return the documents to their proper storage places and file the completed form.

Document Retrieval from Storage

Document Request Form
[Company Name]

A   **Requestor Information:**

Name: _____   Department: _____

Phone: _____   Division: _____

B   **Requested Document Retrieval:**

	Index No.	Document Description (only if specific document needed)	Return Initials
☐ Entire box ☐ Specific document	_____	_____	_____
☐ Entire box ☐ Specific document	_____	_____	_____
☐ Entire box ☐ Specific document	_____	_____	_____
☐ Entire box ☐ Specific document	_____	_____	_____
☐ Entire box ☐ Specific document	_____	_____	_____
☐ Entire box ☐ Specific document	_____	_____	_____

Request Approval:

Manager
Signature: _____   Date: _____

C   **Delivery Receipt:**

Recipient
Signature: _____   Delivery Date: _____

Print Name: _____

DOC-102

Exhibit 13.2   Document Request Form

Recipient Name	Index No.	Date Withdrawn	Description	Department Manager
Barstow, W.	2005-20	7/15/08	A/R—H to N	Willis, M.
Barstow, W.	2005-21	7/15/08	A/R—O to R	Willis, M.
Higgins, J.	2003-14	7/21/08	P/R—3rd Quarter	Willis, M.
Higgins, J.	2003-15	7/07/08	P/R—4th Quarter	Willis, M.

Exhibit 13.3   Withdrawn Documents Report

Policy/Procedure Statement	Retrieval No.:	DOC-06
Brasto Publishing	Page:	1 of 1
	Issue Date:	10/28/0X
	Supersedes:	N/A
Subject: Document Destruction		

1.   PURPOSE AND SCOPE

This procedure is used by company employees to ensure that documents are destroyed in accordance with the company document retention policy.

2.   RESPONSIBILITIES

DOC MGR   **Document Manager**

3.   PROCEDURES

3.1   DOC MGR   **Review Documents Scheduled for Destruction**

1. Sort the index database by document destruction date and print a report listing those storage boxes scheduled for destruction.
2. Using the scheduled document destruction report, pull from storage all boxes with currently scheduled destruction dates.
3. Open and review the contents of each box to ensure that the contents should be destroyed. If there is some uncertainty, contact the controller, who will send an accounting representative to review any questionable documents.
4. If some documents are to be retained, store them in a new box, labeled to match their new destruction date. Enter the new box number in the indexing database.

3.2   DOC MGR   **Destroy Documents**

1. Print the Authorization for Destruction of Records form, which can be downloaded from the company intranet site. An example is shown in Exhibit 13.4.[2] In Section A of the form, complete the form number (sequential from the prior form number) and the current date. In Section B, itemize the boxes recommended for destruction, including their index number, general contents description, document date range, recommended retention period for these types of documents, and the minimum age of any document in the box. Sign the field entitled "Destruction recommended by" and forward to the controller for an approval signature.

[2]Adapted with permission from Willson et al., *Controllership 5E*, John Wiley & Sons, New York, 1995, p. 1405.

> 2. Upon receipt of the approved form, complete the document destruction. Sign and date the form in Section C, and have a witness sign and note the location.
> 3. Make a copy of the form and retain it in a permanent file (see the "Storage Box Indexing" procedure for a description of how to label a box containing permanent file documents).
> 4. Forward the original of the document destruction certificate to the legal department.

Document Destruction

A

Authorization for Destruction of Records
and Cremation Certificate
[Company Name]

No. _____

Date: _____

To: (Controller)
Authority is requested for destruction of the following records:

B

Box Index Number	Description of Records	Date of Records		Recommended Retention Period	Minimum Age	
		From	To		Yr.	Mo.

Destruction recommended by: _____

Destruction approved by: _____

C

Date: _____

I hereby certify that I have this day destroyed, by cremation, the
accounts, records, and memoranda listed above, and further that no accounts,
records, or memoranda other than those named were destroyed herewith.

_____   _____
Witness   Signed

_____   _____
Location   Title

DOC-100

Exhibit 13.4 Document Destruction Certificate

Policy/Procedure Statement	Retrieval No.:	DOC-07
	Page:	1 of 1
Brasto Publishing	Issue Date:	10/28/0X
	Supersedes:	N/A
Subject: Storage Area Layout		

1.   PURPOSE AND SCOPE

This procedure is used by company employees to properly plan all aspects of the records storage area, including layout, maximization of storage space, record segregation, security, control systems, and insurance.

2.   RESPONSIBILITIES

DOC MGR   **Document Manager**

3.   PROCEDURES

3.1   DOC MGR   **Long-Term Planning for Document Storage**

1. The company does not wish to acquire additional storage space more frequently than once every three years, so estimate storage requirements for the current facility under that assumption, based on anticipated document retention policies, company growth rates, and anticipated storage for records related to acquisitions.

2. Plan for changes in the storage media, such as the use of CDs and DVDs instead of traditional paper-based storage, while considering the long-term storage needs of these types of media. Also consider the need for some backup storage of underlying paper documents in addition to advanced media storage systems, based on both legal issues and the risk of lost data on the newer storage media.

3. Consider the use of leased versus purchased storage space as part of the long-term planning process, including in the decision the loss of physical control over records and the storage environment if a third party manages the records.

4. Consider the impact on the aisle and bin numbering scheme (see next item) of any likely storage area expansion. For example, if racks will probably be added to one side of aisle A, consider giving aisle A a higher letter designation to allow for the expansion.

3.2   DOC MGR   **Aisle and Bin Location Numbering System**

1. Assign a unique location code to every storage location. A common coding pattern is to assign a letter to each aisle, followed by a number for each rack within the aisle, and then a letter to each level within the rack. Thus, the location code for the third level of the second rack in the fifth aisle from the left would be E-2-C.

		2.	Number the racks sequentially from left to right and back again as you proceed down an aisle so the first rack on the left is number 1, the first rack on the right is number 2, the second rack on the left is number 3, and so on. Because putaway and picking reports are generally sorted in ascending numerical order by rack number, this allows the warehouse staff to reduce their travel time, moving sequentially down an aisle until they reach the highest required rack number needed to complete their activities.
		3.	Verify that a location code has been assigned to *every* possible storage area location.
		4	If there is a need for real-time data entry of document storage transactions, consider adding a large bar code next to each location label, so scanners can be used to enter location codes.
3.3	DOC MGR		**Maximization of Storage Space**
		1.	Install racking systems that maximize the use of vertical storage space, extending to just below the rafters but without interfering with any fire-suppression systems.
		2.	Enclose building supports within the storage racks, so they do not intrude in the aisle areas. This allows for better access for forklifts through the aisles.
		3.	Avoid aisles located adjacent to exterior walls, since this does not maximize storage space. Instead, always have storage racks on the outside walls, so that all aisles have storage located on both sides.
		4.	Match aisle width to the system used for document storage and retrieval. For example, if a forklift is used, the aisle width must be sufficient for it to maneuver without damaging storage cases. However, if storage functions are conducted manually, aisles can be substantially narrower.
3.4	DOC MGR		**Segregation of Record Types**
		1.	Confidential documents shall be stored in a special locked area within the storage facility. No labeling of this area is required if the document manager feels that it will improve the security of the documents.
		2.	Permanent file documents shall be stored in a segregated area that is prominently labeled as such. Consider the use of additional barriers, such as chain link fencing, to reinforce the segregation of these records. The primary goal is to ensure that the records are not destroyed as part of the scheduled record destruction process for regular company documents.
3.5	DOC MGR		**Storage Security**
		1.	The storage area shall be built on a concrete slab, so there is no possibility of unauthorized access from a subfloor compartment or access tunnel.
		2.	There shall be no window access to the storage area, or else windows shall be covered by bars secured by bolts driven through the walls and secured on the inside.
		3.	Walls shall extend to the roof, and be constructed of brick or concrete blocks.
		4.	The storage area shall have biometric palmprint access for confidential and permanent files. A simple deadbolt lock mechanism is allowable for the main storage area.

3.6	DOC MGR	**Temperature and Humidity Controls** 1. The temperature in the storage area shall be set to 68 degrees with allowable variability of no more than 2 degrees. 2. The humidity in the storage area shall be set to 25%, with allowable variability of no more than 10%. 3. The temperature and humidity levels shall be electronically transmitted to the document manager's office, where they will be prominently displayed for constant monitoring.
3.7	DOC MGR	**Fire Controls** 1. If storage cases and filing cabinets are waterproof, consider the use of overhead sprinkler systems as a fire control. However, this is unlikely to apply in most situations. 2. In the event that storage cases are constructed of cardboard or use standard filing cabinets, install a gas-based fire suppression system that is linked to and triggered by an automated fire detection system. The system should also include an automated warning message to the local fire department, as well as to the document manager.
3.8	DOC MGR	**Insurance** On an annual basis or whenever the size of the record storage area changes appreciably, review all insurance policies related to document storage and verify that coverage is sufficient. In particular, verify that fire suppression systems meet the minimum requirements of the fire insurance policy. It may be necessary to have an insurance agent review the records storage area and recommend changes to insurance policies to match the existing warehouse configuration.

Storage Area Layout

Chapter 14

USER MANUAL

14.1 INTRODUCTION

The user manual is a conglomeration of documentation that relates to the wide array of transactions with which employees will deal in a typical work week. Some of these transactions are closely linked to the accounting department, while others involve only a slight interaction with this area. The user manual is designed to address the broad range of employee activities, rather than have a narrow focus on accounting activities. Examples of activities that may be addressed are:

- Complete the annual budget form for operations.

- Approve hiring an applicant for employment.

- Terminate an employee for cause.

- Requisition a commodity or service through the purchasing operation.

- Request service or supplies from another department.

- Prepare or approve employee time reports.

- Count inventory for the accounting system.

- Complete material receiving reports.

- Complete travel expense reports for reimbursement.

There are certainly other transactions too, but these are enough for starters. Every one of the actions listed results in one or more pieces of paper being received in accounting as a transaction input document. These documents usually are reports providing information or forms requiring some action to be taken and recorded. The problem is that many of these reports and forms are designed or prepared by accountants but are used by people who are not accountants—hence the need for a user manual. It is a training manual for new line and staff supervisors and for the employees who are using the reports and forms. It is a reference manual when a rare or unusual event occurs. It is an information manual to inform the users about company policies and the procedures for completing accounting forms.

14.2 STARTING THE MANUAL

If you have a policy/procedure statement system in place, start by reviewing each statement and ask if officers, department managers, or individual employees are involved in the receiving of data, forms, or reports from accounting. If yes, then mark that statement for possible inclusion in the user manual. Then review each accounting form and ask if information is initiated or processed by an outside user before the form reaches accounting. If so, that form should be selected for the manual.

If the policy/procedure system and forms manual are not in place, then review the list of actions at the beginning of this chapter and list those in use at your operation. Continue beyond these lists and identify other forms or actions with which the non-accounting employee may be involved. Either way, you now have a list of potential accounting policies, procedures, or forms that may be included in the user manual.

One other approach for formulating the contents of a user manual is tracking the number of recurring input document errors or the number of inquiries received daily or weekly from employees initiating the addition of information to the accounting forms at their respective locations. Steadily recurring errors on input documents is a positive sign that a user manual is needed.

Before going further, make a rough list of the potential distribution of such a manual. Is it every senior officer and department manager? Is it just selected departments? Could it be all employees above a certain classification level? Is it all professionals in a professional service organization? Or will just one copy go to each branch office? This list could range from a few dozen locations or persons to hundreds.

If the list is extremely diverse, you may elect to issue different manuals to different users. For example, there could be a factory user manual that includes only policies and procedures that affect those operations. The factory manual may cover only hourly payroll procedures and forms, while the travel policies and cash and accounts receivable sections may be deleted. A special section on inventory control forms may be included in this manual.

Likewise, the manual for branch operations may be expanded to cover special problems such as procedures for shipping goods from the home office and receiving them at the branch. There may also be special provisions for transmitting data and for the automatic deposit of payroll checks of branch employees. The procedure for handling and reporting branch deposits of cash would be included here.

Another user manual may be the administrative department accounting manual. This manual may cover special reports prepared by the sales department, forms for reporting customer credit ratings, or special reports covering research and development located only at the company's primary office.

14.3 OUTLINING AND UPDATING THE USER MANUAL

The next step is to outline the manual, generally by accounting function such as payroll, accounts payable, cashier, accounts receivable, receiving, and so on. A sentence outline should provide enough information to select the various policy and procedure documents and to write explanations or rewrite existing form instructions or other information.

Putting the user manual together is now a matter of selecting the available documentation, adding or deleting information where needed, preparing an index, and printing and publishing the manual. Unlike a book, the index or contents should be on the cover where it is immediately available. Each topic, instruction sheet, and form should be indexed by name and page number. The user manual is usually between 20 and 100 pages long; any longer manual tends not to be used.

Study the materials brought together for the user manual. Some policies or procedures may be quite long, with extensive introductions as well as copies of laws and regulations. If the materials are adequate as originally printed, use them as is. If not, prepare a condensed version for the user manual, stripping out material of little interest to the departmental user.

The manual may be printed on both sides of the paper, but printing on only one side is recommended. Printing on one side leaves the back of the preceding page available for user notes, additions, deletions, and changes until a new manual is published. Use standard white paper and provide an index and date of issue on the cover. After collating, the manual should be held together with a single staple in the upper left corner unless it is placed in a three-ring binder.

If the manual is to be issued to department supervisors, provide a second copy of the manual marked "Office Copy," for most accounting documents prepared at remote locations will be done by the departmental secretary under the direction of the supervisor. It will be the secretary who will be calling the accounting department for assistance with a problem.

Distribute the manual to the selected recipients through the normal delivery system used in the company. The first time the user manual is distributed, a cover letter explaining its purpose and use would be helpful.

Periodically updating parts of the user manual by issuing corrected insert sheets is not generally recommended. Users tend not to delete superceded pages or add new pages to a previously published manual. One way of notifying such users of changes is through interoffice correspondence to the original holders of the manuals. The *From* section of the correspondence would be the accounting department, and the *Subject* section would indicate the specific page and item to be changed. The first paragraph could explain the addition or change in detail; the second paragraph notes the exact location of the change in the user manual. In most cases, the user can reference this correspondence while updating the manual in writing.

The user manual should be fully updated and published annually, especially if the document continues to receive a large number of changes on an ongoing basis.

14.4 SAMPLE USER MANUAL

There are many types of user manuals that can be made specific to certain functions within a company, such as one that is tailored to the needs of the receiving staff, detailing how to inspect incoming materials, write up return documentation, and match receipts to authorizing purchase orders. Rather than provide a sample of a user manual that is specific to a single function, this section contains a more general user manual containing information that is most likely to be used by the majority of a company's employees, containing information about travel policies, filling out expense reimbursement forms, and so on. This information can be used as the core of a general user manual, and can be substantially modified to create user manuals for more specific functions. The example is shown in Exhibits 14.1 through 14.10.

General User Manual	Retrieval No.:	GUSE-01
	Page:	1 of 1
	Issue Date:	10/28/0X
Subject: Contents	Supersedes:	N/A

GENERAL USER MANUAL

CONTENTS

1. Listing of key employees by function and phone number
2. Company holidays
3. Time reporting
4. Travel policies
5. Expense reporting
6. Accounting codes for expense reports
7. Benefit contact information
8. Requisitioning supplies
9. Recording petty cash transactions

Exhibit 14.1   Sample User Manual, Contents

General User Manual		Retrieval No.:	GUSE-02
		Page:	1 of 1
Brasto Publishing		Issue Date:	10/28/0X
		Supersedes:	N/A
Subject: Key Employees			

Type of Problem	Go To—Primary	Go To—Secondary
401(k)	Mitch Bothward	Anne Boardman
Computer Problem	James Teacher	Peter Vanders
Copier Problem	Caitlin Ward	
Customer Service	Sally Dunne	Jim Evans
Dental Insurance	Mitch Bothward	Anne Boardman
Expense Reports	Anne Boardman	
Fax Problem	Caitlin Ward	
Harassment	Mitch Bothward	Anne Boardman
Marketing	Alexandra Wright	
Medical Insurance	Mitch Bothward	Anne Boardman
Network Problem	James Teacher	
Office Supplies	Caitlin Ward	
Paycheck	Anne Boardman	
Phone List	Caitlin Ward	
Phones	Caitlin Ward	
Quality Assurance	Carrie Archer	
Sales	Mark Chowdry	Tim Mannesman
Time-keeping System	Peter Vanders	Anne Boardman

Exhibit 14.2 Sample User Manual, Key Employees

General User Manual	Retrieval No.:	GUSE-03
Brasto Publishing	Page:	1 of 1
	Issue Date:	10/017/0X
Subject: Company Holidays	Supersedes:	N/A

The following holidays are recognized by the company for the year 200X. These holidays match those required by the federal government, which the company follows as part of its obligations as a federal contractor.

	2002 Date of Observance
New Year's Day	January 1, Monday
Martin Luther King Day	January 21, Monday
Washington's Birthday	February 18, Monday
Memorial Day	May 27, Monday
Independence Day	July 4, Thursday
Labor Day	September 2, Monday
Columbus Day	October 14, Monday
Veterans Day	November 11, Monday
Thanksgiving Day	November 28, Thursday
Friday after Thanksgiving	November 29, Friday
Christmas Eve (1/2 Day)	December 24, Tuesday
Christmas	December 25, Wednesday

Exhibit 14.3 Sample User Manual, Company Holidays

General User Manual	Retrieval No.:	GUSE-04
	Page:	1 of 1
Brasto Publishing	Issue Date:	10/28/0X
Subject: Time Reporting	Supersedes:	N/A

Policies: Each employee is responsible for recording his or her time in the time-keeping system. No one may record hours worked on another's time record. Tampering with another's time record is cause for disciplinary action, including possible dismissal, of both employees.

If an employee does not record his or her time in the time-keeping system, then the company has no way of tracking vacation time taken. If this happens, the company will assume that an employee has taken all of his or her vacation time, rendering that person unable to carry forward any vacation hours to the next year; nor will an employee be paid any accrued vacation hours at such time as he or she leaves the company.

Submission Notes, Specific: The following items relate to the blocked identifying letters listed on the sample expense report form shown on the next page:

A.   Enter the name of the employee whose time is recorded on the form.

B.   Enter the employee number (located on the bottom of the employee badge) of the employee whose time is recorded on the form.

C.   Enter the date on which time was worked.

D.   Enter the start time of the activity.

E.   Enter the time at which the activity stopped.

F.   Enter the difference between the start and stop time for the activity. Be sure to include a grand total at the bottom of this column after all line item entries have been made.

G.   Enter the job or project code against which time is to be charged.

H.   Enter the earnings code, located in the table at the bottom of the form, that corresponds to the hours worked.

I.   Have the employee's immediate supervisor sign and date the form.

Exhibit 14.4   Sample User Manual, Time Reporting

Brasto Publishing

Time and Attendance Report

Employee Name: _____ [A]

Employee ID Number: _____ [B]

Date	Start Time	Stop Time	Net Time	Job Code	Earnings Code
[C]	[D]	[E]	[F]	[G]	[H]

Total Time Worked

I hereby certify that the time reported above is a true statement of hours worked:

_____   _____
Name   Date

Earnings Codes:

REG	Regular Hours	JUR	Jury Duty
OT	Overtime	SIC	Sick Leave
HOL	Holiday	VAC	Vacation Leave

Exhibit 14.4 Sample User Manual, Time Reporting (Continued)

General User Manual	Retrieval No.:	GUSE-05
Brasto Publishing	Page:	1 of 2
	Issue Date:	10/28/0X
Subject: Travel Policies	Supersedes:	N/A

Policy: Employees are reimbursed for reasonable and necessary expenses incurred during approved travel.

Authorization: Travel requires approval of the department manager. The Permission to Travel form is required for conferences, conventions, and professional meetings, and must be submitted at least two weeks in advance of the departure date. Requests for foreign travel of the same type must be submitted at least four weeks in advance. The form is not required for business travel.

Change or Cancellation of Travel Request: An amended Permission to Travel form must be submitted to change the place or date of a meeting, or to cancel it.

Advance Payment of Conference Registration Fees: To pay registration fees in advance of a conference, the request should be made at least 20 days in advance of the conference date on an expense report. Literature concerning the conference and fee amount and a copy of the Permission to Travel form must be attached to the voucher.

Reimbursement of Travel Expense: Immediately upon returning from a trip, an employee should submit an expense report for reimbursement. All expense reports require an approval signature from an employee's immediate supervisor. Expense reports will be reimbursed within five business days.

Lodging: If more than one person is indicated on the lodging bill, the single room rate should be shown; otherwise, reimbursement will be made at 50% of the room charge. Lodging reimbursement will be made for the final evening of the trip if the traveler is not able to return home by 9 P.M.

Meals: Reimbursement for meals is on a per diem basis, and is tied directly to the federal government's Federal Travel Regulation rates, which should be consulted regularly to view updates.

Mileage: Mileage for the use of a personal vehicle on company business matches the standard Internal Revenue Service rate. Employees will be notified once a year of changes in this rate. Private vehicle mileage reimbursement cannot exceed the cost of round-trip air coach fare to the named destination.

Public Carrier: Airline tickets must be purchased through the corporate travel office. Certification that coach fare was not available is necessary when tickets are purchased for first-class travel. Business-class seats are allowable for flights exceeding six hours in duration. A ticket coupon is required to document the cost of a flight

Registration Fees: Fees are reimbursed on an expense report when supported by a paid receipt.

Exhibit 14.5 Sample User Manual, Travel Policies

General User Manual	Retrieval No.:	GUSE-05
Brasto Publishing	Page:	2 of 2
	Issue Date:	10/28/0X
Subject: Travel Policies	Supersedes:	N/A

Tips: Tips for meals, taxis, and other services should be noted on the expense report. Tips can include baggage-handling tips when arriving or departing a hotel or airport, and should not exceed $1 per bag.

Taxi and Limousine: Actual charges, including tip, are reimbursable. The cost of a private limousine should not exceed the cost of similar taxi service.

Parking and Tolls: Actual parking charges and road and bridge tolls are reimbursable if using a personal vehicle or rental car on company business, but not if the charges are incurred during a daily commute to the office.

Car Rental: The actual cost of a car rental is reimbursable if a receipt is attached to the expense report. The company will only reimburse for the cost of a mid-sized car, with the incremental cost of any upgrades to larger vehicles being charged back to employees. Do not accept optional insurance coverage when renting a car on company business, because this is covered by a company insurance policy. Car rental should be made through the corporate travel office to take advantage of corporate volume discounts.

Exhibit 14.5   Sample User Manual, Travel Policies (Continued)

General User Manual		Retrieval No.:	GUSE-06
		Page:	1 of 1
Brasto Publishing		Issue Date:	10/28/0X
		Supersedes:	N/A
Subject: Expense Reporting			

Purpose: To reimburse employees for approved travel and other expenditures.

Submission Notes, General: To be reimbursed for all authorized expenses, you must submit an expense report accompanied by receipts for all expenses incurred, and with an approval signature by your manager. Please submit your expense report promptly after incurring an expense. Expense reports with errors or missing documentation will be returned to employees for correction.

Submission Notes, Specific: The following items relate to the blocked identifying letters listed on the sample expense report form shown on the next page:

A. Enter your name, social security number, and department.

B. Enter your employee number, official job title, and the name of your immediate supervisor.

C. Enter the pay periods during which the expenses reported on this form were incurred.

D. Enter the date on which an expense was incurred. This should be the date listed on the receipt.

E. Enter the account number to which the expense should be charged. The most commonly used charge codes are listed later in this manual under the heading "Accounting Codes." Accounting codes used should only be those for your department. If any expenses are to be charged to a different department, then the supervisor of that department must also sign off on the form.

F. Briefly describe the incurred expense. If the expense was a meal, list the name of the people attending and the purpose of the meal.

G. Seven categories of commonly used expenses are listed. Please enter the amount of the expense in the category that most closely indicates the purpose of the expense. If none of the categories match the expense, then list it in the "Other" category. Once entered, the total expense will automatically appear in the "Total" column.

H. Enter the amount of any offsetting advances already issued to you, and against which no expenses have yet been charged.

I. Have your immediate supervisor sign in this block.

Prior to submitting your expense report, please make a copy for your records.

Exhibit 14.6 Sample User Manual, Expense Reporting

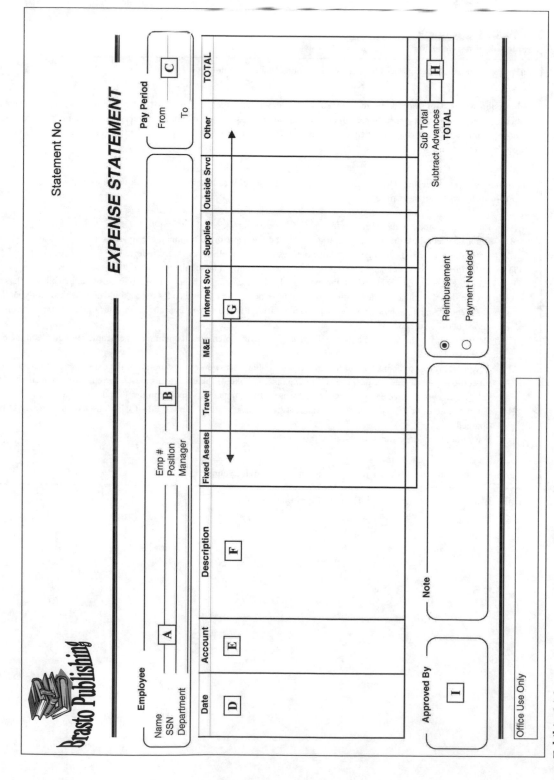

Exhibit 14.6 Sample User Manual, Expense Reporting (Continued)

General User Manual	Retrieval No.:	GUSE-07
	Page:	I of 2
	Issue Date:	10/28/0X
Brasto Publishing	Supersedes:	N/A
Subject: Accounting Codes		

Use the following account codes when filling out your expense report:

Account Number	Account Description
60500-01	Dues and Publications—G&A
60500-02	Dues and Publications—Development
60500-03	Dues and Publications—Consulting
60500-04	Dues and Publications—Marketing
60500-05	Dues and Publications—Production
60500-06	Dues and Publications—Sales
60950-01	Licenses and Fees—G&A
60950-02	Licenses and Fees—Development
60950-03	Licenses and Fees—Consulting
60950-04	Licenses and Fees—Marketing
61050-01	Meals—G&A
61050-02	Meals—Development
61050-03	Meals—Consulting
61050-04	Meals—Marketing
61050-05	Meals—Production
61050-06	Meals—Sales
61150-01	Postage—G&A
61150-02	Postage—Development
61150-03	Postage—Consulting
61150-04	Postage—Marketing
61150-06	Postage—Sales
62200-01	Supplies—G&A
62200-02	Supplies—Development
62200-03	Supplies—Consulting
62200-04	Supplies—Marketing
62200-05	Supplies—Production
62200-06	Supplies—Sales
62300-01	Telephone—G&A
62300-02	Telephone—Development
62300-03	Telephone—Consulting
62300-04	Telephone—Marketing
62300-05	Telephone—Production
62300-06	Telephone—Sales
62350-04	Trade Shows
62400-01	Training—G&A
62400-02	Training—Development
62400-03	Training—Consulting
62400-04	Training—Marketing

Exhibit 14.7 Sample User Manual, Accounting Codes

General User Manual		Retrieval No.:	GUSE-07
Brasto Publishing		Page:	2 of 2
		Issue Date:	10/28/0X
Subject: Accounting Codes		Supersedes:	N/A

Account Number	Account Description
62400-05	Training—Production
62400-06	Training—Sales
62450-01	Travel—G&A
62450-02	Travel—Development
62450-03	Travel—Consulting
62450-04	Travel—Marketing
62450-05	Travel—Production
62450-06	Travel—Sales

Exhibit 14.7 Sample User Manual, Accounting Codes (Continued)

General User Manual		Retrieval No.:	GUSE-08
Brasto Publishing		Page:	1 of 1
		Issue Date:	10/28/0X
Subject: Benefits Contact Information		Supersedes:	N/A

The staff of the human resources department should be able to answer most of your questions regarding benefits. However, if you are more comfortable contacting the benefit provider directly, or if your question arises after hours, please use the following contact information:

401(k) Plan Customer Service	800-621-8912
Cafeteria Plan Customer Service	800-702-3597
COBRA Payments	800-593-0421
Dental Reimbursement	800-555-8543
Life Insurance Customer Service	800-391-8371
Medical Account Representative (Susan Allen)	800-423-8010
Medical Customer Service	800-341-9020
Medical Reimbursement	800-877-9777

Exhibit 14.8 Sample User Manual, Benefits Contact Information

General User Manual	Retrieval No.:	GUSE-09
	Page:	1 of 1
Brasto Publishing	Issue Date:	10/28/0X
	Supersedes:	N/A
Subject: Requisitioning Supplies		

Purpose: When supplies or equipment are needed, one should complete a requisition form. The original copy is sent to the purchasing department and the canary copy is retained by the requisitioning department for later comparison to the purchase order. When the purchase order is prepared by the purchasing department, one copy is sent to the requisitioning department.

Submission Notes, Specific: The following items relate to the blocked identifying letters listed on the sample expense report form shown on the next page:

A. Enter the date on which the requisition was filled out.

B. The purchasing department will fill in the purchase order number, unless the requisitioning employee has obtained the number in advance.

C. Enter the account code or name to which the requisition will be charged.

D. Enter the date by which the service or product must be received.

E. Enter the name of the person to whom delivery should be made.

F. Enter the reason why the service or product is being ordered. If available, enter the project name or number for which it is being used.

G. Enter the contact information for any suggested suppliers.

H. Enter the quantity, description, and estimated price of each item being requested. The actual price and total extended price will be entered by the purchasing department.

I. If the amount being requested is under $5,000 then only the signatures of the requesting person and budgetary authority (the person against whose budget this expense will be charged) are needed. If the amount exceeds $5,000 but is less than $50,000, then the signature of the chief financial officer must be added. If the requisition exceeds $50,000, then the signature of the president must be added.

Exhibit 14.9   Sample User Manual, Requisitioning Supplies

REQUISITION

Date: ___ A ___   Purchase Order No. ___ B

Account to Charge: ___ C ___   Required Delivery Date: ___ D ___

Deliver to: ___ E ___   To be used for: ___ F ___

Name and Address of Suggested Suppliers:

1 ___ G ___

2 ___

3 ___

4 ___

Quantity	Description	Estimated Price	Actual Price	Total
	H			

Authorization:

Requested By: ___ I ___

           Name   Date

Budgetary Authority: ___

           Name   Date

Chief Financial Officer: ___

           Name   Date

President: ___

           Name   Date

Exhibit 14.9   Sample User Manual, Requisitioning Supplies (Continued)

General User Manual	Retrieval No.:	GUSE-10
Brasto Publishing	Page:	1 of 1
	Issue Date:	10/28/0X
	Supersedes:	N/A
Subject: Petty Cash Transactions		

Purpose: To obtain cash for emergency purchases under $50.

Discussion: If a department has a petty cash fund, disbursements are accumulated until the fund is nearly depleted. The receipts and one copy of the petty cash voucher form are brought to the finance department. The cashier will issue cash to replace the amount of expenses itemized on the petty cash voucher.

If a department has no petty cash fund, a receipt under $50 can be brought to the finance department and exchanged for cash or a company check.

Distribution of Completed Form: The completed petty cash voucher form is filed with the accounts payable vouchers.

Exhibit 14.10   Sample User Manual, Recording Petty Cash Transactions

PREPARING A PETTY CASH VOUCHER

Complete the form according to the following instructions.

A. Department — Enter the complete account title.

B. Date — Enter the date the voucher is prepared.

C. Date — Enter date of each transaction.

D. Vendor — List the name of the vendor on each transaction.

E. G.L. — Enter general ledger code of each transaction.

F. Object Code — Enter object code of each transaction.

G. Department — Enter the department account number for each transaction.

H. Amount — Enter the total of each transaction.

I. Total — Enter total to be reimbursed.

J. Summarize information in E, F, G, H.

K. Submitted By — Name of individual to receive the reimbursement.

L. Approved By — The signature of the budgetary authority as listed in the Chart of Accounts.

M. Verified By — For accounting use only.

N. Approved By — Approved signature by accounting department.

O. Date — Enter the date the voucher is approved by the Accounting Department.

P. Petty Cash Authorization No. — Accounting enters the number of the authorization.

(Continues)

Exhibit 14.10   (Continued)

Petty Cash Voucher

DEPARTMENT ___A___ DATE ___B___

DATE	VENDOR	G.L.	OBJECT	DEPARTMENT	AMOUNT	
C	D	E	F	G	H	
				TOTAL	I	

DEPARTMENT

SUBMITTED BY ___K___

APPROVED BY ___L___

FINANCIAL AFFAIRS

VERIFIED BY ___M___

APPROVED BY ___N___

DATE ___O___

P.C. AUTHORIZATION NO. ___P___

G.L.	OBJECT	DEPARTMENT	AMOUNT	
J	J	J	J	
		TOTAL	I	

Exhibit 14.10 Sample User Manual, Recording Petty Cash Transactions (Continued)

Index